ID0909753

International Advertising

International Advertising

Realities and Myths

EDITED BY

JOHN PHILIP JONES

Sage Publications, Inc.
International Educational and Professional Publisher
Thousand Oaks ■ London ■ New Delhi

For information:

Sage Publications, Inc.
2455 Teller Road
Thousand Oaks, California 91320
E-mail: order@sagepub.com

Sage Publications Ltd.
6 Bonhill Street
London EC2A 4PU
United Kingdom

Sage Publications India Pvt. Ltd.
M-32 Market
Greater Kailash I
New Delhi 110 048 India

Printed in the United States of America

Library of Congress Cataloging-in-Publication Data

Main entry under title:

International advertising: Realities and myths/edited by John
    Philip Jones.
        p. cm.
    Includes bibliographical references and index.
    ISBN 0-7619-1244-4 (acid-free paper).—ISBN 0-7619-1245-2 (pbk.:
    acid-free paper)
    1. Advertising. 2. Advertising media planning. 3. Advertising.
Comparison. I. Jones, John Philip.
HF5823.I59 2000
659.1—DC21   90-6528

00 01 02 03 04 05 06 8 7 6 5 4 3 2 1

Acquiring Editor: Harry Briggs
Production Editor: Astrid Virding
Typesetter/Designer: Danielle Dillahunt
Indexer: Janet Perlman
Cover Designer: Ravi Balasuriya

Contents

Part II
An International Circumnavigation

This series of handbooks is dedicated to David Ogilvy (1911-1999).

While the volume of advertising is still growing in the
United States, it is growing faster in the rest of the world,
and America is no longer top nation professionally. The
tortoises are overtaking the hare.

—David Ogilvy, 1983
Ogilvy on Advertising

1

Introduction

The Vicissitudes of
International Advertising

John Philip Jones

This volume follows three recently published companions: *How Advertising Works, The Advertising Business* and *How to Use Advertising to Build Strong Brands*. This present work, which is devoted to the international aspects of advertising, will be joined shortly by a final volume describing the main professional organizations and publications in the advertising field worldwide. These five books comprise a battery of more than 200 individual chapters. All of the contributions to these volumes have intellectual substance and are intended to describe in reasonable detail a large proportion of what is known about advertising at the end of the 20th century.

Like the other volumes, this book is the combined effort of a number of specialists, mostly prominent figures in their fields. It is the product of 26 authors: 20 practitioners and 6 full-time academics, professors in well-known universities in the United States, Australia, and Scandinavia. Appropriately, in view of the subject, 20 of the contributors work outside of the United States. The other 6 authors, who are based in the United States, all have significant experience of international advertising operations.

The book is divided into three sections. This introduction and Part I (Chapters 2 through 8) contain material describing general aspects of international advertising—that is, the discussion is not focused on individual countries. Within Part I, Chapters 6, 7, and 8 address a common topic: the demographic and psychographic harmonies between specific countries—harmonies that provide opportunities for common advertising approaches, a matter of great potential importance.

The remaining two parts of the book are devoted to specific countries. I have been selective in my choices and have made no attempt to cover the world comprehensively. The countries included are Australia, China, France, Germany, India, Japan, the smaller countries of the Pacific Rim, Russia, the Scandinavian countries, South Africa, and the United Kingdom. In making my selections, I have been guided by two considerations: (a) the present importance and future potential of each country as an advertising market, and (b) my knowledge of innovative research work that is being carried out there.

The contributions to Part II (Chapters 9 through 18) describe and analyze advertising and the advertising business in selected countries. Part III (Chapters 19 through 27) is devoted to work from individual countries that contributes to the extension of the frontier of our knowledge.

International Marketing and Advertising Companies

Contrary to popular belief, the transfer of advertising campaigns across national frontiers is a process that has not proceeded smoothly, continuously, and incrementally. Rather, the popularity of such transfers has progressed and receded in response to significant (and perhaps unexpected) changes in advertisers' and advertising agencies' opinions regarding the merits of international advertising.

The merits of this type of advertising constitute a topic that cannot be considered in isolation. It is one part of the wider subject of international business organization. Theories of international business have been described, analyzed, and fought over with relentless enthusiasm by generations of management gurus and academics. Businesspeople at the "sharp end" have also contributed their opinions. Enlightenment nevertheless continues to elude us, and the reason is simple. The vigor of the views expressed has invariably been greater than the extent and quality of the empirical data used to support them.

To establish some parameters for the discussion, I offer below definitions of various types of organizations that operate across national borders, with particular regard to how those organizations handle brands. There are five different types of such organizations, and they fall along a continuum. The three marked with asterisks in the following list are widely recognized. The two remaining categories have come about as a result of relatively recent academic analysis that was undertaken because it had become increasingly obvious that the three more widely recognized organizational systems were unable to provide good enough guides for new or evolving types of business.[1]

1. *Global organizations*:* The role of overseas operations in global organizations is to "implement parent company strategies"—in other words, to use uniform techniques to market brands that are developed centrally.

2. *International organizations*:* In these types of organizations, overseas branches "adapt and leverage" parent company competencies; this allows a degree of flexibility in the adaptation of centrally developed brands.

3. *Transnational organizations:* In these organizations, overseas operations make different contributions to integrated worldwide operations by focusing partly on the local market and partly on how this can influence the firm as a whole. This will encourage but not force a convergence of brands across the markets.

4. *Permanent alliances:*[2] In permanent alliances, local operations remain independent, but alliances are cemented by the drive and self-interest of the decision makers in each country. Brands remain local, but convergence may possibly take place in the long term.

5. *Multinationals*:* In such organizations, the role of overseas subsidiaries is to "sense and exploit" local opportunities. Brands remain local.

There is, of course, more to these types of organizations than the single matter of the roles of their overseas operations and how their brands are affected. In particular, their assets and capabilities are differently configured, and there may be different philosophies regarding the development and diffusion of knowledge. However, my concern in this chapter is advertising

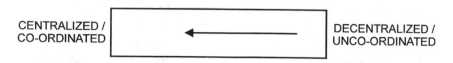

Figure 1.1. International Advertising: Early Years After World War II

strategy, hence the emphasis on these organizations' different ways of managing brands.

During the first two or three decades after World War II, there was a clearly marked movement toward the global extreme, a move driven by cost and control considerations. Business organizations were moving toward the international/global end of the continuum represented by the list above. This move, as it affected advertising strategy, is illustrated in Figure 1.1.

The following quotation provides a typical expression of the underlying philosophy of globalization. This was written from an advertising agency perspective, but large numbers of manufacturing companies have justified their policies with the use of the same types of arguments. This (slightly truncated) quotation dates from 1984, but similar points continue to be made today, although less insistently than in the past:

  i. Coordination offers cost-savings. . . .
 ii. It facilitates the sharing of experience. . . .
iii. It enables effective control. . . .
 iv. The international importance of the business will ensure that it has the benefit of top resources. . . .
  v. Most important, consistency of approach means that a positioning and image for a product can be built over time and across territory, a consideration of growing importance as internationally received media become more commonplace.[3]

Although such views have been and are shared by both practitioners and academics, the latter have often led the charge and have done so with considerable panache. In the words of Theodore Levitt: "A powerful force now drives the world toward a single converging commonality, and that force is technology. It has proletarianized communication, transport, and travel . . . homogenizing markets everywhere."[4] How alluring a picture is painted by the prophecies of such zealots. But, regrettably, their words do not contain

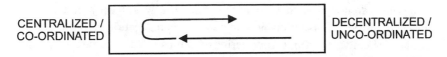

CENTRALIZED /
CO-ORDINATED

DECENTRALIZED /
UNCO-ORDINATED

Figure 1.2. International Advertising: Trend During the 1980s

even the smallest reference to the only person who is able to turn these visions into reality. I refer, of course, to the consumer.

The problem with the whole concept of globalization is that it is, to an extreme degree, producer driven rather than consumer induced. I am reminded of the apocryphal remark of the suburban householder to the grass-seed salesman: "Don't tell me about your grass seed. Tell me about my lawn." Focusing on the lawn is what consumer orientation is all about, and the consumer holds the key to the future of most businesses. Manufacturers have often paid a breathtaking price for misjudging the importance of this point.

Trends in International Advertising

As the best-informed observers are aware, the pendulum some time ago began to swing the other way, a movement that can be illustrated by a single indicator of global philosophies and how widely they are followed by major firms operating on the world scene—their use of standardized advertising. In this, a substantial change seems to have occurred during the 1980s, since when there has been no reversal.[5]

- The proportion of "substantially localized" campaigns increased from 20% to 35%.
- The proportion of partly standardized and partly localized campaigns rose from 10% to 55%.
- The proportion of "fully standardized" campaigns fell from 70% to the remarkable low of 10%.

The trend during this period is described in Figure 1.2.

If the data provided by the surveys referred to here are even approximately correct, what we saw during the 1980s was not so much a trend as a *volte-face*.

The figures do not prove that global branding itself was sharply cut back, but they certainly show an entirely new degree of circumspection in its implementation. The evidence from earlier periods (as illustrated in Figure 1.1) demonstrates that the global extension of brands at that time applied to all aspects of the marketing mix, and that the adaptation tended to be extremely literal and inflexible.[6] The advertising industry soon shook itself free of such rigidity.

The reasons for the change that took place are not too difficult to explain. The inflationary business conditions of the 1970s played a part by discouraging long-term thinking—an unwillingness to wait for the eventual benefits of globalization. More important, hard experience led to a dawning of reality. The history of many forays into international markets, such as Procter & Gamble's unfortunate early moves into Japan, employing American brands and unadapted marketing methods, bit deep into the consciousness of marketers. The effects were felt by all observers, not just by those who had paid dearly for the experience: The advertising industry has developed the study of the competition into an art form. In evaluating the new situation—the apparent retreat from globalization—the marketing gurus very quickly appreciated what was happening in the marketplace and brought ingenuity to their attempts to explain it.

There are two interconnected notions that recur in debates on the subject: transnationalism and pluralization. *Transnationalism* (described above) is less a type of organization than a mind-set, a way that managers are schooled to look at markets and brands. It embraces at least some elements of a firm's corporate culture. The concept focuses on the goals and problems of cross-border management, and it encourages pragmatism in exploiting local opportunities and solving local problems. But what managers are trained to think about ultimately is the overall health of the company. They work to exploit local possibilities, "to become insiders in each market,"[7] and to build strong brands there. However, they are taught to take a broad perspective, so that in the long term they are able to engineer (or at least encourage) an international convergence of brands, which it is thought will open the way to major economies of scale.

The idea behind *pluralization* is the acceptance of the obvious fact of market fragmentation, but it ingeniously suggests that this fragmentation follows uniform patterns in country after country: "The kinds of small market segments common in Switzerland now also appear in Sri Lanka and Swaziland. . . . Though consumption thus gets pluralized and miniaturized, its global aggregate gets magnified."[8]

This is a plausible doctrine, but it is difficult to answer two questions about it. First, where is the broad-scale empirical validation? In the original paper on the topic (again by Levitt), the only example of pluralization provided concerns minor varieties of food. Food is not the best example to choose. In the past, successful brands of food that have been uniformly positioned internationally have been much scarcer than brands of toiletries, detergents, clothing, gasoline, or airlines. The second point is that, even if consumers in Switzerland, Sri Lanka, and Swaziland develop coincidentally a taste for pizza, sushi, and tapas, what mechanism is available to exploit the scale economies in production and marketing? It is one thing to centralize manufacture of high-volume goods like detergents and high-value items like automobiles. There is a large leap from these things to the small, niche, perishable products that Levitt cites.

There is some truth in the doctrines of transnationalism and pluralization, but there is a great need for the underlying arguments to be formulated more fully, and, most important, amplified with a far broader range of specific examples.

If the voices from the American academic ivory tower have not yet provided a clear picture of what is going on in international markets, American consumers have at least provided a number of explicit lessons, which may or may not be relevant to other countries. Historically, the United States has been much the richest source of marketing experience, and many of the ways in which the U.S. domestic market has developed in the past have been followed by similar movements abroad, after an appropriate time lag.

Many observers predict that in the future, the United States will be less a model that will be followed than it has been. But even if we accept the emergence of the so-called Triad of coequal trading partners (North America, Western Europe, and Japan), there will be some delay at least before the United States loses its preeminence. It is no coincidence that it is Kenichi Ohmae, the Japanese analyst who developed the Triad concept, who also coined the delightful word *Californianization,* meaning that the ideal consumption patterns, in the eyes of the rest of the Triad, are those of California.[9]

In one respect at least, the United States still leads the world. This is in the maturity of its consumer goods markets. Logic points very strongly to similar patterns emerging in other countries when per capita income levels of substantial numbers of these countries approach that of the United States.

Two important things have happened in American consumer goods markets during recent decades:

1. Product categories have progressively flattened, until an estimated 90% of consumer purchasing takes place in fields that show no growth beyond the 1-2% percent associated with population increase.[10]

2. Connected with point 1, manufacturers have reacted in frustration to the lack of aggregate market growth by searching for and exploiting market niches, some very small. Many of these have been caused by demographic shifts, such as the increase in the numbers of older people and the growth in the numbers of male homemakers. This strategy has led to a dramatic fragmentation of markets and a splintering of consumer franchises—a generalization that holds for virtually every consumer goods category measured by Nielsen. There is very little chance that the trend to fragmentation will reverse,[11] although the pace of splintering is certainly less at the end of the 1990s than it was at the beginning of the decade.

In addition, three other developments have taken place, all to some extent influenced by the two important changes described above:

3. The launch of new brands, always a formidably difficult undertaking, has become more problematic than ever as a consequence of the lack of market growth. It should be remembered that in the past, the majority of successful international brands were introduced as innovations in a single country and subsequently rolled out into others. In most, although not all, cases, the American launch came first.

4. Manufacturers' advertising and promotion budgets moved sharply in relative terms from advertising (above-the-line activity) to sales promotions (below-the-line activity) in the two decades ending in 1992. Advertising has not subsequently regained its share. The increase in promotions came in response to short-term competitive pressures on sales volume against a background of a gradual growth of concentration in the retail trade, bringing an increase in retail buying power vis-à-vis manufacturers.

5. American network television—the major advertising medium for delivering the mass coverage needed by packaged goods advertisers—has progressively lost much of its audience.

These movements mean that manufacturers have had to learn to operate more opportunistically than they have in the past. Entrepreneurship is the rallying cry in colleges of business administration. Scale economies from long production runs and from the mass marketing of single product lines are now less evident than in the past. In 1999, in supermarkets in all parts of the United States, the housewife can choose from among at least six separate varieties of Tide laundry detergent, each quite distinct from the others in functional terms; 50(!) varieties of Crest toothpaste; and eight varieties of Coca-Cola.

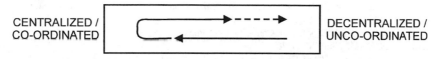

CENTRALIZED /
CO-ORDINATED

DECENTRALIZED /
UNCO-ORDINATED

Figure 1.3. International Advertising: The Future?

If these trends are to spread to the rest of the Triad, are they likely to spur an even further and sharper retreat from globalization? Is there going to be a continued movement of the type illustrated in Figure 1.3? This outcome is by no means certain. It ignores the reactive powers of business. Many organizations have in the past been subtle listeners and have responded with great effect to faint and poorly articulated signals sent out by consumers. Myriad illustrations could be provided. Examples, *in the United States,* include small Japanese cars, mineral water, and soft drinks containing fruit juice; *in Britain,* muesli, beer brewed in the Continental fashion, and Oriental food; *in Japan,* herbal shampoo, French wine, and golf; and a wide range of products in every country responding to the tastes of teenagers (see also Ford and Phillips, Chapter 8, this volume).

However, how much benefit companies will gain from sensitive monitoring of market trends depends on the effectiveness of manufacturers' and advertising agencies' local antennae. It also depends on how much managers are encouraged to listen to the signals from the markets and on how quickly the firms react. There have been many cases in the past in which large companies have responded to important opportunities with bureaucratic sloth. The long-term future—what will happen in the 21st century—might bring a considerable convergence of consumer tastes and needs, and consequently a significant extension and strengthening of international brands. But it is the consumer who is going to dictate the extent of this. And, as usual, the most successful manufacturers will not be those whose mission is to sell what they can make, but those whose mission is to make what they can sell—especially if they are able to find out about the things they can sell in advance of their competitors.

Notes

1. Christopher A. Bartlett and Sumantra Ghoshal, *Managing Across Borders: The Transnational Solution* (Boston: Harvard Business School Press, 1989), 58, 65.

2. Kenichi Ohmae, "The Global Logic of Strategic Alliances," *Harvard Business Review,* vol. 89, March/April 1989, 143-154.

3. Chris Ambler, "Benefits of Centrally Coordinated Campaigns," *Viewpoint* (Ogilvy & Mather, New York), Winter 1984, 30.

4. Theodore Levitt, "The Globalization of Markets," in *The Marketing Imagination* (New York: Free Press, 1983), 20.

5. The data are variable in quality, although this does not invalidate the conclusions, which are based on the extreme shifts in the numbers. Robert E. Hite and Cynthia Fraser, "International Advertising Strategies of Multinational Corporations," *Journal of Advertising Research,* August/September 1988, 9-17.

6. See, for instance, Ralph Z. Sorenson and Ulrich E. Wiechmann, "Probing Opinions: How Multinationals View Marketing Standardization," *Harvard Business Review,* vol. 75, May/June 1975, 39.

7. Kenichi Ohmae, "Managing in a Borderless World," *Harvard Business Review,* May/June 1989, 152-161.

8. Theodore Levitt, "The Pluralization of Consumption" (editorial), *Harvard Business Review,* May/June 1989, 7-8.

9. Ohmae, "The Global Logic of Strategic Alliances."

10. John Philip Jones, *How Much Is Enough? Getting the Most From Your Advertising Dollar* (New York: Simon & Schuster-Lexington, 1992), chap. 2.

11. Ibid.

Part I

The Realities of
International Advertising

2

International Advertising Developments

Ashish Banerjee

Usage and Contexts

Advertising is a worldwide business activity today. As marketers expand into countries they have previously not explored, and as media proliferate across countries, advertising is gaining impetus around the world. For those of us who travel a lot, advertising is the most visible manifestation of the globalization of business in general and of brands in particular.

The term *international advertising* is widely used to denote cross-border advertising, and it may have a number of context-specific connotations. One of the contexts in which the term is often used is in the description of or in reference to advertising that originates in a country other than the one the person using the term is from. To an American, all advertising created outside the United States may constitute "international" advertising; to a German, all advertising conceived and developed outside Germany might be "international." Because what constitutes "international" in this context is a function of where one happens to be in geographic terms, there is room for a lot of ambiguity. Therefore, such usage is best avoided. I would suggest that advertising originating in a particular country be referred to with the name of that country as a qualifying prefix. Advertising from the United Kingdom would therefore be referred to as British advertising, and so on.

Another sense in which the term *international advertising* is used is in the context of discussions regarding the scale and scope of the advertising business on a worldwide, continental, or country-by-country basis. I shall discuss this use in much greater detail in the next section.

The widest usage of the term *international advertising* is in the context of advertising for brands that are marketed in many countries. Such advertising is also referred to as *global, multinational, multicountry,* or *cross-national advertising*. A few definitions that may help differentiate among these terms vis-à-vis nuances of usage, as well as a more exhaustive treatment of this subject, will appear later in this chapter.

Scale and Scope of the Advertising Business Worldwide

Per Robert Cohen of McCann-Erickson Worldwide, in 1998 marketers invested an aggregate of $405.3 billion worldwide in advertising. The United States, the world's largest advertising market, accounted for $201.6 billion: 49.7% of the global total. Country-by-country advertising expenditure figures are published periodically by most of the major network advertising agency organizations. Worldwide advertising expenditure figures are available from *Advertising Age* as well as from the International Advertising Association.

Aggregate advertising expenditures vary widely from country to country. These variations are caused by three major factors: the size of the buying population, the state of the economy, and the extent of competitive activity in the branded goods and services sector of the economy. Data from selected countries appear in Tables 2.1 through 2.3.

Cross-country comparisons of the extent of advertising activity in different countries are often made using data on advertising expenditure per capita. However, this seemingly foolproof method is not without its pitfalls, because it depends primarily upon the currency's exchange rate vis-à-vis the U.S.

TABLE 2.1 Advertising Expenditure, 1995: Americas, Top 15 Countries

Country	Total Expenditure (U.S.$ millions)	Expenditure per Capita (U.S.$)
United States	174,933	674
Canada	9,740	325
Brazil	8,600	56
Argentina	3,229	99
Mexico	2,284	25
Colombia	1,838	51
Venezuela	1,050	48
Peru	999	42
Chile	622	44
Puerto Rico	394	106
Costa Rica	133	40
Trinidad and Tobago	124	98
Ecuador	101	9
Guatemala	78	7
Bolivia	30	4
El Salvador	69	13

SOURCE: Data from McCann-Erickson Worldwide.

dollar, the buying power of the currency, and media costs, which vary across countries.

A more useful way of examining the relative extent of advertising activity in a country is to compute a ratio between the total amount of advertising moneys expended in a given year and the country's gross national product (GNP) or gross domestic product (GDP). Because this measure is based only on economic factors (unlike advertising per capita), it offers a better basis for making comparisons across countries—certainly across those with similar GDP figures.

The International Monetary Fund recently released a new method of calculating GNP/GDP that takes into account the buying power of the local currency in each country, based on the cost of living. This new methodology has resulted in substantial rerankings of many countries—most notably China and India, which have moved up considerably in the rankings. It is not inconceivable that a similar method for calculating aggregate advertising expenditures, based on buying power, or in terms of number of TV commercials or print ads or the number of people reached, will be developed in the near future by the advertising industry.

TABLE 2.2 Advertising Expenditure, 1995: Europe, Top 20 Countries

Country	Total Expenditure (U.S.$ millions)	Expenditure per Capita (U.S.$)
Germany	16,345	200
United Kingdom	15,720	269
France	11,912	205
Italy	6,217	109
Spain	3,299	84
Switzerland	2,446	354
Netherlands	2,409	156
Sweden	1,985	225
Greece	1,861	181
Austria	1,515	188
Belgium	1,504	148
Russia	1,150	8
Finland	1,049	205
Denmark	1,031	196
Norway	985	226
Portugal	912	93
Poland	615	16
Turkey	600	9
Ireland	431	119
Hungary	383	38

SOURCE: Data from McCann-Erickson Worldwide.

Advertising has traditionally prospered in most countries characterized by free market economies. Until the early 1990s, more than 50% of total worldwide advertising expenditures were in the United States—the one economy that adheres to the strictest principles of capitalism and free market economics.

Factors Influencing Advertising Expenditures in Various Countries

Aggregate advertising expenditure is directly related to the extent to which an economy has developed. The United States and most Western European economies are characterized by relatively higher advertising-to-GDP ratios than the rest of the world. On the other hand, most Eastern European economies (which, until recently, were characterized by communist or socialist economic systems) exhibit some of the lowest advertising-to-GDP ratios,

TABLE 2.3 Advertising Expenditure, 1995: Asia/Pacific, Top 15 Countries

Country	Total Expenditure (U.S.$ millions)	Expenditure per Capita (U.S.$)
Japan	45,000	357
South Korea	5,573	123
Taiwan	3,346	156
Australia	2,809	154
Hong Kong	1,943	313
India	1,722	2
Thailand	1,624	27
Indonesia	1,466	7
New Zealand	910	252
China	805	1
Singapore	657	199
Malaysia	613	29
Philippines	479	7
Pakistan	75	1
Guam	68	444
Vietnam	68	1

SOURCE: Data from McCann-Erickson Worldwide.

because branded competition in these economies is a fairly recent phenomenon. Developing or "newly industrialized" economies (China, India, Brazil, Nigeria, and the like) are typified by advertising-to-GDP ratios that lie between the higher extremes of the more developed economies and the lower extremes of the formerly socialist Eastern European economies.

The general rule is that the more developed the economy, the greater the extent to which advertising plays its part in "oiling the economic engine." Usually, growth in a nation's productive capacity (in terms of its ability to add economic values) leads to increasing per capita income levels, which give people the means to afford lifestyles that encompass basic needs plus not-so-basic wants. Advertising is characterized by its ability to build preferences in the domain of wants, by informing the consumer about the benefits that each brand offers, in product categories comprising many brands that provide comparable functional utilities but differing nonfunctional utilities ("added values").

The size of the buying population also influences the extent of advertising activity in an economy. Countries such as Switzerland and Kuwait have relatively high standards of living, but relatively small populations. This leads to lower advertising-to-GNP ratios, because advertisers think in terms of modest expenditures to reach the relatively few residents of these countries. On the other hand, countries with comparable per capita income levels but larger populations, such as Germany, Japan, and the United States, are characterized by aggressive attitudes on the part of advertisers, which drives up the advertising-to-GNP ratios.

The size of the buying population has an additional effect on the extent of advertising activity when it is considered in conjunction with the media options available in a country. Typically, highly developed economies also exhibit higher levels of media development, media availability, and media fragmentation, and consequently, higher media costs on a per unit basis. The United States has the most widely developed and fragmented media landscape of any country and also has on average the highest media cost on a per TV spot or per magazine page basis. The higher media costs in the United States are largely attributable to the fact that they help marketers reach a large buying population with relatively high disposable income levels and only partly attributable to the strength of the dollar versus other currencies (which, again, is a function of the country's economic strength).

The extent of competitive activity in the branded goods and services sector also has a markedly large influence on the extent of advertising activity in a country. Advertising is a major means by which marketers communicate the uniqueness of their brands to their prospects. The greater the extent of branded competition in the marketplace, the higher the need for brand differentiation and, therefore, demand for advertising space and time. This leads to increases in the cost of advertising, makes competition advertising-intensive in nature, and, eventually, when replicated over a large number of product and service categories, pushes up the advertising-to-GNP ratio for the economy as a whole.

Scale and Scope of the Worldwide Advertising Agency Networks

Advertising is a marketer-led activity, and over the years since the 1920s, a number of U.S.- and U.K.-based agencies have followed their major clients in expanding their operations overseas and setting up offices in many countries. More recently, they have been followed by major Japanese and French agencies. These overseas operations have evolved into fairly sophisticated networks of offices in many countries. Different overseas offices often service the same client companies and work along similar (or identical) operational, strategic, structural, and cultural principles—all established by guidelines emanating from the head office.

In terms of ownership, these offices may be wholly owned by the parent agency, partially owned (majority or minority equity stake) by the parent agency, or set up as nonequity partnerships. All three of these forms of ownership structure continue to this day, but the number of nonequity partnerships is on the decline, because parent agencies usually want to own at least part of their affiliate agencies.

The older American agencies have consolidated their positions over time with mergers, acquisitions, and expansions, and it is fair to say that they dominate the business at the global level. Of the world's top 25 advertising agency networks, 19 are of American origin, 3 are Japanese, 2 are French, and 1 is British.

Client companies with operations in many countries usually align their brands with one or more of the worldwide agency networks in order to realize economies of scale, consistency of strategic thinking and advertising development, and efficacy of executional implementation in terms of creation, production, and media placement. As an example, Unilever, one of the world's largest marketers and advertisers of branded packaged goods across many product categories, uses a "club" of four worldwide agency networks—J. Walter Thompson, Ogilvy & Mather, Ammirati Puris Lintas, and McCann-Erickson—usually on a brand or category basis. In 1999 Unilever's Lux toilet soap is serviced by J. Walter Thompson in all the countries where it is advertised and where the agency operates. The other "club" agencies have similar brand alignments. In some cases actual brand names may differ from country to country, but the packaging and brand positioning are uniform.

Table 2.4 presents 1997 financial data for the world's most "internationalized" advertising agency networks (characterized by a significantly widespread operating presence). Table 2.5 provides worldwide advertising expenditure data for the top 25 multinational advertisers in 1997.

Because the larger worldwide agency networks are able to provide their multinational clients with a generally uniform quality of talent, resources, and services around the globe, the worldwide agency landscape is tilted somewhat in their favor, because multinational marketers and their brands account for a significant proportion of overall advertising spending in every country and therefore worldwide. In other words, the agency networks with the widest and strongest nets traditionally have caught the most fish.

TABLE 2.4 World's Top 25 Agency Networks, 1997: Income and Volume Figures (in U.S.$ millions)

By Income Rank 1997	Rank 1996	Agency	Worldwide Gross Income 1997	1997-1996 % Change	Worldwide Volume 1997	1997-1996 % Change
1	1	Dentsu	$1,927	0.9	$14,192	1.9
2	2	McCann-Erickson Worldwide	1,451	12.7	11,016	20.5
3	3	J. Walter Thompson	1,120	4.5	7,637	4.6
4	4	BBDO Worldwide	990	5.7	8,059	3.3
5	6	DDB Needham Worldwide	920	5.4	6,882	6.2
6	8	Grey Advertising	918	9.1	6,125	9.0
7	9	Euro RSCG Worldwide	883	7.2	6,536	7.7
8	7	Leo Burnett Co.	878	1.4	5,977	2.7
9	5	Hakuhodo	848	−5.5	6,476	−3.0
10	10	Ogilvy & Mather Worldwide	838	5.7	7,375	6.2
11	11	Young & Rubicam	781	10.4	8,004	8.9
12	12	Publicis Communication	625	−7.1	4,058	−11.9
13	13	Ammirati Puris Lintas	621	2.5	4,449	4.2
14	14	D'Arcy Masius	607	14.0	5,807	13.3
15	15	Bates Worldwide	520	2.4	6,424	1.7
16	17	Foote, Cone & Belding	511	21.9	5,418	10.0
17	16	Saatchi & Saatchi	490	5.9	5,730	2.1
18	18	TBWA International	476	15.1	3,403	13.5
19	19	Bozell Worldwide	404	25.1	3,077	22.1
20	20	Lowe & Partners Worldwide	301	3.3	2,083	−0.9
21	22	Carlson Marketing Group	285	11.5	2,277	11.8
22	23	Wunderman Cato Johnson	281	10.4	2,032	4.6
23	27	TMP Worldwide	264	23.4	1,758	23.1
24	25	Rapp Collins Worldwide	261	17.8	1,789	17.2
25	24	Asatsu	230	−0.4	1,886	0.7

SOURCE: Adapted by permission from data that appeared in the April 27, 1998, issue of *Advertising Age*. Copyright Crain Communications Inc., 1998.

Advertising in the Context of Brands Marketed and Advertised in Many Countries

As noted earlier, a number of terms are used to refer to advertising of brands marketed in many countries. Let's examine each of these terms.

TABLE 2.5 Top 25 Global Marketers, 1997

Rank 1997	Advertiser	Headquarters	Non-U.S. Ad Spending 1997 (U.S.$ millions)	1997-1996 % Change	Country Count
1	Procter & Gamble Co.	Cincinnati, U.S.	5,755	13.3	63
2	Unilever	Rotterdam/London	3,434	7.7	62
3	Nestlé	Vevey, Switzerland	1,782	–8.5	63
4	Toyota Motor Corp.	Toyota City, Japan	2,106	16.6	52
5	Coca-Cola Co.	Atlanta, U.S.	1,737	18.6	61
6	General Motors Corp.	Detroit, U.S.	4,044	26.7	46
7	Volkswagen	Wolfsburg, Germany	1,103	–1.5	44
8	PSA Peugeot Citroen	Paris, France	871	–9.6	39
9	Nissan Motor Co.	Tokyo, Japan	1,413	–1.1	50
10	Mars Inc.	McLean, VA, U.S.	1,480	16.2	38
11	Ford Motor Co.	Dearborn, MI, U.S.	2,106	8.8	47
12	Sony Corp.	Tokyo, Japan	1,547	23.9	53
13	L'Oréal	Paris, France	1,407	28.8	44
14	Philip Morris Cos.	New York, U.S.	2,889	–6.8	52
15	Renault	Paris, France	700	5.3	36
16	Fiat	Turin, Italy	655	12.3	26
17	Honda Motor Co.	Tokyo, Japan	1,204	16.3	39
18	Henkel	Düsseldorf, Germany	619	2.3	25
19	McDonald's Corp.	Oak Brook, IL, U.S.	1,646	–0.7	49
20	Kao Corp.	Tokyo, Japan	619	–0.6	9
21	Ferrero	Perugia, Italy	567	–7.2	31
22	BMW	Munich, Germany	706	9.6	39
23	Colgate-Palmolive Co.	New York, U.S.	913	7.8	55
24	Danone Group	Levallois-Perret, France	569	37.1	21
25	Johnson & Johnson	New Brunswick, NJ, U.S.	1,320	4.0	55

SOURCE: Adapted by permission from data that appeared in the November 9, 1998, issue of *Advertising Age*. Copyright Crain Communications Inc., 1998.

Global advertising. This term is usually used to refer to advertising for universally ubiquitous brands, such as Coca-Cola, Marlboro cigarettes, Kodak photographic film, Benetton apparel, Gucci accessories, Sony home electronics, and Perrier bottled water. Typically, the term *global* should be used as a qualifier only when the brand is available in a very large number of countries (i.e., when it is a "global brand") and employs the same advertising execution(s) in almost all of those countries.

The number of truly global brands is very limited. Further, it is not always necessary for a global brand to use global advertising executions. Coca-Cola and Pepsi usually do, with some modifications to accommodate local norms, tastes, and preferences. On the other hand, Levi's jeans, very much a global brand, uses "localized" advertising executions that vary immensely depending upon the country in question. The term *global advertising* is widely misused, and the reader is urged to use it with some caution.

International advertising: Depending upon the context, this term could refer to advertising from another country, or to global advertising, or to the international dimension of the advertising agency business. Because of the overall ambiguity of the term, the reader is urged (despite the title of this chapter) to use it sparingly, and use more precise terms instead.

Multinational advertising: This is a term typically used to refer to the advertising for multinational brands—brands that may not be as ubiquitous as global brands, but are nevertheless available in a large number of countries. Examples include Impulse body spray; Ivory, Camay, and Palmolive soaps; Head & Shoulders, Sunsilk/Gloria/Sedal, and Pert Plus/Wash & Go shampoos; the L'Oréal hair-care line; Colgate and Crest toothpastes; Vaseline Intensive Care and Nivea body lotions; Pond's, Oil of Olay, and L'Oréal Plenitude facial skin-care lines; Nescafé instant coffee; some of Kellogg's cereal brands; and most major airlines (e.g., Lufthansa, British Airways, Swissair, Singapore). Usually, the development of advertising for such brands is somewhat centralized, with the "lead agency" of a major worldwide advertising network (usually the New York, London, or Paris office) being responsible for strategic planning and creative development.

Transnational advertising: This is a more recent and evolutionary term used to connote advertising (for multinational brands) developed in a more participatory, decentralized manner, with the input of consumers, the agency network's personnel, and the client's marketing personnel from the various countries where the advertising will eventually be exposed. Developments on these lines are taking place in the food field as well as in hair care.

Multidomestic advertising: This term refers to the advertising used for a multidomestic brand—a brand that might have the same name across a number of countries but is characterized by different states of brand development and a relatively low degree of brand standardization across those countries. Necessarily, the advertising for such a brand would vary widely from country to country, depending upon the marketer's strategic intent and the set of circumstances contingent upon the brand in each country. This is a burgeoning activity and is to be found in beer as well as in some food categories.

Multicountry Advertising Campaign Development

As the term suggests, multicountry advertising campaigns are employed by marketers mainly when a particular brand is at a sufficiently significant level of development and sales in a fairly large number of countries. For such a set of circumstances to exist, the brand usually has to tap into certain basic commonalities of consumption patterns and demographic, psychographic, sociological, cultural, economic, and lifestyle-related factors among its target consumers in each country where it is marketed.

Such commonalities seldom manifest themselves as identical across countries. What is often found are similarities on some of the parameters listed above and differences on others. A "good," effective multicountry advertising campaign focuses convincingly on the similarities while making allowances for the differences. As an example, the widely acclaimed campaign for Gillette's Sensor shaving system uses compelling visual vignettes of what the experience of maleness ("being a man") is all about while demonstrating the functional superiority of the brand. The executions are rounded out with the tag line "The best a man can get," which addresses two key benefits: (a) This is the best shaving system your money can buy (functional), and (b) it helps you look and be your best (nonrational/emotional/psychological).

Most of the vignettes in the Sensor commercials are deeply rooted in the human condition from a male perspective. They depict various aspects of relationships, such as fatherhood, achievement, and success, because these are universally relevant and acceptable values and visual portrayals. Gillette and its agencies, BBDO and McCann-Erickson, keep the commercials culturally relevant by modifying some of the other vignettes, especially those relating to sports; for example, the commercials used in Latin America and Europe depict soccer, whereas those used on the North American continent depict American football.

The development process for such multinational campaigns is complex, because it involves many stages and many people in many countries. The advertising development process can run two ways:

1. *Single-country development, subsequent testing, and rollout:* A commercial is developed and exposed in one country, usually the brand's "lead market," where it generates the largest volume of sales. If it successfully meets or exceeds its communication and effectiveness action standards, it is then tested in all other countries where the brand is marketed. If it tests well, management will usually decide to run the same commercial unchanged or with minor modifications to suit social, cultural, or executional differences across countries. Currently, minor (but sometimes major) modifications are the norm.

2. *Multicountry development and exposure:* More recently, agencies have begun to use multicountry teams to develop both advertising strategy and creative executions. This process ensures strategic and executional consistencies in the advertising used across all the markets, but is usually employable for a limited number of brands in circumstances where the brands' constituencies of consumers are reasonably similar across countries.

Strategic and Creative Considerations

In terms of the manipulation of strategic and creative (executional) variables, there are a number of options available to the multinational marketer. The choice of option is usually dictated by the circumstances, contingent upon the brand and the marketer's long-term objectives for it. A simplified representation appears in Table 2.6.

It is useful to visualize an individual brand as a point on a continuum. At one end of the continuum, the brand is a multidomestic; at the other end, it is global. Most multinational brands marketed today are at neither extreme of this continuum, but at a point somewhere in between the extremes. In many instances, such a brand is carefully led through a managed evolution over a part of the continuum, as more and more elements of the brand are brought into harmony ("standardized") across the countries where it is marketed. The representation in Table 2.6 attempts to depict the same notion for the advertising for such brands. The reader can discern how the advertising strategy

TABLE 2.6 Brand and Strategy Options

Brand Type	Advertising Strategy Option Across Countries	Creative Execution Option Across Countries
Global	same	same
Multinational (evolved)	same	similar ("pattern")
Multinational (evolving)	similar	similar
Multidomestic	different	different

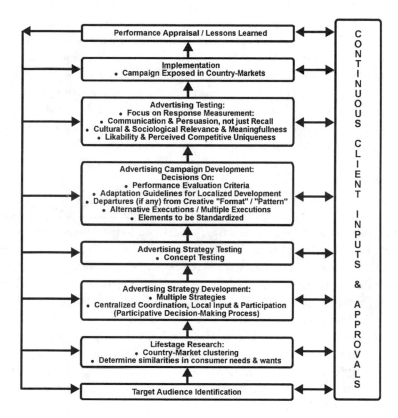

Figure 2.1. Multinational Advertising Development and Management: Banerjee's Operational Process Framework

and creative execution for a brand will become increasingly harmonious and standardized as a brand evolves along the continuum. Figure 2.1 presents a generalized representation of the various stages in the multicountry campaign development process for major multinational brands.

Worldwide Media and Programming Development

Much of the advertising activity for major multinational brands is contingent upon reaching similar groups of consumers across many countries. One of the best ways of doing this is to use media and vehicle options available in similar forms in many countries, because it stands to reason that the prototypical loyal *Baywatch* viewer in the United States is likely to exhibit reasonable similarities to the prototypical loyal *Baywatch* viewer in Germany.

The argument can be extended to print media as well, because the readers of magazines such as *Elle, Cosmopolitan, Vogue,* and *Playboy* tend to exhibit some similar characteristics across borders. The different national editions of these magazines are targeted to a somewhat common reader profile, offer similar editorial environments, and are usually read by similar people across national boundaries.

Generally speaking, fashion, lifestyle, and business-oriented magazines and newspapers are able to find multicountry audiences, as are music, sports, and youth-oriented TV programming, in addition to traditional drama-based soap operas (called *telenovelas* in Latin America, where they are extremely popular), and sitcoms. Cable News Network (CNN), of course, is ubiquitous, as are the *International Herald Tribune,* the *Economist,* the *Financial Times,* and regional editions of *The Wall Street Journal* and *Time* magazine.

Each of these media options offers the advertiser access to audiences on a worldwide basis—today, it is possible to buy space or time across a number of countries by placing a single phone call and signing a single contract. In fact, the 1992 launch commercial for Gillette's Sensor razor aired at exactly the same time in 19 countries around the world via a staggered exposure schedule on CNN.

With the rapid proliferation of satellite television, there have been vast increases in available programming capacity and a consequent need for "good" programming that is well received across borders. In many instances, advertisers are producing programming (or underwriting program production costs) and selling or bartering these programs to major media outlets. The *Wide World of Sports* is a program that is aired in more than 100 countries via such satellite channels as British Sky Broadcasting (across Europe) and STAR TV (across Asia and the Middle East) and is supported by charter advertisers like Gillette. Satellite channel operators in each of these countries guarantee the charter advertiser prime commercial time and placement in exchange for the rights to air the program.

In addition to television programming and print title options, certain television channels are now accessible in a large number of countries via satellite. CNN is viewed in more than 100 countries and MTV in even more;

other channels, such as ESPN International, Prime Sports, STAR Plus, and BBC World Service TV, are also beamed to a large number of countries.

The Future

With continued globalization and integration of the world's economies, multinational brands will be marketed in increasingly larger numbers of countries. Such manufacturing scale and geographic scope will generate scale economies to lower costs, and advertising standardization will provide one way of lowering overall production and marketing expenses. Accordingly, it is generally accepted that the use of standardized advertising campaigns will continue to increase as brands penetrate new markets and seek to lower their costs. Additionally, some major multinational marketers (Unilever, Gillette, Nestlé, Procter & Gamble, Colgate-Palmolive, and the like) are now investing in brands conceived as panregional (usually pan-European) entities that are launched simultaneously in a large number of countries or are rolled out very quickly across a continent, adding further impetus to the earlier argument.

The rapid proliferation of satellite television with "wide-footprint" coverage (STAR TV's footprint ranges from Turkey to Tokyo) is adding further impetus to the use of standardized advertising campaigns. Many of these campaigns employ predominantly visual messages, obviating the need for language translation (and possible miscommunication) across borders. As satellite proliferation progresses, the use of standardized cross-border advertising will continue to increase.

Recommended Further Reading

de Mooij, Marieke, *Advertising Worldwide: Concepts, Theories and Practices of International, Multinational and Global Advertising,* 2nd ed. (Englewood Cliffs, NJ: Prentice Hall International, 1994).
NTC Publications, *World Advertising Trends* (Henley-on-Thames, UK: NTC, 1996).
Rijkens, Rein, *European Advertising Strategies* (London: Cassell, 1992).

3

International Advertising

How Far Can It Fly?

Roderick White

Only two countries' advertising communities have the arrogance to believe that their advertising is the best in the world: those in Britain and the United States. This belief has encouraged marketers on both sides of the Atlantic to make a simplistic translation of Levitt's concept of global marketing into global advertising. The fact that English is becoming the primary worldwide lingua franca, at least for business, is then amplified by the post-imperialist instincts of the British and the neo-imperialist impulses of the Americans. But does this make sense? Or, at least, how should we make sense of it?

The arguments in favor of globally—or at least internationally—common and coordinated advertising campaigns are several, with varying degrees of merit. In this chapter, I will look at most of them, in the context of my experience in planning advertising for a variety of clients internationally and my observation of debates about the subject since the 1970s.

It should be noted from the start, however, that strict polarity (global versus non-global) is spurious: Reality shows a continuum from tightly coordinated (Alfa Romeo in Europe) to wholly local (most Japanese multinationals), and a consensus view appears to be developing that "Think globally, act locally" (i.e., adapt global concepts to local conditions) is the most promising route to follow.

Why Advertise Globally?

The arguments for some form of global advertising fall into several categories.

Marketing Arguments

- For a brand marketed in a common format to similar customers in different countries, it is logical that its communication should be the same in all these countries. Why should it be any different?
- There are, increasingly, identifiable groups of people, across national boundaries, who have common interests, values, needs, and frames of reference; it is sensible to appeal to them in the same way in all countries.
- Increasingly, international media enable international advertising; these range from specifically multinational publications and satellite TV channels to the situation in much of Europe, where one country's TV stations have footprints that cover some or all of one or more neighboring countries. This is an opportunity to be exploited and a sign of things to come. If we put out different messages in media that overlap national boundaries, we will confuse people.
- The growth of global tourism (and business travel) means that our customers are increasingly exposed to our advertising outside their home countries. If the advertising gives conflicting messages, this will damage the brand.

Economic Arguments

- Making a commercial, or series of commercials, is expensive, especially if celebrity talent is involved. Better to make one commercial for $1 million,[1] and translate and run it worldwide, than to make six, or a dozen, each for $250,000, to satisfy the whims of individual countries. This also applies, usually on a smaller scale, to photography.

- Using centralized creation, production, and control to develop advertising leads to economies of effort: fewer marketing people involved in agency contact, spending less time on it; less time spent on creation by agencies, so the client can reduce agency remuneration overall.
- Global media companies, such as Time Warner, News Corporation, and Bertelsmann, give advertisers the opportunity and the need to produce global campaigns, to capitalize on cross-border media opportunities and the production economies that accompany them. These media owners' muscle needs to be matched with equivalent buying power.

Control Arguments

- The people who understand the brand are at corporate headquarters. If they control the brand's advertising worldwide, they can be sure that brand values are correctly carried through to all the corporation's markets.
- Given a central corporate team and globally coordinated agency team, both parties to the process will work in harmony, and control will be facilitated.

Creative Arguments

- There are few good creative ideas, and very few great ones. If we have a great idea, we owe it to ourselves to exploit it fully, in every market in which we operate.
- Good creative ideas travel—look at Hollywood films. Why should this not be true of advertising?

The Fashion Argument

- (This one is not actually an argument; rather, it is a bandwagon effect.) If everyone else is doing it, it must be right, and we should not be left behind.

All these arguments have some merit, even the last. They are all, however, open to challenge, and one of the most valuable things an intelligent marketer can do is to challenge received wisdom.

The Marketing Issues

Advertising is only part of marketing—although for most consumer businesses it consumes a conspicuous share of the communications budget. We should not automatically assume that what applies to marketing overall applies equally to all parts of the mix.

We need, however, to look hard at marketing itself before we accept the pressure to go global. The idea of global marketing is compelling, and as transnational corporations multiply and prosper, more and more products and services can be found selling in an increasing proportion of the world's 200-odd countries. If the corporation can sell the same specification in every market, this makes possible hitherto unheard-of economies of scale and freedom of action. Apart from constraints imposed by the sheer cost and time scale of creating a plant to service the world, production can be located to fit financial and geographic convenience, and scale economies may be gained by producing for the world from just a few plants. How much simpler, too, if all the elements of the product can be homogenized for the world, down to and including brand names, packaging designs, brochures, and instruction leaflets.

There are companies that, in effect, operate like this, and they are probably growing in number, although this is not easy to monitor. But markets remain stubbornly national. In spite of the massive size of transnational corporations, their effective penetration of many market sectors remains low on a global or even continental scale. Further, even where a brand has established a near-universal presence, its market share, and often consumer perceptions, may vary wildly. A classic example is Levi's, which is more or less a mass-market brand with limited cachet in the United States but is brand leader, with a distinct quality image and a price premium, in much of Europe. Things can be much more extreme. Yardley's English Lavender is a brand of fragranced toiletries that is considered dated, elderly, and a gift for your grandmother in the United Kingdom. In France, it embodies a more positive, upmarket English chic. And in South America, it is an extremely macho brand for men.

Thus positionings within markets can vary, even for major brands. There are countries where the Pepsi Challenge, which is a number 2 brand strategy, is irrelevant because Pepsi is number 1—not many, but they exist. Further, there are countries—and, in particular, regions within countries (e.g., Scotland)—where the worldwide dominance of colas in the soft drink market is far from local reality. You have to question whether even global marketing can be strictly imposed in these circumstances.

A further problem—one that is being very gradually eroded on a world scale by the development of international agreements under the World Trade

Organization—is the diversity of legal systems, standards, and advertising regulatory frameworks. It is often not possible to market the identical product in the identical packaging, let alone advertise or promote it in the identical way, across national boundaries. This applies even in the European Union, where the "single market" has supposedly been in existence for 7 years. (The forthcoming EU directive on advertising regulation moves this situation forward only a little.)

With communications, things become considerably more difficult. Quite apart from the different legal requirements and market situations, there's the problem of culture. This is where opponents of global advertising can have a field day, because they can argue that the very idea of global advertising runs counter to the marketing concept: it takes insufficient notice of the requirements, needs, attitudes, mind-sets, traditions, and expectations of the target group in the individual country. This attitude is best detailed in a recent book by Marieke de Mooij, a Dutch analyst with years of experience, chiefly with BBDO.[2]

De Mooij's arguments can be summarized, very briefly, as follows. It is a demonstrable fact that the cultural value systems of different national populations vary widely. This is shown both by personality profiles and by the ways in which people receive and interpret communications, including advertising, and is reflected in recognizable national advertising styles. Below this generality, there are significant differences in modes of thinking, in body language and gesture, and in how language is used. Advertising that fails to tune in to the nuances of the national character, and of the subgroup within the culture that is being targeted, will by definition be sub-optimal. In other words, the consumer should be recognized as king at the national level (see de Mooij, Chapter 6, this volume).

The counter-argument is like the old contrast between an individual who sees the glass as half full and one who sees it as half empty. De Mooij, it can be argued, is looking for *differences,* but it is the job of the international marketer to look for *similarities.* If we do this, we will be able to find sufficient common ground to develop strategies and executions that will transcend national differences. Hence the proliferation of international market research agencies carrying out carefully standardized research in many countries simultaneously and programs such as VALS or RISC that apply a common framework of analysis to attitudinal material from a wide range of countries.

A more specific rebuttal to de Mooij's argument is the idea that certain audiences are, worldwide, effectively homogeneous. Business travelers and teenagers are most often cited, and it has become customary to talk of these groups as "tribes" with similar interests, needs, values, and frames of reference. You reach business travelers, of course, through in-flight magazines, CNN, and increasingly the Internet; you reach teenagers through MTV and pop concerts. Easy, isn't it?

Here again, however, a moment's thought should give us pause. Anyone who has spent time in multinational business meetings will have noticed how people from different countries fail—consistently—to communicate effectively with each other. Even where language barriers appear to have been eliminated, either by simultaneous translation or because everyone speaks good English, at some time during the meeting you suddenly realize that each country's representatives seem to be singing from a slightly different hymnbook. Surprisingly often, they revert to something remarkably like national stereotypes—even though we all know that these stereotypes are caricatures.

Similarly, an Italian teenager may be just like a Dutch teenager when he or she is listening to music or wondering which brand of trainers to buy, but most of the time, and in most purchasing situations, a teenager is distinctively and differently Italian or Dutch. We ignore this at our peril.

The media arguments seem to be fundamentally weak. Although the presence of a medium may present an opportunity, media are purely means to an end. The marketing strategy and its translation into communications strategies and campaigns are what matter. If there are media that facilitate implementation of the strategy, fine, but the strategy should never be dictated by the media.

Adducing global tourism as an argument for global advertising has always been a straw thrown to someone drowning. It fails to allow for three key facts: (a) People on vacation are not in a mood that has much to do with their domestic purchasing behavior, so the relevance of any advertising they see is limited ("Oh, honey, do you see they have Gillette here? How wonderful!"); (b) they are rarely exposed to local media anyway; and (c) any local advertising they see is usually in a foreign language they do not understand well enough to know whether or not the ads are saying the same things as at home.

The Economic Issues

There is undoubtedly force behind economic arguments for globalization of advertising. The production costs argument is seductively simple and appears compelling. In some circumstances, there are demonstrable and clear advantages to be gained, but the situation is rarely as clear-cut as might be supposed. Much of the detail will depend on negotiations with actors, because much of the cost of airing commercials is made up of repeat fees (residuals) for the artists, and these can be very substantial—even if a global buyout is negotiated.

More important, however, are the physical problems that arise from translating commercials into several languages. It is not a simple matter to take 30 seconds of celluloid, carefully crafted into an English-language selling message, and turn it into the same thing in Finnish or Chinese. For a start, different languages take different numbers of words, of different lengths, to say the same thing. This means that to get it right, translation requires skilled and expensive creative talent. This leads, in turn, to a complex and often frustrating process in which local, regional, and headquarters people from agency and advertiser can find themselves going around in ever-decreasing circles, clocking expensive hours.

In sophisticated advertising markets, too, it is regarded by consumers as an insult if a commercial is dubbed: you must either film in several languages (and so must set up translation at a very early stage in production) or limit yourself to voice-over.

It is far easier to produce centralized still photography—although even here it is essential to consult with the key markets for the campaign, to ensure that there is a sufficient bank of shots available to provide subjects that are culturally acceptable and to cover foreseeable tactical needs.

All this suggests that, even if there are savings in production, these will not be of the scale implicit in the notion that the cost of producing an international campaign need be only the same as that of producing a single-country campaign. In relation to the overall budget, the savings may turn out to be negligible.

Similar arguments apply to media. Although some agency chiefs have said that a large global organization is essential to stand up to global media power,[3] there is little evidence—yet—that the global media groups have the ability either to coordinate selling efforts to extract a high price from advertisers or to deliver coordinated media packages across a wide range of countries. Both could conceivably happen—there are at least some global deals being struck, and News Corporation in April 1998 appointed its first global media sales chief.

Finally, it seems that major packaged goods advertisers, such as Unilever, actually pay their global agencies more, rather than less, for multinational service.

The Control Issues

There is a long-standing debate in the management literature about how best to manage a global corporation, and there are observable differences between theorists and practitioners. Modern theory—well and briefly summarized in an advertising context by Banerjee[4]—favors decentralization or regionalization in the marketing field, on the classical marketing grounds that it is essential to build upward from the consumer (see Banerjee, Chapter 2, this volume). In practice, a large proportion of companies that operate multinationally appear to take the view that, just as their production and finance management has become progressively more centralized (if it ever was not), so should their marketing.

The underlying assumption is that the man from the head office knows best—and, indeed, knows everything. If you are in Madison, Wisconsin, and aiming to market a brand in France or Tajikistan, it is actually a fair bet that you do not know everything about these markets: indeed, in the latter case you probably know next to nothing.

It seems clear that some centralization, albeit with the aid of teams of people, from both advertiser and agency, who can and do work together, is essential. Central control, rigorously applied, seems folly; centralized control that exploits local and regional knowledge, and that allows adequate rein for local and regional inputs, makes sense.

The Creative Issues

Certainly, there are few great creative ideas. Indeed, there are arguably so few that most advertising is by definition unoriginal. Cynics have observed that the main purpose of international award jamborees like the Cannes festival is to provide the world's creative directors with a fresh bank of ideas from other countries that they can rip off.

Unilever, in particular, has quite successfully institutionalized the exploitation of creative ideas internationally,[5] but has done so without, necessarily, internationalizing the rest of the marketing mix. Often the same idea appears in different markets attached to different brand names—Unilever's management's task includes that of identifying which brands in a given market can best use a successful new creative idea, given local market conditions and the brand portfolio available.

It is easy to talk about "creative ideas" in the abstract. The key issue is how they translate to, or how they need to be adapted for, a given market. The idea and its execution may well have to be considered differently. For the most part, a strong underlying proposition will usually travel, although a Unique Selling Proposition—if genuine—may have been pre-empted in some markets,[6] and sometimes the proposition may turn out to be addressing a problem that is not especially relevant to the market concerned.

For example, Tic Tac mints have successfully advertised in North America on a platform of "2 hours' freshness for less than 2 calories," using a female presenter in a straightforward selling commercial. In the United Kingdom, breath freshness owns a tiny segment of the mint market, with no motivating interest to most mint eaters, and calorie counting is a marginal concern. The result, for a small brand in the United Kingdom, is that the U.S. advertising acts like a promotion for Tic Tac: it creates short-term sales but produces no long-term brand-building benefit—in fact, surveys show the brand is becoming progressively marginalized and dated. On a broader scale, British Airways never succeeded in finding a way to run some of the ads from its "World's Favorite Airline" campaign in Japan.[7]

Further problems occur with actors and models, and with body language: Different people are seen differently in different countries. Ford got into trouble with the U.K. race relations authorities when a newspaper discovered that the company had identified Asian employees as Caucasians in a brochure adapted for Poland. This was a commercially correct decision, given Polish consumer attitudes, but Ford mishandled the PR. Similarly, many of the gestures that we take for granted are interpreted quite differently in other cultures.[8]

This is true, too, of the structure of communications. This may apply to the use of metaphor (almost universal in U.K. advertising but rare in Germany) or to the pace of a TV commercial.[9] It is by no means certain that a commercial that appears modern, stylish, and clever in one country will be perceived as such elsewhere—and it may, of course, be simply unintelligible: It is hard to see the British spot for Blackcurrant Tango traveling very far, although it's a great idea.

In the same way, national expectations and sophistication may change. When Russia opened up to the West, Western brands' advertising tended to be simple and informational.[10] It then became clear that Russian audiences were used to Western commercials shown on pan-European satellite TV and resented not seeing the very latest ads. Now there is a backlash developing, and consumers are looking for "Russian" ads.[11]

So, Where Do We Go From Here?

There is a tide flowing toward more international coordination of advertising planning and management. A large proportion of major account moves have a transnational (regional, at the least) component,[12] and this has encouraged the development of agency structures designed to cope with multinational assignments. As with all tides in advertising, there will undoubtedly be reverses, but the globalization of relationships seems set to continue.

Hard evidence is difficult to find, but my impression is that (as Banerjee suggested several years ago)[13] there are fewer attempts by large and sophisticated advertisers to develop tightly coordinated international campaigns; they are paying more attention to tailoring campaigns to fit local/regional consumer attitudes and market situations. At the same time, the language of globalization remains strong in the media, in the business press, and in management thinking.

Newcomers to the international advertising scene—including, for example, the growing range of Webvertisers—may therefore believe that all they need is a global campaign, and that such a campaign can happily be created in New York or London or even Moscow. (I omit Tokyo because the Japanese, who have been among the world's great consumer marketers for 30 years, almost routinely do not coordinate their advertising, and it is only relatively recently that the big Japanese agencies like Dentsu and Hakuhodo have established widespread agency networks.)

I believe that the only sensible route is to think locally, even if you then act globally:

- Recognize that the marketing concept is still fundamental: the (local) consumer matters. In an age when marketing communications are increasingly being thought of as at least potentially one-to-one, it is ludicrous to imagine that a single approach will do for the whole world.
- It pays, however, to be pragmatic. A brand *positioning,* if it is any good, should travel to most countries. A creative *idea,* if it is excellent, can work nearly everywhere (and creative chiefs from all the world's agencies pirate each other's

ideas at international awards festivals). But you have to look at the idea through the eyes of the locals—either through specific, tailored research or through colleagues in the market. Even the best ideas are likely to need some tweaking in *execution,* in order to get into the mind-set, or to respect the cultural values, of the local target group. This requires input from cooperative, quality creative people, in the market. And you have to recognize that translation for advertising is not the same as translation for literature: the aim is to communicate effectively with the target audience in the receiving country, not to enable the audience to empathize with the author.

- If your advertising does not connect with the target group in another country, accept the fact. Don't fight it. Ads that are shoehorned into an alien environment really do no one any favors. Experience suggests that, among major markets, this is likely to be a particular problem in Australia, Britain, and Japan.[14]

- Recognize, too, however, that it is always possible to suboptimize—to divide your world into segments of countries with apparently similar characteristics and consumer expectations. There are plenty of ways of doing this,[15] and one may be appropriate to your needs and may fit your material.

- There will, of course, be times when an ad or campaign clearly can and will travel everywhere. When this happens, rejoice! But it is naive to believe that it is routinely possible to set up an ad "factory" in the United States (for example), and simply roll the ads out worldwide—an idea that Bond and Kirshenbaum seem to advocate,[16] contrasting the approach used by Nike, through Wieden & Kennedy, favorably with more orthodox global agency networks.

International advertising is not an easy way out. Getting the most from it requires sensitivity, intelligence, inspiration, and great management skill. Be prepared for disappointment and frustration—but also a complex and enriching learning experience.

Notes

1. According to *Advertising Age,* April 20, 1998, Schweppes's latest global commercial cost $1.6 million.

2. Marieke de Mooij, *Global Marketing and Advertising: Understanding Cultural Paradoxes* (Thousand Oaks, CA: Sage, 1998).

3. Martin Sorrell, "Beyond the Millennium," *Admap,* January 1997.

4. Ashish Banerjee, "Transnational Advertising Development and Management: An Account Planning Approach and a Process Framework," *International Journal of Advertising,* May 1994.

5. Ibid.

6. Ann Green and Colin Aubury, "Global Copy Testing: Lessons From Experience," *Admap,* October 1997.

7. Rita Clifton, "International Account Planning," in Alan Cooper (ed.), *How to Plan Advertising* (London: Account Planning Group, 1997).

8. De Mooij, *Global Marketing and Advertising.*

9. See, for example, Ian Beccatelli and Alan Swindells, "Developing Better Pan-European Campaigns," *Admap,* March 1998.

10. Lucy Banister, "Global Brands, Local Context," *Admap,* October 1997.

11. *Observer* (London), March 10, 1998.

12. Clifton, "International Account Planning."

13. Banerjee, "Transnational Advertising Development."

14. See, for example, de Mooij, *Global Marketing and Advertising*; John Philip Jones, "Rational Arguments and Emotional Envelopes," *Admap,* April 1998.

15. See, for example, Banerjee, "Transnational Advertising Development."

16. Jonathan Bond and Richard Kirshenbaum, *Under the Radar: Talking to Today's Cynical Consumer* (New York: John Wiley, 1998).

4

Alice in Disneyland

A Creative View of International Advertising

Jeremy Bullmore

I n the course of the next few pages, I'd like to touch on the crucial importance of continuing to reinvent the wheel, why there is no such thing as a client, and what Detroit and the Cabbage Patch Doll have in common, and ponder the fact that we use the words *we* and *us* to mean at least five quite different and often mutually exclusive things—and why we should continue to do so.

I'd also like to point out that the Swap Shop is not so much a store where you can make exchanges as it is a metaphor, reveal the true reason for choosing

NOTE: This chapter is an edited version of a presentation made to a J. Walter Thompson world managers' meeting in Orlando, Florida (home of Epcot Center and Disney World), in May 1984. It is adapted from a chapter first published in Jeremy Bullmore, *Behind the Scenes in Advertising* (Henley-on-Thames, UK: NTC Publications, 1991).

Alice in Wonderland as our theme, suggest that the person who would have been most fascinated by J. Walter Thompson might have been Charles Darwin, ask you to consider the true significance of what you are wearing this morning, and raise the possibility that we might abandon our organizational structure a matter of months before it becomes the most admired model in the next generation of management textbooks.

In the time left, I'd like to suggest that the most important person in the company is someone you've never heard of, that J. Walter Thompson is neither an owl nor a hawk but a unicorn, that postrationalization is quite different from retrospective sense making, and that if there is one person who really should have been with us this week, it's Harvey F. Kolodny.

Finally, I'd like to consider the difference between a paradox and a contradiction, recommend that anyone who wants to work for only one boss should probably look for another job, celebrate the value of failure, and argue that we have a great deal to learn from both F. Scott Fitzgerald and the bicycle.

Most people would consider this to be a menu of eclectic ideas. What have they got in common? And what is their relevance to advertising, particularly international advertising? I shall try to explain.

What We Have Learned

The reason all—or nearly all—the subjects I've listed are relevant to the title of my talk is that, as you may by now have guessed, I don't intend to deal with international advertising absolutely directly. By which I mean, I don't intend to talk about how we've learned to plan: to set strategy, to invent solutions to specific advertising briefs. Rather, I intend to talk about how we create and maintain the right climate, the right culture, the right environment in which good advertising is most likely to be created more often than not—and even more important, more often and more consistently than our competitors.

I have two main reasons for this slight shift of emphasis—both of them personal. First, it has been a very long time since I was directly responsible for creating advertising, and there are people here today—and even more who are not here today—who can talk about the planning and execution of advertising with at least as much knowledge and much more current relevance than I can.

The second reason stems from the first and contains my first paradox. The only justification for an advertising agency's existence, let alone profit, is that we take our clients' money, use it to make advertising and to place advertising, then satisfy those clients that they are more successful—by whatever measurements they and we can apply—than they would have been if they hadn't entrusted us with that money in the first place. It follows, therefore, that those in the company who create advertising that works are the most important people we have.

And yet—since I stopped being directly involved in the making of advertising, I've been given more important titles and much greater rewards than I ever had before. This is no cause for complaint—and in the sort of job I do I am not alone in the advertising business. But put as plainly as that, it does seem, to put it mildly, a curious state of affairs. Why should this company be prepared to pay me more for doing less?

If a reason exists at all, it must be something to do with that culture, that climate, that environment I spoke about earlier. It's impossible to measure; no adequate vocabulary exists to describe it—but I think it indisputable that all companies do have cultures and that company cultures can be benign and encouraging or malign and restrictive.

One small piece of anecdotal evidence: I suspect everyone here has had the experience of losing a person to another agency—but without much regret because he or she seemed to be of no more than adequate talent. A month or two later we discover that the person we said goodbye to with so little sense of loss has been responsible for quite exceptionally good work on behalf of his or her new agency. We fool ourselves, I think, if we assume that this particular individual has suddenly, overnight, become more talented. It seems more sensible, if a lot more painful, to accept that what has changed is not the individual but the environment. It wasn't the individual's fault that he or she was no more than adequate. It was ours.

Of course, it can and does happen the other way: People leave us as stars, and within months their work has become mediocre and their new employers are baffled and bitter.

Yes, of course, we must continue to attempt to attract and maintain more than our fair share of the best people. But if it is true, and I'm sure it is, that the difference in quality between the output of one agency and the output of another is due at least as much to the culture of that agency as to the inherent ability of its individual members, then it is a priceless commodity and worth examining in considerable detail.

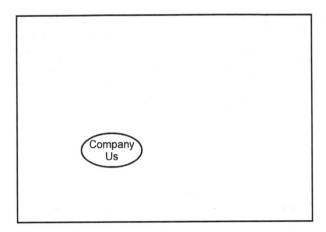

Figure 4.1. The First "Us"

What is *our* culture? Like it or not—and I personally like it very much—the J. Walter Thompson Company seems to me to have an almost infinite number of different cultures, and some of them seem at first sight to be contradictions or conflicts.

Let us look at some of the ways people in this company use the words *we* and *us,* because those words nearly always imply a sense of identification and belonging. First there is the company "us," the J. Walter Thompson Worldwide "us" (Figure 4.1). At this meeting this has so far been the most common use of the word, which is hardly surprising, given that's what "we're" here for. Yet, all around the world, the thousands of other people who aren't here won't be saying, "I wonder what 'we're' up to at Epcot." They'll be saying, "I wonder what 'they're' up to at Epcot."

The company "us" is of very considerable interest to our top management—and rightly so. Even more important, it's of considerable interest to certain clients, usually at the very top—or the very center—of certain large multinational companies. They want to know what "we"—the whole company—can offer them, and why "we" aren't offering them more.

Then there's a regional "us," by which I mean our own definition of regional, as in the Asia Pacific, Latin America, Europe, and the United States (Figure 4.2). I am not sure whether the regional "us"-es, the regional cultures, are getting stronger and more distinctive, although I sense they are, if only because many of our clients are themselves thinking in regional terms. In

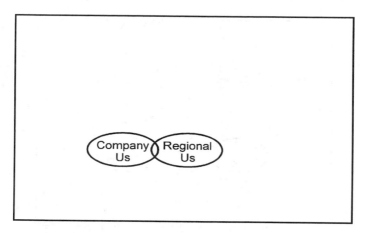

Figure 4.2. The Second "Us"

Europe, I can think of Kellogg's, Kraft, and Ford who want a European "us"—although, as we shall see, not all of them and not all the time.

The "us" that, for all sorts of reasons, most of our people identify with most of the time is the office "us" (Figure 4.3): "we in Tokyo"; "we in Melbourne"; "we in Chicago"; "we in Copenhagen." Each of these offices, along with all the rest, has a distinct culture, a distinct style. We sometimes debate whether this is good or bad, whether it is perversity or brilliant marketing or unplanned inertia. I think that it is an inevitable consequence of spending most of your time in one particular building, with one particular group of people.

Within each office, and depending on size, there can be found a series of even more complicated "us"-es (Figure 4.4). The account group "us": "We strongly recommend," "We are totally united in thinking," "We haven't the slightest idea what the bloody brief means." At its best, the account group "us" is the single most important unit of them all. The people who work in account groups and, above all, the people who run them well generate the advertising on which the total company's reputation, growth, and success ultimately depend. Yet consider the problems.

Only in very few cases is the composition of that group exclusive or permanent. The writer works on three or more accounts—and identifies with each one—sometimes in the course of a single day. And so do the art director, the television producer, the production person, the account executive, the media person, the planner. The person who runs accounts usually runs more

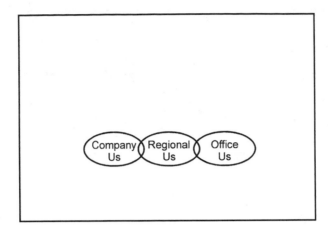

Figure 4.3. The Third "Us"

than one—often five or six. He or she is in constant competition with other account directors for total agency resources: for the time and the commitment of the most talented. Everyone who works in account groups has many bosses—including, of course, his or her departmental boss. That in turn leads me to another culture, another "us"—the departmental "us" (Figure 4.5).

Because a department, unlike an account group, is composed of people of similar skills, there is—or should be—a culture and a sense of craft endeavor

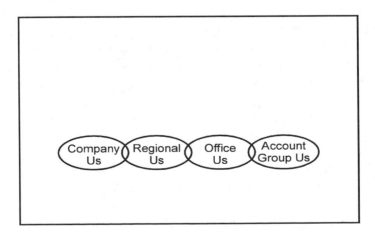

Figure 4.4. The Fourth "Us"

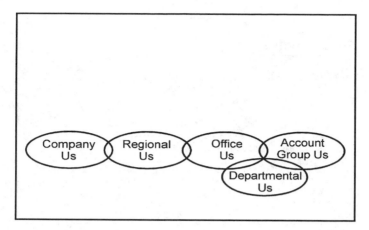

Figure 4.5. The Fifth "Us"

with which each individual also identifies, and that at times may be opposed to the account group culture. As Figure 4.5 shows—and you haven't seen anything yet—the departmental culture draws from and contributes to both the office culture and the account group culture.

That's the simple bit—I'll come back to the organogram later. But what is already quite obvious is that, long before the phrase was invented, long before it became even modestly fashionable, the J. Walter Thompson Company evolved—in a way that would have fascinated Charles Darwin—into what is now known as a matrix organization. And *evolved* is precisely the right word. I can't believe that anybody thought of it, or wrote it into a 5-year plan, or got it agreed to by the Operations Committee. It just happened—and if it hadn't happened, we would have died.

Harvey F. Kolodny is a professor of organizational behavior at the University of Toronto. In a 1981 piece titled "Managing in a Matrix," he cited three conditions that research shows justify a matrix design:

- Outside pressure for a dual focus
- A need to process large amounts of information simultaneously
- Pressure for shared resources[1]

I think Professor Kolodny would be proud of us. We've got all three conditions—and we've got them in spades.

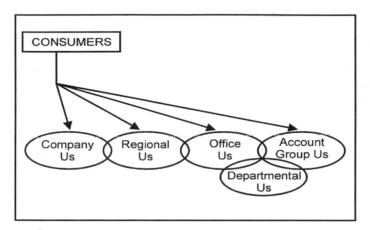

Figure 4.6. Consumers

"Pressure for shared resources" we've already touched on. "A need to process large amounts of information simultaneously" we all know only too well. So let's return to "outside pressure for a dual focus" (and wouldn't it be nice if it were only dual?).

Although there are a lot of things wrong with my diagram, the most obvious flaw is the absence of outside pressures and influences. So let's add some.

Consumers, Agency Clients, Agency Competitors, the Work

First, consumers: They remain a tiresome and undisciplined bunch of people who have scant regard for the problems of running an advertising agency. Yet unless we understand them, and the relationship they have with our clients' brands, we can't operate.

In many ways, consumers are growing more alike, and we all know why. Mass communications, travel, multinational companies, the whole apparatus of the global village. So some bits of "us," the company "us," the regional "us," have got to be more aware of these similarities than ever before. Not only are consumers affecting offices and account groups—as they always have—they are affecting our other "us"-es and cultures as well (Figure 4.6).

Unfortunately, or perhaps fortunately, these same people—consumers—are simultaneously striving for greater individuality. More and more people want cars, which is a move toward sameness. More and more people want a particular car for *them,* which is a move toward difference. So far, the answer to that paradox (*not* contradiction), from Detroit and elsewhere, has been *options*: the same basic car (with all the economies of scale in production) *plus* bits and pieces to satisfy the individual.

Increasingly, I believe, we are going to feel the impact of flexible manufacturing processes. Production lines already exist that can produce quite different products with no loss of efficiency and at no higher cost. Any color you like, any modification you like, with no price penalty. As it progresses, this revolution—and revolution it is—will make "global marketing" much more of a nightmare and much more fun.

More and more people want to travel abroad and can afford to do so, which is a move toward sameness. More and more people want to go where nobody else is going, which is a move toward difference. So the holiday companies are now promoting holidays that allow you to go where you want, and do what you want, when you want to do it. Which is much the same solution as Detroit's basic low-cost model—with lots of options, tailor-made. When we go to work, most of us here today wear fairly similar clothes. Yet look at us now, in our leisure wear: an extremely vivid, if not totally pleasing, demonstration of our own, personal individualities. The Cabbage Patch Doll has sold in the millions by the simple method of being simultaneously similar and individual.

None of this is going to go away. Our clients must be growing increasingly perplexed as they read about global marketing in the morning and the growth of individualism in the afternoon. This is very good news for us: A perplexed client needs help. And that is why, at least as much as consumers, our clients affect our various cultures and "us"-es—perhaps at more levels than ever before (Figure 4.7).

Maybe there never was a time when clients were single-minded. They certainly aren't now, and what is more, they won't and can't become so. Many of our clients' organizations are getting almost as complex as ours—but they haven't had the practice we've had.

There is no such thing as a client. There's a client company, containing dozens of different people, each with his or her own views and priorities, most of them both sensible and paradoxical. A company's world coordinator will have one view; his marketing director in the United Kingdom will have one

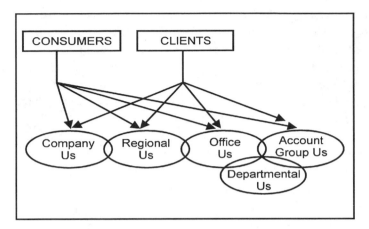

Figure 4.7. Clients

view. And if these two happen to coincide, the chances are that one of them is wrong.

Management consultants are our greatest allies, although quite unintentionally. They advise centralized companies to decentralize. They advise decentralized companies to centralize. Bafflement and perplexities grow more neurotic every day. That, too, is excellent news for us.

Now, we must include our competitors (Figure 4.8). Some of these competitors are the Y&Rs and Ogilvys and FCBs and McCanns; some, the more recently established multinationals like the Saatchi brothers. Some are so new and young and national that only if you live and work in their countries will you have heard of them. So competitors, too, come in different forms and affect different bits of our total company. Whatever they are, and wherever they may be, we ignore them at our peril.

It's no surprise to find that consumer behavior, client behavior, and competitive activity are following the same trends and countertrends: more similarities and more differences. If that's the way that people are going, then that's the way that marketing companies and advertising agencies must go as well. The process of evolution continues.

Figure 4.8 is the simplest diagram I could devise to illustrate where we seem to be at the moment. There is only one more bit to add, which is, of course, *the work:* the planning, the research, the media, the advertising. Somehow, it needs to emerge from that apparent jungle, and somehow it does

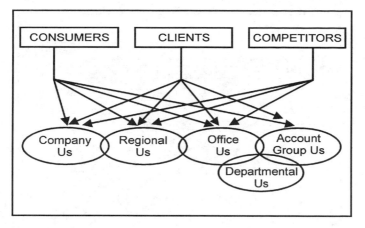

Figure 4.8. Competitors

(Figure 4.9). But if we are dissatisfied with what we do, which we are, and if we believe we can do a lot of it better, which we do, how can we help those all-important account groups to be as good as they can be? Do we try to clear the jungle, make lines of communication simpler and shorter? Or do we become even better at learning how to manage the extraordinary muddle?

My own view is that we should spend most of our time and effort improving our ability to manage muddle. Many of you will be familiar with that excellent book *In Search of Excellence,* by Thomas Peters and Robert Waterman. Chapter 4 of that volume is all about managing muddle—although it is actually titled "Managing Ambiguity and Paradox." On the first page of the chapter, the authors write: "The old management theories were attractive because they were straightforward and not laden with ambiguity and paradox. On the other hand, the world isn't like that." [2]

This startling insight comes at least 50 years after this company—the total "us"—had not only recognized it but had learned to cope with it. (Lewis Carroll discovered it even earlier, which is the real reason for the theme of this talk and this meeting.)

Peters and Waterman go on to say, "Most important, we think the excellent companies, if they know any one thing, know how to manage paradox." [3] (And let me give you the dictionary definition of *paradox:* "a statement apparently inconsistent or absurd, yet really true." So a paradox is not a contradiction; it is only an apparent one.)

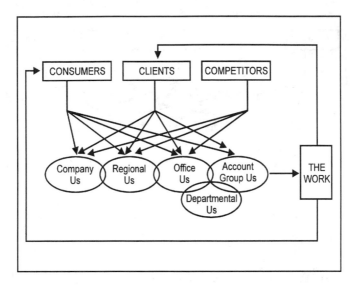

Figure 4.9. The Work

Paradoxes

One paradox is *profit*. It is perfectly true, as both we and our clients so often say, that "we're only in business to make a profit." But it is also *not* true, because if it were exclusively true, we might look for quite different businesses to be in that might make more profit. (Indeed, this organization tried and failed, and should never forget the huge value of those failures.)

Peters and Waterman say, "In a piece of research that preceded this work, we found that companies whose only articulated goals were financial did not do nearly as well financially as companies that had broader sets of values." They quote one executive who said: "Profit is like health. You need it, and the more the better. But it's not why you exist." [4]

Then there is the paradox of structure. Peters and Waterman write: "We are confronted with an extraordinary conundrum. Most current theory is neither tight nor loose enough." [5] They say:

We need new language. We need to consider adding terms to our management vocabulary: a few might be temporary structure, ad hoc groups, fluid organizations, small is beautiful, incrementalism, experimentation, action orientation, imitations, lots of tries, unjustified variations, internal competition, playfulness, the technology of foolishness, product champions, bootlegging, cabals, and shadow organizations. Each of these turns the tables on conventional wisdom. Each implies both the absence of clear direction and the simultaneous need for action.[6]

Again, I find these words encouraging—not because they tell us how we should reorganize ourselves, but because they help us understand why we would be mad if we did. We don't use the words, but we've got all those groups and techniques and methods in successful operation already.

It's easy enough to *accept* things, whether the existence of television or a company structure. But for a real understanding of *how things work,* it is, I think, absolutely essential to keep on reinventing the wheel. I know the internal combustion engine works, but if I am to understand *how,* I have to take one apart and put it together again.

That, I suppose, is what I have tried to do so far in what I have been saying: to take our extraordinary culture apart and put it together again, to show that there is some method in our madness and to suggest not only that it is justifiable, but that it is even beginning to acquire a certain academic respectability.

How Does This Relate to International Advertising?

It was a good choice of the authors of *In Search of Excellence* to start their Chapter 4 with a quotation from F. Scott Fitzgerald: "The test of a first-rate intelligence is the ability to hold two opposed ideas in mind at the same time and still retain the ability to function." [7] That, I think, is at the heart of what we can offer our people and our clients.

We have spent a lot of time at this meeting talking about global campaigns. But no client company, however multinational, however centralized in approach, can afford to be without a deep and sensitive knowledge of every market in which it operates. A sensitive client in an important packaged goods company once described how "an international product fell flat on its face" because neither his own people nor his agency had bothered to notice some very local differences. We should never be guilty of that—we are rightly and properly contaminated by failures of that kind, and those failures make a mockery of our claim to have a network of strong offices, each with a close and sensitive knowledge of its own market.

Yet I am equally sure that we are guilty from time to time of rejecting ideas from other markets for less respectable reasons. Even if we aren't, we can and do give that impression—which is just as damaging.

The believed reasons for resistance or rejection are usually summed up by the phrase "not invented here." It is certainly true that using other people's advertising is not what most people are in this business for. If we can think of a reason for being against it, we probably will.

If it can, however, be *reinvented*, then that's a lot better. If you can take the idea apart, see how it works, put it together again, and judge it against your own knowledge of your own market, then not only will you have behaved very responsibly indeed—because that's what you should do with any idea—but you're now a partial author; you actually *contributed* to it.

This seems to me to be a wholly sensible and responsible way to behave. What's more, if we apply a little retrospective sense making (which is the respectable way of describing postrationalization), we can see that this is how every single campaign idea begins to cross borders successfully.

An idea can *only* emerge as the solution to a single market problem. After savage scrutiny, total understanding, and perhaps some necessary modification, it may then apply to a second market—and then perhaps to many more. Or it may remain as a single-market solution.

That's the history of the Marlboro cowboy and the Pepsi Challenge, and I think that's what we should both say to and do with at least some of our multinational clients. Not all clients will be local clients, but all clients need to be served locally.

I don't think we should apologize for being a paradoxical and ambiguous company. I think we should celebrate the fact. We already talk about our flexibility—particularly to multinational clients. I suspect we feel a bit apologetic about that as well, because saying you're flexible can often sound as if you don't know what the hell you are up to. I believe we can be extremely and positively flexible, *as long as we remember that without an account group, nothing will ever happen.* Just as there is an infinite variety of national or office account groups, so there can be regional, multinational, global, or even galactic groups—as long as there is someone in charge, creating the sense of unity and purpose, and fighting for shared resources.

I believe that when senior clients come to us in a state of confusion, we should say: "Of course it's confusing; we've been managing confusion for 80 years. Now just lie down and tell me everything and you'll soon feel better." I do not believe that we should pretend to our clients that we know how to eliminate conflict and paradox; we should say only that we know how to use them fruitfully.

Paradox and ambiguity can be managed with our clients, at all their many different levels. And I think we should be equally open and positive with our people. Of course they'll have more than one boss. If they want only one, they should join the Foreign Legion. Of course they'll get different views from different people—and different views from the same people at different times. That's inevitable; and if it's inevitable, it's manageable.

Of course there will be more people in the client company with the power to say no than there are with the power to say yes. How in any complex business could it be otherwise? But aren't we in the persuasion business? If someone asks, "Which is the most important—national business or multinational business?" We should cheerfully answer, "They're both more important—and vice versa." If they don't understand, ask them which is the more important wheel on a bicycle. Is it the back wheel because it provides drive, or the front wheel because it provides direction? Then remind them that if they don't have both, they'll fall over.

Tell them about the infinite number of "we"s and "us"-es they can belong to, in sequence or simultaneously or both. Not only is there a very large stage on which to perform, but they can play every role in it they want, without going through the hassle of changing jobs. As members of the total, worldwide company "us," we have access to an astounding variety of people, experience, ideas, and experiments. I do think the Swap Shop is at least as much a metaphor as it is a marketplace. If our main job is to help the people who produce the work on which we all depend, we've got an Aladdin's cave as well as a Wonderland to let them play in, and learn from, at no cost.

The days when all ideas came from some omniscient central source are gone, and gone for good. That's fine—as long as we recognize it.

Most of the smaller "we"s and "us"-es seem remarkably fit and healthy and fun to work in. There are, however, some needs and great opportunities to get greater synergy between these necessary subcultures, to form new and perhaps bigger "us"-es. And a large part of this will be achieved only if we share our knowledge more successfully than we do at the moment. And the most effective ways of doing this will be the time-honored ways: persuasion, guile, flattery, blackmail, selfishness, bribery, and blatant appeals to other people's self-interest. Luckily, we will be greatly aided by the intelligent use of new technologies.

Now, where does all this leave us? Revisit the menu of ideas I went through at the beginning and that I hope I have to some extent explained during this talk. Does the thought perhaps occur that effective advertising demands that its practitioners think outside the confines of conventional theory, outside the comprehensible, seemingly helpful but in reality sterile and deadening rules of the advertising game? And does not the additional thought enter your mind that this need to think "outside the box" is even more pressingly important if we are to exploit successfully the international possibilities of the advertising enterprise?

Notes

1. Harvey F. Kolodny, "Managing in a Matrix," *Business Horizons,* March 1981, 17-24.

2. Thomas J. Peters and Robert H. Waterman, Jr., *In Search of Excellence: Lessons From America's Best-Run Companies* (New York: Harper & Row, 1982), 89-90.

3. Ibid., 91.

4. Ibid., 103.

5. Ibid., 106.

6. Ibid., 106-107.

7. Quoted in ibid., 89; from F. Scott Fitzgerald, "The Crack-up," in Charles R. Anderson (ed.), *American Literary Masters,* vol. 2 (New York: Holt, Rinehart & Winston, 1965), 1007.

5

Brand and Consumer Values in Global Marketing

Harold F. Clark, Jr.

Global marketing is a hot topic. For 20 years, *multinational, globalism,* and *galacticism* have been alluring buzzwords that guarantee large attendance at any symposium or meeting. People flock out of a sense of nervous ambition: "If I'm in a relatively mature and stagnant market here at home, can't I make a lot of money cashing in overseas?"

Many companies are truly global and are making money around the world—give or take a few local economic crises. But an equal number seem to struggle and over and over again fall prey to classic kinds of global marketing mistakes. A few recent examples (kept anonymous to protect careers):

1. One successful U.S. brand with a very descriptive brand name (like Janitor in a Drum, or Head & Shoulders—but not either of these) was introduced into China. The parent company instructed its Chinese company to translate the brand name into Mandarin. The words were translated into symbols that had the same

descriptive meaning as the original name, but didn't sound like the original English name. The Chinese company was ordered to change the name into the phonetic words in Mandarin that would sound exactly like the English name. The result was meaningless (and unpronounceable) in Mandarin.

2. Prior to a new product launch in Europe, another multinational company did attitude and usage research in the United Kingdom and France and assumed that it was valid for all Europe. The rationale was that in the United States, it is not necessary to do the same piece of research in every one of the 50 states.

3. A successful U.S. company with a brand that has been on the market and advertised for more than 40 years introduced that brand into Europe and insisted on running the contemporaneous U.S. advertising, which presupposed 40 years of experience and knowledge of the brand. The company wondered why the brand failed.

4. Scandinavians routinely see advertising for U.S. brands—advertising that does not feature blond models, which are of course the norm in Scandinavia.

These kinds of experiences are not new. Many successful multinational marketers know what to do, or what not to do, in marketing a brand successfully around the world. Why can't others learn and avoid these kinds of costly mistakes?

In this chapter I provide practical advice to the new global marketers by (a) examining the best practices of some of the successful ones, (b) considering what global marketers should do instead of what they like to do, and (c) recommending a necessary course of action if they are to succeed in the future.

How Experts Define Global Marketing

In the minds of many people, global marketing has to do with manufacturers who have branches that make and/or sell products in a number of countries. They seek common methods to produce, distribute, and share knowledge or products across borders.

Some time ago, a study conducted among 25 major worldwide marketers revealed how these companies viewed global marketing and what they did as a result.[1] Given that both their attitudes and their practices persist today, the study remains as relevant as ever. It is interesting in what it reveals and in what it does not reveal.

First, the study asked respondents to define *global marketing*. They described it in the following ways:

We are going to have markets established on the basis of priorities and those market priorities will be certain things from mature markets and another set of things in a developing market and another set in an emerging market.

We have global brands and therefore those brands, when marketed anywhere in the world, are marketed the same no matter what the market is, no matter what the continent is. They are fundamentally positioned the same; the underlying strategic principles that guide the management of the business are the same.

The strategies that count, that form part of the total strategy, are country and regional strategies.

If you have success in one marketplace, one country, you could try to transfer that success from another country and so on. This is how you create a global product.

Global marketing is a result, a common outcome, of some of the parts. It's not the planning.

We let the locals change any part of the marketing mix they feel is necessary.

These responses make global marketing sound like a process conducted by the corporate center in a pretty haphazard way. There is a holdover of the old arrogance embedded in such phrases as "let the locals" and "no matter what the market is." They are reminiscent of the days of export departments, peopled by men and women who sat at the center, surrounded by many opinions, few facts, and the desire to ship their products around the world.

One executive in a top global company said with unusual candor, "We would rather make money than be right." Implicit in this response is the notion that global marketing is another profit opportunity. "We do it to make money. And if we use the same materials in every market, we can save money in the process."

These comments all reflect views of global marketing based on how the center of the corporation views the world and what it does. Global marketing is all about how the corporation should best organize itself to sell more product. It's about the transfer of systems, technology, and solutions from market to market.

The study asked respondents to rank a number of elements of global marketing in order of importance; their priorities reveal the depth of interest

TABLE 5.1 Respondents' Rankings of the Most Essential Elements of Global Marketing (in percentages)

Ranking	*To implement effective global marketing, it is absolutely essential:*	*Strongly Agree*	*Strongly Disagree*
1	to find the right balance between headquarters and local control.	100	0
2	to stimulate the right degree of communication and exchange on an ongoing basis.	100	0
3	to find people with the right talent, experience, and philosophy to carry out global marketing.	96	4
4	to develop products that make sense as global brands.	86	14
5	to get company people worldwide to believe in the global marketing approach and support it fully.	82	18
6	to train and develop people to be effective global marketers.	82	18
7	to establish the right organizational structure worldwide.	82	18
8	to integrate the marketing research function on a global basis so that information obtained from national markets is comparable.	68	32
9	to establish packaging, pricing, and product specifications that make sense on a global basis.	54	46
10	to find an ad agency network that can be an effective partner in carrying out a global strategy.	54	46
11	to develop advertising that can be effective on a global basis.	46	54

SOURCE: Data are from a private study conducted by Warren Keegan Associates, Inc., for J. Walter Thompson.

in the organizational aspects, as Table 5.1 shows. Their number-one issue is the old global marketing chestnut: whether it is better to develop product concepts locally or to impose a worldwide view from the center. That was the issue they wanted to talk about most. On this question of centralism versus decentralism, most came down firmly in the middle. As one respondent noted, "The successful companies combine vision at the top, in-depth knowledge of each local market, and the ability to merge these two perspectives in an organizational culture that respects each perspective."

In fact, most successful global companies work comfortably within a matrix or grid structure and have long since rejected the outdated notion of an export department or international division dictating marketing direction. They have been very successful at developing, manufacturing, distributing, and selling products quickly and cost-effectively in a number of markets simultaneously. They do not make the kinds of mistakes cited at the beginning of this chapter; they have more experience than that (or they made their mistakes years ago). They learned how to market around the world—and it has worked.

Their insights about what they learned are instructive:

- One must learn to live with a number of apparently conflicting perspectives at one time.
- A global selling strategy is an absolute requirement for survival at home. The cost of new product technology requires that successful marketers look beyond their home borders for a sufficient market to earn a rapid return on investment. The ability of competitors to copy product advantages and features quickly and devastatingly creates pressures never encountered before. A competitive advantage lasts months, not years. Companies must launch quickly in as many markets as possible in order to take maximum advantage of their own short-lived innovations.
- Global communications and technology are shrinking the world and accelerating global selling and marketing. Technology is a measurable universal. At any time there is a best available technology, and a global marketer ought to use it everywhere in the world. Research, information technology, engineering, and manufacturing commonalities should be able to drive down costs by concentrating efforts on single solutions to multinational problems. All this works to create brands with the greatest possible value to the corporation.
- A successful global strategy depends on the nonjudgmental interchange of knowledge, ideas, and expertise. Only two things inhibit this process: (a) management myopia that refuses to recognize and seize appropriate opportunities regardless of country of origin, and (b) organizational culture that resists suggested solutions from somewhere else ("not invented here").
- There are market differences. Human needs and wants may be universal, but their expression is deeply rooted in cultural differences. Some form of local autonomy is necessary.

Most of this advice concerns what ought to be done, not how to do it. The dilemma in the last point is particularly revealing. Even though there was agreement that local opinions matter, there was little consensus on how to solicit, evaluate, or use this input. Respondents had no agreed-upon formulas for managing a brand effectively with their colleagues around the world. They recognized that power shifts from the center out and back, but they recognized equally that absolute power neither can nor should be exercised on every issue.

Missing in all of their discussion was the importance of understanding consumers. When consumers were mentioned, they did not seem so important as the corporate process issues (how to transmit technology, how to share power, how to improve communications, and how to streamline management decisions in a very complex system of manufacture, distribution, and sales). Respondents offered no insights on how to relate optimally to the needs, wants, and desires of a potential target group.[2]

If marketing is an activity involved with satisfying the needs and wants of consumers, then in some form, global marketing must be involved with consumers. To understand more about the critical importance of local input, perhaps we should look at the global consumer.

The Global Consumer
Consuming Global Brands

Who are the global consumers? There are more than 2 billion of them and, according to one observer, they are all herded into one global village because that is where the process of global homogenization can most easily be accomplished. All people get thirsty; therefore it follows that they all buy colas for the same reason. All people want to spare their children the pain of soap in the eye; therefore it follows that they all buy baby shampoo for the same reason. What does not follow is that because they may have similar needs and wants in some product categories, they are all part of the same "global target group."

Indeed, it could be argued that there is no such thing as either a global target group or a global brand. Let's look at a few simple truths.

1. Consumers are not "global" themselves. What would a global consumer be, anyway? I once knew a man who was born in China of Canadian parents, married an Englishwoman, had children born in the United States and Brazil, and lived in Germany. I suspect he was as close to a multinational consumer as I have ever met. But when he, or any other consumer, sits in front of the television set in Frankfurt or São Paulo or London or Chicago or wherever he happens to be this week, there is nothing much "global" about him. He is one person in one place. He has a uniquely personal set of experiences, values, beliefs, cultures, and mores. He chooses and values brands based on that uniqueness. So does everyone else.

2. People do not buy brands or products because they are *global*. It is of no matter where else in the world the same brand is available so long as it is in my local store.

3. Increasingly, people do not care much where a brand was manufactured. Does it matter to a housewife in Düsseldorf that her Lux Toilettenseife is made in the same place as the Lux Toilet Soap that her British cousin buys in Leeds? It does not occur to her to ask. Once, "made in the USA" had a certain cachet, but as product quality escalates around the world, consumers no longer believe the best products or product improvements necessarily come from someplace beyond their borders. Indeed, many people are suspicious of anything "foreign." Not being made here would be a barrier to overcome, not an automatic plus. In some product categories, country of origin has become a value (France for wine, Japan for high tech and cars, and the United States for cola drinks), but generally manufacturers do not loudly proclaim the factory location as a consumer benefit.

4. What people do everywhere is search for familiar brands, found in familiar stores, down the aisles where those brands have always been. They develop patterns that they feel no need to alter. They are not in the market for global brands; they are in the market for dependable and relevant brands that meet their needs and that they can find where they have always found them.

5. Because what consumers value is personal and individual, they are naturally attracted to brands that appear to reflect those values. The heart of marketing in any country is finding a way to relate a brand to what is important to consumers in that country.

Every consumer has attitudes and opinions about the brands she or he buys; the brand means something. This is the concept of the *brand idea*—what a brand stands for in the mind of the consumer. (It is, in fact, what brand managers all over the world should be trying to influence.) Those brands that a person feels strongest about are those that matter the most, because by consistently and reliably meeting important needs, they relate to what that person values.

The great global brands are firmly established around the world cultures because their brand managers have created a consistent brand idea and brand values in every market around the world. These are brands that elicit the same response wherever their names are mentioned; Lux, Coca-Cola, Nike, and Johnson's Baby Shampoo evoke consistent, recognizable brand ideas from market to market and are valued by consumers everywhere for the same kinds of reasons.

Kellogg's Corn Flakes is positioned in consumers' minds in every market as the "sunshine" breakfast. The rich, wholesome values of Kellogg's Corn Flakes are consonant with the rich, wholesome values found in every country and the brand has succeeded as a result. The same design elements, typefaces, and visual symbols are used everywhere. Today, if you show people a script letter *K,* they will respond *Kellogg's.* In the late 1960s, Kellogg's could have positioned Corn Flakes as an evening snack and thereby accelerated its acceptance in Europe. But the company avoided these easy sales—"Corn Flakes is a breakfast cereal and that is what it will be; we don't care if it takes until the millennium" (which seemed a long way off then). Kellogg's understood the elements of its successful brand idea and never wavered in its goal, which it reached well before 2000.

Ford has always been the hardworking car for hardworking people, a sensible car for "Everyman"—well built to appeal to his practical nature and stylish enough to appeal to his aesthetic needs. Yet consider how different the actual automobiles are from country to country.

Eastman Kodak, selling film and cameras around the world, carefully orchestrated the values of its name and products. Consumers value and trust Kodak because it is consonant with their own values. The company's care to keep the emblematic yellow packaging provides travelers the reassurance of these values around the world.

At the core of these examples and many, many more is the understanding of the manufacturer of what that brand should stand for everywhere it is sold.

6. Manufacturers, however, do not own the brand ideas. Those belong to the people who think about the brands in their own markets. Sometimes, they let their individuality affect the values they place on the brands they buy. They contribute actively to the personae of the brands in their countries.

Blue jeans in the United States began as sturdy and practical work clothes. In many parts of the world they have evolved into a symbol of Western culture. Today, tourists in Russia barter jeans for long, heavy, woolen military coats.

The Marlboro cigarette brand idea began in the United States as an attempt to rid the filtered cigarette of its feminine connotation. The cowboy context was an association with masculinity. In Europe, the cowboy symbolizes America in one country and the strength of a strong filtered cigarette in another. The brand idea that looks very much the same from market to market has significant nuances of difference as a result of people bringing their own personal associations to it.

Pepsi-Cola created "the Pepsi Generation" to describe and appeal to the young people in America who were bright, clean, well scrubbed, and playing volleyball on the beach. In many parts of the world, however, "the Pepsi Generation" has taken on far broader associations and has become representative of rebellion against the establishment. Elsewhere it means the first daring breakaway from the safety of childhood lemonades to the more forbidden, caffeine-laden, and darker cola drinks.

7. To succeed in any market, a brand must do more than meet a need—its brand idea must add value to the consumer. These additional brand values may encompass meaningful competitive advantages—functional differences, social differences, psychological differences, or economic differences. They may suggest that important values in a brand are those that give rise to the "representational" role that the brand can play in the life of its purchaser. These values are what sustain a brand over time.

How do these values manifest themselves? Consumers choose some brands that are like old friends: safe, reliable, and trustworthy. Sometimes these brands have always been there, like Ivory Soap, Tide, or Persil and Oxo (both the latter in the United Kingdom). Women used these brands 40 years ago, and today their daughters have no reason to choose different ones. In every case, there are several perfectly acceptable alternatives and, if they are required to, they might be quite happy to take one. Preferably, however, they feel most comfortable with their old friends. Who doesn't?

Most people purchase subsequent cars from the same companies that made their first cars. They value that relationship. They appreciate the consistent and reliable service they have received. Because a person has formed a valuable relationship with a particular maker of automobiles, he or she buys a newer model from the same manufacturer.

People value those brands with which they have the most successful experience. Those are the ones they feel personal relationships with. A host of factors beyond personal experience also affect brand relationships. Some are cultural, historic, social, or psychological; others are more direct (e.g., what other people say, positively or negatively; retailers' recommendations;

service). Communications (through advertising, promotion, packaging, Website, and so on) work to create relationships.

Why consumers value one brand over another is a very subjective and personal matter. It derives, first, from their direct personal experience of the brand; second, from what that brand has come to mean for them; and finally, from the nature and depth of the relationship they have developed with that brand. It is a compilation of their feelings—how well that brand seems to match what they value as important in that category. Over time, if the manufacturer is successful in developing a link between the brand values and the consumer's own values, that consumer will say that brand is "for me." A vital relationship will be established. The manufacturer has a customer.

In any market, the fundamental role of marketing is to build as many relationships as possible. The greater the number of relationships, the bigger the brand. Global marketing is no different. It's about building relationships all over the world.

If we accept the premise that marketing aims to build relationships, there really is no such thing as a global brand. There are global products that belong to manufacturers who sell them all over the place. But brands are local because relationships are individual; brands relate to consumers—one at a time—regardless of where they are. Consumers do not see global brands, do not expect or want them, and do not respond to them in any global way. They value their brands for their own personal reasons; they own them.

It is difficult to develop value-adding relationships with people if we do not take the time and effort to get to know them and what makes them unique. And we need to know more than their attitudes, beliefs, and feelings; we need to know how they behave.

How People Buy Things and the Role Advertising Plays

If people buy those brands to which they have the closest and most loyal relationships, then the buying process must be equally personal and singular. How people buy is complex, and attempts to reduce it to predictable patterns should be resisted. One key influence is advertising, and understanding the different ways advertising influences the attitudes and buying behavior of consumers can clarify how brand relationships turn into sales.

Let us place ourselves in the same attitude of mind and physical location where people generally relax and consume media. Perhaps they are reading a magazine or watching television—or watching television and knitting (since more than 65% of people do something else while they watch TV). Maybe one or two people are sharing the space. As they turn the pages of the magazine or look at the box, they are indiscriminately attracted to certain images, words, headlines, and sounds. The reasons may vary widely: They may be new, entertaining, unusual, familiar (the promise of a known reward), or immediately relevant (the mention of a particular buzzword). People notice paint advertisements when they also notice how shabby their living room walls look.

People do not set out to "notice advertising." They are not expecting to buy anything. Certainly, they do not sit down and say, "Tonight, I'm going to change my attitudes." If an advertisement or, more likely, part of an advertisement makes an impression on them, then the process of awareness has begun. Attitudes shift about a certain brand—however slightly—and the advertisement has overcome its most formidable barrier, active indifference.

Some learning undoubtedly occurs—possibly below the conscious level and seldom as an act of will or a deliberate decision to change attitudes. After several exposures, a person is more apt to recall advertising, but it cannot be said to have worked until that person consciously decides that something in the advertising is worth remembering. At that point the person still has not decided to *do* anything; that will come when the need becomes acute or a buying opportunity occurs.

It is tough for advertising to work in this environment. Add the growing cynicism of consumers toward all advertising and you appreciate just how difficult it is for advertising to be "effective."

In projecting ourselves into this domestic scene of advertising consumption, we have left out all references to location. This response is much the same regardless of whether the living room is in Granville, Ohio; Grantham, England; or Grafton, Australia.

Cutting through indifference is difficult enough in one market; it is geometrically more difficult in many markets.

Yet all these consumers purchase things. They do develop loyalties to clusters of brands that they find acceptable in any product category. They make choices all the time, easily and frequently. Advertised brands do prosper as a result of this exchange. So something is going on that offsets the rather passive at-home response. Let us speculate further on the kinds of steps a consumer is apt to go through from the easy chair to the shopping mall to examine the effect of advertising in this cycle.[3]

When a man wants a three-piece wool suit, he checks out familiar, known stores first to see if they have what he wants. The choice of store will determine what price he is willing to pay. He probably has a store that he favors—because of its high quality, its name/prestige, its selection, its low prices, or the fact that the people there call him by name.

In preparing to buy his suit, he has not looked at an advertisement—at least not consciously. He has absorbed the general fashions of the times and perhaps knows whether lapels and necktie widths are shrinking or expanding. He might have noticed advertising that announced what stores are beating the season with early sales. He is not consciously looking for a specific brand of suit. The retailer is primary and the brand is secondary.

Buying a first car—also a considered purchase—is very different. Our male consumer may already have an idea of the car he would like to own. The names Volvo, BMW, and Chevrolet all evoke specific attitudes that have been created over the years by a mixture of personal experience, word of mouth, and advertising. People have told him their war stories about cars. He has looked at the cars his friends drive, and he understands that whole business of the statements that cars make about individuals and their progress in life. He may select one or two dealers to visit, having determined by browsing the Internet where he is apt to get the lowest price. Here it is clear: He makes up his mind about the brand first and then seeks the dealer where he can get the best deal. Advertising may have played a role—but probably early in the process, when his first attitudes were formed.

In buying a cereal, his wife behaves quite differently. There are a number of acceptable cereals the family likes, maybe different ones for different family members. She purchases these brands in a store that has a huge selection of brands. She seeks the store out because it offers her this convenience of choice. While in the cereal section, she might see a new brand that she has never tried before; she might remember that she has heard of it somewhere (a TV commercial, perhaps?) and decided to try it on impulse. For most of her shortlist, advertising reinforces her preconceptions, like a "hand wave" from an old and good friend.

Most of her choices of repeat-purchase packaged goods do not consume much of her active thought process. Advertising may be important because it helps sustain the friendship and gives a personality to a brand so that it stays on the shortlist.

There are, of course, buying decisions for which consumers want or need to know more before buying. Here, they search out advertising according to its reliability. Classified advertisements, personals, department store newspaper ads, and the Yellow Pages are all examples of advertising that performs a very necessary service. Buyers rely on other sources as well: friends' recommendations, retailers' advice, past experience, reputations of manufacturers, Websites, customer hot lines, and so on. They make expensive or complex purchases only when they have gathered enough information to make their decisions.

Every one of these decisions is different. The roles of the brand, the retailer, and the manufacturer are different in each case. Advertising plays a different role in each case. Every purchase is the result of different factors or influences that occur at different times. The consumers are the same people in every case, yet they behave differently and do different things from category to category. There is hardly a homogeneous behavior pattern within even one person, much less among people all over the world.

As personal and individual as buying decisions are, there are of course categories in which consumers around the world behave in similar ways. Choices among spark plugs, tubes of caulking, and leaf rakes are probably pretty much the same for most people everywhere. Individuals rarely have too much of themselves invested in such culturally imposed products.

At the top end of the economic scale, consumers around the world may also behave in similar ways. Decisions to buy designer dresses, luxury watches, or cruises in Glacier Bay may work in the same way around the world and unite consumers in these categories. When someone in New York, London, Sydney, Tokyo, or Hong Kong buys a Rolex watch, one could argue quite persuasively that *at that moment* that person's expectations and desires are the same as those of other consumers buying the same brand elsewhere. But as soon as the same consumers buy something else—say, a beer in a bar, pub, kneipe, or watering hole—the similarities break down. They are not buying with similar expectations, and they are very unlike other Rolex purchasers somewhere else.

Consumers move in and out of product categories all the time. Certainly, there is nothing wrong with considering the target group for Rolex watches around the world. This does not mean, however, that all Rolex purchasers are becoming homogeneous.

Consider what this brief review of the relationships between people and advertising tells us:

1. Consumers in any market focus on what is relevant to their needs at any given time.
2. They are not interested in advertising per se but will look at it if it is relevant—that is, if it speaks to specific needs they have at the moment.
3. They are not interested in global brands because such brands are global. They are not even global people. They do not behave as a consistent group of purchasers in any category.
4. Consumers go through individual decision processes in the purchase of anything. This is not a conscious process and it is affected by a number of factors.
5. Over time, they will buy brands that add real value to their lives. This value can derive from their personal experience with the brands, their perception of the brands' value, or how the brands reflect what the individuals stand for.
6. Consumers use communication vehicles differently, according to the kind of purchase and when in the purchase cycle they encounter that communication.
7. The communications to which people are most apt to pay attention are those that are in sync with their values.

It is a large leap from this rather personal and intimate process of valuing and choosing brands to the homogenization of consumers and the plan to sell them global brands from the center. These marketing truths bear repeating because of their implied imperative, which global marketers ignore at their peril: *To market a product or service successfully to consumers in any single market, a manufacturer must invest the time, money, and sensitivity to discover, understand, and relate to those consumers' needs, attitudes, values, emotions, and behavior.*

Returning to the marketers who were surveyed in the investigation described earlier in this chapter, we can hypothesize why they have succeeded in their quest for great global brands. They have learned (some of them the hard way) the importance of listening to, learning from, and accepting the validity of the point of view of the local market.

Successful Execution Requires Local Knowledge and Input

When respondents in the study mentioned above were asked to rank those elements that they would be most reluctant to change for a local country, they set quite sensible priorities. Their answers appear in Table 5.2.

- *Question:* With an existing global product/brand, which parts of the marketing mix would your company be the most reluctant to change for a local country? What is the headquarters role and the local role in determining a final decision on each of these points for a global product/brand?

TABLE 5.2 Respondents' Rankings of Elements They Would Be Reluctant/Willing to Change (in percentages)

Cluster	Resist Change	Readily Change	Dominant Role: Headquarters	Dominant Role: Local
Brand name and logo	85	7	82	0
Product specifications	68	14	57	7
Product positioning and strategy	43	29	50	14
Packaging (surface design)	39	21	43	14
Advertising strategy	32	35	25	35
Packaging (functional)	25	39	21	46
Pricing	14	64	17	68
Advertising execution	14	54	11	61
Public relations program	11	57	7	61
Package sizes	7	64	10	64
Budget allocation to advertising/promotion/ PR for a given brand	7	64	18	54
Types of distribution outlets	3	82	4	86
Trade promotion programs	0	86	4	86
Specific media choice	0	86	4	86
Media strategy	0	79	4	71
Consumer promotion programs	0	78	4	79

SOURCE: Data are from a private study conducted by Warren Keegan Associates, Inc., for J. Walter Thompson.

The brand name and logo were by far the most vital elements the respondents noted they would keep consistent. 85% would refuse to change the brand name and logo to meet local country needs. It is the center that has the dominant responsibility to protect these elements (often for quite understandable legal and copyright reasons). Interestingly, nearly a third of the respondents felt that product specifications could be changed to meet local needs, and 14% said that they would "readily" change product formulation. Everything else falls off from this point as the respondents showed great flexibility in handling all the other elements.

At the lower end of Table 5.2 (those parts of the marketing mix that the respondents would be least reluctant to change) are all the executional elements—advertising execution, public relations, package size, advertising-to-sales ratios, promotion programs, and so on. This finding dovetails with the rankings in Table 5.1, where the lowest of the top 11 essential elements of effective global marketing was the development of advertising that can be effective on a global basis. Successful global marketers are not looking for, do not expect, and/or are quite willing to forgo one-world commercials or the conference room wall decorated with the single print execution in 15 different languages. Only 14% would resist changing advertising execution. They recognize the technical difficulties, and they do not sense that there are cost savings.

Indeed, their goal is not consistent execution at all. Rather, their goal is a global brand idea: a brand that stands for the same things in every country where they operate around the world. To achieve this goal, they rely on their colleagues in every local market to provide compelling insights about their consumers' attitudes, behavior, feelings, and values in that market. Using this knowledge, they create communications that are relevant, competitive, and most likely to evoke the global brand idea in that local market.

This kind of sensitivity to local market differences within one global brand idea is what keeps brands vibrant in every market. The stories of successful brands marketed in more than one country share this common thread: Those manufacturers who maintain consistent worldwide brand ideas and have the responsiveness to allow for the local expression of those ideas have a greater chance of success than those whose approach to the world is more inflexible.

The greatest challenge facing global marketers is to find the right people for both sides of the equation—people who have the ability to understand consumers, who take the time to appreciate differences and uncover similarities, who get excited about how individual people choose and value the brands they use.

What the Successful
International Marketers Require

The key to successful marketing is the development of people who are willing to learn how to do it. Table 5.1 shows that 96% of respondents felt that the essential element for successful global marketing is "to find people with the right talent, experience, and philosophy to carry out effective global marketing." The responses displayed in Table 5.2 suggest that these people have two critical roles: (a) to understand and protect what the brand stands for in the minds of consumers (what I have been calling the brand idea, and (b) to encourage local marketers to use their full range of marketing and communications tools to generate that consistent brand idea in their markets.

So what are these people like? What makes them successful?

- They understand not only the global brand ideas of the brands in their custody, but also the cultures and values of those consumers to whom they hope to market those brands.
- They hold themselves accountable for shepherding their brands consistently through each individual marketplace by discovering how to make the values inherent in their brands relevant to the values held by the consumers in each marketplace.
- They recognize that a consumer purchase anywhere is a very personal, intimate choice based on individual needs and perspectives.
- They respect the ability of technology to move ideas quickly around the globe, but they also know that technology does not increase sensitivity. In fact, they worry because technology can obliterate or ignore critical consumer values and differences.
- They are fascinated with the ways words, symbols, and sounds work differently in different cultures.
- They want to know more about how brands work differently as a result of different values in different markets.

For these marketers, global marketing is not about organization or local versus central control. It is not a question of worldwide brand positioning statements or whether the same television execution will work in every market around the world. It is not about debates over organizational control and power. Global marketing is about people, values, and ideas.

We appear to be developing a new generation of international brand managers who do not fully appreciate the importance of grooming this kind of multinational intelligence. They do not focus on the individual needs, attitudes, values, emotions, and behavior of consumers in every individual market. Their goal is to develop global positioning statements and global advertising executions rather than global brand ideas.

Their role models a generation earlier were people who might have been the respondents to this early survey, those men and women who felt that global marketing is all about global organizing: the *management* of global brands. What young people saw, learned, and now may believe to be true was that global marketing is only about effective control, transfer of information, power, and systems (see Table 5.1).

The economic exigencies of the past few years have slowed down the number of people who have been able to move to and work in countries other than their own. Indeed, the growth of the professional expertise of local nationals around the world has meant that there is much less need for expatriate marketers than there might have been 20 years go. But where people learn the truths of marketing is in the marketplace. To the degree that we are not asking them to live and work in different markets around the world, we are making it harder for them to learn about global marketing. Traveling to a market is not the same as living in it, working with the trade, speaking the language, talking to customers in shops, and getting to know consumers, as marketers so eagerly and readily do at home.

One long-term consequence of this practice of training fewer and fewer people in many different world markets is the lack of training of future senior management in multinational corporations. Those who will take over the leadership of multinational corporations in 10 to 15 years may never have grappled with the real issues of building global brands. By not giving them experience in countries other than their own, companies are making it more difficult for them to succeed down the line.

Men and women who have lived in other countries are critical to the success of global marketing. As it becomes more and more difficult to find such people, those multinational corporations who wish to succeed in the global marketplace will need to set aside the resources to train individuals and develop their expertise in that marketplace and to motivate them to stay for the long term.

It is expensive to invest in the growth and development of people, and there is always the lingering worry that they may jump ship and accept better offers elsewhere. But the far greater cost is to entrust the management of a global opportunity to people who are untrained in the values required for successful global brand marketing.

The debate on global marketing has long been about the structure and process, the management, development, manufacture, distribution, and sales of products around the world. But the important link between consumers and marketers is the link of values. Because successful marketers understand both consumer values and brand values in every market, they are capable of developing brands that work effectively across borders.

Now the debate needs to be about how we are going to find and develop those people who will understand and nurture those values. They are the key to building the next round of great global brands.

Notes

1. An independent research company in the United States conducted the study at the request of the J. Walter Thompson Company. It began with a panel of experts who selected the top global marketing companies. Of the 25 companies selected, 8 of the top 10 and 18 of the top 25 companies participated in the study.

2. It must be acknowledged that the drafters of the questionnaire did not seem to consider knowledge of local customer attitudes and behavior important enough to be included in the list of elements of effective global marketing.

3. J. Walter Thompson in the United Kingdom has conducted extensive research on the effects of the buying system for numerous products and services and how the role for advertising differs within that process.

6

Mapping Cultural Values for Global Marketing and Advertising

Marieke de Mooij

The Influence of Culture on Global Marketing and Advertising

Globalization and modernization have led international companies to think that marketing, branding, and advertising strategies should be standardized. The argument is that with the globalization of markets, information, and communication, people's wants, needs, and motives will become so similar that this will justify targeting uniform brands and advertising campaigns to

NOTE: This chapter is adapted from a paper that appeared in the published proceedings of the 50th Annual Congress of ESOMAR, September 1997, Edinburgh, Scotland. Copyright © ESOMAR® 1999. Permission for using this material has been granted by ESOMAR® (European Society for Opinion and Marketing Research), Amsterdam, The Netherlands. For further information please refer to the ESOMAR ® website: www.esomar.nl

77

consumers across cultures. Converging incomes across borders are expected to lead to similar consumption patterns, and the global flows of information and communication are expected to lead to similar value patterns. However, standardized global advertising campaigns rarely work as well as do campaigns reflecting local values. This is because of differences in value patterns across borders, which appear not to be converging.

My hypothesis is that converging income levels will not result in converging value patterns across borders and that patterns of national culture will be a better explanation of differences in consumer behavior across borders.

This chapter presents evidence that consumer behavior varies with culture patterns and that this variance is stable over time and will become increasingly manifest. Consumption behavior, decision making, media behavior, and advertising behavior are culture-bound and are expected to remain culture-bound because values of national cultures are stable. Other analysts, notably Hofstede and Inglehart, have demonstrated the stability of values of national cultures.[1]

Apart from testing my hypothesis about the importance of national culture, I demonstrate in this chapter how Hofstede's model of culture can be applied to international marketing strategy. If culture is the dominant influence on consumer behavior, global companies need tools to analyze cultural patterns to avoid the pitfalls of extending a strategy from one market to others where it does not fit. They need a tool to map values of national culture in order to differentiate strategies according to well-defined culture clusters.

My plan of study has the following steps:

- Linking Hofstede's data on values of national culture to data on consumption and attitudes across countries from a number of large surveys: OECD data and data from 16 European countries in four large surveys conducted between 1970 and 1997.[2] (Income data are World Bank estimates based on purchasing power parity.)
- Calculating rank order correlations, expressed in Spearman's rank correlation coefficients, which reduces the potential influence of single extreme scores. (Significance levels are indicated as follows: $*p < 0.05$ [lowest], $**p < 0.01$, $***p < 0.005$ [highest].)
- Applying the findings to (a) consumption patterns over time to demonstrate that for segmenting global markets, cultural values are better criteria than income; (b) product usage and buying motives for two product domains, clothing and the home; (c) the underlying philosophy for differentiation and positioning strategies—the psychological concept of self; and (d) media behavior.

- Providing maps combining product usage, buying motives, and national values for three product domains: personal care products, cars, and insurance.

Hofstede's Dimensions of National Culture

Hofstede has distinguished five dimensions of national culture: power distance (PDI), individualism/collectivism (IDV), masculinity/femininity (MAS/FEM), uncertainty avoidance (UAI), and long-term orientation (LTO). For those who are unfamiliar with his model, short descriptions follow:

- *Power distance:* This is the extent to which less powerful members of a society accept that power is distributed unequally. In large power distance cultures, everybody has his or her rightful place in society, there is respect for old age, and status is important to show power. In small PDI cultures, people try to look younger and powerful people try to look less powerful.
- *Individualism/collectivism:* In individualist cultures people look after themselves and their immediate families only; in collectivist cultures people belong to in-groups that look after them in exchange for loyalty. In individualist cultures, values are in the person; in collectivist cultures, identity is based in the social network to which one belongs. In individualist cultures there is more explicit, verbal communication; in collectivist cultures communication is more implicit.
- *Masculinity/femininity:* In masculine cultures the dominant values are achievement and success. In feminine cultures the dominant values are caring for others and quality of life. In masculine societies performance and achievement are important; status is important to show success. Feminine societies have a people orientation, small is beautiful, and status is not so important. In masculine cultures there is large role differentiation between males and females; in feminine cultures there is small role differentiation.
- *Uncertainty avoidance:* This is the extent to which people feel threatened by uncertainty and ambiguity and try to avoid situations in which those feelings arise. In cultures of strong uncertainty avoidance, there is a need for rules and formality to structure life. Competence is a strong value, resulting in belief in experts, in contrast to weak uncertainty avoidance cultures, with their belief in generalists. People in strong uncertainty avoidance cultures have higher levels of anxiety than do people in weak uncertainty avoidance cultures, and showing emotions is accepted.
- *Long-term orientation:* This is the extent to which a society exhibits a pragmatic future-oriented perspective rather than a conventional historic or short-term point of view. The values of the LTO dimension are similar to the Confucian values of East

Asia and include acceptance of change, perseverance, thrift, and pursuit of peace of mind. The opposite is the short-term orientation of the Anglo-Saxon world.

These dimensions are measured on index scales from 0 to 100, although some countries may have scores below 0 or above 100 on some dimensions because they were measured after the original scale was defined. Hofstede's original data were based on an extensive IBM database for which, between 1967 and 1973, 116,000 questionnaires were used in 72 countries and in 20 languages. Later, in 23 countries an additional Chinese value survey was conducted by Michael Harris Bond.

The results were validated against about 40 cross-cultural studies from a variety of disciplines. Hofstede gives scores for 56 countries; others have extended the list to 85 countries. The combined scores for each country explain variations in behavior of people and organizations. The scores indicate the relative differences between cultures.

Cultural Values Instead of Economic Criteria to Segment Global Markets

Four examples demonstrate that, despite economic development and modernization, differences in consumer behavior in the global marketplace remain culture-bound and are driven more by culture than by income.

Consumption of Mineral Water

People's concern for health can be recognized in consumption patterns that vary by culture. People in weak uncertainty avoidance cultures, for example, have a more active approach to health and exercise relatively more than do people in strong uncertainty avoidance cultures. In Eurodata 91, the proportion of respondents who participated in neither sport nor exercise correlates significantly with UAI (.80***). People in strong uncertainty avoidance cultures have a more passive approach to health and relate it to what they eat and drink. One manifestation of this is the consumption of mineral water. Between 1970 and 1997, in the same 15 countries, consumption of mineral water appears to correlate significantly with UAI. The Reader's Digest Association's 1970 survey reported differences in the consumption of mineral water for 15 countries (Greece was not included in 1970). Drinking mineral water ("one of the drinks taken in the past year") in 1970 correlates with UAI (.44*). There is a similar correlation between the Eurodata 91 answers ("frequent drinking of bottled mineral water") and UAI (.46*). EMS 95 reports regular consumption of mineral water, which also correlates with UAI (.45*). Euromonitor 1997 reports sales volume of mineral water for 1996, which correlates even more strongly with UAI (.70***). All correlations are for the same 15 countries.

Main Food Shoppers

Eurodata 91 splits main food shoppers into males and females. According to the degree of masculinity of cultures, differences in role differentiation are expected to explain differences in food shopping. In masculine cultures, more females will do the daily food shopping, and in feminine cultures, fewer females will do it. In feminine cultures, males will be more involved in the daily household chores than in masculine cultures. For 16 countries in Europe (Eurodata 91) there is a significant correlation between the proportion of main food shoppers who are women and MAS (.63***). When the more traditional countries of Spain, Portugal, and Greece are excluded from the calculation, significance becomes even stronger (.91***). Thus, along with modernization and economic development, latent cultural differences become manifest.

Ownership of Personal Stereos

In the beginning of the products' life cycles, sales of specialty goods such as consumer electronics will be influenced by income. When they become commodities, cultural differences appear to prevail. Using a product such as a personal stereo is a very individualist habit. Even without looking at the statistics, one can see the difference between young people in the Netherlands and Spain, for example. Whereas at Dutch universities plenty of youngsters can be seen carrying personal stereos, this is not so in Spain. In 1990, ownership of personal stereos, as measured by Eurodata 91, correlated both with individualism (.48*) and income (.58*). Euromonitor 1997 sales data on personal stereos (per capita) show a similar correlation with IDV (.49*) but no significant correlation with income (.19).

Home Computers and the Internet

The division between private and public life varies according to the degree of individualism, and this influences the use of home computers. Whereas in individualist cultures people may want to take work into their homes, this is not the usual behavior in collectivist cultures. Usage and ownership of home computers and connected activities are related to IDV. Whereas 1990 ownership of personal computers (Eurodata 91) correlates with both IDV (.69***) and income (.63***), 1995 data (World Economic Forum) of numbers of computers per 100 people for 12 developed countries (United States, Australia, Canada, United Kingdom, the Netherlands, Singapore, Germany, France, Hong Kong, Japan, Taiwan, and South Korea) show significant correlation with IDV (.90***), but not with income (.27).

Usage of the Internet is also culture-bound.[3] Naturally, Internet usage is linked with computer ownership. Data for 1997 show that worldwide (data for 45 countries), both computer ownership and Internet usage strongly correlate with income (.89*** and .88***, respectively) and IDV (.76*** and .79***), but also correlate negatively with uncertainty avoidance (−.33* and −.38*). When correlations are calculated for the 15 European countries where incomes are converging, computer ownership correlates with income (.63**), but at similar significance negatively with uncertainty avoidance (−.63**). Internet usage does not correlate with income, but it correlates negatively with uncertainty avoidance (−.74***), power distance (−.65***), and masculinity (−.47*).

In linear regression analysis (stepwise regression) femininity appears to be the first predictor for Internet usage. Generally, cultures with a combination of small power distance and weak uncertainty avoidance are more innovative, causing people in those cultures to embrace new technologies faster than people in cultures of large power distance and strong uncertainty avoidance. The feminine cultures, where quality of life is an important value, appear to be the leaders.

Product Usage and Buying Motives

Consumption decisions can be driven by functional or social needs. Clothes may satisfy a functional need, but branded clothing or fashion satisfies a social need. People may dress fashionably to satisfy a number of different needs: the need for status, the need to differentiate oneself from others or to be in harmony with the group, the need to be well-groomed. The need for status is the need to express either one's success or one's position in society and is thus related to masculinity and/or to power distance. Correlations with usage of other products demonstrate the two relationships. EMS 95 included questions about the number and value of the watches people own or intend to buy. Members of feminine cultures tend to buy lower-priced watches than do members of masculine cultures, according to the answers to a question about the approximate value of the main watch owned. The answers "under £100" correlate negatively with MAS (–.51*). Wearing expensive watches, however, appears to appeal to the other status need. The answer "over £1,000" to the question about the amount the respondent is willing to spend on a watch correlates positively with PDI (.62**).

Another significant correlation is between Euromonitor 1997 data on sales (value per capita) of real jewelry and MAS (.66***). There is no significant correlation between income and sales of real jewelry (.23). If fashion is perceived as "foreign," the need for status can be derived from its foreignness. People in feminine cultures are less attracted to foreign goods than are people in masculine cultures. The answers of "strongly disagree" to the statement "Foreign goods are more attractive than our own" (EMS 95) correlate negatively with MAS (–.52*). Dressing fashionably can also be part of the need to be well-groomed. Members of small power distance and weak uncertainty avoidance cultures are generally not so well-groomed as members of large power distance and strong uncertainty avoidance cultures. Particularly in cultures of this configuration, people are well-groomed. It is one way of expressing status (one's rightful place in society) and facing a threatening world. Observant travelers in Europe may have noticed the difference between the careful way of dressing of the Belgians, French, and Italians (high on PDI/UAI) as opposed to the carefree (sometimes sloppy) way of dressing of the Dutch, Danes, and British (low on PDI/UAI).

Another example is how people relate to their homes. Values relating to the home vary considerably by culture. A house may service a functional need; a home serves a social need. Culture influences the types of houses people live in and the activities in and around people's homes. In individualist cultures, people prefer one-family houses with private gardens. Every home should have its own garden, however small. Members of collectivist cultures prefer to live in apartment buildings and own relatively few private gardens. In

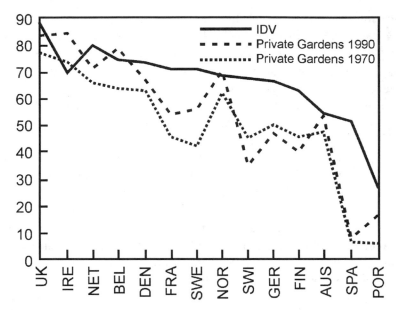

Figure 6.1. Correlation Between Ownership of Private Gardens and Individualism/
Collectivism

SOURCE: Data from the Reader's Digest Association's Survey of Europe Today, 1970; Eurodata 91
(Eurodata is a consumer survey of 17 European countries sponsored by the Reader's Digest Association,
Inc.); and Geert Hofstede, *Cultures and Organizations: Software of the Mind* (New York: McGraw-Hill,
1991).

NOTE: UK = United Kingdom, IRE = Ireland, NET = Netherlands, BEL = Belgium, DEN = Denmark, FRA
= France, SWE = Sweden, NOR = Norway, SWI = Switzerland, GER = Germany, FIN = Finland, AUS =
Austria, SPA = Spain, POR = Portugal.

collectivist cultures, much social life takes place outside the home, in public
places. Both the 1970 Reader's Digest Association survey and Eurodata 91
include data on "possession of private garden," which (in 14 countries in
Europe) correlate with IDV (1970, .73***; 1991, .82***). The two correlations are illustrated in Figure 6.1.

At face value, possession of a private garden may be viewed as a luxury
and thus may be expected to correlate with income. This is not so: There is no
correlation between possession of a private gardens and income (1970, .02; 1991,
.06). Although in the years between 1970 and 1990 incomes in the European
countries converged, the differences between countries with respect to ownership of private gardens remained the same. Living in a one-family house is
another item that could be expected to correlate with income, yet there is a small
negative but not significant correlation between income and "living in a whole

house" in Eurodata 91 (–.29). In line with possession of a private garden, the proportion having "accommodation comprising whole house" correlates positively with IDV (.62**), whereas the proportion having "accommodation of apartment/ flat" correlates negatively with IDV (–.61**). Whereas economic development in individualist cultures leads to building more one-family houses, in collectivist cultures it leads to building more luxury apartment buildings.

Decision Making and Buying Behavior

Buying decisions are rarely purely individual. There are a number of influences. The role of the group, its reference function, and the individual's place and role in the group vary by culture. The degree of uncertainty avoidance will play a role in the type of reference group that is most influential: professional or formal rather than informal. In collectivist cultures, where group conformity is strong, if a person makes a decision he or she will make it in consensus with the group—thus it is not an individual decision. Consensus seeking also plays a role in feminine cultures, as does the small role differentiation between males and females. In feminine cultures, the partner plays a strong role in decision making. This is demonstrated by the negative correlation (–.63***) between masculinity and involvement of the partner in the choice of make and model of the main car in the household (EMS 95), as illustrated in Figure 6.2.

Figure 6.2 shows how countries that are geographically close can show very different behavior—which can have important consequences for advertising. Denmark and Germany, although sharing a geographic border, are far apart on this chart, and so are Belgium and the Netherlands. The Dutch can be characterized by small role differentiation, although in this particular chart the Dutch show a dip. This is because in the EMS 95 survey, the Dutch were found to have a high percentage of company cars, for which the company is a more important partner in decision making.

An example of how strongly this difference can affect automobile advertising is a 1996 television commercial for the Renault Mégane. It depicts a man who wants to surprise his wife with the new Renault Mégane and to demonstrate the car's short braking distance. He stops in front of what he thinks is his house, which he enters shouting, "Darling, I've bought the Renault Mégane," but it appears he has gone into his neighbor's house instead

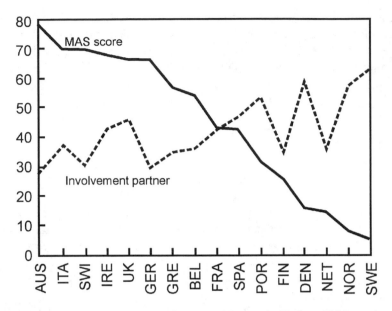

Figure 6.2. Correlation Between Involvement of Partner in Choice of Make and Model of Main Car and Masculinity/Femininity

SOURCE: Data from EMS 95 (copyright Inter/View); and Geert Hofstede, *Cultures and Organizations: Software of the Mind* (New York: McGraw-Hill, 1991).

NOTE: AUS = Austria, ITA = Italy, SWI = Switzerland, IRE = Ireland, UK = United Kingdom, GER = Germany, GRE = Greece, BEL = Belgium, FRA = France, SPA = Spain, POR = Portugal, FIN = Finland, DEN = Denmark, NET = Netherlands, NOR = Norway, SWE = Sweden.

(which is similar to his own) because he is not used to the car's short braking distance. The text of this Belgian commercial was changed radically for the Netherlands, although the Netherlands and half of Belgium share the same Dutch language. In Belgium, a husband can buy a car without consulting his wife—this is not done in the Netherlands.

The Concepts of Self, Personality, and Identity

A core element of Western marketing is the focus on product/brand attributes, benefits, and values that distinguish the user's self from others. The underlying philosophies are based on psychological theories about the self. People will buy products that are compatible with their self-concepts, or rather that enhance their "ideal self" images. Frequently mentioned drives related to the ideal self are self-esteem, self-actualization, and the need for achievement. Implicit in the concept of personality is the individualist notion that people should distinguish themselves from others as opposed to conforming to the group as is found in collectivist cultures.

The self-concept, as the term is used in consumer psychology, is based on a psychoanalytic theory of the self and personality that was mainly developed in the United States. According to the mental health model prevalent in the United States, a young person has to develop an identity that will enable him or her to function independently in a variety of social settings, apart from the family. Failure to do so can cause an identity crisis. The mental health models of collectivist cultures are different. Indian and Japanese models, for example, stress encouragement of dependency needs in the earlier phases of childhood and negotiated adaptation to complex familial hierarchical relationships.[4] The mental health model of masculine cultures is based on the need for success. Success must be shown; the successful must "shine." This is opposed to the mental health model of feminine cultures, where people must be liked. In this case, modesty is an essential virtue and those who shine too much are disliked.

Contrary to what is suggested in much of the literature of consumer psychology that attempts to explain consumer behavior and marketing models, there is no single concept of "self" applicable across all cultures. All of Hofstede's dimensions play potential roles in the concept of self, but the most important are individualism and masculinity. Differentiating oneself from others is a basic aspect of individualist culture. Masculinity adds to that in the sense that people want to distinguish themselves. EMS 95 asked about agreement with the statement "I like to stand out in a crowd." The percentage of "strongly agree" responses correlates with MAS (.49*) and UAI (.51*). The multiple correlation coefficient is $R = .63***$. Wishing to stand out in a crowd is not a value for members of feminine cultures, to whom modesty is a core value. On the other hand, it is a typical value of masculine cultures, and in combination with strong uncertainty avoidance, it leads to overt display of oneself as a successful person.

Because of the different concepts of self, one has to be careful in extending concepts relating to the American view of self to other cultures, particularly collectivist ones. Examples include such personal drives as self-esteem, self-confirmation, self-consistency, self-actualization, recognition, exhibition, dominance, independence, and the need for achievement. Culture's consequence is that the concepts of *brand personality* and *brand identity* are metaphors that are less understandable and thus less useful to collectivist cultures than to individualist cultures. Words for the concepts *identity* and *personality* do not even exist in the Chinese and Japanese languages.

Understanding this can be helpful for those who seek to develop global brand strategies. Relationships between consumers and brands, and the very functions of brands, vary across cultures depending on the type of self-concept. Because of the influence of the group, brand loyalty is stronger in collectivist societies. In cultures where trust in the company and long-term relationships between consumers and companies are more important than strong product/brand personalities, focus on the company brand will be a more effective strategy than the development of separate product brands. Indeed, most successful Asian brands are company brands, whereas U.S. brands rarely carry the names of their companies. Corporate branding and endorsement strategies will be more effective in Asian markets than a product-brand approach of strongly positioned brand personalities. The minimum thing to add to brands in Asian advertising is the company's name, as I have seen done by Procter & Gamble in China and by Nippon Lever in Japan. On the other hand, now that Asian products are increasingly entering Western markets, Asian companies may do even better in Western markets by developing more differentiated brands.

Media Behavior

Within any culture, media behavior is related to communication styles. Individualist cultures, for example, are more verbally oriented; collectivist cultures are more visually oriented. The verbal orientation of individualist cultures is demonstrated by the correlation between EMS data on the personal use of teletext services and IDV (.51*). (The low proportion in France, due to the existence of Minitel, influences the level of significance. Excluding France, the correlation is .67***.) More verbally oriented cultures tend to read more. Both Eurodata 91 and the Reader's Digest Association's Survey of Europe Today 1970, asked questions about book readership. The percentages answering "12 or more books read in the past year" in 1991 and "8 or more books read in the past year" 1970 (13 countries) both strongly correlate with

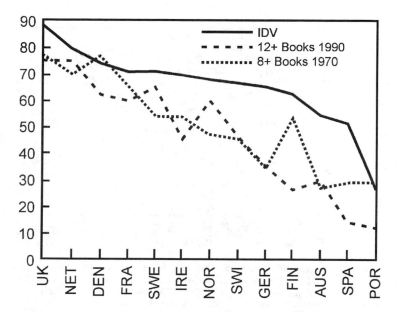

Figure 6.3. Correlation Between Reading More Than 12 Books in the Past Year and Individualism/Collectivism

SOURCE: Data from the Reader's Digest Association's Survey of Europe Today, 1970; Eurodata 91 (Eurodata is a consumer survey of 17 European countries sponsored by the Reader's Digest Association, Inc.); and Geert Hofstede, *Cultures and Organizations: Software of the Mind* (New York: McGraw-Hill, 1991).

NOTE: UK = United Kingdom, NET = Netherlands, DEN = Denmark, FRA = France, SWE = Sweden, IRE = Ireland, NOR = Norway, SWI = Switzerland, GER = Germany, FIN = Finland, AUS = Austria, SPA = Spain, POR = Portugal.

IDV (.91*** and .97***). This again demonstrates the stability of culture's influence.

In individualist cultures there are larger numbers of national and regional daily newspapers. There is a very significant correlation between the existence of daily newspapers and IDV worldwide, as measured for 35 countries (.75***).[5] With respect to the press also, the relationship between power distance and the number of different titles people read is revealing. Data from three different sources show a negative correlation between power distance and readership of newspapers for 16 countries in Europe. The correlations between the various measurements of readership of newspapers and power distance are as follows:

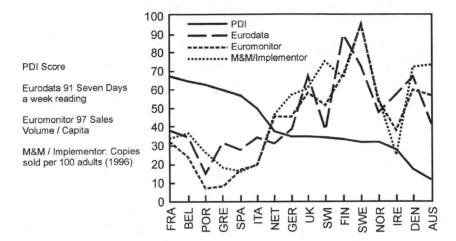

PDI Score

Eurodata 91 Seven Days
a week reading

Euromonitor 97 Sales
Volume / Capita

M&M / Implementor: Copies
sold per 100 adults (1996)

Figure 6.4. Correlation Between Press Consumption and Power Distance

SOURCE: Data from Eurodata 91 (Eurodata is a consumer survey of 17 European countries sponsored by
the Reader's Digest Association, Inc.); Consumer Europe 1997 (Euromonitor); "European Planning Guide
1996-97," *Media and Marketing Europe,* August 1996; and Geert Hofstede, *Cultures and Organizations:
Software of the Mind* (New York: McGraw-Hill, 1991).

NOTE: FRA = France, BEL = Belgium, POR = Portugal, GRE = Greece, SPA = Spain, ITA = Italy, NET =
Netherlands, GER = Germany, UK = United Kingdom, SWI = Switzerland, FIN = Finland, SWE = Sweden,
NOR = Norway, IRE = Ireland, DEN = Denmark, AUS = Austria.

- Eurodata 91 measurement of "read any yesterday" = –.66*** and of "seven days
  a week reading" = –.69***.
- Data on press consumption as published in the *European Planning Guide
  1996-97*;[6] number of copies per 100 adults = –.64***.
- Euromonitor 1997 sales data on number of daily newspapers (volume per capita):
  –.75***.

The three correlations are illustrated in Figure 6.4.

Members of small power distance cultures are heavy readers of newspapers
but they do not have as much confidence in the press as do members of large
power distance cultures. There is a positive correlation between Eurodata 91
respondents confirming "a great deal/quite a lot of confidence in the press"
and PDI (.55*). In large power distance cultures, people view the press as an
authority. In small power distance cultures, people have less confidence in the
press, which results in the need to consult more and different sources. The
small power distance cultures are also democracies with more citizen involvement in government. This involvement implies that people have to be in-

formed. And, as they do not have confidence in their sources, they have to consult a number of different ones.

Mapping Product Usage and Buying Motives According to National Values

The most interesting practical application of Hofstede's model to international marketing and advertising is the possibility of mapping cultures according to needs, motives, product usage, media usage, and the like. I present below examples for three different product categories: cosmetics and personal care products, automobiles, and insurance.

Cosmetics and Personal Care Products

Cosmetics satisfy two primary needs: the need to differentiate oneself from others and the need to look young. However, basically the use of cosmetics and body products goes against nature or is a potential harm to the skin. Thus most of these products are less easily adopted by members of strong uncertainty avoidance cultures, who are concerned with purity. This concern with purity can also be found in usage and attitudes toward other products, such as mineral water (as discussed earlier).

Both the Reader's Digest Association survey of 1970 and Eurodata 91 asked questions about usage of a variety of cosmetics and personal care products. In both surveys, the percentage of agreement of all women that they use deodorants, various lip products such as lipstick or lip gloss, and hair care products such as hair conditioner, gel, or mousse correlate to various degrees with PDI, IDV, UAI. Correlations with sales data on the same products in Euromonitor 1997 deviate with respect to the correlation between usage of lip products and IDV, because figures for the Netherlands and Belgium are relatively low and seem to be biased. If these are not included in the calculation, the correlation for 13 countries is significant (.63**). Table 6.1 presents correlations for the three product categories: deodorants, lip products (lipstick, lip gloss) and hair conditioner, gel, and mousse.

What does this mean? An important need satisfied by deodorants is the need for privacy. In individualist cultures people don't want to smell other people, whereas in collectivist cultures they do not mind so much. But

TABLE 6.1　Cosmetics and Personal Care Product Correlation With Power Distance, Individualism/Collectivism, and Uncertainty Avoidance

Products	Power Distance			Individualism/Collectivism			Uncertainty Avoidance		
	Reader's Digest 1970	Euro- data 1991	Euro- monitor 1997	Reader's Digest 1970	Euro- data 1991	Euro- monitor 1997	Reader's Digest 1970	Euro- data 1991	Euro- monitor 1997
Deodorants	−.40	−.56*	−.41	.49*	.58*	.59*	−.74***	−.89***	−.77***
Lip products	−.22	−.64***	−.44*	.82***	.58*	.33 (.63**)	−.70***	−.90***	−.49*
Hair products	−.50*	−.47*	−.55*	.22	.12	.37	−.51*	−.52*	−.72***

SOURCE: Data from the Reader's Digest Association's Survey of Europe Today, 1970; Eurodata 91 (Eurodata is a consumer survey of 17 European countries sponsored by the Reader's Digest Association, Inc.); Consumer Europe 1997 (Euromonitor); and Geert Hofstede, *Cultures and Organizations: Software of the Mind* (New York: McGraw-Hill, 1991).

deodorants are an artificial means to control body odor. There is a negative correlation with UAI. Lip products satisfy the need to look young and to differentiate oneself. Hair products such as hair conditioner are mainly means to look younger. Usage of both lip and hair products correlates negatively with UAI. This expresses the need for purity and distrust of the artificial. It explains the frequently used scientific data and arguments in advertising for hair care, toothpaste, and other personal care products in Germany and also the existence of "scientific" brands such as Laboratoire Garnier in France and Dr. Best in Germany. Scientific data and arguments are expected to be more effective in strong uncertainty avoidance cultures than in weak uncertainty avoidance cultures. The preoccupation with purity related to cosmetic products has also been recognized in Japanese society, which is very high on the uncertainty avoidance index.[7]

Figure 6.5 depicts four culture clusters. Heavy usage of cosmetics is found in the cultures of the configuration with small PDI/weak UAI. This also is a cluster of IDV cultures. Medium to heavy usage will be associated with large PDI/weak UAI. Cultures in this cluster are also collectivist. Status brands will be important in this cluster, and brand loyalty will be strong. Medium usage is found in the culture cluster small PDI/strong UAI. This cluster includes medium individualist cultures. Small power distance means people will use cosmetics to look young, whereas strong uncertainty avoidance limits acceptance of some types of cosmetics. Products or brands focusing on naturalness

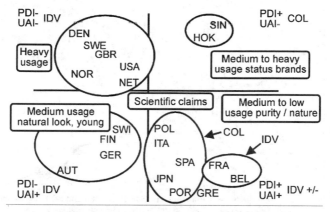

Figure 6.5. Clustering for Deodorants, Cosmetics, and Hair Care

NOTE: AUT = Austria, BEL = Belgium, DEN = Denmark, FIN = Finland, FRA = France, GBR = Great Britain, GER = Germany, GRE = Greece, HOK = Hong Kong, ITA = Italy, JPN = Japan, NET = Netherlands, NOR = Norway, POL = Poland, POR = Portugal, SIN = Singapore, SPA = Spain, SWE = Sweden, SWI = Switzerland, USA = United States.

and purity, preferably if they are scientifically controlled, will sell best in this cluster of cultures. In the culture cluster large PDI/strong UAI, sales will have to be stimulated more than in the other clusters, and both the scientific approach and status brands would be expected to sell best. This cluster includes individualist and collectivist cultures, so the approach will have to be differentiated for the two subclusters. Figure 6.5 presents a map for deodorants, cosmetics, and hair care products on three dimensions for 20 countries.

Cars

Income is generally assumed to be the main influence on the choice between a new or a secondhand car. The choice also appears to be influenced by culture. The respondents to EMS 95 reported culture-bound behavior with respect to buying secondhand automobiles. This influence of culture is confirmed by Eurodata 91. There is a strong correlation between buying new cars and strong uncertainty avoidance, demonstrated by a negative correlation between UAI and buying secondhand cars in both the 1970 Reader's Digest Association survey and Eurodata 91 (−.83*** and −.87***, respectively) and in EMS 95 (−.84***). The respondents of Eurodata 91 reflect the whole

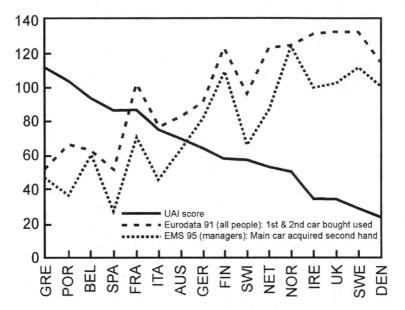

Figure 6.6. Correlation Between Buying Secondhand Cars and Uncertainty Avoidance

SOURCE: Data from Eurodata 91 (Eurodata is a consumer survey of 17 European countries sponsored by the Reader's Digest Association, Inc.); EMS 95 (copyright Inter/View); and Geert Hofstede, *Cultures and Organizations: Software of the Mind* (New York: McGraw-Hill, 1991).

NOTE: GRE = Greece, POR = Portugal, BEL = Belgium, SPA = Spain, FRA = France, ITA = Italy, AUS = Austria, GER = Germany, FIN = Finland, SWI = Switzerland, NET = Netherlands, NOR = Norway, IRE = Ireland, UK = United Kingdom, SWE = Sweden, DEN = Denmark.

population, whereas the respondents of EMS 95 reflect businesspeople with higher income levels. Culture overrides income as an influence on decisions. For this high-level target group, income is not the decisive factor. Figure 6.6 illustrates the correlations between buying secondhand cars and UAI.

Other factors found to be culture-bound are the body type of car, the design of the car, and interest in the engine of the car. In EMS 95 the percentage of respondents strongly agreeing "I like cars with individualistic styling" correlates with PDI (.47*), as illustrated in Figure 6.7. From content analysis of car advertising, I have also found that in large power distance cultures design and style of a car are used more frequently as arguments than in other cultures. Obviously the design of a car is a powerful motive for these cultures, reflecting the need for status.[8]

The size of a car's engine is not an equally important motive to members of all cultures. In feminine cultures, people are less interested in the engine

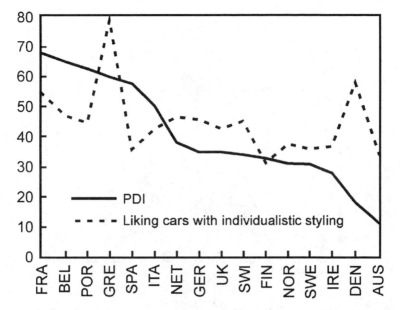

Figure 6.7. Correlation: Preference for Individualist Styling of Car and Power Distance
SOURCE: Data from EMS 95 (copyright Inter/View); and Geert Hofstede, *Cultures and Organizations: Software of the Mind* (New York: McGraw-Hill, 1991).
NOTE: FRA = France, BEL = Belgium, POR = Portugal, GRE = Greece, SPA = Spain, ITA = Italy, NET = Netherlands, GER = Germany, UK = United Kingdom, SWI = Switzerland, FIN = Finland, NOR = Norway, SWE = Sweden, IRE = Ireland, DEN = Denmark, AUS = Austria.

size than they are in masculine cultures. Members of feminine cultures more often do not know the engine sizes of their cars. The percentage giving no answers to questions about the engine size of people's cars in Eurodata 91 correlates negatively with MAS (−.60***). Also in EMS 95, with high-income respondents and a larger percentage of males, the "don't know" answers to the question about the engine size of the respondent's main car correlate negatively with MAS (−.52*). The correlations are illustrated in Figure 6.8. The relative differences between Eurodata and EMS 95 may be explained by the fact that a larger proportion of the EMS respondents are male, as the EMS target group is businesspeople, whereas the Eurodata population is all people. In all cultures, males will be more interested in technology than are females.

These findings confirm the existence of very different motives for buying automobiles, which can be clustered by culture as in the diagram in Figure 6.9. The upper left-hand quadrant shows the configuration UAI low/FEM. In this culture cluster, people have a preference for safety to protect the family

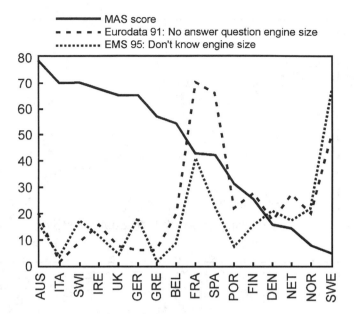

Figure 6.8. Correlation: Knowledge of Engine Size of Car and Masculinity/ Femininity

SOURCE: Data from Eurodata 91 (Eurodata is a consumer survey of 17 European countries sponsored by the Reader's Digest Association, Inc.); EMS 95 (copyright Inter/View); and Geert Hofstede, *Cultures and Organizations: Software of the Mind* (New York: McGraw-Hill, 1991).

NOTE: AUS = Austria, ITA = Italy, SWI = Switzerland, IRE = Ireland, UK = United Kingdom, GER = Germany, GRE = Greece, BEL = Belgium, FRA = France, SPA = Spain, POR = Portugal, FIN = Finland, DEN = Denmark, NET = Netherlands, NOR = Norway, SWE = Sweden.

and for saving money. Saving money is a frequent claim in advertising in these cultures. There is no interest in the size of the engine or other technical aspects. The upper right-hand quadrant shows a cluster of cultures of the configuration UAI low/MAS. People in these cultures tend to need status to show success. There is a preference for cars with big, powerful engines. The right-hand lower quadrant shows the cluster of cultures of the configuration UAI high/MAS. People of strong uncertainty avoidance cultures are fast drivers, and they prefer cars with fast acceleration. This seems paradoxical, as one would expect to see risk aversion translated into a safety motive, but the explanation is that people of strong uncertainty avoidance cultures build up stress that they also want to release. Fast driving functions as an emotional safety valve. A high score on the MAS dimension also adds the need to drive aggressively. And cars must be technologically advanced, well designed, and well tested. In the

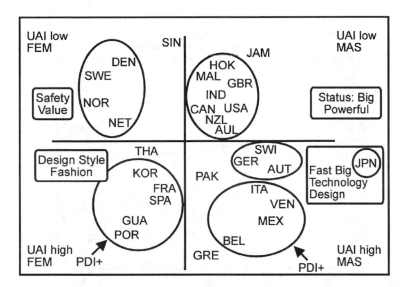

Figure 6.9. Clustering of Buying Motives for Automobiles

NOTE: AUL = Australia, AUT = Austria, BEL = Belgium, CAN = Canada, DEN = Denmark, FRA = France, GBR = Great Britain, GER = Germany, GRE = Greece, GUA = Guatemala, HOK = Hong Kong, IND = India, ITA = Italy, JAM = Jamaica, JPN = Japan, KOR = Korea, MAL = Malaysia, MEX = Mexico, NET = Netherlands, NOR = Norway, NZL = New Zealand, PAK = Pakistan, POR = Portugal, SIN = Singapore, SPA = Spain, SWE = Sweden, SWI = Switzerland, THA = Thailand, USA = United States, VEN = Venezuela.

lower left-hand quadrant, the configuration UAI high/FEM, one sees the need for "sporty" driving and fast acceleration, but not aggressiveness. This is combined with a preference for design, but more in the art/fashion sphere, embracing pleasure and enjoyment. Both lower quadrants include cultures of large power distance, which reinforces the appeal of the design of a car, a status function.

Insurance Products

The need for insurance products is influenced in various ways, in general by the degree of individualism. In collectivist cultures the extended family or other in-groups function as a safety net. Figure 6.10 illustrates the correlation between IDV and Eurodata 91 data on ownership of whole life insurance (.82***) and home insurance (.82***) among home owners in Europe. No significant correlation was found between income and ownership of whole

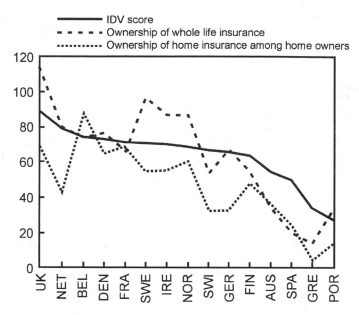

Figure 6.10. Correlation: Whole Life and Home Insurance and Individualism/
Collectivism

SOURCE: Data from Eurodata 91 (Eurodata is a consumer survey of 17 European countries sponsored by
the Reader's Digest Association, Inc.); and Geert Hofstede, *Cultures and Organizations: Software of the
Mind* (New York: McGraw-Hill, 1991).

NOTE: UK = United Kingdom, NET = Netherlands, BEL = Belgium, DEN = Denmark, FRA = France,
SWE = Sweden, IRE = Ireland, NOR = Norway, SWI = Switzerland, GER = Germany, FIN = Finland, AUS
= Austria, SPA = Spain, GRE = Greece, POR = Portugal.

life and home insurance (.33 and .31). Data on ownership of whole life insurance
in the 1970 Reader's Digest Association survey also show a significant correlation
with IDV (.53*) and no significant correlation with income (.38).

At face value, one would expect that individuals of strong uncertainty
avoidance cultures would own more insurance products than would members
of weak uncertainty avoidance cultures, whereas it appears to be the opposite
with respect to private insurance. Personal ownership of insurance and pension-related investments (as reported in EMS 95) and ownership of private
pension saving plans (in Eurodata 91) appear to correlate negatively with UAI
(see Figure 6.11). This implies that individuals of strong uncertainty avoidance cultures tend to buy fewer insurance- and pension-related investments
personally. This demonstrates that uncertainty avoidance is not the same as
risk avoidance. Insurance products eliminate risk. Members of weak uncer-

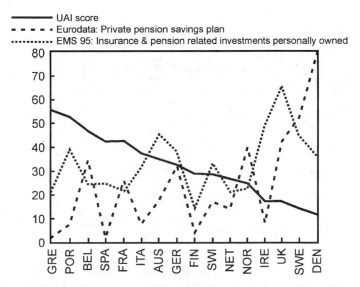

Figure 6.11. Correlation: Personal Pension Products and Uncertainty Avoidance

SOURCE: Data from Eurodata 91 (Eurodata is a consumer survey of 17 European countries sponsored by the Reader's Digest Association, Inc.); EMS 95 (copyright Inter/View); and Geert Hofstede, *Cultures and Organizations: Software of the Mind* (New York: McGraw-Hill, 1991).

NOTE: GRE = Greece, POR = Portugal, BEL = Belgium, SPA = Spain, FRA = France, ITA = Italy, AUS = Austria, GER = Germany, FIN = Finland, SWI = Switzerland, NET = Netherlands, NOR = Norway, IRE = Ireland, UK = United Kingdom, SWE = Sweden, DEN = Denmark.

tainty avoidance cultures may make cool calculations of risk and insure themselves. For members of strong uncertainty avoidance cultures, it is a more emotional reaction.

In strong uncertainty avoidance cultures people will expect the government or their companies to take care of their pension plans. This is confirmed by 1995 OECD data for 15 European countries on public pension spending as a percentage of GDP, which correlate positively with UAI (.66***). This phenomenon is related to competence as a citizen—the degree to which people tend to organize their lives themselves or wait for the authorities to organize things for them. A related correlation is between UAI and the answer "strongly agree" to the Eurodata 91 item "Welfare is the responsibility of government" (.46*).

The different needs and motives for buying insurance products can be mapped according to the configuration IDV/UAI, as in Figure 6.12. The culture cluster of the configuration COL/weak UAI will include low users, but if they buy insurance products, it will be a rational, calculated decision. The culture cluster COL/strong UAI will include low users who will have to be

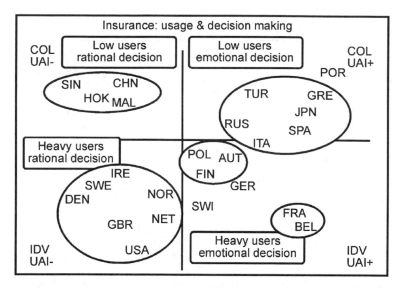

Figure 6.12. Clustering for Insurance Usage and Buying Motives

NOTE: AUT = Austria, BEL = Belgium, CHN = China, DEN = Denmark, FIN = Finland, FRA = France, GBR = Great Britain, GER = Germany, GRE = Greece, HOK = Hong Kong, IRE = Ireland, ITA = Italy, JPN = Japan, MAL = Malaysia, NET = Netherlands, NOR = Norway, POL = Poland, POR = Portugal, RUS = Russia, SIN = Singapore, SPA = Spain, SWE = Sweden, SWI = Switzerland, TUR = Turkey, USA = United States.

persuaded in an emotional manner. The configuration IDV/strong UAI will include a need for insurance products, but decision making will be an emotional matter. The cluster of cultures of the configuration IDV/weak UAI will include heavy users who also make rational, calculated decisions. Television commercials for Norwich Union Insurance in France show richly rewarding French family life characterized by *savoir vivre* and the claim that this should not be lost at retirement age. The approach in the United Kingdom is different. The United Kingdom is part of the cluster IDV/weak UAI, where buying life insurance is a matter of calculated risk, much less an emotional decision.

Conclusion

The research described briefly in this chapter demonstrates that values of national culture are important influences on consumer behavior and that they are expected to remain of importance, or even become more important with

converging income levels. Along with globalization and modernization, countries may be converging with respect to income levels, but they are not
converging with respect to values of national culture. A large number of
significant correlations between Hofstede's dimensions of national culture
and patterns of consumer behavior demonstrate the influence of culture on
behavior. Consistency over time with respect to the relationship between
Hofstede's dimensions and specific products and services demonstrates that
the influence of national culture is stable. The application of Hofstede's model
to international marketing and advertising is a powerful tool to compare
cultures with respect to product usage, needs, and motives, and subsequently
to adapt marketing activities and advertising approaches to the similarities and
differences found.

Notes

1. Geert Hofstede, *Cultures and Organizations: Software of the Mind* (New York: McGraw-
Hill, 1991); Ronald Inglehart, *Culture Shift in Advanced Industrial Society* (Princeton, NJ:
Princeton University Press, 1990).

2. Geert Hofstede, *Culture's Consequences: International Differences in Work-Related Values*
(Beverly Hills, CA: Sage, 1980); Hofstede, *Cultures and Organizations.* The data on consumption
and attitudes are from the following sources: (a) Euromonitor's Consumer Europe 1997 survey
(Euromonitor 1997; Euromonitor International plc, 60-61 Britton Street, London EC1M 5NA,
United Kingdom), which provides sales data in value and/or volume for a number of product
categories in the 15 countries of the European Union plus Switzerland and Norway; (b) the
European Media & Marketing Survey 1995 (EMS 95; conducted by Inter/View International),
which is a research survey of print media readership and TV audience levels within the upscale
consumer group in Europe (European Union, Switzerland, and Norway); (c) OECD data for 1994
and 1996; (d) the Reader's Digest Association's 1970 Survey of Europe Today, a study of
consumption habits and attitudes in 16 European countries; and (e) the 1991 Reader's Digest
Association Eurodata Survey (Eurodata 91), a study of the lifestyles, consumer spending habits,
and attitudes of people in 17 European countries.

3. July 1997 data on computers per 1,000 people and Internet hosts per 10,000 people are from
World Bank, *World Development Report 1998-99* (Washington, DC: World Bank, 1999).

4. A. Roland, *In Search of Self in India and Japan* (Princeton, NJ: Princeton University Press,
1988), 314.

5. *Benn's Media Directory, 1992* (New York: Nichols, 1992), as cited in Marieke de Mooij,
*Advertising Worldwide: Concepts, Theories and Practices of International, Multinational and
Global Advertising,* 2nd ed. (Englewood Cliffs, NJ: Prentice Hall International, 1994).

6. "European Planning Guide 1996-97," *Media and Marketing Europe,* August 1996. Implementor is the source of these data; the base is copies bought within a publication period.

7. C. Becker, "Hair and Cosmetic Products in the Japanese Market," *Marketing and Research
Today,* February 1997.

8. Marieke de Mooij, *Global Marketing and Advertising: Understanding Cultural Paradoxes*
(Thousand Oaks, CA: Sage, 1998).

7

Women as
an Advertising Target

An International Overview

Rena Bartos

I t is a truism that effective marketing and advertising must be built on understanding of the consumer. Yet sometimes perceptions and assumptions about people and about countries prevent marketers from responding to the opportunities inherent in social change. There are two subjects about which everyone in the marketing and advertising communities has strong opinions and preconceptions. One of them is women. The other is international marketing.

It isn't too many years ago that markets in the United States were clearly separated by gender. The assumption was that men were the targets for all the

NOTE: This chapter is based on data that has appeared in Rena Bartos, *Marketing to Women Around the World* (Cambridge, MA: Harvard Business School Press, 1989). Adapted and reprinted by permission of Harvard Business School Press.

expensive, big-ticket products and services, such as cars, travel, and financial services. On the other hand, women were sold food, household products, fashions, and cosmetics. It is remarkable to recall that at that time, working women were invisible in marketing and advertising plans. Most advertisers thought of women consumers as housewives. The usual target definition was "any housewife, 18 to 49." Occasionally, they would recognize young, single women, who in those days they described as "girls," as natural targets for cosmetic and fashion products. These two perceptions of women dominated marketing approaches to women in those days.

The surge of women entering the workforce has revolutionized the way we define the consumer marketplace:

- We find that men are crossing over into the supermarket and shopping for food and household products that used to be the exclusive responsibility of the housewife.
- We find that women are crossing over into the big-ticket product categories. They have become good customers for financial services, for travel, and for cars.
- We find that not all working women are young, single girls, and not all housewives are married.

In short, our perception of the total consumer marketplace has been turned upside down as a result of this one simple demographic fact.

The concept that effective advertising and marketing must be built on understanding of the consumer is particularly relevant to the international marketplace. The stereotypes and assumptions that marketers in the United States used to hold about consumers in their own country are compounded when they move overseas.

Some believe that consumers are fundamentally the same around the world and that strategies that work in one market can be transported to others. Some concede that rapid change has occurred in the United States, but they believe that consumers in other parts of the world are still motivated by traditional values. Still others think that there are such strong cultural differences between countries and regions that every marketing effort should be based on indigenous cultural patterns and lifestyles.

The changes in the women's market in the United States have been documented extensively. The question is, Have these changes occurred in other parts of the world or is this a uniquely American phenomenon? Do the traditional assumptions about the women's market hold up in Europe? In Latin America? In the Far East? In Canada?

Even if some women in these countries have, in fact, entered the workforce, is it because they are so driven by economic necessity that they are not very good customers for advertised products and services? Or even if the surface manifestations of demography are similar to those in the United States, are the underlying attitudes and perceptions of women in those countries markedly different from those of American women? The answers to these questions are essential if marketing and advertising in different parts of the world are to remain relevant to their target consumers.

J. Walter Thompson has examined the status of the women's market in 10 countries around the world: Canada, the United States, Brazil, Mexico, Venezuela, Great Britain, Italy, West Germany, Australia, and Japan. There are a number of basic demographic facts, such as occupation, marital status, presence of children, and age, that help us to define the consumer marketplace and understand the dynamics of how both working women and nonworking women use products and services and respond to media. In the data gathered in this study, this basic demography is intertwined with attitudes and social values that are clues to aspirations and motivations.

The first simple demographic fact is, of course, the presence of women in the workforce. But in looking at demography around the world, we find there is no such thing as a simple demographic fact in international research. We observe wildly conflicting estimates of the number of women working in each country. For example, the estimate for the United States ranges from 54% to 63%, and that for Canada from 46% to 62%.

There is no space here to discuss the nature of the data sources and the reasons for their diversity. It was decided to use the most recent population census of each country as the basis for this study. So, although the demography is not simple and may not be precisely parallel, anywhere from 27% to 55% of women in these 10 countries go to work. Although there are more working women in the United States than in the other countries, there are places in the world that have higher levels of working women. For instance, relatively more women in the Eastern Bloc and Scandinavia are in the workforce than in any of the countries discussed here.

- The highest proportion of working women is in North America. Some 55% of all women in the United States and 52% of women in Canada go to work.
- The level of working women in Japan, Great Britain, and Australia is also high. In those countries, from 49% to 46% are working women.
- West Germany is in the middle at 39%.

- Relatively fewer women in Italy and the three Latin American countries are in the workforce.

How does this compare with the past?

- Between 1960 and the 1980s, the most dramatic increase occurred in North America—in Canada and the United States—followed by Australia.
- Although there are currently more English than Italian women in the workforce, the relative gain has been more intense in Italy than in Great Britain.
- Although slightly fewer women in the three Latin American countries go to work, there has been real change in that region. The proportion of working women almost doubled in Venezuela and rose sharply in Mexico and Brazil.
- On the other hand, there were minor declines in Japan and West Germany. In each of these countries the population is trending older, and each has a retirement age of 60. There are relatively fewer women of working age available to work. However, there have been major structural changes in the nature and quality of the women's workforce in Japan and in West Germany.

Not All Nonworking Women Are Housewives

We might assume that in each of these countries the women who don't work must be at home keeping house. Therefore, they must be our traditional target consumers, the homemakers. However, when we consider the occupational profiles of all women in these countries, we see that some women are neither keeping house nor going to work. These "others" include schoolgirls who are too young to be at work or to be married, and retired/disabled women who are out of the mainstream.

It is frustrating that we don't have precise occupational profiles for all the countries in our study, but here is a report on those for which we do have these data:

- The highest proportion of nonactive women or "others" is in West Germany, where 25% of women are neither working nor keeping house. The majority of these are past working age.
- The second-highest level of "others" is in Italy, mostly retirees.
- In Australia, 22% of women are out of the mainstream, again mostly retirees.
- In Japan, 19% of women are retired, disabled, or still in school.

- In Venezuela, 16% of women are neither at work nor keeping house. The majority of these are still in school.
- In the United States, 15% of women are neither keeping house nor in the workforce.
- A smaller proportion of women in Canada are labeled "others." Only 10% of women in that country are either retired or still in school.
- Great Britain reported the lowest level of women who are out of the mainstream—neither at home keeping house nor going to work outside of the home.

We do not have any of this kind of information for the other Latin American countries.

The Ratio of Working Women to Housewives

Once we remove the schoolgirls and grandmothers from our consideration and confine our attention to active women—that is, those who are either full-time homemakers or in the workforce—we get a truer picture of the ratio of working women to housewives.

- This proportion has shifted rapidly in the United States. In the early 1970s, slightly more women were keeping house than going to work. Currently, the ratio of working women to housewives is 65:35.
- Japan, Australia, Canada, and West Germany have more working women than housewives. In Canada the ratio is 58:42.
- There are slightly more full-time homemakers than working women in Great Britain, but the difference is extremely slight. The ratio of housewives to working women is 50.5:49.5! Italy is the only country with relatively more housewives than working women at a ratio of 57:43.

Will the Trend Continue?

Will this trend toward women's working continue, or has it been a temporary blip? There are four reasons it is likely to continue.

First, there is a clear correlation between women's education and their presence in the workforce. The more education a woman has, the more likely she is to go to work. This refutes the notion that economic necessity is the only reason women work.

Clearly, better-educated women come from more affluent households, and those who are married tend to marry the highest-achieving men. Conversely, women with the lowest levels of education are probably most in need of income, and yet they are least likely to be in the workforce. There is consistency in this pattern from country to country. We do not have information on this for every country, and the educational systems and educational terminology vary from country to country; nonetheless, the pattern is remarkably consistent.

Because of the dramatic finding that the more education a woman has, the more likely she is to work, it can be speculated that the level of women's educational achievements in each country would correlate with their labor force participation. This analysis has been limited to the top two categories of educational achievement, "completed secondary school" and "completed postsecondary."

Although there is no direct correlation between women's educational achievements and their presence in the workforce, the patterns are intriguing. The three countries with the highest proportions of working women—the United States, Canada, and Japan—also have the highest proportions of women who have graduated from college or gone beyond.

Overall, although the correlation between women's educational achievements and their presence in the workforce is not totally consistent, the pattern suggests a tenuous relationship. Certainly, in those countries where women have achieved the highest levels of advanced education, they are most likely to be in the workforce, and in those countries where women have the lowest levels of education, they are less likely to go to work.

The second reason the trend toward women's working is likely to continue is that in recent years there has been an increase in women seeking advanced education and in the extent to which they have studied professions that used to be the exclusive bastions of men. This is also true for the five countries for which we have these kinds of trend data.

A third reason this trend is likely to continue is that in the United States currently more than half of the students enrolled in colleges and universities are women. This is up substantially from a generation ago. In the eight countries for which we have this kind of information, some comparisons are based on 1960 and others on the 1970s. In spite of these variations in time span, the direction of the trend is clear. In every one of these countries there were more women enrolled in colleges and universities in the 1980s than there were in the 1960s or early 1970s. The most striking change occurred in Canada, where in 20 years women moved from 33% of college students to a dramatic 55%. This is a bigger gain than that of the United States, which moved from 39% to 51% in the same period.

In every one of the eight countries for which we have trend data, more women participated in college education in the 1980s than had done so in the preceding 15 or 20 years. Although the level of women's college enrollment appears somewhat lower in Japan, the report from that country excluded junior college and graduate school from the definition of college enrollment.

The fourth reason the trend toward women's working is likely to continue is that women's aspirations are changing. The surge of women into the workforce is one indicator of change. However, it may be a manifestation of more fundamental change in women's aspirations and feelings about themselves and their roles in life.

Why Women Work

Women's aspirations are revealed, in part, by a consideration of the reasons women work. The obvious answer is economic: They work because they need the money. It is true that there are strong economic reasons women go to work:

- *Necessity:* Some women work for reasons of sheer economic necessity. These are women who must work if they or their families are to survive. They include unmarried women with no husbands or fathers to support them. Some have never married and have always had to work for a living. Others had their marriages interrupted by death or divorce and were suddenly thrust into the working world. Still others are married to men whose incomes simply cannot support their families.
- *A second paycheck:* Although many married women may not absolutely need the money, a second paycheck in the household enables them to maintain or improve their families' standard of living. This reason for working tends to be far more universal than that of sheer economic necessity.

But there are motivations beyond the paycheck that attract women into the workforce. The emotional and psychological rewards of work are intertwined with women's economic reasons for a job.

- *Broader horizons:* For many women, particularly those who are working for the second paycheck, the attraction of work is more a matter of what they are getting away from than what they are going to. The sense that the life of a housewife is a very narrow one is a perception that transcends national boundaries. These women feel that there must be "something more to life than the kitchen sink." Even though many of these women don't have highly stimulating or responsible jobs or professions, they share the sense that going out to work is far more satisfying than staying at home. The social stimulation that occurs in the workplace and the enhanced sense of self that comes with working explain why many of these women say they would rather work than stay at home.

- *Achievement:* A small number of women work for the same reasons that have always motivated ambitious men. They work because their work gives them a sense of achievement and because they enjoy the stimulation of the work itself. These fortunate women have found work that gives them psychic rewards as well as economic ones. The real difference between these women and those who are motivated by the combination of economic incentives and broader horizons is that they actually enjoy the work they do.

The Aspirations of Housewives

Some young housewives also want to be involved in the larger world outside the limits of the hearth and home. Although the traditional notion was that a woman's occupational goal in life should be to become a wife and mother, there is increasing evidence that women, particularly younger women, seek to combine marriage, work, and children.

This yearning for "something more" is quite universal. It occurs in every one of the countries studied. The attitude was summed up by one young Japanese housewife who said: "I feel that I want to get involved in society. Get out there. It would be a good opportunity for me to learn about things in the everyday world . . . and, besides, the working mothers I see look so alive. I feel that working would give me a chance to use the energy that has been bottled up in me."

Why Women Don't Work

Not all housewives share these aspirations, however. The reasons these women don't go to work or care to work are a direct reflection of their belief that women's proper role or function is to be at home caring for their husbands and children. Some say that their husbands would not allow them to work or that their husbands can afford to have them stay at home. This implicitly endorses the traditional perception of male and female roles, that the husband should work to support the family and the wife should stay at home and care for the house and children. Others say they are unable to work for reasons of health or reasons of age. These women have put themselves out of the running, so to speak.

The New Demographics

There is a way of segmenting the women's market that goes beyond occupation. It is based on the attitudes of housewives and working women toward work. I call this typology *the New Demographics*. It is based on a pair of questions that originated in the *Yankelovich Monitor* some years ago.

How Housewives Feel About Going to Work

The question asked of housewives was whether they ever planned to go to work: near term, in the next 5 years, sometime in the future, or not at all. We designate those housewives who say they do not ever plan to work as "stay-at-home housewives" and those who choose any of the other responses as "plan-to-work housewives." This expression of a desire to work is not necessarily a prediction that a particular woman will do so, but it is a very sensitive indicator of different attitudes and predispositions that, in turn, translate into differences in the marketplace.

The New Demographics typology of the stay-at-home housewife reflects that traditional homemaker's perception of her role. The plan-to-work housewife documents the aspirations of some young housewives to move beyond the narrow confines of their domestic roles.

- Almost three out of four housewives in Great Britain (73%) opt to stay at home.
- Housewives in West Germany and Japan are also far more likely to say they would prefer to stay at home than go to work (69% and 68%, respectively).
- Approximately two out of three housewives in Mexico, Venezuela, and the United States say they would rather stay at home than go to work (at 65%, 64%, and 63%, respectively).

- Although more housewives in Italy choose to stay at home (54%), a sizable proportion of Italian housewives yearn to enter the workforce (46%). As a matter of fact, there are relatively more plan-to-work housewives in Italy than in the other European countries or in Mexico, Venezuela, the United States, or Japan.
- The pattern is sharply reversed in Brazil, where 77% of housewives say they want to go to work.
- Housewives in Canada are far more likely to want to work than to stay at home. Some 60% of Canadian housewives say they plan to go to work.
- We have two sources of data about the New Demographics in Australia. Just over half of the housewives in Sydney and Melbourne (51%) say they plan to go to work. On the other hand, if we consider housewives in the five mainland capital cities, almost three opt to stay at home for every one who says she plans to go to work (ratio of 73:27).

How Working Women Feel About The Work They Do

Working women were asked whether they consider the work that they do "just a job" or a career. This question does not relate to their occupations, but rather to their attitudes toward their work. The differentiation between just-a-job working women and career women reflects the achievement orientation and ambition of career women. This is a very discriminating reflection of different values and lifestyles that, in turn, translate into real differences in the ways they buy and use products.

- When we consider working women, we see that the highest level of career perception occurs in Venezuela, where 57% of working women in the country are career oriented.
- Working women in Canada are similarly highly career oriented: 56% say their work is a career, whereas only 44% think it is "just a job."
- Australian women in Sydney and Melbourne show a somewhat similar picture. Just over half of working women (52.5%) in those cities are career oriented. On the other hand, when we consider working women in the five mainland cities, just over a third (36%) consider themselves career women, whereas 64% think their work is "just a job."
- In the United States more women who work consider the work they do "just a job" than perceive their work as a career. Nonetheless, two out of five designate themselves as career oriented.
- Great Britain, Brazil, and Mexico have fairly similar proportions of career-minded women. Almost two in five women in these countries see their work as a career.

- In Japan there are two working women who think their work is "just a job" for every one who considers it a career.
- By more than two to one, working women in Italy see their work as "just a job" rather than a career.
- The lowest level of career orientation occurs in West Germany, where only one working woman considers her work a career for every three who say that it is "just a job."

Melding Attitudes and Demographics

The size of the New Demographic segments is defined by setting the attitudes of housewives and working women toward work in proportion to the actual ratio of housewives and working women in the population of each country.

- If we consider career orientation among working women and the desire to work among housewives as evidence of ambition and aspiration, it is striking to note that both Canada, and Sydney and Melbourne in Australia have the highest proportions of career-oriented working women and plan-to-work housewives. This suggests that the quiet revolution is boiling up in each of these countries and has not yet reached its full expression.
- The high proportion of plan-to-work intentions among housewives in Brazil points to potential for change in that country.
- By the same token, women in Venezuela rank next in this level of ambition and aspiration.
- Although the United States has the highest ratio of working women to house-wives, the combined proportion of career women and plan-to-work housewives is 40%.
- Although there are relatively fewer working women in Italy than in the United States, there are almost identical proportions of "outward-bound" women in Italy (39%). This is due to the strong presence of plan-to-work housewives who yearn to enter the workforce.
- There are very similar proportions of "outward-bound" women in Mexico, Japan, Great Britain, and the five mainland cities of Australia, but the emphasis differs. Plan-to-work housewives in Mexico are the source of aspiration potential in that country. In Japan, Great Britain, and the five mainland cities of Australia, there are relatively more career-oriented working women than plan-to-work house-wives.
- Women in West Germany are the least likely to express this combination of aspiration and ambition. There are slightly more plan-to-work housewives than career-oriented working women in West Germany.

In the United States we have many years' worth of evidence that the four New Demographic segments really differ from each other demographically, attitudinally, and in the ways they behave in the marketplace. The two key demographic characteristics that differentiate them seem to be age and education. Stay-at-home housewives are the oldest and least well educated of all women, plan-to-work housewives are the youngest, and career women are the best educated and most affluent.

An examination of the demographic profiles of the segments in these countries parallels the observations we have made about the New Demographics in the United States. Although the proportions of the New Demographic segments vary from country to country, they reflect a spectrum of values ranging from the most traditional attitudes held by stay-at-home housewives to the most nontraditional perspectives expressed by career women. In many cases, plan-to-work housewives were far more like the two segments of working women than their stay-at-home counterparts.

Conclusions

This chapter has offered a brief glimpse into the fascinating subject of women around the world. Even this surface examination shows that there is enormous diversity in their levels of participation in the workforce and the extent of their ambition and aspirations.

But this is only the tip of the iceberg. In order to understand fully the status of the women's market in these 10 countries, we need to identify the women's positions in the life cycle. Whether or not they are married and whether or not they have children affect their needs as consumers, their lifestyles, and their market behavior. The life-cycle framework adds a discriminating dimension to the analysis of the consumer behavior of working women and housewives.

We also need to understand their self-perceptions and value systems. We need to learn not just whether or not they are married and whether or not they have children, but how they feel about their roles as women, as wives, and as mothers. We need to understand the dynamics of how their family roles affect or restrain their entrance into the workforce, and how this in turn affects their lifestyles and their needs as consumers. We need to understand how husbands feel about all these issues and how their attitudes affect the ways family purchase decisions are made.

To link this understanding to marketing applications, we need to learn how women's positions in the life cycle and their situation in the New Demographics typology affect how they buy and use products and how they respond to media.

If I had to use one word to describe the state of the women's market in the 10 countries we studied, that word would be *diversity*. Women are not a monolithic group. In every country we studied, there is a diverse spectrum of segments representing a range of values and attitudes and a range of marketplace behavior.

There were some universal elements that transcended national boundaries, and there were distinctive cultural nuances that differentiated women in each country from women in other countries. Women are not unidimensional. Even women in those countries that were most supportive of traditional values were surprisingly in favor of some very nontraditional types of behavior and lifestyles.

New values and old values coexist in varying proportions in every country studied. Those values and the behavior that reflects them appear to be changing rapidly. I believe that there are ways that international marketers can harness those changes to their marketing procedures.

The only constant in the world of the international advertiser is change. Consumers are changing. Markets are changing. And the cultural context is changing. On the other hand, the flip side of change is opportunity for the marketer with the courage and vision to seize the challenge.

8

Media May Be Global, but Is Youth?

Rosemary Ford
Adam Phillips

In 1983, Theodore Levitt wrote in a celebrated article, "The globalization of markets is at hand." [1] Well, now it is here. Its advantages are obvious and can be summed up as "economies of scale." The impact of globalization on the media has meant that not only are the same movies and television programs available simultaneously in many countries, but more and more people are able to receive international media brands delivered by satellite (such as CNN and MTV) or buy international publications that are produced in different languages (such as *Reader's Digest, Vogue,* and *Cosmopolitan*). Manufacturing companies operating in several different countries can at least consider using the same or similar advertising across borders, and worldwide media conglomerates can potentially offer media-buying packages on the same basis.

However, this type of approach can work only if the target for a product is the same across national boundaries and if different cultural values do not interfere with the way in which the media product or the advertising is received. These are two big "ifs," and the need for information in these two areas is absolute if major and embarrassing mistakes are to be avoided. At the simplest level, there are problems of translation to consider: "Nothing sucks like an Electrolux" presumably did little to aid Electrolux vacuum cleaner sales in America. The problems of identifying and understanding marketing targets are rather more challenging.

We are not in a position, yet, to talk about youth at a global level. But we can speak with some knowledge about youth in the European Union. Euroquest, with which we are professionally associated, has recently published a survey titled Teenagers Europe 1997 that can be used to identify and understand youth targets, giving marketers and advertisers more information than they have ever had before about young Europeans' attitudes, values, and behavior. The study is based on interviews with 10,000 11- to 19-year-olds in Germany, France, Italy, and Great Britain. These four countries account for two-thirds of teenagers in the European Union (full methodological details are provided in Appendix A). The coverage of the survey included use of and attitudes toward media (television, press, cinema, radio, and the Internet), use of about 150 product fields, and a wide range of attitudinal data. In short, it is the most comprehensive study of teenagers ever undertaken in Europe. In this chapter, using data from this study, we will demonstrate that it is possible to take a "global" approach to youth, at least within Europe, because we have been able to identify "types" of teenagers that transcend national boundaries. We will demonstrate how this typology can help an advertiser understand the users of its brand *and* how to reach them, while at the same time taking important national differences into account.

And those national differences should not be underestimated. It is by no means our intention to suggest that a "global" approach is always appropriate. Before we describe the different types of teenagers that exist in all four countries, let us first take a moment to remind ourselves just how different these countries can be.

National Differences

Space does not allow a detailed enumeration of the legal, behavioral, and attitudinal differences that exist among Britain, France, Germany, and Italy,

TABLE 8.1 Income and Working Status Variations by Country

	Great Britain	*Germany*	*France*	*Italy*
All 11-19-year-olds				
(unweighted samples)	4,055	2,023	2,021	1,971
Average weekly income ($)	87	72	67	42
Education status (%)				
School/college/university	85	86	92	94
Apprenticed	3	9	3	2
Permanent job	9	2	1	3
Regularly receive money from[a] (%)				
Regular job, full-time	15	20	5	4
Regular job, part-time	43	20	19	10
Pocket money/allowance				
from parents	50	69	69	85
Pocket money/allowance				
from grandparents	12	22	34	36
Grant	6	2	6	2
Don't get any money	3	5	7	3

SOURCE: Data from Teenagers Europe 1997.

a. This group consisted of 15-19-year-olds only (total 5,407 unweighted).

but we can give some illustrations. At the most fundamental level, there are differences in the age at which people are allowed to take part in various activities. A 14-year-old in Italy can use the "pulling power" of a moped to attract the opposite sex and legally have sex at the end of the evening. A French 14-year-old can do all the attracting he likes on his moped, but theoretically has to wait another 4 years before having sex. The British have to wait until age 16 to do both, whereas the Germans can legally have sex and leave school before they are allowed their own wheels. More seriously perhaps, German and Italian teenagers still have conscription looming on the horizon as they grow up, which has not been the case for British teenagers since 1962 and after 2002 will no longer be the case in France.

Data from the Teenagers Europe study indicate that British and German teenagers typically have more money to spend than do their French and Italian counterparts, and Table 8.1 shows that this appears to be related to the fact that British and German teenagers start work younger. Working teenagers in Germany are more likely to be apprenticed than are those in Britain, and this may account for their income being a little lower. However, another factor is that British teenagers are the most likely to earn money from part-time jobs.[2]

TABLE 8.2 Television Viewing by Country

	Great Britain	France	Italy	Germany
All who watch television (unweighted samples)	4,046	1,978	1,956	1,925
Average hours watched on				
Weekdays	4.0	3.5	3.1	2.5
Saturdays	4.3	3.0	2.5	3.0
Sundays	3.7	2.8	2.9	3.0
Average hours per day	4.0	3.3	3.0	2.6

SOURCE: Data from Teenagers Europe 1997.

So the constraints upon teenagers imposed by society vary quite widely from one country to another, and although it is the case that across the European Union there are trends toward a longer period in education and leaving the family home at a later age, there are still marked differences in the patterns of education and beginning work.[3]

We have also observed wide variations in behavior, of which one of the most outstanding is the extent to which young people watch television. Table 8.2 shows the average number of hours 11- to 19-year-olds claim to watch television on weekdays, Saturdays, and Sundays. British teenagers typically watch around 4 hours of television every day of the week, which is consistently at least half an hour more than teenagers elsewhere and, on average, about 1.5 hours more than German teenagers.

As one might expect, attitudes as well as behavior vary from one country to another. Respondents were presented with a list of 26 items and asked to select those that they thought were "really important in life." Teenagers in all four countries were unanimous in placing "friendship," "health," and "love" as the top three items, but there were considerable differences in the extent to which they considered other things important; some examples appear in Table 8.3.

British teenagers were the most likely to rate "meeting new people," "having an adventurous life," and "lots of free time to enjoy myself" as important, but were also the most likely to select "knowing how to save" and "leading a healthy life." German teenagers placed more emphasis on "physical beauty" than others, albeit still at quite a low level compared with other things, and were also the most likely to choose "having lots of money," "having a peaceful life," and "an independent job." They were the least likely to select

TABLE 8.3 Things That Are Most Important in Life: Highlights From 26 Possible Items (in percentages)

	Great Britain	Italy	France	Germany
All 11-19-year-olds (unweighted samples)	4,055	1,971	2,021	2,023
Friendship	96	93	94	91
Health	87	82	88	82
Love	84	75	83	71
Achieving success on my own merits	66	48	72	55
Leading a healthy life	70	51	44	52
Meeting new people	65	45	49	52
Lots of free time to enjoy myself	65	34	51	54
Having children	49	47	58	34
Reading, studying	44	51	56	31
Having lots of money	34	30	40	47
Having an adventurous life	47	25	39	35
Knowing how to save	47	35	27	33
An independent job	31	27	23	42
Having a peaceful life	29	19	26	41
Physical beauty	19	22	28	33
Religion	15	38	16	11

SOURCE: Data from Teenagers Europe 1997.

"having children," and perhaps rather contrary to the stereotype, they were considerably less likely than others to select "reading, studying." In contrast, the French were the most likely to choose this as well as the most likely to choose "having children." They were also considerably above average in choosing "achieve success on my own merits." Almost 4 in 10 Italian teenagers picked out "religion" as being one of the most important things in life, compared with fewer than 2 in 10 in the other three countries.

This is just a taste of the attitudinal differences we can highlight from the data in Teenagers Europe. We could go on to talk about how the British are the most likely to agree that "Sundays are boring"—in strong contrast to the Italians, whose tradition is of Sundays that have a much more social nature. We could also talk about Italian enthusiasm for sport and the pronounced concern for the environment displayed by German teenagers. To summarize, we have evidence of major differences among the lives and attitudes of teenagers across Europe, and yet we can also demonstrate common patterns.

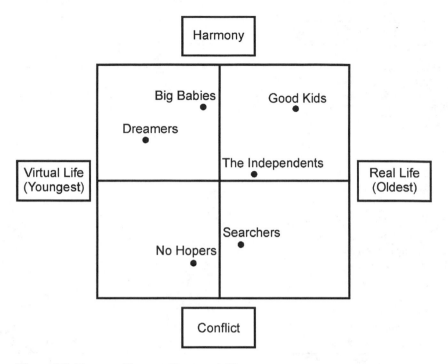

Figure 8.1. European Teenage Clusters: A Map

Pan-European Commonalities

Eurisko, our Italian partner in Europe, has carried out factor and cluster analysis of the Teenagers Europe data. A total of 65 variables were used in this analysis, taking into account objective variables (such as sex, age, education/work status) and also attitudinal and behavioral variables (see Appendix B for a list of these variables). The aim of the analysis was to see if it was possible to identify groups of respondents that were internally homogeneous in terms of these variables and clearly distinct from each other.

The analysis produced six clusters of respondents that can be thought of as six different "ways" of being a teenager in Europe today. A map derived from principal-components analysis is the simplest way to begin to describe the differences among these groups, as illustrated in Figure 8.1.

The analysis differentiated the groups on two key dimensions that form the axes of Figure 8.1. The vertical axis is linked to family relations, namely, whether the respondent is more in a state of harmony or in conflict with his or her family. The horizontal axis is defined by attitudes and behaviors that indicate the extent to which the individual lives in the "real" world as opposed to the world of his or her imagination. This axis is also linked to age, with the youngest groups, who have less experience of the real world, living more in their imaginations and dreams of what life will be like.

The two clusters with the youngest profiles, "Dreamers" and "Big Babies," sit in the top left quadrant of the map, where the family is still an important reference point and where "life" is still largely imagined. Dreamers are enthusiastic children who are media and technology fans and are curious about everything. They are confident and have dreams they believe they can fulfill—becoming another Bill Gates, or being a famous footballer. They are social and have friends while living happily within their families. They spend their money on computers, video games, clothes, music, sports, and entertainment outside the home.

The Big Babies also have good family relationships, but have much more limited horizons than the Dreamers. Dreamers are confident they can achieve their dreams, but Big Babies are quite insecure and tend to shelter within the world of school and home. Studying and family are important to them, and their leisure time is spent mostly at home. They spend their money mainly on gifts for others, on clothes, and on records/CDs. They do not have much money ($41 per week), probably because they are the youngest group.

In the top right segment there are older teenagers, in particular the "Good Kids," a group that can probably be summed up as every parent's dream—in harmony with their families, able to think intelligently for themselves, and well equipped to deal with the real world. They tend to be in the middle age range of teenagers, are often students, and have the most upscale background of all the six groups. They have many interests and friends, but maintain their individuality within their friendship groups. They have ideals and ethics, but also know how to enjoy themselves, and their spending is varied, including music, clothing, sports, and books.

The "Independents" also tend to the top right-hand quadrant of the map, but are less in harmony with their families. They have the oldest profile, are composed of more women than men, and have a medium-low profile in socioeconomic terms. The majority of teenagers who no longer go to school

TABLE 8.4 Distribution of Teenage Clusters Across Europe (in percentages)

Cluster	Total Europe	Great Britain	Italy	France	Germany
All 11-19-year-olds (unweighted sample)	10,070	4,055	1,971	2,021	2,023
Dreamers	15	27	9	13	13
Big Babies	15	12	9	15	20
Good Kids	16	10	27	13	15
Independents	14	17	10	15	16
Searchers	20	18	30	22	14
No Hopers	19	16	14	23	22

SOURCE: Data from Teenagers Europe 1997.

are concentrated in this group, and they are the most likely to be in work. Consequently, their lifestyle is quite free, with family having little influence or authority. They have the highest personal income of these six groups, averaging $117 per week. Their focus is on entertainment, fun, friends, and fashion, and this is reflected in their relatively high spending on clothing, entertainment, and music. Their values tend to be material rather than idealistic.

"Searchers" sit toward the bottom right quadrant, in conflict with the adult world and their families and seeking to create a "different" life from that of their parents, with new rules and values. They have an average age and sex profile. Their orientation is more toward their peer group than toward their families. At the same time, these teenagers are eager to explore and are full of interests. Their emphasis is on experimenting and experiencing new things. Music is very important to them, and they spend quite a lot on it, together with spending on clothing, entertainment, magazines, and books.

In the bottom left quadrant, we find the "No Hopers"—every parent's nightmare. They are in conflict with the adult world and seek escape from real life, with a "no problem," apathetic attitude. Their age profile is average, and they are slightly biased toward the male sex. There is little communication at home, but there is also little that really interests or stimulates them outside the home, and they do not seem to be comfortable with friends, either. They are not interested in the future and seem to have the attitude of waiting to take whatever life brings. They generally do things and consume a bit of everything, but in a limited way, with little enthusiasm.

Table 8.4 shows the sizes of all of these groups and also their distribution across countries. All six are relatively substantial in size, with Searchers and

No Hopers forming the largest groups, each accounting for one in five teenagers. All six types appear in all four countries, although there are substantial variations.

Almost 30% of teenagers in Britain fall into the cluster of Dreamers, and this cannot be accounted for by demographic differences, as the profile of British teenagers is close to average in terms of age. Britain is also above average in the proportion of Independents in its teenage population. Good Kids are the smallest group in Britain, accounting for just 1 in 10 teenagers.

Germany has a high proportion of Big Babies, and this may partly be accounted for by demographics, as the German age profile is a little younger than average. The proportions of Independents and No Hopers are also above average in Germany; No Hopers in fact form the largest group.

France is similar in this respect, with almost a quarter of teenagers falling into the No Hoper cluster. Conflict, or at least some lack of harmony, would appear to be highest in France, as the next largest group there is the Searchers, accounting for another 22% of French teenagers.

The two largest groups in Italy are the Good Kids and the Searchers. Italy has the lowest proportion of No Hopers and of the other three groups.

So there are variations in the extent to which these groups are present in the four countries, but it is the case that all six are to be found everywhere. These groups can therefore be used as a pan-European market segmentation, and later in this chapter we will illustrate just how this can work in practice. First, however, we will look at the relationships these different groups have with various media.

Media Behavior Among
the Pan-European Clusters

There are clear differences among the clusters in terms of their attitudes toward and use of media. The most pronounced differences relate to television. Dreamers are attracted to anything conveyed to them through a screen, and this extends to video games, computers, and cinema. Their hours watching television are almost 7 per week more than the average for 11- to 19-year-olds; more than half of them live in homes with three or more TVs, and almost two-thirds have TV in their bedrooms. A quarter also have VCRs in their rooms, as shown in Table 8.5.

TABLE 8.5 Television Variations Among Clusters

Cluster	Average Hours Watched per Week[a]	3 or More TVs in Home[a] (%)	TV in Bedroom[a] (%)	VCR in Bedroom[b] (%)
All 11-19-year-olds	22.3	42	52	20
Dreamers	29.1	54	64	25
Independents	26.2	47	63	27
Searchers	23.8	46	53	18
No Hopers	20.9	36	48	21
Big Babies	18.6	31	43	14
Good Kids	16.4	37	44	15

SOURCE: Data from Teenagers Europe 1997.
a. Base = all who watch television (9,905 unweighted).
b. Base = all who have VCR in home (8,946).

The attitudes of Dreamers toward television tie in with their behavior. They tend to agree with all the statements the survey asked about television, whether those statements were positive or negative. So although they have criticisms, they are also extremely positive about the medium. For example, they were the most likely to agree with the item "There aren't enough programs for people of my age" (59% versus an average of 45%), but they were also the most likely to agree that "I love watching TV" (69% versus 55%). We have already described Dreamers as tending to live in the virtual world of the imagination rather than in real life, and one indicator of this is that 3 in 10 agree that "TV is more exciting than real life"—twice the average level of agreement.

Table 8.5 also shows that the Independents watch a relatively large amount of television, and, like the Dreamers, they are above average on other television-related variables. However, their attitudes are much closer to the average, so that one senses less involvement with the medium than we find among Dreamers. In Britain, Independents (rather more girls than boys, and out for fun and enjoyment rather than agonizing over moral issues) have high indices for liking soap operas and are more likely than other teenagers to watch MTV and VH1. In contrast, young Dreamers have high indices on *Mighty Max* (a cartoon baby character who has fun/adventure fantasies) and *Scratchy & Co* (a Saturday morning children's program "hosted" by a mock cartoon character—a mixture of competitions, sketches, cartoons, and other children's programs over a period of a couple of hours). A number of sports programs are also popular with Dreamers. Good Kids, whose viewing levels are considerably lower than those of other groups, also favor quite different programs. The program with the highest index among the older Good Kids is *Cutting Edge* (a current affairs investigative/documentary program), and no other group has a higher index on *Winnie the Pooh.* (Because Teenagers Europe covered television programs and titles relevant within each country, we have largely confined ourselves to commenting on differences between the clusters in Great Britain.)

So the pan-European clusters show significant differences in terms of their viewing behavior, their attitudes, and their selection of programming. There are also differences among the groups in their relationships with press media. For newspapers, readership often appears to be a reflection of parental social class, with Good Kids, our most upmarket group, being most likely to mention quality press titles. Although almost a fifth claim to buy papers themselves, the vast majority do not, and this must influence what titles are available to them.

Good Kids seem to have the closest relationship with newspapers, with almost 9 in 10 agreeing that "newspapers help me know what's going on in the world" (average agreement for all 11- to 19-year-olds is 74%) and only a quarter agreeing that "newspapers are boring"—about half the level of agreement among Dreamers. Good Kids, together with Searchers, are the most likely to say that they buy papers themselves.

Good Kids and Searchers are the most likely to read magazines, although reading magazines is in fact high overall, with more than 85% of all groups claiming to read them. More than three-quarters of Searchers and Independents claim to buy their own, compared with only 60% of Big Babies, whose parents are quite commonly the purchasers.

For women's magazine titles, Independents seem to read a wider variety of magazines than other groups, usually having the highest index on each of the British titles the survey covered. The title with the highest index among this group was *New Woman,* followed by *Woman's Own, Bella, Take a Break,* and *Woman.* The highest indices for Searchers were quite different, led by *Hair Flair, Company, 19,* and *The Clothes Show Magazine.* Good Kids are different again—they are most likely to read *Elle* or *Marie Claire.*

Teenagers Europe has extensive title coverage for each local market, and here we have commented only on our findings in the British women's magazines sector. Other sectors also reflect the differences we have found among the different groups. Reflecting their enthusiasm for computers (described toward the end of this section), Dreamers tend to have the highest

TABLE 8.6 Radio Listening by Cluster

Cluster	Listen to the Radio[a] (%)	Average Hours Listen per Week[b]
All 11-19-year-olds	92	18.7
Independents	96	24.7
Searchers	95	23.2
Good Kids	94	17.3
Dreamers	92	16.3
Big Babies	87	11.7
No Hopers	86	16.5

SOURCE: Data from Teenagers Europe 1997.
a. Base = all respondents (10,070 unweighted).
b. Base = all who listen to the radio (9,334 unweighted).

indices on all the computer magazine titles, rivaled in only a couple of cases by the rather older Independents and Searchers on two PC titles: *Personal Computer World* and *What PC.*

Listening to the radio is a common activity for all teenagers, although least so among No Hopers and Big Babies. Independents and Searchers listen for the most hours, as shown in Table 8.6. Reflecting their interests, Dreamers are more likely than some other groups to listen to radio for sports programming, and they are not so keen on news—too much tainted by the real world! Searchers also use the radio for sports, but also for music and talk shows. No Hopers, another group that tends toward the virtual rather than reality, are like Dreamers in being below average in listening to news. So in this medium, too, the pan-European clusters are separated by the extent to which they use the medium and by what they use it for.

Dreamers are attracted to the cinema as well as to television. They are the most likely to agree that "I love going to the cinema" (52% versus average of 37%), but because Dreamers are relatively young and have less money to spend, it is the Searchers and the Good Kids who are the most likely to have been to the cinema in the past year. Among those who have been, however, the average frequency of going is almost as high for Dreamers as for Good Kids and Searchers. Overall, at least 80% of all the groups had been to the cinema in the past year.

The pattern of whom they go to the movies with again mirrors other findings about these groups. Dreamers and Big Babies are more likely than others to go with parents or siblings; Independents are most likely to go with boyfriends/girlfriends, whereas Searchers and Good Kids are the most likely groups to go with friends. No Hopers are the most likely to go alone to the cinema—although it should be noted that we are talking about 5% falling into this category compared with an average of 3%.

Finally, we can look at variations in Internet use among these groups. More than two-thirds of 11- to 19-year-olds claim to use computers, and more than half have computers at home. These figures are considerably higher among Dreamers, 83% of whom use computers and 63% of whom have computers at home. They use computers predominantly for school/college work or for playing games. Games are a close second for all teenagers, except for the two youngest groups (Dreamers and Big Babies), for whom games use is the most important; using a computer for school/college work is still a major second, but a little more so for Dreamers than for Big Babies.

Using computers to access the Internet was mentioned by 11% of the sample overall and was slightly more common among Dreamers and Searchers. Dreamers are the most likely to have computers at home (63% say their families have computers, compared with an average of 52%) and these computers are more likely to have modems and access to the Internet. Good Kids are the next most likely group to have computers at home (58%), which is slightly surprising given that their families are probably more able to afford them than are the families of Dreamers. Clearly, there is something about Dreamers (and perhaps their families) that draws them to computers and to the Internet.

To summarize, the pan-European clusters we have generated from Teenagers Europe do have distinct media consumption profiles. All teenagers watch TV, read magazines, go to the cinema, and listen to the radio, but membership in these groups does discriminate in the extent to which they do these things and their *choice* of individual programs, subject areas, and titles. It would theoretically be possible to target any one of these groups on a pan-European basis if one had a genuinely pan-European media product or brand. There are no international magazine titles that are targeted at the teenage market, but we have been able to look at the few pan-European television channels and programs to see if the same groups are attracted to the same programming in each country.

The figures in Table 8.7 are indices calculated from claimed viewing measures. Thus if the viewing of a channel in a particular cluster is the same as that for the total sample, the index would be 100. To the extent that it is higher or lower, the index will be greater or less than 100. When looking at

TABLE 8.7 Cable Channels and Programs by Cluster

	Independents	Searchers	Dreamers	Good Kids	Big Babies	No Hopers
MTV						
Great Britain	120	125	104	95	51	86
Germany	114	116	116	128	72	77
France	143	128	116	109	49	67
CNN						
Great Britain	89	109	136	102	63	68
Germany	94	107	150	129	78	71
France	78	177	71	107	44	90
Eurosport						
Great Britain	82	101	144	89	53	86
Germany	100	110	128	114	91	76
France	132	119	112	110	67	72
The X-Files						
Great Britain	91	113	123	96	92	91
France	92	114	121	89	79	101
Italy	75	117	177	93	76	77
Baywatch						
Great Britain	81	111	200	56	53	93
Germany	114	103	188	86	75	66
Italy	115	101	182	101	92	57
Star Trek						
Great Britain	66	98	111	90	133	100
Germany	68	118	118	73	96	124
Italy	44	88	199	110	94	84

SOURCE: Data from Teenagers Europe 1997.
NOTE: Base = all respondents (total 10,700, unweighted), except for *The X-Files* and *Baywatch,* for which base = all 15-19-year-olds (total 5,407, unweighted).

indices, one should keep in mind that one is looking at a ratio rather than at absolute figures.

Table 8.7 shows that there are signs that some television programming is reaching the same targets across Europe. All television programs and cable channels tend to be high among Dreamers because of their high general viewing levels, but MTV also appears to appeal consistently to Independents and Searchers in all four countries and not to Big Babies and No Hopers. This is rather as we might expect, given the fun/entertainment focus of Independents and the importance of music for Searchers. There is rather less consistency of appeal for CNN and for Eurosport.[4]

In terms of individual programs, there is little consistent appeal for *Star Trek,* which has widely differing indices within five of the six clusters. *Baywatch* has high penetration among Dreamers and average penetration among Searchers in each country, but there is less consistency among the indices for other clusters. However, when we look at *The X-Files,* we can see that it appeals to Searchers in all three countries where it is shown, as well as to Dreamers, whereas other clusters are distinctly less likely to watch it. The indices for *The X-Files* within each cluster for each country are remarkably similar, indicating that this program clearly appeals to, or fails to attract, similar types of teenagers wherever it is shown.

The analysis we can do in this respect is relatively limited, because there are few media products that are genuinely international. Where they do exist, we can see that some are reaching similar targets in all countries, but others are not. So how do pan-European consumer brands fare in this type of analysis?

Brand Use Among Pan-European Clusters

Table 8.8 shows some brand use information analyzed by cluster. The figures are indices calculated as before, but this time based on usership. If we look at the figures for Calvin Klein, it appears that Searchers are more likely than average to choose the brand and, with two exceptions, the same is true of Good Kids and Independents; Big Babies, Dreamers, and No Hopers are less likely to choose it. The pattern of indices for Britain generally matches the European picture. In contrast, Yves St. Laurent (YSL) consistently appeals to Independents but otherwise there is little similarity among the figures for Britain, France, and Germany. We can also look at deodorants and see that Impulse in Britain tends to attract the same types of users (Searchers and Good Kids) as in the rest of Europe. We are only able to compare two countries for Brut, but in both Britain and France, Brut appeals to Dreamers and not to Independents, Good Kids, Big Babies, or No Hopers. Another market where a product tends to attract the same types of users in Britain as elsewhere is treatments for acne, where the clusters that are attracted to Clearasil are very similar in Britain, France, and Germany.

TABLE 8.8 Brand Use by Cluster

	Independents	Searchers	Dreamers	Good Kids	Big Babies	No Hopers
Perfume						
Calvin Klein						
Great Britain	185	144	58	138	36	60
Italy	72	132	67	127	38	68
France	200	119	70	94	45	75
Germany	147	182	56	147	29	74
YSL						
Great Britain	185	115	71	91	23	108
France	179	102	58	146	72	65
Germany	205	178	143	37	34	54
Deodorant						
Impulse						
Great Britain	125	119	85	110	100	73
Italy	93	111	75	120	67	80
Germany	156	158	74	116	60	64
Brut						
Great Britain	76	101	164	64	55	72
France	97	147	133	91	35	88
Acne Treatment						
Clearasil						
Great Britain	95	120	115	97	90	68
France	138	113	120	83	68	83
Germany	101	148	110	92	76	91

SOURCE: Data from Teenagers Europe 1997.
NOTE: Base = all respondents (total 10,070, unweighted).

What these results suggest is that some brands appeal to the same types of users in every country, whereas others do not. The obvious conclusion is that some brands are genuinely international, in the sense that they have the same values independent of the countries in which they are sold, whereas others are not. Clearly, as people travel more and are exposed to international media, it is the brands that have the same values everywhere that are likely to be more successful, because their users are less likely to be confused by different positionings in different countries.

These findings are not exclusive to packaged goods brands. Table 8.9 shows a similar pattern for retailers. It can be seen that there is quite a close fit between the strong clusters for Benetton in Britain and the other countries. However, the match is less close for Kookai.

TABLE 8.9 Clothes Shops Visited in Past 6 Months

Shops	*Independents*	*Searchers*	*Dreamers*	*Good Kids*	*Big Babies*	*No Hopers*
Benetton						
Great Britain	125	150	72	170	39	73
Italy	82	106	99	118	79	78
France	114	123	90	121	89	71
Germany	106	152	79	140	64	82
Kookai						
Great Britain	171	154	46	217	32	41
Italy	73	125	160	100	58	53
France	150	136	55	107	61	81

SOURCE: Data from Teenagers Europe 1997.
NOTE: Base = all respondents (total 10,070, unweighted).

Obviously, we have chosen a selection of brands to illustrate the points we are trying to make. However, we have seen similar patterns in other markets where the purchaser, or strong influencer, is the teenager.

To sum up, we believe that we have demonstrated that in the main countries in Western Europe, at least, there is an international market where young people have the opportunity to use brands that are the same everywhere. However, the brands in the market are frequently positioned differently in different countries, even when they have the same name. Groups of young people of different nationalities can be identified who are more similar to each other in terms of their attitudes and behavior than they are to their compatriots in different groups and ages. Where international brands exist, groups of young people are likely to be as attracted to buy the same brands as are people of their type in other countries. These different groups also have very different media consumption habits. As with branded goods, different groups are more attracted to different newspapers and television programs, and there is some evidence that some international television programs and channels have been able to create the same kind of common international appeal to particular groups that we have detected with branded goods.

Language is clearly a major barrier, but the expansion of digital broadcasting should go a long way toward ameliorating this problem. It will be interesting to see whether the press will be forced to respond.

In answer to the question posed in the title of this chapter: Media production is increasingly global, and there are clearly groups of young people in each of the main European countries who are much more similar to each other than the obvious differences of language and national culture would suggest. However, most media and consumer brands are not yet tapping into these different teen cultures as much as they might. As globalization continues, media and brand owners who can do this effectively will be the ones who will be the most successful. Or, as Theodore Levitt said in the early 1980s, "Companies that do not adapt to the new global realities will become victims of those that do." [5],Fortunately, in Europe at least, there still seems to be time to adjust to meet the changes that are coming.

APPENDIX A
Methodology

The universe for this study was 11- to 19-year-olds living in France, Great Britain, Germany, and Italy. Although the precise sampling details varied from country to country, the same principles applied throughout: a nationally representative sample in terms of age, sex, and social grade within 11- to 19-year-olds. No more than one child was interviewed per household. Sample sizes were 4,000 in Great Britain and 2,000 in each of the other countries.

Information was collected using self-completion questionnaires—either postal or with interviewer placement and collection. Fieldwork was conducted between April and June 1997 in all countries. The fieldwork was conducted by CSA in France, BMRB International in Great Britain, Basisresearch in Germany, and Eurisko in Italy.

The same basic questionnaire was followed in all countries. In France and Great Britain, a separate questionnaire was developed for younger and older respondents, deleting questions not relevant to younger respondents, simplifying language, and taking out inappropriate attitude statements (e.g., regarding contraception). In Germany and Italy the same questionnaire was used for all age groups, with instructions inserted as appropriate. Although the questionnaire was harmonized as far as possible, brand lists and certain questions varied to suit specific country conditions.

Results have been weighted for each country to ensure that the achieved sample is balanced to be fully representative of age, sex, and region. The total analysis has been weighted in proportion to distribution of the teenage population across the four countries covered by the survey. Sources for the total 11- to 19-year-old population in each country were as follows: France,1990 census; Great Britain, ONS (formerly OPCS); Germany, Mikrozensus 1995; Italy, ISTAT 1996.

APPENDIX B
Variables Used in Cluster Analysis

- Viewership of television on weekdays, Saturdays, and Sundays
- Listening to radio on weekdays, Saturdays, and Sundays
- Cinema visiting
- Agreement with
  - I want to be famous.
  - I consider myself an expert on new technology.
  - Having a career is very important to me.
  - I would like to have my own family.
  - I like to enjoy life and don't worry about the future.
  - It's important to work hard at school.
  - I hate being the center of attention.
  - I don't want responsibility, I'd rather be told what to do.
  - It's important to me to feel part of a group.
  - I'm always the first to try out new things.
  - I like spending time on my own.
  - As long as I study and do well at school, I can do what I want.
  - We don't speak much in my house.
  - I get on with one of my parents and get on less with the other.
  - I get on with my parents.
  - Sometimes I lie so my parents don't get worried.
  - Overall we all get along in my family.
  - My parents don't understand me.
  - My parents don't trust me enough.
  - My ideas are very different from my parents'.
  - In my house, everyone is free to get on with their life and interests.
  - I have a lot of freedom.
  - I really like to be with my family.
  - Protection of nature is more important than growth in the economy.
  - Everybody has a responsibility to the environment.
  - I'd like to go somewhere different on holiday each year.
  - I love traveling abroad.
  - I like to do a lot when I'm on holiday.
  - I hate going on holiday with my parents.
  - I like to go on holiday with a large group of friends.
  - Discos are boring.
  - Sundays are boring.
  - I go out a lot.
  - I enjoy hanging out with my friends.

- I really enjoy reading books.
- I don't get enough privacy.
- I enjoy spending time on a computer.
- I love playing sport.
- In the past 7 days, in free time
  - Attend religious service
  - Sleep over at a friend's house
  - DIY
  - Travel with friends
  - Knit, sew
  - Build objects, models
  - Eat snacks
  - Eat out
  - Window shopping/shopping
  - Play a musical instrument
- In the past 6 months
  - Visited the theater
  - Attended a sporting event
  - Visited museum/exhibition
- Computer usage
- Play any of listed sports
- Sometimes have discussions about politics
- Member of a religious organization
- Member of a youth organization
- Take part in rallies, meetings, etc. about social, civil, or environmental problems
- Follow political programs on TV/radio
- Agreement with
  - Sport is important to keep healthy.
  - Sport is part of my social life.
  - I like spending time with my family.
  - I would rather spend time at home than go out partying.
- Number of books read
- School
- University
- Training/apprenticeship scheme
- In paid employment
- Unemployed
- Age
- Sex

Notes

1. Theodore Levitt, "The Globalization of Markets," *Harvard Business Review,* vol. 61, May/June 1983.

2. Questionnaires were checked and back-translated to minimize the possible biases of inconsistent wording of questions.

3. "Youth in the European Union: From Education to Working Life," *Eurostat,* March 1997.

4. Italy is excluded from the average for cable channels because penetration of cable and satellite were very low in Italy at the time the survey was conducted.

5. Levitt, "The Globalization of Markets."

Part II

An International
Circumnavigation

9

Rational Arguments and Emotional Envelopes

American and British Advertising Compared

John Philip Jones

A t an *Admap* conference in London in January 1998—one of the more serious forums for marketing and advertising professionals who are interested in the state of the art—there was a good deal of discussion, some quite heated, about the relative value and relevance of rational and emotional appeals in advertising. Given that many people evidently disagreed with my views, I resolved to address this issue on my return to the United States. This chapter is largely, although not totally, concerned with repeat-purchase pack-

NOTE: An earlier version of this chapter was originally published as an article in ASMAR (April, 1998), and is reproduced by permission.

141

aged goods, known in Europe as fast-moving consumer goods (fmcg), and my argument embraces all media, especially television, which in the United States as in Britain is the most important advertising medium for major brands of repeat-purchase packaged goods.

However, I shall begin by discussing three American print advertisements, each of which appeared in 1998 in leading women's weekly magazines. Figure 9.1 shows black-and-white reproductions of the color ads. The three campaigns shown also have appeared on television, and I have reason to believe that all three have been successful in the marketplace. (I employ print ads here in preference to stills from television commercials because print ads make it easier to illustrate my arguments.) Incidentally, American brands of repeat-purchase packaged goods use magazine advertising more widely than do similar British brands, for the rather obvious reason that magazines are able to reach the 40% of the television audience that spends little time in front of the television screen. (Magazine advertising represents 9% of aggregate media expenditure in the United States, compared with 6% in Britain).

I shall discuss a double-page spread for Sears Roebuck and reprinted by courtesy of that company (Ad 1), a single-page ad for Procter & Gamble's Metamucil (Ad 2), and a single-page ad for Lever Brother's Dove (Ad 3). All three advertisers are big players in the national marketplace. More important, my three examples can be taken as typical. I could find literally hundreds of American advertisements to illustrate the points I wish to make.

Advertisements typified by Ad 1 focus exclusively on the consumer. Ad 1 aims to persuade women to modify their attitudes toward Sears and to encourage the belief that this enormous mass-market store chain sells much more than the power tools and washing machines with which it is usually associated: It is also in the fashion business. There is no emphasis at all on the merchandise. The advertisement does no more than offer a mirror to the potential shopper. She can see herself in it and she will (it is hoped) be encouraged to go to Sears and explore for herself.

Ad 2 (like all the advertisements it typifies) is focused on the functional properties of the brand, in this case Metamucil, the leading laxative in the United States. The argument that Metamucil can be mixed with fruit juice to make it palatable counters a serious problem of perception that applies to all laxatives. Other brands can also be mixed with juice, but the fact that Metamucil is the first brand whose advertising proposes that it should be drunk mixed as a fruit cocktail preempts the claim. (This is a creative technique first exploited by Claude Hopkins 80 years ago.)

Figure 9.1. Three American Advertisements for Leading Brands of Repeat-Purchase Packaged Goods (Ad 1 at top, Ad 2 middle, and Ad 3 at bottom)

Ad 3 (again a typical example) is concerned with functional claims for the brand, but this time within the specific context of what the consumer is looking for. The style of Ad 3 straddles the styles of Ads 1 and 2. It represents what I have attempted to communicate in the title of this chapter—functional claims enclosed within an emotional envelope.

Two Countries Separated by a Common Advertising Language

In this chapter I attempt to hypothesize the similarities and differences between advertising in the United States and advertising in Britain; I will use the three advertisements in Figure 9.1 as points of reference.

As far as similarities go, all of the major American marketers operate in Britain and many of the leading British marketers also operate in the United States. There is a huge overlap of similarly positioned brands, many marketed with the same brand names. What is strange but true is that American-originated campaigns are used only rarely in Britain, and British-originated campaigns are even more rarely used in the United States. The same media are used, mutatis mutandis, for the same brands in the two countries, but the campaigns differ.

American product categories are more dense and crowded than are equivalent categories in Britain, which means that individual American campaigns must lay greater stress on basic identification of the brands than is the case generally in Britain. But there are more reasons for the differences in the two styles of advertising than can be accounted for by the single factor of category fragmentation, although this factor alone means a much tougher marketing environment in the United States than in Britain.

Ad 1 seems to me to represent a style of advertising more common in Britain than in the United States; on the other hand, Ad 2 represents a style more common in the United States than in Britain. However, Ad 3 represents the most popular pattern of all in both countries, although there are differences in emphasis: In Britain there seems to be a greater emphasis on user imagery, whereas in the United States there is more emphasis on product functionality. The notion that American advertising is more product focused than British advertising is a blinding glimpse of the obvious, and few analysts with any knowledge of advertising in both countries would disagree with this hypothesis. A content analysis of the papers assembled by the Institute of Practitioners in Advertising (IPA) for its Advertising Effectiveness Awards suggests that less than 20% of the submissions are "largely rational"—an extremely low figure by American standards.

However, I must make an important point about American advertising: It has changed a lot over the past decade. British observers need to refresh their acquaintance with the type of product-based advertising actually exposed in the United States in the late 1990s. The painful stereotypes of American advertising of the 1960s have all but disappeared. There are no more scientists in white coats. The Unique Selling Proposition (USP) is treated largely as an out-of-date doctrine, with intermittent revivals. (There was an ephemeral experiment with broadening the USP to embrace a brand's "Unique Selling Personality" and Ted Bates is currently attempting to revive the original USP, despite its anachronism.) The notorious slice-of-life technique, which was invented with the purpose of generating high day-after-recall scores, disappeared a decade ago when the advertising industry abandoned recall testing in favor of persuasion, which many American advertisers consider a totally viable predictive system—one that is underused by advertisers outside the United States, to their serious detriment.

There is no doubt whatsoever that American advertising has evolved. And I believe that this evolution has led to advertising that is not only strategically relevant (which American advertising always was), but also to campaign styles that are friendly to the viewer, which was generally not true until the mid-1980s, when the extensive research on the value of likability began to be propagated. I fear that British views of American advertising are all too often informed by out-of-date knowledge.

The special style of British advertising is of course greatly influenced by British account planning, with its extensive use of qualitative research and its emphasis on distinguishing brands by their personality and nonfunctional qualities. (I caught a frisson at the *Admap* conference that British practitioners actually consider functional claims to be indecent!)

British advertising has many interesting features that are perhaps more apparent to overseas observers than to British ones. Much of the emotional and/or humorous advertising communicates at a subtle level, and the sometimes surreal fantasy has high attention value and perhaps more besides. British advertising strikes me as more *national* than that of any other country, with the possible exceptions of Japan and Australia. American advertising, by contrast, is more variegated. This is, first, a reflection of the volume of advertising exposed in the United States, which is much greater than in any other country; second, an expression also of the multifaceted nature of American society; and third, and not least, a result of the overriding importance in most product categories of rooting the advertising in brand differentiation.

The most important negative feature of British advertising is that—unlike American advertising—it has not evolved. When on my frequent visits to London I study British advertising, I am always struck by déjà vu. I am invariably brought back to the world I knew when I was working in the London office of J. Walter Thompson during the 1970s.

It is difficult to draw conclusions about the relative effectiveness of the American and British styles of advertising. But there is no evidence, beyond prizes in creative competitions, that British advertising is in any way superior. The failure rate of new brands is equally (and deplorably) high in both countries. According to comparative analyses of A. C. Nielsen data measuring the immediate sales effectiveness, or Short-Term Advertising Strength (STAS), of brands, the immediate effects of British campaigns are no greater than those of American ones. Indeed, at the top end, American campaigns seem to be clearly superior (see Table 9.1).[1]

British practitioners will probably point (with justifiable pride) to the IPA Advertising Effectiveness case studies that I have already mentioned. These provide a corpus of evidence that has no equal anywhere in the world. But it is unfortunately true that the hundreds of cases (approximately twice as many unpublished as published) represent a minuscule fraction of all the British advertising campaigns that have been exposed during the past 18 years. The IPA cases, fascinating and important as they are, cannot be taken as typical of British advertising as a whole. (These case studies are described by Chris Baker in Chapter 27, this volume.)

In the last analysis, what it all comes down to is what David Ogilvy described 30 years ago as the "ruthless salesmanship" of classical American advertising copy (he was talking about the work of Claude Hopkins).[2] It is a quality he greatly admired and one that he expressed in many of his own campaigns, although in writing these he always added his own unmistakable elegance and polish.

Rather importantly, the differences between British and American advertising are connected with the respect that American advertisers pay to the functional differences between brands, the importance of which is underscored by substantial aggregations of Nielsen evidence:

TABLE 9.1 STAS Deciles

	United States (Jones STAS)	United Kingdom (McDonald Adlab)	Germany (Jones STAS)
First	236	184	154
Second	164	129	127
Third	139	119	116
Fourth	121	114	108
Fifth	116	110	106
Sixth	108	107	101
Seventh	103	102	100
Eighth	97	98	98
Ninth	89	93	92
Tenth	73	73	83

- Most of the small number of new brands that succeed in the marketplace are characterized by functional innovation.[3] "On a blind product test of your new brand versus leading brands already on the market, you should not ordinarily consider trying to build a consumer franchise with the product unless you have a 60:40 preference—and 65:35 would be preferable."[4]

- The majority of market leaders that lose their leadership lose it to competitive brands that make functional improvements, and the losers are unable to keep up. "It is a cardinal fact that a consumer franchise *will not* protect a brand against a well-advertised technical breakthrough by competition."[5]

- Many if not most successful brand relaunches are based on functional improvements.[6]

- Other important aspects of marketing, such as retail distribution and the impact of the manufacturer's sales force in the retail store, are underpinned by evidence of consumer preference for the functional properties of the brand. All parts of the marketing mix therefore operate synergistically.[7]

- There is a widely known and widely emulated emphasis on functional superiority in the operating principles of leading marketers of consumer goods. Procter & Gamble is the shining example.[8]

Are British Advertisers Missing Important Opportunities?

The well-developed and pervasive culture of the British advertising industry does indeed have four inhibiting effects on the actual and potential success of many brands. The people who ultimately suffer are the advertisers, whose brands pay an opportunity cost in unexplored avenues of growth.

Unexploited Functional Advantages

Everything I have said in this chapter reinforces my point that British brands with competitive functional advantages are sacrificing opportunities for increased profit by their failure to exploit these functional advantages in their advertising. The problem does not stop there. The general lack of interest on the part of agencies in the functional properties of the brands they handle discourages them from taking a proactive role with their clients in persuading them to spend money, time, and talent on product R&D. Rosser Reeves made this point in the early 1960s in one of the relatively few sensible recommendations in a book that is otherwise (alas) full of questionable doctrine:

> The agency can induce the client to change his product, improve his product. We have done this on numerous occasions. . . . A great advertising man of three decades ago once said "A gifted product is mightier than a gifted pen." How right he was! This is not a secondary road. It is often the first, and the best road to travel.[9]

Lack of Aggressiveness

In Britain I am often forcibly struck by the prevalence of such remarks as "Sales growth is not our primary goal," "All we can accomplish is to decelerate decline," and "We are only interested in the long term." Such comments appear to communicate profundity. In most circumstances, however, they demonstrate little more than a passive acceptance of the status quo.

Attitudes in the United States are strikingly different. In the American marketing environment the comments quoted above would be looked upon as ludicrously flaccid. American optimism and aggressiveness are often defeated by the forces of the marketplace, but they sometimes succeed against the odds. American product categories show even less aggregate growth than those in Britain. They are also more difficult to handle because of their fragmentation. But in these seemingly impossible circumstances, huge American brands often actually succeed in increasing their sales. Three striking recent examples are Tide, Coca-Cola, and Marlboro.

A lack of aggressiveness can permeate the culture of an organization. No brand can boost its sales unless the people responsible for marketing it believe (or persuade themselves) that growth is possible and then plan—and invest— accordingly.

Vulnerability to Competition From Store Brands

The British food trade has a number of striking characteristics, the main one being the importance of store brands, which account for 30% of volume, compared with 15% in the United States. The high share in the United Kingdom is not entirely the result of retail concentration. Sweden and the Netherlands, which have similarly concentrated food trades, have much smaller shares accounted for by store brands. American retail concentration in the food trade is a regional phenomenon, and on this basis it has developed far, as is apparent to visitors to Chicago, Washington, D.C., central New York, and other important regions.

I believe that the ferocity of the competition between manufacturers' brands in the United States—a competition driven mainly by functional differentiation—has held back the competition from store brands. By contrast, I believe that the softer competition between manufacturers' brands in Britain has made them gradually but increasingly vulnerable to the grittier, price-driven competition from the retailers' brands. Aggregated American data give some support to this hypothesis.[10]

Artificial Restrictions on the Use of Market Research

British advertising agencies, which rely to a great degree on account planning, confine their use of developmental research in the main to qualitative focus groups and "one-on-ones." These techniques are necessary for the development of effective advertising, but on their own they are insufficient. Quantitative pretesting can make an equally necessary contribution by providing an insurance policy against exposing ineffective advertising at sometimes enormous expense.

There is still a deeply entrenched emotional prejudice against all quantitative pretesting in British agencies. This is really based on the fear that the main influence on advertising decisions will eventually be passed from the agency

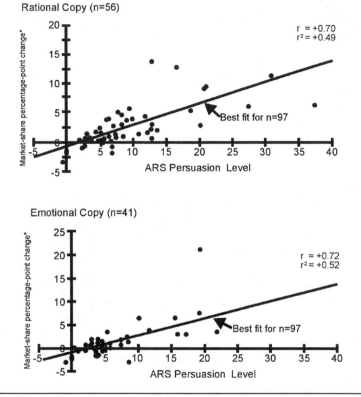

Figure 9.2. ARS Persuasion® Testing: Rational and Emotional Copy

to the research organization. I have always been aware of this prejudice, especially during the years I worked in the agency business in London. In retrospect, it seems to be an attitude more than a little tinged by insecurity.

A more reasonable objection to *recall* testing is that it discriminates in favor of explicit copy, "which communicates concrete, product-related benefits," and against implicit copy, "which communicates less tangible or more *psychological* benefits." [11] However, it should be emphasized that this objection does not—repeat *not*—apply to quantitative persuasion testing.

The two diagrams in Figure 9.2 display a total of 97 cases researched by the best-known American pretesting organization, ARS. For each case, they relate the size of the ARS Persuasion® score to the sales (measured by scanner research) of each brand immediately following the exposure of the tested advertisement. The brands form a "census collection" of cases that were not chosen selectively; all examples with the appropriate sales measurement were included. On the basis of a content analysis of the advertisements, the campaigns were divided into 56 that were predominantly rational and 41 that were predominantly emotional. As is obvious from the regressions in the two diagrams, this pretesting technique can predict the sales effectiveness of emotional copy as well as it can predict rational copy. There is therefore no reason to believe that quantitative persuasion pretesting is inappropriate for the majority of British advertisements.

It seems regrettable that British advertising, which is in some ways so striking and has been so effective in a number of well-documented cases, should be so curiously inhibited against employing rational arguments. The situation will not easily change. The attitudes of British agency practitioners are profoundly conservative, although I suspect that clients are more open-minded. Advertisers must realize, however, that a renewed emphasis on functional claims in their advertising will mean that they will need to pay a substantial price in terms of increased R&D in order to justify their advertising claims. In a competitive marketplace, this is a price that must be paid. And for the most successful operators it is a price well worth paying.

Notes

1. STAS is a quantitative measure of the immediate sales-generating effect of an advertisement. See John Philip Jones, *When Ads Work: New Proof That Advertising Triggers Sales* (New York: Simon & Schuster-Lexington, 1995).

2. David Ogilvy, *Confessions of an Advertising Man* (New York: Atheneum, 1964), 114.

3. James O. Peckham, Sr., *The Wheel of Marketing*, 2nd ed. (privately published, 1981; available through A. C. Nielsen, New York), 76.

4. Ibid., 92.

5. Ibid., 73.

6. Ibid., 83.

7. Ibid., 15.

8. David Ogilvy, *Ogilvy on Advertising* (New York: Crown, 1983), 156.

9. Rosser Reeves, *Reality in Advertising* (New York: Alfred A. Knopf, 1961), 55.

10. Susan R. Ashley, "How to Effectively Compete Against Private-Label Brands," paper presented at the ESOMAR seminar, Building Successful Brands: The Need for an Integrated Approach, Amsterdam, 1994.

11. Shirley Young, "Copy Testing Without Magic Numbers," *Journal of Advertising Research*, February 1972, 21-23.

10

The Power of Advertising, Myths and Realities

Evidence From Norway

Thorolf Helgesen

Perceptions of advertising as a strong marketing force seem to be widespread, both within business communities and among the general public. These perceptions tend to be founded not on empirical evidence, but on myths about advertising effectiveness. In order to explore what constitutes the belief in advertising as a "strong force," a Norwegian study was undertaken in 1994 based on interviews with large Norwegian advertisers. In this chapter, I relate the results of that study to recent research into advertising effectiveness.

NOTE: This chapter is adapted from an article that appeared in *Marketing and Research Today,* May 1996. Copyright © ESOMAR® 1999. Permission for using this material has been granted by ESOMAR® (European Society for Opinion and Marketing Research), Amsterdam, The Netherlands. For further information please refer to the ESOMAR® website:www.esomar.nl

The Image of Advertising

Each year, large sums are spent by companies that wish to boost their sales by means of advertising. The exact size of advertising expenditures worldwide is not known, but available statistics indicate that the aggregate amount of advertising expenditures is most impressive and continually increasing over time. For example, in 1997, media advertising in the United States amounted to $111 billion (up from $77 billion in 1992). This would put the world advertising expenditure in 1997 in the ballpark of $300 billion.

These figures evidently reflect a pervasive belief in advertising as a major means of promoting and selling goods and services. More specifically, advertising is frequently seen as an effective instrument for influencing people's needs, beliefs, opinions, attitudes, and buying behavior. Such opinions are held by a large proportion of the general public, as frequently expressed in opinion polls. They are also shared by many journalists, politicians, and other public opinion leaders. And they are continually supported and elaborated by representatives and spokespersons for the advertising industry who argue for advertising as an efficient marketing tool, and also in some contexts as a means of enhancing social welfare.

Another important source of influence is consumer organizations, which contribute to the faith in advertising as a strong force, albeit a negative one. According to consumer organizations and consumer protection spokespersons, advertising can "mold the minds" of consumers and "create artificial needs." Thus advertising is presented as a powerful but also harmful instrument for manipulating consumers.

The sheer amount of advertising may be an important source of the belief in its power. A popular notion is that business companies would never use all the money they do for advertising unless they knew its power and effect. Although the lack of strong evidence makes this a very doubtful proposition, the large amount of advertising reflects advertisers' strong *belief* in advertising as a viable means of selling goods and services.

Alternative Perspectives on Advertising Effectiveness

The widely held beliefs in advertising as a powerful force are contradicted by an almost complete lack of empirical documentation of advertising effects and effectiveness, at a general level. To quote Kotler: "Good planning and control of advertising depend critically on advertising effectiveness. Yet the amount of fundamental research on advertising effectiveness is appallingly small." [1]

In recent years, we have witnessed a discussion about advertising as a strong force versus advertising as a "weak force." Jones has advocated that advertising in most cases operates as a "weak force," that is, that advertising in most cases does not create any substantiated effects in the marketplace.[2] Ehrenberg takes this criticism even further, by arguing that advertising *always* operates as a weak force. According to Ehrenberg, advertising may at best contribute to brand awareness, as one of many stimuli. Eventually, it may also enhance the *trial* of a brand, whereas repeated purchases mainly depend on personal experience with the brand. After trial, advertising may again play a certain role by contributing to brand loyalty, but only as a force of minor importance.[3]

Ziff, as a practitioner, supports these views, pointing to a number of factors that have gradually reduced over time the power of advertising. According to Ziff, modern advertising has an emphasis on image instead of content, without appeal to a growing number of sophisticated and information-seeking customers. He concludes that after "years of systematic, optimistic, reckless overstatement of all the things that advertising could supposedly do," the time has come for an "agonizing reappraisal" of advertising's roles and potentials.[4] Recently, more sophisticated methods for measuring the sales effects of advertising have been developed. One outstanding contribution is the work of Jones.[5] Based on single-source techniques and using television meters and home scanners to retrieve the necessary data about advertising exposure and corresponding buyer behavior, he has demonstrated how advertising for fast-moving consumer goods can trigger short- and long-term sales. According to Jones, such advertising has created positive short-term sales effects in 70% of the studied cases and long-term sales (1 year) in 46% of these cases. This does not demonstrate, however, that all these campaigns are also profitable. That is a different question altogether.

Schultz, Tannenbaum, and Lauterborn "challenge business to confront a fundamental dilemma in today's marketing—the fact that mass media advertising no longer works," to quote an introductory blurb in their book *Integrated Marketing Communications*.[6] Instead, they introduce a method for measuring sales responses to combined communication efforts. A major implication is that advertising may work or may not work, depending on, among other factors, the right combinations of advertising and promotional efforts directed to specific target groups registered in databases. On this basis, Schultz et al. demonstrate how the return on marketing communication investments may be calculated. A similar perspective on combined communication efforts has been adopted by, among others, Jones, Roberts, and Brandes.[7] Each has demonstrated how advertising, combined with sales promotions, in a number of cases has produced significantly greater short-term sales than advertising alone.

Seemingly, we have been moving from a period with little or no fundamental research on advertising effectiveness through a period characterized by a growing concern and skepticism among an increasing number of researchers and into a period where a new kind of empirical documentation demonstrates that advertising may in fact work—but by no means always—and that there are vast differences in advertising performance.

However, any corresponding soul-searching activities among practitioners are rare. As a consequence, there seems to be a great and possibly growing distance between the widely held beliefs of advertising effects and effectiveness on one side and findings from recent research on the other. One possible explanation for this discrepancy is the lack of contact and dialogue between practitioners and researchers. A second possible explanation is that the advertising industry is a much more powerful and influential source of attitude formation than are researchers in this field. A third explanation may be that our empirical and verified knowledge of how advertising works is still tentative and limited.

In this situation, myths about advertising effects and effectiveness are pervasive. Although myths are not necessarily wrong, they are widely held beliefs without empirical substantiation. As generally used, the term *myth* applies to any belief that has no foundation in fact. As far as advertising is concerned, this definition applies to the present state of the art.

Secondary Effects of Advertising

I have confined the discussion above to advertising effects on *end users,* which is by far the most frequently adopted perspective on advertising's power and influence. But advertising often has other important functions, mainly the way it can influence company employees and intermediaries. For example, in the case of advertising for national brands, one aspect of growing importance is its influence on retailers in order to get access to their shelves. From the retailers' point of view, brands with heavy advertising support are normally considered more advantageous choices than brands with little or no advertising support—regardless of advertising's actual effects on end users. Thus, in the words of Ehrenberg, "advertising is a price firms pay just to survive. It is the cost of doing business." [8] If a promise of advertising support de facto leads to distribution, advertising may also work on end users via *distribution channels and corresponding exposure of the brands.*

Among the secondary effects of advertising are also those of motivating and legitimating salespeople and other employees, and generally contributing to a positive company profile. Advertising may also stimulate the word-of-mouth process. As demonstrated by Park, Roth, and Jacques, such effects may be important, but still they are frequently overlooked by both practitioners and researchers.[9]

Finally, advertising may function as a barrier to entry—that is, by hindering potential entrants from attacking a market. Potential entrants may consider advertising to be a necessary admission ticket to a market already heavily backed by advertising, and may find the price tag exorbitantly high. In such cases, advertising may work as an efficient tool to *defend and protect market shares,* regardless of its direct effects on the end users.

Against this background, a Norwegian study was undertaken among large national advertisers in order to explore their opinions on advertising effects and effectiveness. The aim of the study was to reveal to what extent, on what grounds, and in which respects the advertisers consider advertising a potent marketing force. Before presenting the research design and the findings from this study, it may be useful to have a closer look at the Norwegian advertising market and its practices.

Norwegian Advertising Practices

The population of Norway is 4.3 million. Categories are therefore of limited size, which is also reflected in the sizes of the advertising budgets. On the other hand, Norway is ranked among the top countries in terms of per capita income, which in 1993 amounted to Nkr170,000, or approximately US$26,000. Against this background, one might expect advertising expenditures per capita, by international standards, to be high. That is not the case, however.

This may partly be explained by a lack of advertising media. For example, television advertising was not introduced in Norway until 1992 (as in Sweden). Radio advertising is a similar case. On the other hand, direct mail, the largest single media channel in Norway, is not reflected in official statistics. Additionally, there are many legal restrictions on advertising in Norway. For example, advertising for alcohol, tobacco, and prescription pharmaceuticals is banned, as is advertising directed at children. And in the field of promotions, most of the usual types found in other countries are prohibited, including coupons, sweepstakes, and promotional gifts. These practices reflect a widespread, culturally conditioned skepticism about advertising and promotions—as seems to be the case also in the other Scandinavian countries.

A substantial part of the Norwegian advertising for branded goods is for products of foreign origin, the marketing of which is largely handled by Norwegian subsidiaries of international companies. Thus—and with the modest market size in mind—it is understandable that many campaigns of foreign origin appear in the media, especially on television, although a considerable degree of national adaptation occurs.

This international aspect also applies to the advertising agencies. The 10 largest agencies—accounting for approximately 80% of the total turnover—all have Anglo-American ownership. On this basis, it might be expected that international advertising practices would be a predominant trait also in the Norwegian advertising industry. To what extent this is true is not known, but the practices of large Norwegian advertisers and advertising agencies have been explored in two studies.[10]

The first study focused on the decision-making process in large advertising companies. The rationality of advertising decisions suffers from severe deficiencies, among which are a lack of marketing information, a corresponding lack of clear advertising goals and strategies, and an absence of advertising effectiveness tests. Also, it has become clear that the methods of fixing advertising budgets and selecting advertising media are highly arbitrary.

The other study aimed at exploring the relationship between advertisers and their advertising agencies. From this study—based on interviews with 40 directors of large agencies—there is convincing evidence that the agencies' strategies and practices are dominated by a strong culture of creativity, which seems to serve the agencies' own ends, but not necessarily those of their clients, who are basically concerned with advertising's impact on their markets in terms of sales, market shares, and profitability. The latter study also focused on the issue of research—to what extent the work of the agencies is based on and controlled by advertising research. The results indicate a lack of research orientation among both agencies and clients. For example, 28 out of 40 agency representatives said that they never receive sufficient marketing information from their clients. And as far as advertising tests are concerned, the respondents' attitudes were vague and skeptical. Advertising tests were not frequently used, the main arguments being lack of time, money, and valid research methods. These findings correspond to those of Flandin, Martin, and Simkin in the United Kingdom.[11]

In order to explore knowledge about advertising research and where to find it, the Norwegian respondents were asked about their readership of advertising journals. Specifically, they were asked about the *Journal of Advertising Research* and the *International Journal of Advertising*. Not one of the respondents had ever read these journals. The first was completely unknown to all of them, and only two respondents had heard the name of the second.

Against this background, it may be argued that the level of professionalism among Norwegian advertisers and advertising agencies leaves much to be desired. An important aspect of the study described in this chapter is whether this possibly low level of professionalism is reflected in the advertisers' beliefs about the power of advertising.

The Perceived Power of Advertising

I describe below the results of a survey of a sample of 240 of the largest Norwegian advertisers undertaken in 1994. The sampling frame was provided by a study of large Norwegian advertisers as registered by the Norwegian Association of Advertising Agencies in 1993. The largest advertisers were identified from the Norwegian Bureau of Advertising Statistics database, which includes virtually all Norwegian advertisers of branded goods and services. Among the categories covered were detergents and toiletries, food and beverages, cars, oil and chemicals, data equipment, banks, insurance, and telecommunications companies. In each organization, the person responsible for advertising decisions was identified. Most frequently, this person was at a marketing director level. The study was carried out via a postal survey. With 143 completed questionnaires, the response rate was 60%.

Preceding the main survey, a pilot study was carried out in the form of extended semistructured interviews with representatives of advertisers, advertising agencies, advertising media, consumer organizations, and research institutions. Generally, all respondents expressed viewpoints representing the strong theory, based on their subjective opinions and attitudes. When asked about references, none of the respondents was able to underpin the opinions expressed by means of empirical substantiation.

The next step was the design of the questionnaire to be used in the main survey. In this questionnaire, attitudes toward advertising were measured along a 5-point Likert scale, covering 43 items expressing different aspects of advertising's capacity to influence people and enhance a company's marketing performance. Among the items were the following: "People do not notice advertising messages any longer"; "Advertising can make people buy things they don't need"; "Heavily advertised brands sell better"; "Much advertising is wasted"; and "We are influenced by advertising without knowing it." Of the 43 statements, 16 were considered to be core items related to advertising effects and effectiveness, according to whether advertising was perceived as a "strong force" or a "weak force." These formed the basis for the data analysis presented below. Broadly, these core items can be divided into two groups: one group of items related to the inherent potential force of advertising per se and one group of items related to advertising effectiveness as a function of professional standards. The questionnaire also contained background information covering company size as measured by turnover, the markets in which it was operating, the size of its advertising budget, and advertising expenditure as a percentage of turnover. All figures relate to the operating year 1993.

Findings

Table 10.1 shows the frequency distribution of the scores on the 16 core items related to the issue of advertising power. (From this table, scores for "agree strongly" and "agree somewhat" have been added together in the ensuing discussion. The same applies to "disagree strongly" and "disagree somewhat.") As this table shows, the respondents' opinions on advertising clearly reflect their beliefs in advertising as a strong force. A large majority of the respondents agree strongly or somewhat that advertising has a strong influ-

TABLE 10.1 Opinions on Advertising Power (in percentages)

	Agree Strongly	Agree Somewhat	Neither Agree nor Disagree	Disagree Somewhat	Disagree Strongly
Positive statements					
Advertising has a strong influence on brand choice.	42.0	54.5	2.1	1.4	—
Advertising is more powerful with involved customers.	60.3	34.0	3.6	0.7	1.4
People are influenced by advertising without knowing it.	50.0	43.0	4.9	1.4	0.7
Advertising is necessary for effective competition.	48.6	41.6	3.5	1.4	4.9
Expenses for advertising are a profitable investment.	30.7	51.0	16.1	0.7	1.4
Advertising can create needs.	31.4	37.1	9.8	12.6	9.1
Advertising can make people buy things they don't need.	12.6	43.3	21.6	16.8	5.7
The more advertising, the more sales.	3.5	31.7	29.6	28.9	6.3
Without advertising, trading activities will stop.	11.4	21.8	21.1	33.1	10.6
Negative statements					
People don't pay notice to advertising messages anymore.	—	4.2	6.3	47.2	42.3
I am little influenced by advertising myself.	0.7	5.6	14.7	53.8	25.2
Expenditures for advertising are often wasted.	2.1	8.4	16.1	33.6	39.8
The power of advertising is exaggerated.	2.8	27.3	28.0	32.8	9.1
People are fed up with advertising.	2.1	25.9	34.2	32.2	5.6
Advertisers' belief in advertising is too strong.	5.6	13.4	45.0	29.6	7.0
Much advertising is mistaken.	26.6	46.1	18.2	6.3	2.8

ence on brand choice (96.5%), that people are influenced by advertising without knowing it (93.0%), and that advertising can create needs (68.5%). They also believe that advertising is necessary for effective competition (90.2%) and that expenses for advertising are a profitable investment (81.7%).

Conversely, they disagree that people don't pay notice to advertising any longer (89.5%) and that expenditures for advertising are often wasted (73.4%).

Still, there seem to be second thoughts on advertising's effectiveness, as expressed in the 72.7% agreement with the statement "Much advertising is mistaken." A possible explanation of this seemingly contradictory result may be that the widely held belief in advertising as a strong force may reflect the respondents' views on advertising's inherent potential per se, whereas the statement about advertising being mistaken may reflect shortcomings in the professional state of the art. It may also reflect a belief in personal competence as contrasted with many of the current practices in other companies. One interesting point is the scores for "I am little influenced by advertising myself." As many as 79% of the respondents disagree, which is contrary to the viewpoints often expressed by advertising practitioners and the general public. This indicates a degree of consistency in these respondents' attitudes toward advertising, and may also be interpreted as supporting evidence for their belief in advertising as a strong force.

Underlying Attitudes Toward Advertising

To explore the underlying patterns in the answers, a factor analysis was made of the principal components. Five factors emerged that explain 53.6% of the variance. The strongest loadings are demonstrated in Table 10.2, and Table 10.3 attempts to interpret the five factors.

According to conclusions based on the data in Table 10.3, one of the main factors underlying the respondents' attitudes toward advertising as an instrument for exercising market power and influence is the assumed susceptibility of consumers to advertising claims (Factor 1). Thus advertising is supposed to have an inherent persuasive power (Factor 3), albeit its potential is limited by the less-than-perfect professional standards of practitioners (Factor 2). Finally, in a marketing context, advertising is seen as an important element (Factor 4) and specifically as a driving force behind sales (Factor 5).

As a next step in the data analysis, a cluster analysis based on Ward's method was performed, using the centroid and Euclidean distance model. The purpose of this analysis was to see whether clusters of respondents would emerge holding different viewpoints on advertising strength. The result, based

TABLE 10.2 Factor Analysis of the Respondents' Reactions

Statement	Factor 1	Factor 2	Factor 3	Factor 4	Factor 5
We are influenced by advertising without knowing it.	0.401				
Advertising has a great influence on brand choice.	0.380				
People are fed up with advertising.		0.477			
Advertisers' belief in advertising is exaggerated.		0.415			
Much advertising is mistaken.		0.377			
Advertising can make people buy things they don't need.			0.628		
Advertising can create needs.			0.492		
Without advertising, trading activities will stop.				0.567	
The more advertising, the more sales.					0.688

on a two-cluster solution, is presented in Table 10.4, which shows that the respondents in Cluster 2 score consistently higher than those in Cluster 1 across all statements (more positive on positive statements, more negative on negative statements). The respondents in Cluster 2 hold extremely high beliefs in advertising as a "strong force." By contrast, those belonging to Cluster 1 hold more moderate opinions. The findings are significant at a 95% level of confidence.

TABLE 10.3 Factor Interpretation of Loadings

Factor	Eigenvalue	Factor Loading	Cum
Factor 1: Susceptibility of Consumers/ End Users	2.9753	0.186	—
Factor 2: Practical Limitations to Advertising Efficiency	1.8311	0.114	0.300
Factor 3: Inherent Persuasive Power of Advertising	1.3608	0.085	0.385
Factor 4: Importance of Advertising as a Marketing Instrument	1.3077	0.082	0.467
Factor 5: Importance of Advertising as a Sales Driver	1.0941	0.068	0.536

TABLE 10.4 Cluster and Centroid Values in a Two-Cluster Solution

Statement	Cluster 1	Cluster 2	Grand Centroid	p Values
People don't pay notice to advertising messages any longer.	4.0678	4.4167	4.2727	0.0088
Advertising can make people buy things they don't need.	3.1017	2.2381	2.5944	0.0000
Expenditures for advertising are often wasted.	3.5763	4.3095	4.0070	0.0000
Advertising can create needs.	3.3051	1.6071	2.3077	0.0000
Without advertising, trading activities will stop.	3.2542	2.9167	3.0559	ns
Much advertising is mistaken.	2.1186	2.1310	2.1259	ns
Expenses for advertising are a profitable investment.	2.2712	1.6548	1.9091	0.0000
Advertisers' belief in advertising is too strong.	3.1186	3.2381	3.1888	ns
People are fed up with advertising.	3.0339	3.2024	3.1329	ns
Advertising is necessary for effective competition.	2.2542	1.3690	1.7343	0.0000
Advertising has a strong influence on brand choice.	1.8644	1.4643	1.6204	0.0088
The power of advertising is exaggerated.	2.8475	3.4167	3.1818	0.0000
Advertising is more powerful with involved customers.	1.6271	1.3929	1.4895	0.0000
People are influenced by advertising without knowing it.	1.9322	1.3690	1.6014	0.0000
The more advertising, the more sales.	3.1864	2.9167	3.0280	ns
I am little influenced by advertising myself.	3.6949	4.1667	3.9720	0.0011
Numbers of respondents	59	84	143	

The two clusters were analyzed against the following background data: company size in terms of turnover, size of advertising budget, and advertising budget as a share of turnover. No significant differences were found. Out of the 143 respondents, 135 could be identified by name/sex. There were 104 males and 31 females. There were more women in Cluster 2 than in Cluster 1—27% against 17%. This may indicate that women may hold a somewhat stronger belief in the power of advertising than do men, but this cannot be proven from the data.

Conclusions

The findings from this study strongly indicate a widespread belief in advertising as a strong force among large Norwegian advertisers. Of 143 respondents, 84 hold extreme opinions of advertising as a strong force, whereas 59 hold more moderate opinions. No adherents of advertising as a weak force were identified. This result is not surprising. After all, all respondents were working in companies with large advertising budgets, and they were responsible for the decisions made on advertising activities. People without an ardent belief in advertising as a strong force can hardly be expected to invest large sums in this kind of marketing effort.

On the other hand, it is fairly well documented that much advertising does not work. Much advertising suffers from inferior planning, including lack of relevant marketing research and valid testing procedures, even in large marketing companies.[12]

Against this background, the advertisers' belief in advertising as a strong force is somewhat surprising, and contrary to what might have been expected. But part of the explanation may be found in the dominating culture within the advertising industry. This culture has an emphasis on creativity rather than research, as manifested in the search for "the Big Idea," which—according to Leo Bogart—"is in the realm of myth, rather than reality." [13] Thus the advertisers' belief in advertising as a strong force may reflect their quest for "the Big Idea" that can release the inherent persuasive power of advertising. Another explanation is that practitioners in advertising have only limited contact with academia. Hence the concern about advertising effectiveness expressed in many academic reports has not penetrated to the practitioners. By contrast, much closer relationships between academia and practitioners can be observed in such professions as medicine, engineering, and law.

Most academic studies on advertising effectiveness are, however, concerned solely with advertising effectiveness related to final consumers. As I have noted above, advertising may have many other effects that can eventually justify its use regardless of the effects on end users—securing distribution, motivating and legitimating the sales force, stimulating recommendations from dealers, raising the advertiser's profile among important target groups of intermediaries, and scaring off potential entrants.

In the last analysis, the latter types of effects may have influenced the answers to items such as "Advertising is necessary for effective competition" and "Expenses for advertising are a profitable investment." From an Ehrenbergian perspective ("Advertising is the cost of doing business"), such considerations may be part of the explanation of the respondents' attitudes toward advertising. It is to be hoped that new studies on this subject will explore the relationship between advertising myths and more rational considerations of advertising's primary and secondary effects.

In conclusion, advertisers believe in advertising as a stronger force than is justified by empirical findings. On the other hand, the power of advertising may in fact be growing due to an increase in the professionalism and effectiveness of planning and execution, based on research. In most professional enterprises, technical advances take place slowly but inexorably. It would be a surprise if this did not apply also to advertising.

Notes

1. Philip Kotler, *Marketing Management,* 8th ed. (Englewood Cliffs, NJ: Prentice Hall International, 1994), 646.

2. John Philip Jones, "Over-promise and Under-delivery," *Marketing and Research Today,* November 1991.

3. Andrew S. C. Ehrenberg, comments in "How Advertising Works," *Marketing and Research Today,* November 1992.

4. W. B. Ziff, Jr., "The Crisis of Confidence in Advertising," *Journal of Advertising Research,* vol. 32, no. 4, 1992, RC5.

5. John Philip Jones, *When Ads Work: New Proof That Advertising Triggers Sales* (New York: Simon & Schuster-Lexington, 1995). See also John Philip Jones, "Single-Source Research Begins to Fulfill Its Promise," *Journal of Advertising Research,* vol. 35, May/June 1995, 9-15.

6. D. E. Schultz, S. I. Tannenbaum, and R. F. Lauterborn, *Integrated Marketing Communications: Pulling It Together and Making it Work* (Chicago: NTC Business Books, 1994).

7. Jones, *When Ads Work;* Andrew Roberts, "What Do We Know About Advertising's Short-Term Effects?" contribution to the ASI European Advertising Effectiveness Symposium, Barcelona, 1995; B. Brandes, "Single-Source Data," contribution to the ASI European Advertising Effectiveness Symposium, Barcelona, 1995.

8. Andrew S. C. Ehrenberg, as quoted in Stephen S. Bell, *Advertising, Reinforcing, Not Persuading,* Report 88-107 (Wellesley, MA: Marketing Science Institute, July 1988).

9. C. W. Park, M. S. Roth, and P. F. Jacques, "Evaluating the Effects of Advertising and Sales Promotion Campaigns," *Industrial Marketing Management,* vol. 17, 1988.

10. Thorolf Helgesen, "The Rationality of Advertising Decisions," *Journal of Advertising Research,* vol. 32, no. 6, 1992. See also Thorolf Helgesen, "Advertising Awards and Advertising Agency Performance Criteria," *Journal of Advertising Research,* vol. 34, no. 4, 1994.

11. M. P. Flandin, E. Martin, and L. P. Simkin, "Advertising Effectiveness Research: A Survey of Agencies, Clients and Conflicts," *International Journal of Advertising,* vol. 11, no. 2, 1992.

12. Leo Bogart, as cited in Randall Rothenberg, *Where the Suckers Moon: An Advertising Story* (New York: Alfred A. Knopf, 1994). See also Helgesen, "The Rationality of Advertising Decisions."

13. Rothenberg, *Where the Suckers Moon.*

11

Print Advertising—
and How an American
Creative Man Learned
to Operate in an
International Environment

Jonathan Brand

There are those of us who started before television took over and played out our careers with hardly a nod to the tube. We are the "print specialists." And proud of it, let me say, sourly grapeful for the vicissitudes of assignment that come when you work for the world's largest, most far-flung agency and have a Swedish-born wife. J. Walter Thompson's executive vice president international told me, "When we send a man abroad, the most important thing isn't that the man is happy, it's that his *wife* be happy."

Denmark, Norway, and Sweden didn't have commercial broadcasting when I arrived in 1968. I remember the editor of this volume (he who recruited me to be creative director for JWT-Scandinavia) telling clients at least once every 6 months, "We expect TV to come in 2 years." He and I were there to pioneer not only an agency but a medium. But we were both long gone when economics and technology—access to other countries' advertising via TV dish and cable—forced the issue in the late 1980s.

My greatest regret about leaving New York wasn't that I would forget how to do advertising, as one of my colleagues admonished me, but that I would have to empty my closet of 8 years' worth of *The New Yorker, Esquire, Time,* and *Life.* Just how valuable they were—or will be—I am realizing only now as I wander about flea markets and antique fairs in the Northwest. One booth has a stack of *Ladies' Home Journals* from just before World War I. "Why is this one $20 and another $18 or $16?" I ask the woman. "It depends which Cream of Wheat ad is in it," she says. "The one you're holding is illustrated by N. C. Wyeth."

Imagine! People will pay good money for advertising that clients only grudgingly paid for in the first place. And as I look around I see booths springing up devoted solely to tear sheets. Automobile ads from the 1920s are big sellers—at $15 a pop. Did I say pop? Just look at the acres of Coca-Cola and Pepsi-Cola ads. And the books that tell you which ones to collect at what prices (watch out for the reproductions of tin trays).

For my money, the most valuable magazine I threw out in 1968 was at the bottom of the pile. It was from 1960, when, barely a month in the business, I opened it to the headline, sitting under a picture of a Volkswagen, "Lemon." This ad marked the great divide in modern advertising, and I was to see up close how it divided J. Walter Thompson. I ran with the magazine to my boss on the Ford account. "They just committed suicide!" he shrieked, and pronounced it the worst ad he'd ever seen. An hour later we went to a meeting with an art group supervisor, who greeted us with the same ad: "You see this? This is the most important ad in the last 25 years. It's going to change advertising as we know it."

What was wrong and right about "Lemon"? It broke the first rule of advertising: Never say anything remotely negative about your product. The rule makers didn't believe anybody would read farther than that "suicidal" headline. The rule breakers believed everybody would be curious enough to read a paragraph or two and get the point. It begins:

This Volkswagen missed the boat.

The chrome strip on the glove compartment is blemished and must be replaced. Chances are you wouldn't have noticed it; Inspector Kurt Kroner did.

For the next 20 years or so I read every word of every Volkswagen ad I could get my hands on. And I suspect that millions of other people—consumers, not just ad folk; women, not just men—did the same. There was always a reward for us in the last line. In the original ad, after learning about the extraordinary quality control at VW—3,389 inspectors for the 3,000 cars produced daily—we were left with this: "We pluck the lemons; you get the plums." Or try this one on for smiles: "It doesn't go in one year and out the other."

Volkswagen—and Doyle Dane Bernbach, its upstart advertising agency—taught America to "Think Small" (another headline that turned hyperbole on its head) and to laugh at the pretentiousness of American cars and their advertising. Instead of a color spread showing gorgeous this-year's models (car and admiring couple), VW offered a black-and-white page, unpopulated and propless apart from what looked like the same old People's-car. But people actually bought the Bug (or Beetle) masquerading as a vehicle; it became a gray badge of courage.

A more recent Volkswagen theme, "The most loved cars in the world," is a disappointment, and although intuitively we know the reason, J. Walter Thompson gets credit for putting it down on paper. A canon of the "T-Plan," a J. Walter Thompson method of developing advertising strategy, was, "It's not what you put into the advertising that counts, it's what consumers get out of it." To say—baldly—that your product is the most loved isn't likely to get the desired effect. You've got to earn their love, as those classic VW ads did week after week in a hundred new ways. And if you want your love up front, well, Volvo, shepherded by Scali McCabe Sloves, took care of that one. The problem there was not that Volvo was unloved but that it was so successful in promoting its Swedish engineering excellence, it didn't have a human face.

Was Volkswagen unable to back up its lovability claim? Yes, and these days it had better be able to. Perhaps Volkswagen did a survey in 81 countries. But Americans are the world's most jaded ad watchers, and if a car can't make it here, it doesn't matter to us how it does everywhere. Or was what we were seeing a latent image, some leftover affection that adhered to the brand thanks to "Lemon" and its brethren? Not even *"Fahrvergnügen,"* the fahr-out VW campaign that preceded "most loved," can erase the good will engineered into the product by Helmut Krone (art director), Julian Koenig (copywriter), and Bill Bernbach in the 1960s. And by dozens of others who did their brilliant executions of the creative strategy. (I asked a Volkswagen dealer what he thought of "*Fahrvergnügen.*" He replied, "I thought it was good, good for the dealership. People came in and said, 'What the heck does *that* mean?' ") Fortunately, what goes aground sometimes comes back. The New Beetle, introduced in 1998, is thoroughly modern on the inside but all nostalgia on the outside and in its advertising by Arnold Communications. One ad displays a green car above the headline "Lime." Another asks, "Hug it? Drive it? Hug it? Drive it?" The original Bug got you there—just about; the new one reminds you with "0-60? Yes." And, getting down to a technical advance, you have, "The engine's in the front, but its heart's in the same place." It looks like a campaign that could go on and on with (so far) a sales curve that goes up and up.

Notice that I credited the art director on VW before the copywriter. In 1960 this would have been unthinkable at J. Walter Thompson or any other mainstream agency. It was understood that the copywriter came up with the idea, got it approved by his boss, then scribbled the headline together with an instruction as to the desired visual on a piece of paper, and slipped it under the distant door (often on a different floor) of the "layout man." Doyle Dane Bernbach changed all that. It became an "art director's agency." Bob Gage, the founding art director, had a hand in that—he was conceptually a match for his writing partners. And (my surmise) they all saw the obvious: These days, when people are dropping their newspapers and magazines and staring blankly at the television, it takes a visual "stopper" to get their attention. Of course, mere stoppers weren't going to turn the tide of TV; it would take terrific visuals and headlines working together (as opposed to saying the same thing) to form powerful advertising ideas.

In the 1960s, the days of copywriter kings were numbered, though it took most agencies several years to realize it. But some copywriter princes—or junior copywriters, as they were then called—wanted to move faster, and they sent their résumés and samples over to Doyle Dane Bernbach only to learn that the agency had hired an electrician for the job. DDB didn't want people with bad habits (that is, training), and, being the persistent type and having a friend there, I wanted to know why. She looked at my portfolio and said, "You're as good a writer as I am, Jon, but I've learned to focus on the product, the idea is inside the product. And over here we sit with our art directors and knock ideas back and forth and don't answer the phone. Then, when we've got the solution, we don't have a whole series of hurdles to get over, ending with a review board [J. Walter Thompson's review board was infamous]. If Bill [Bernbach] likes it, that's it."

She didn't have to add the line attributed to Bernbach that, supposedly, rang in the ears of his account executives: "If you can't sell it to the client, don't come back." Years later, when I was running a creative department, I realized why that story was apocryphal: Doyle Dane Bernbach managed to get great advertising through to print partly because the copywriters and art directors had a lot of contact with the clients. Who understood or could explain better why they had produced what they did? Incredibly, a big part of the industry was still functioning into the 1970s on the assumption that creative people are best left behind at the agency, where they won't embarrass anybody. You were supposed to wait (productively) at your typewriter or drawing board until the account person returned from a meeting with the changes the client required (it was his product, after all, and if he lacked aesthetic sensibility, well, it was his money down the drain).

"Doyle Dane," as it was known around town, followed its Volkswagen campaign with a number of other successes: a more frontal underdog approach for Avis Car Rental ("We try harder. We've got to, we're only No. 2."); status symbol advertising for Chivas Regal scotch that delighted readers into plunking down the extra two bucks; a "We want you to live" series for Mobil that transformed corporate into public interest advertising; work for Polaroid that brought instant attention; Levy's Rye Bread advertising that "You don't have to be Jewish to love"; image ads for Ohrbach's that revolutionized retail advertising and drove the store uptown (from 14th to 34th Streets); and on and on. These were the classic campaigns of "The Golden Age of American Advertising" (subtitle of Larry Dobrow's book *When Advertising Tried Harder*).[1]

These were mostly print campaigns. But the fact was, and is, that if you do a print ad well, you can probably do television just as well. Another way of turning it: Good print advertising translates into good television much more easily than the other way around. And most creative people will tell you that print is harder to do. At least, it puts the responsibility right on you—you can't rely on a trendy director and glitzy effects to make your dumb idea shine.

Amazingly, television is bringing back the strongest argument for print: You have something in your hands to look at as long as you like, whereas TV now gives you a remote to mute or channel surf with, and the omnipresent VCR lets you record first and zap later. A dinner guest recently announced proudly that he could go an entire evening without seeing a commercial. Say goodbye, you who said hello to "the captive audience" only a few years ago. The new situation is a flip-flop of the days when the downside of print was that people could flip the page on you. Now there's hope for a rebirth of print, assuming creative people brought up on TV themselves are willing to work with the dictionary (Merriam-Webster has a CD-ROM) and T-square (make that QuarkXPress).

For all the ballyhoo about 500-channel TV, print is the real targeter. The "big" weekly magazines, *Life, Look,* and *The Saturday Evening Post,* left us in the 1970s, but they were replaced many times over by specialized titles. Now the people making the advertising can assume some intelligence—or at least prior knowledge and interest—as well as wherewithal in the readers. Give them ads as gripping as the editorial content, and you've got them.

One who realized people would read advertising worth reading—and is the only postwar advertising figure who can be mentioned in the same breath with Bill Bernbach—is David Ogilvy, a Britisher. In campaigns for Rolls-Royce, Mercedes-Benz, the Commonwealth of Puerto Rico, Guinness Stout, Shell Oil, KLM, the eye-patched "Man in the Hathaway Shirt," and himself (among others), Ogilvy let the words flow, and his readers followed. He boasted, "I never write fewer than sixteen headlines for a single advertisement." [2] And no wonder, there were (it seemed) at least 16 words in each of them. His legacy includes a vendetta against billboards that deform the landscape and this most-memorable line: "The consumer isn't a moron; she is your wife." [3]

Unlike Bernbach and his offspring, Ogilvy believed in research, and he looked back. *Ogilvy on Advertising* reprints ads long ago left for dead, including "A Hog Can Cross the Country Without Changing Trains—But YOU Can't!" for the Chesapeake & Ohio Railway. "This may well be the best advertisement about a public issue that has ever appeared," he wrote.[4] He loved to count words—and results! About an advertisement with the headline "What Everybody Ought to Know . . . About This Stock and Bond Business," Ogilvy commented: "This advertisement contains 6,540 words—the most anybody has ever used in a single page. When it appeared in the *New York Times,* it pulled 10,000 responses to an offer of a booklet buried near the end. It was written by the late Louis Engel of Merrill Lynch." [5]

Ogilvy invoked the giants of earlier generations: James Webb Young, Helen Resor, Raymond Rubicam, John Caples, and especially Claude Hopkins, whose *Scientific Advertising* he reprinted with an introduction by himself (he also put his own portrait on the back cover).[6] Ogilvy reveled in the old rules (and made up some of his own) that his contemporaries reviled. But you couldn't depend on him to stick to them: in *Confessions of an Advertising Man* (published in 1963—the first bestseller in adman history), he writes: "One of the most provocative advertisements which has come out of our agency showed a girl in a bathtub, talking to her lover on the telephone. The headline: 'Darling, I'm having the most extraordinary experience . . . I'm head over heels in DOVE.' " Five paragraphs later, he writes: "Some copywriters write tricky headlines—puns, literary allusions, and other obscurities. This is a sin." [7]

I must confess for my part that Claude Hopkins was an unknown antecedent for me until I left the daily battle and started teaching copywriting (when I worked on Pepsodent toothpaste I was merely carrying forward his campaign, which uncovered plaque and made him a million dollars). But the spirit of Helen Resor lingered in the hats that Women's Group heads at J. Walter Thompson still wore in the office (once I glimpsed Mrs. Resor herself). And James Webb Young entered my pantheon on Day One. Personnel equipped me with Young's book *A Technique for Producing Ideas,* which outlines how the great man with the common touch did it: "The first step [is] . . . the gathering of materials. Part of it, you will see, is a current job and part of it is a life-long job . . . a constant enrichment of your store of knowledge. Second, the working over of these materials in your mind. Third, the incubating stage, where you let something beside the conscious mind do the work of synthesis. Fourth, the actual birth of the Idea—the 'Eureka! I have it!' stage. And fifth, the final shaping and development of the idea to practical usefulness." [8]

I suspect that since advertising became a subject studied at universities, this little book has been a runaway bestseller. And now I see the proof of it, "Over 100,000 copies sold!" on the cover of the paperback edition I bought at a yard sale. And what's this, a foreword by William Bernbach!

The only part of Young's regimen that I consciously practiced was the unconscious part—going to sleep with a piece of paper and pencil next to me. It couldn't have been easier—I'd wake up in the morning and write it all down. The key to it was programming myself at bedtime. It happened in Copenhagen that I woke up in the middle of the night shaken by a deadline I'd forgotten, given to me by an art director and copywriter who'd hit a brick wall on two Carnation products, Kisser (Little Friskies) and Coffee-mate. I fumbled around in the dark, found a stub of pencil, went into the bathroom, sat down, and wrote 10 headlines for each problem on toilet paper (they had specified 10, echoing my dictum that quality comes out of quantity). We were able to decipher enough of them to provide campaigns for both brands for 2 years.

But the first—"Why does fishmonger Hansen feed his cat Kisser?" and "Why does butcher Jensen feed his cat Kisser?" featuring kittens in the arms of Hansen and Jensen—got us in big trouble. The Danish food inspectors didn't allow pets in fish and meat markets.

Every worker on an assembly line develops techniques to improve his or her personal production. I started heading for the toilet early—JWT assigned me, and dozens like me, to a cubicle in a wide hallway, where I could monitor a hundred telephone calls a day. I found solitude—and my best ideas—in the unmarked men's room. In Copenhagen I passed along my secret to a Scottish account supervisor, who derived endless pleasure from ordering me to "Go to the men's room and lay us a golden egg." When I encouraged writers to sit at the typewriter and "knock off 50 headlines," it didn't mean I lacked confidence in them (I chose my people carefully; I could only afford beginners). I knew that the great idea was lurking in the corner of your brain and had to be rattled loose, and that body copy was infinitely easier to write when you had 20 decent headlines but space for only one. Usually you'd save your second best for last, for what is called the "button line." And when a writer couldn't deliver a terrific headline? I told him or her to go ahead and write the body copy; there was sure to be a headline in there somewhere. But the most efficient producer of headlines has always been a good visual idea; that's why working with an art director was such a logical advance. Once the strategy becomes clear, you can "shoot first and think later," a cliché of both hunter and street photographer that I advise writers and art directors alike to adopt. Shoot "around" a subject and the possibilities for ads jump out at you.

My own proclivity in print advertising was to make it as natural and true to life as possible. To achieve this, it mattered not at all if the production budget was next to zero, because I knew the art directors would then ask me to take the pictures. Or, if an illustration was called for, they might do it themselves (we had amazing luck in Copenhagen—three out of six art directors could draw). Even when we had a decent budget, we didn't always spend it. The point was, you had total control, didn't have to argue with outside artistic temperaments. And you saved time, always a rare commodity in advertising. My favorite example is our introduction of Pepsi-Cola to Denmark, a campaign unknown in the United States outside Purchase, New York. (Word came back to us that the heads of Pepsi were calling it "the best print advertising in the history of the brand." Somebody even called it "the Volkswagen of soft drink advertising." Another compliment that kept us going came from a Danish client: "J. Walter Thompson knows how to make advertising that sells things to people who hate advertising.") At that time Coca-Cola was beginning to pour money into "It's the Real Thing." Translated into Danish, this slogan became, in back-translation, "It's just the thing." Five months after our campaign broke, recall of our slogan, "Pepsi. That's also us" ("Pepsi. Det er osse os"), was four times greater than Coke's. And it never appeared in a headline—we put it down at the bottom with the logo.

Our slogan was the brainchild of an account representative-turned-copywriter in his first writing assignment. I hated to lose him as account rep, he was the best I ever worked with. He had a way of infusing belief-in-the-product into you that made doing ads for it almost a moral duty. The art director was another young Dane who didn't mind working day and night. I started them out with this: "Don't copy Coke with its smiling, dancing, American-looking kids. Do us a real Danish campaign."

They had about a month to do their research (happily, student riots were just reaching Denmark, and the besieged university was where this creative duo spent many of their days). They brought me piles of rough layouts that disappointed me. But I wasn't worried, I knew we'd have plenty of time the night before the big presentation—that was when we always came through. Finally they appeared with "the boy on the bicycle," as he came to be known; he was relaxing on the roadside next to his bike, drinking a Pepsi. But it was the *headline* that grabbed me: "What I thirst after is peace and quiet." This became 1 of 14 ads we presented—most of them with finished photography. We found our "model" (bearded, the perfect student protester) peddling a girl's bike down the cobblestoned street right in front of the office. I stopped him, asked if he'd stand with his bike "over there against the wall" and hold the bottle. Three rolls of film, and he rode off. We'd forgotten to get a model release! Two years later, after he'd appeared full page in most of Denmark's newspapers and on billboards, our art director spotted the fellow peddling past JWT and took him upstairs to sign the release and receive his fee.

The following January, we drove to northern Jutland to do the next summer's advertisements, but this time the copywriter on his first outing was another young Dane; the original writer and his wife, another of my writers, had quit to go to Provence to cook, paint, and "live." We had no headlines, no visuals, no models, and no light. A week later, we returned with 15 finished ads (well, the body copy wasn't written). Again the client's representatives assembled, and this time they rejected an ad. It had a nice enough headline: "We share everything. Also taste." But the picture I had taken was of the copywriter and a girl we found in a bar; they were cavorting stark naked in the shower drinking Pepsi. The Danish product manager fought for the ad, telling his superiors, "You don't understand the Danes." "Good, put it in your portfolio," replied the president of Pepsi-Cola Europe. We reshot with clothes, though not in the shower.

The idea of the campaign was simple: Pepsi drinkers (real people, caught in realistic situations) have a thirst for life, experience, call it what you like. That comes first. When they have a physical thirst, it's for Pepsi. The slogan "Pepsi. That's also us" refers to the Danish expression "[Fill in the blank], that's me." It's whatever the individual considers the essence of him- or herself—walks in the country or going fishing or enjoying a good book. "The Real Me," you might say. The modesty of putting Pepsi second in a world of screaming advertising is what connected with the public. Also, our client was open to widening the target—we didn't have to feature youth in every ad. (We photographed two old ladies and their nephew in the formal parlor of their farmhouse, enjoying Pepsi. Headline: "We don't drink so much coffee anymore.") And then there's the magic of those words in Danish, "osse os," which immediately got onto everybody's tongue and went into the language. Years later, when the original Danish copywriter on Pepsi, now a freelance copywriter, showed his work to prospective clients, he didn't show Pepsi. But he mentioned it. "Oh, yes, that's when social realism came to Danish advertising" was a reaction he got.

Whither print? Onward and upward, naturally. Also outward—print is where the regional agencies show their stuff. Chiat/Day electrified the world from the West Coast, adopting the British "account planning" and proving that research could be creative's best friend. Humphrey Browning MacDougall, best in a fiercely creative market, called itself "Boston's New York Ad Agency." When HBM bit the dust, some of its partners regrouped at Arnold and, most recently, gave us the new-old Volkswagen Beetle advertising. Fallon McElligott's work for small clients (a hair cutter, a restaurant, a church) put Minneapolis on the map, and after they took big awards, they took big accounts, even *The Wall Street Journal*. Richardson, Myers and Donofrio opened an office in Philadelphia (I was the copywriter), grabbed most of the local awards and a Clio, saw that Fallon McElligott was doing just fine by staying at home, and retreated to Baltimore. Then it was Goodby, Silverstein in San Francisco, from nothing to *Advertising Age*'s 1990 "Agency of the Year" in a flash. (Chiat/Day, meanwhile, passed the "1984" milestone and became "Agency of the Decade.") Now back to New York, there's Kirshenbaum & Bond elbowing its way up. And don't forget the British: Some say they do it best, and that David Abbott is the Shakespeare of our trade. (Too bad they don't read Swedish; they'd be amazed at the work that was done in the 1960s and 1970s by the Arbman agency. The Swedes did it the way Vikings have always done it—they sent their people to New York to hang around Doyle Dane Bernbach. And they captured Carl Ally and Jerry Della Femina and brought them back and picked their brains.)

The first words creative people learn—and the last they want to use in their ads—are "Now!" and "New!" Still, those are the words that motivate every generation of ad makers. They want to do something they and the world have never seen before (I call that a healthy attitude). Emulate the elegant Bernbachian headlines/visuals or the correct Ogilvyesque formulations? Hell, no, they're ancient history—as is everything since. One of my University of Oregon students (at 26 an associate creative director at Kirshenbaum & Bond) has already earned a couple of his 15 minutes of fame by telling *Adweek* (they blew it up across a page): "Those Fallon McElligott headlines, they were great, but they're kind of like being lectured by your high school science teacher."[9] I hope he didn't think *I* was teaching him a science.

Notes

1. Larry Dobrow, *When Advertising Tried Harder: The Golden Age of American Advertising* (New York: Friendly Press, 1984).

2. David Ogilvy, *Confessions of an Advertising Man* (New York: Atheneum, 1984), 105.

3. Ibid., 96.

4. David Ogilvy, *Ogilvy on Advertising* (New York: Crown, 1983), 124.

5. Ibid., 84-85.

6. Claude Hopkins, *Scientific Advertising* (New York: Bell, 1960).

7. Ogilvy, *Confessions of an Advertising Man,* 106, 107.

8. James Webb Young, *A Technique for Producing Ideas* (Lincolnwood, IL: NTC Business Books, 1975), 38, 54.

9. Quoted in Debra Goldman, "The Future: Get Used to It," *Adweek,* September 20, 1993, 30.

12

The Emergence
of Advertising in Russia

Ludmilla Gricenko Wells

Western misperceptions about advertising in the former Soviet Union make it difficult for Western firms (firms based or operating in countries with market economies) to create messages and use mass information media to reach potential consumers there. In December 1991, when the Soviet Union ceased to exist, among the common misperceptions were (a) the belief that the Soviets had not created, produced, or used advertising; (b) the belief that advertising agencies did not exist in the Soviet Union; and (c) the feeling that the sole correct advertising system is one based on a free market Western model. By providing some information about those factors in this chapter, I hope to help Western professionals benefit from a more realistic view of advertising in what is now Russia and a diverse group of other independent republics.

Advertising in the former Soviet Union as a whole has not been a focus of study since Philip Hanson wrote his *Advertising and Socialism,* a contemporary history of the advertising process in the Soviet Union from 1968 to 1974.[1]

From 1974 to 1993, there was little research, and no attention given to dispelling some of the Western myths and fallacies about advertising there. Western researchers and professionals essentially ignored the cultural, economic, political, and social implications of introducing a Western model of advertising to the Communist regime of the Soviet Union and expected compliance with preset concepts and procedures. Aside from semantic, historical, economic, and political differences, it was presumptuous of them to believe that Soviet professionals did not understand Western advertising. It was more likely that Western professionals did not understand Russian culture and the role of advertising as an institution in that country.

The role of advertising as an institution in the former Soviet Union has been directly tied to socioeconomic changes labeled *perestroika* and *glasnost*. In concept, perestroika was the process of reformation; in practice, it was a restructuring that included a reinterpretation of socialist ideology and dirigiste economics. Perestroika redefined the role of Soviet mass communication and indirectly the role and functions of advertising. Glasnost is more a means by which society informs itself about government activities through mass information (mass media), oral propaganda (free speech), and visual representations (commercial art).

Perestroika and glasnost have been symbols of economic reform and information dissemination. The West perceived these developments as movements toward democracy and away from Marxism-Leninism. However, these changes were not blasphemy to socialism. The Soviets' acceptance of democratic principles guided the process of political and economic self-determination, but the process did not necessarily replicate the democracy and capitalism embraced in the West.

Advertising in the Soviet Union

The first advertising organizations in the former Soviet Union began to develop before the 1917 Revolution and the implementation of Marxist-Leninist doctrine.[2] "Advertising Is the Engine of Trade" sounds like a battle cry of the Western advertising industry during the late 1800s, when the train was the dominant mode of travel. Actually, this slogan was created and used by Metsl, the first Russian to open an "advertising organization" office in Moscow in

1878.[3] Around the time Metsl started to offer advertising services in Russia, Calkins and Holden began to do the same in the United States, in the 1890s. Both the Russian and the American agencies brought together the craftsmanship of copywriting and illustration to provide creative services for advertising.

Before 1988, access to Soviet consumer and product market information was, in most cases, restricted. Yet the resulting lack of information did not deter Western advertising agencies from establishing a tentative presence in the Soviet Union. Since 1988, perhaps the most visible symbol of changing perceptions of the economic value of advertising has been the acceleration of joint-venture operating agreements among Western and Soviet industrial manufacturing and raw material processing firms, import/export organizations, publishing firms, and advertising agencies. February 1988 became a milestone in advertising history when headlines announced the opening of joint-venture advertising agencies and enterprises in the former Soviet Union aimed at introducing Western advertising protocols for "correctly" organizing management functions in the advertising industry.

Although the broad function of advertising is communication, the underlying Western function of advertising is to sell products and services.[4] Advertising agencies confronted the problem of transporting uniquely Western advertising processes, developed within free market systems, into the former Soviet Union, with its underdeveloped economy and consumer market. The arrival of Western advertising agencies there had an impact on the structure, function, and process of advertising. Between 1989 and 1991, Western advertising agencies (a) instigated a competitive attitude among individuals in the advertising industry and (b) introduced a Western model of advertising and management that Soviets expected to adopt and incorporate into their existing procedures and operations. By encouraging individuals and enterprises to take new initiative and responsibility for their individual actions, advertising served as a stimulus for collective action in advancing perestroika.

For the most part, Western advertisers and agencies did not consider Soviet advertising to be "real" advertising. Western advertising responds to and reflects the wants and needs of the marketplace—an interaction between the manufacturer and the consumer under the economic paradigm of supply and demand. In general, both the manufacturer and the consumer are represented in the advertising process. Soviet advertising was treated like a commodity. Yet one of the tenets of Western advertising is that it serves to inform, educate, and persuade. In as strict adherence as possible to the assortment of definitions of Western advertising, Soviet advertising did just that: It informed and educated in a persuasive manner. Westerners tend to overlook the fact that definitions of advertising are culturally bound.

The Influence of Glasnost on Advertising

Advertising as an institution in the Soviet Union operated tentatively at first. Former socialist "truths" were questioned, but not discounted. Government censorship had been eased, but not eliminated. To accept new visions of socialism, the Soviet citizenry had to reinterpret their own roles and values in society. These roles were not grounded in terms of economic self-worth or in levels of state control, but in cultural traditions.[5] The Russian culture—a state of consciousness, a mentality—was a significant factor in perestroika, because perestroika "embraced the whole of social life, not just the economy." [6] Ryvkina notes that "cultural influence . . . manifests itself through values and social norms that regulate the activity of the economic institutions—planning, supply, the market, financing. 'Cultural units' that regulate economic development also form the economy in spheres of morality, religion, politics, ideology and law." [7]

Glasnost created greater opportunities for the exchange of information and more open communication among social, political, and economic strata. In turn, advertising took on a new role as an institution of social influence and control. The constant influx of cultural artifacts from the West, such as television programs, movies, music, and literature, and Western concepts of advertising and the images represented in advertising, effected a change in Soviets' individual values, social norms, political orientation, government regulations, and economic development.

Advertising as Cultural Communication

Advertising is a product of "cultural expectations." [8] As a product, advertising is a manifestation, a professionally conceived and executed artifact, of a culture and society. It is a catalyst that joins the informational needs and wants of individuals and the market and stimulates cooperative activity between the market and consumers.[9] In turn, the marketplace responds to the ideas and issues raised by individuals and institutions. Advertising messages, images, and symbols often construct new realities of social life not only as it should be, but as it may be. Advertising as communication and as an institution played a significant role in redefining the Soviets' individual values, social norms, and governing political and controlled economy.

Advertising in the former Soviet Union manipulated cultural constructs of reality based on individual values and traditions into new economic and political realities stemming from Western "freedoms" in the marketplace and a democratic form of government. However, Soviet history—Old Russia, socialism, and Communism—offered Soviets very limited experiences with freedom of individual choice. After 1985, the rapid influx of Western advertising concepts and procedures created a conflict of values among Soviet advertising professionals.

Institutions change as a consequence of individuals' real and perceived choices within the reality of time and space.[10] They represent the symbolic and expressed ideas of individuals and the shared meaning that arises from the interaction between and among individuals and social, political, and economic institutions.

As individuals struggled to define their roles within society, so did Soviet advertising professionals reinterpret and redefine their roles within the emerging communications industry. The new meanings assigned to the symbols of long-standing institutions—government, religion, family, education—created new realities in Soviet society, and Soviet society reinterpreted, redefined, reassessed, and articulated meaning to the role of advertising as an institution.

The Golden Nightingale: Advertising After 1988

After 1988, advertising strengthened its role as an institution. Advertising practitioners wanted advertising not only to gain attention, but to communicate clearly. Metaphorically, they wanted advertising to be their Golden Nightingale:

> We had to find some kind of symbol that could be used to explain advertising in the Soviet Union . . . something very familiar. . . . We thought about the [Golden] Rooster, but he simply crows about advertising, he evokes and provokes attention, but a rooster is rather crass. Then there was the goose that lays the golden

eggs from Pushkin's fable; then there was the Golden Nightingale, which was a little more dignified. It would get the attention of a person and the person would be soothed. We wanted our nightingale to sing in such a way that everyone understands.[11]

A variety of factors influenced the development of advertising and directed it away from the clear vision articulated by the young USSR Association of Advertising Workers. Among these factors were (a) a lack of consistency in defining what advertising was, (b) a scarcity of training and education for advertising, (c) a tendency among Soviet professionals to borrow freely from a Western model of advertising, (d) the influence of foreign biases on message and media strategy, (e) a lack of advertising regulation explicit in the Western model of advertising, and (f) the cultural expectations among Soviet consumers about advertising and the role of advertising in their society. These factors/themes about advertising in the former Soviet Union offer insight into the meanings that Soviet individuals gave to advertising and its developing role as an economic and social institution within the context of their Russian culture, social norms, and individual values.

A Soviet definition of advertising, unlike a Western definition, embraced aspects of both marketing and communications. In addition, the term *advertising* was used broadly to refer to many types of promotional activities. Advertising in the former Soviet Union was viewed as an integral function of marketing. Soviet advertising was not seen as a separate form of communication that "implies selection of idea symbols for imparting meaning," [12] but simply as another mechanism for promoting the distribution of goods and services. Participants described advertising in the Soviet Union in terms of perestroika and the economic and social development of a market system and "civil" society.

Definitions of advertising included publicity, public relations, product promotion/trade films, and participation in trade shows, exhibitions, seminars, or symposia. The differences and the difficulties between the West and the Soviet Union in terms of defining advertising extended to defining advertising in mass media. There were few specialized or narrowly defined terms used in the Soviet advertising industry. Soviet practitioners tended to use synonyms interchangeably to describe similar communication concepts rather than specific channels or functions of mass media. In the former Soviet Union, measured mass-media advertising was not limited to newspapers, magazines, radio, television, or outdoor.

Practitioners often defined advertising in terms that reflected their experiences with advertising, past and present. To some, contemporary Soviet advertising was no longer associated with "bourgeois propaganda," but was closer to market information. To others, advertising was the obvious use of print or broadcast media to encompass a variety of promotional activities. These activities included a wide use of elements that ranged from staged publicity events to trade exhibitions and films, to public relations and symposia. Although these elements were described in terms of communication between producers and consumers, Soviet participants viewed advertising as a form of domestic and foreign marketing.

Professional Qualifications

Even though advertising was broadly defined, many people working in the industry saw the need for professional training and education. Moreover, the greater the exposure to Western concepts, the more the participants attempted to compare or contrast foreign and Soviet advertising systems. The different ways advertising was defined were often based on the sources of information about advertising—that is, in the broadest terms, on formal or informal education.

For the most part, Soviets believed that if there was no formal course of study that concluded with a diploma in that specific field, then advertising could not be recognized as a legitimate occupation or profession. Individuals earned higher-education degrees in disciplines that met the needs of the Soviet Union's economic system.

Transitional Economics:
The Market System and Advertising

Without the benefit of academic or much on-the-job training in advertising, and without a free market system, the onset of perestroika and glasnost, and in particular the decree of February 6, 1988, led Soviet directors and administrators in a position to make advertising decisions to adapt what they knew of the Western model to the Soviet system. The 1988 decree constituted the legal basis for business and advertising activities in terms of developing a free market system.

Radical changes in government funding policies for mass communication and business enterprises were being curtailed, mandating that firms seek other sources of operating and financing advertising. Moreover, advertising practitioners and entrepreneurs began their own perestroika to meet the demands of making the transition to a market system. For some, this created opportunities to take advantage of a popular movement toward a system that promised financial independence and profit revenues. Others, already on the edge of bankruptcy, felt the constraints of reduced government subsidy and high taxes on profits. They were confronted with new operating expenses for such things as employee salaries, new computers and printing equipment, office supplies, rental of office space, and utilities.

The client, the agency, the media, and funding and finance were, on the surface, all redefined in an attempt to simulate Western advertising practices. Advertising professionals acknowledged the hardship of losing government subsidies, yet they did not wholeheartedly embrace the free market as an alternate economic system.

Messages and the Channels of Communication

Soviet advertising enterprises felt strong foreign and domestic economic influences regarding the types of messages and media that would be produced. Foreign firms that approached domestic agencies and media created a dichotomy. From one side, foreign firms wanted to do business in the former Soviet Union—a unique marketplace with its own rules, procedures, and consumer attitudes. From the other side, foreign firms wanted advertising the way they were used to seeing and doing it, because economically developed countries already had successful experience with advertising in their own countries.

Foreign firms with hard currency attempted to impose their own criteria for media selection and creative execution without taking into account the differences in demographic and market conditions. There are two significant factors that foreign firms should not only have recognized but also understood before entering the Soviet marketplace. First, Soviet consumers were not accustomed to advertising, much less Western-style advertising messages. Second, Soviet firms were reluctant to eliminate or reduce symbols of Russian culture in structuring advertising messages or traditional media use, and foreign firms resisted using Russian cultural symbols for their products. Much depended on individuals' perceptions that the symbols extolled a Russian culture, heritage, grandeur, and uniqueness—a tie to the best of what Russia had to offer. As a force acting in the opposite direction, Soviet advertising agencies also attempted to dissuade domestic firms from using Russian symbolism in foreign-market advertising. They were symbols of an old tired system, of failing Communism—the worst of a political and economic system. To be progressive, joint-venture advertising agencies or Soviet enterprises with foreign experience attempted to incorporate Western concepts of advertising and communications into the Soviet domestic market.

Advertising Self-Regulation

The push to adopt a Western model of advertising did not bring with it the regulations and laws that constrain Western advertising. The lack of government regulation that recognized or addressed issues in the Soviet advertising industry had quietly prompted advertisers, advertising agencies, the media, and other organizations to look inward at their own industry. Regulation and ethical behavior are part of the standards and operating procedures of the advertising profession. Soviet advertising professionals guided their business activities using three methods. First, there was a need to create a reputable, voluntary organization that would initiate and standardize professional behavior for its members. Second, self-regulation was employed to establish professional codes of behavior within each advertising enterprise. And the third method was one of "arbitrary rule"—decision-making based on instinct and experience to preserve the integrity of the advertising system and the Soviet society that was exposed to its practices.

Advertising industry practitioners, as a form of self-regulation, became self-appointed "caretakers," from the position of dealing with social issues and responsibility toward society. Here advertising professionals expressed an overwhelming concern for the effects of advertising on Soviet society. Discussions were centered less on the stigma of "censorship" to constrict the flow of information to the public than on the need to preserve Russian social norms and cultural values.

The Enigma of the Russian Culture: Inner Tensions

Although the advertising industry may have been self-conscious about its policies, Russian consumers maintained a set of cultural expectations about advertising that were formed under the centralized planned economy. What they experienced under the emerging market system did not fit with their expectations. Radical policy changes had an immediate effect on the structure and functions of the former Soviet government, economy, and enterprises, but did not take into account the time that would be needed for the people to adjust to these new forms of capitalism.

How advertising was prepared and when and where it was seen and heard affected how Soviet individuals perceived advertising's value in their personal lives. Advertising affected their attitudes toward Soviet enterprises and the media. The public and advertising practitioners alike believed there was a shared responsibility for what was advertised. Advertising started to intrude into the lives of older adults: their habits, their finances. The Soviet middle class was confronted with advertisements for goods at high, unaffordable ruble prices or available only, if at all, for scarce valuta (i.e., convertible currency). Advertising affected the cost of traditional print entertainment and information sources for retirees, the working middle classes, professionals, and their families and relatives. The Soviet Union was already suffering from a shortage of goods at state-controlled prices. Advertisements appeared for goods that were available, accessible, but unattainable. Consumers blamed both the advertisers and the media.

Valuta was not readily available or accessible to the average consumer. The easing of government restrictions to earn valuta was directed at businesses, in order to stimulate economic growth. But it had the opposite effect: It built resentment among the very consumers who would be making purchases. Individuals paid attention to what affected them the most, that is, the prices of goods and the means to buy—valuta. Then other issues surfaced concerning what appeared to be a replication of Western-style advertising. These included the scheduling frequency of advertisements and their content.

For some practitioners, advertising was considered a necessary form of communication to ensure a future for the next generation. Advertising was a form of education that would supplement traditional schooling and upbringing. It would offer opportunities to learn and share in the discovery of people outside the former Soviet Union. For many, it would be the only way to be prepared for the uncertainties that would lie ahead.

Continued Conflicts and Their Resolution

Advertising played diverse roles in the social and economic life of the Soviet citizenry. To some, it was a like a test of wills: the challenge of conforming to Western expectations of the forms and functions of advertising in a country that viewed advertising as an economic proposition, a transition from a centrally planned market system to a free market system. To others, advertising was a paradox of trying to improve the quality of life, raise the standard of living for the Soviet citizenry, while removing some of the cultural artifacts they enjoyed: commercial-free media such as television and radio, newspapers, and magazines.

After 1985, the rapid influx of Western advertising concepts and procedures created a conflict of values among Soviet advertising professionals. Torn between holding on to their Russian cultural values and pressure to adopt new Western images, Soviets were forced to reinterpret and redefine their roles in advertising. Older-generation professionals were reluctantly conforming to Western standards and practices of advertising while the young generation forged ahead to adapt quickly the Western model. In order to advance perestroika initiatives, Soviet advertising industry professionals began to adapt selected concepts and protocols imposed upon them by Western agencies and businesses.

In some instances, Soviet advertising professionals understood the rewards and consequences of their market system, compared to a Western free market system, better than did their Soviet commerce and industry counterparts. The urgent need to make a transition to a market system that demanded valuta currency, and the need to support domestic enterprises with only ruble currency, created pressures on decision makers to decide who would reap the benefits of or pay the penalties for economic restructuring.

Soviet professionals considered advertising an integral function of any market system, including the one that existed under a centralized statist economic paradigm. In order to advance perestroika initiatives, advertising was viewed as a critical component in penetrating Western markets and enticing foreign investments. The underdeveloped domestic market—a consumer market with increasing shortages of consumer goods and services—seemed to be neglected by Soviet enterprises. The advertising that was produced was designed to intensify an exchange of market information between domestic commerce and industry and foreign enterprises. The use of mass information media channels—what are considered to be traditional Western-type measured media for consumer advertising—was clearly not a discriminating factor in structuring business-to-business communications.

The use of mass information media by large foreign and domestic firms tended to monopolize information channels as a preemptive strike against competition to ensure market power. Smaller foreign and domestic firms were relegated to scattered messages via the mass information media as their primary means of business-to-business communication. In both cases, business and industry advertising neglected the Soviet consumer with purchasing power as a vital component who also had an active role in the Soviet economy.

The Soviet consumer was exposed to advertisements either for products that were available only for valuta, which consumers did not have, or for merchandise at high ruble prices that made it unaffordable. This led to a further division of social and economic classes, of poverty and wealth, of the "haves" and "have-nots" in a new Soviet society that did not want to shed socialism or Russian cultural values completely.

Although glasnost opened more avenues for the exchange of information, advertising was perceived by Soviet consumers as an intrusion into their personal lives. They considered advertising as unwanted information about products and services that were either unavailable or unaffordable. This was further exacerbated by their perception that advertising was diminishing the quality and, in some ways, the cultural aspects of their lives. Program broadcasts were interrupted with advertisements for inconsequential products and services; favorite editorial material was being compromised by the media's addressing the needs of "businesses." Soviet consumers essentially felt they were being cheated. They were in some way paying for information they did not want or need.

The role of advertising as an institution of economic and social influence created a demoralizing atmosphere among the Soviet citizenry. Measures of success and individual wealth were evidenced by a proliferation of new enterprises in the service industry: brokerage firms, advertising agents and agencies, commercial banks, and so on. The concept of "fast money" did nothing to improve the quality of life among the public as a whole. Consumer goods were still scarce, and sources of information and entertainment were being replaced with something reminiscent of "bourgeois propaganda." The security of having lived under socialism—a philosophy of equality among social classes—was becoming more fragmented by the creation of extremes between economic classes and social strata.

Changes in the social and economic conditions within the former Soviet Union also affected how advertising training and education were perceived by both young and old professionals. To conform to a Western view of the role and functions of advertising and the market system, the leaders in the Soviet communications industry felt that their educational and professional backgrounds were inadequate. They perceived that in order to produce advertising according to the Western model, advertisers and practitioners had to have specialized and advanced training in advertising. This instilled a sense of inferiority in the Soviet advertising industry. Soviets turned to whatever information and educational sources about advertising were available: self-study, on-the-job training, temporary foreign training, and formal academic courses.

Soviet practitioners felt that a separate, more formal approach to advertising education was critical. Soviet industry and advertising professionals both considered that their specialized training or broad educational backgrounds did not adequately prepare them for a role in the advertising profession. For the most part this was due to their having lived, learned, and worked under a socialist system throughout their formative years and into adulthood. Taking a stance to advance specialized training for young professionals in some ways created another narrowly defined career field. Although they looked to the West for new ideas, they failed to see the diverse educational backgrounds of Westerners as a significant factor in advertising.

Regardless of the amount of information about advertising that had become available in the former Soviet Union, government legislation and industry regulation of advertising content and practice were virtually nonexistent. Soviet advertising professionals for the most part relied on their own ethical standards, those rooted in their Russian culture, to determine the suitable scheduling, placement, and content of advertisements. The growth of professional advertising associations had also spurred the need to establish a code of ethics and self-regulation, as exemplified by Western practitioners and government legislation.

This conflict of values produced a "tyranny of arbitrary rule." To exercise economic freedom to achieve individual and entrepreneurial prosperity, Soviet professionals had to determine to what degree advertising could intrude in children's and adults' private lives. Mass information media in the former Soviet Union supplemented out-of-home educational and cultural information. The West certainly had a significant influence in shaping Soviet perceptions of advertising, but not to the degree that Soviets were prepared to relinquish the rich heritage, individual values, and social norms of their Russian culture.

The meanings attributed to advertising were as diverse in nature as the Soviets were in social, professional, and academic backgrounds. But all, with some sadness, expressed broken ties to the traditions and values extolled in their Russian culture. Struggling with their conflict of values and social and economic paradoxes, Soviets attempted to preserve the good works of socialism and the symbols of their Russian heritage and to replicate them while trying to move toward a form of democracy and free market system.

Soviets understood and accepted that change was inevitable, but felt change should be at its own pace and not at a pace set by the West. What rules existed in the Soviet Union were as much the dictates of government as they were of the older generation in the mass information media, in commerce and academia. Those in the younger generation had the spirit, and in some ways a freedom from preconceptions, to explore and structure their own field of advertising on top of their own Soviet model of advertising and free market system.

More than 10 years ago, the rapid influx of Western advertising agencies into Moscow served as a warning shot for the development of a free market system. So inspired, the first full-service Russian advertising agency, Avrora, opened its doors in 1991. This entrepreneurial spirit motivated others, and by 1997 there were more than 1,500 agencies in Moscow. Large, full-service Russian agencies competed directly with Western agencies for both domestic and foreign clients. And the tide quickly turned to mergers and acquisitions by Western agencies to solidify further stakeholder positions in the advertising industry. In 1997, the top 13 agencies in Moscow were all Western operations, partly or wholly owned. These included the major international names in the industry. The largest agency in billing, although not income, was DMB&B, with a volume of $92 million, a very small figure by American standards.[13]

From such a low starting point, the growth potential for agencies in Russia is obviously very great.

Notes

1. Philip Hanson, *Advertising and Socialism* (White Plains, NY: International Arts and Sciences, 1974).

2. Ibid.

3. Y. Degtyarev and L. Kornilov, *Torgovlaya Reklama: Ekonomika, Iskusstvo* [Trade Advertising: Economics, Art] (Moscow: Ekonomika, 1969).

4. Robert Bartels, *The History of Marketing Thought,* 3rd ed. (Columbus, OH: Publishing Horizons, 1988).

5. David Satter, "Homo Sovieticus: Can Attitudes Change?" *Survey,* vol. 30, no. 3, October 1988, 92-105.

6. Abel Aganbegyan, *The Economic Challenge of Perestroika,* ed. Michael B. Brown, trans. Pauline M. Tiffen (Bloomington: Indiana University Press, 1988), 43.

7. Rozalina V. Ryvkina, "Economic Culture as Society's Memory," *Soviet Review,* vol. 31, no. 1, January 1990, 4.

8. Kim B. Rotzoll and James E. Haefner, with Charles H. Sandage, *Advertising in Contemporary Society,* 2nd ed. (Cincinnati: South-Western, 1990).

9. James W. Carey, *Communication as Culture* (Boston: Unwin Hyman, 1989).

10. John E. Jackson (ed.), *Institutions in American Society: Essays in Market, Political, and Social Organizations* (Ann Arbor: University of Michigan Press, 1990). See also Robert J. Shafer, *A Guide to Historical Research Methods* (Chicago: Dorsey, 1980).

11. Interview, conducted in Russian, with anonymous informant, Moscow, May 1991; my translation.

12. Bartels, *The History of Marketing Thought,* 46.

13. "Agency Report," *Advertising Age,* April 27, 1998, S35.

Recommended Further Reading

Hanson, Philip, *The Consumer in the Soviet Economy* (Evanston, IL: Northwestern University Press, 1968).

Sandage, Charles H., "Some Institutional Aspects of Advertising," *Journal of Advertising,* vol. 2, January 1973, 6-9.

Wells, Ludmilla Gricenko, *The Role of Advertising in the Soviet Union,* unpublished doctoral dissertation, University of Tennessee, 1992.

Wells, Ludmilla Gricenko, "The Socioeconomic Culture and the Advertising Process in the Soviet Union," in Rebecca Holman (ed.), *Proceedings of the 1991 Conference of the American Academy of Advertising* (New York: American Academy of Advertising, 1992), 203-212.

Wells, Ludmilla Gricenko, "Western Concepts, Russian Perspectives: Meanings of Advertising in the Former Soviet Union," *Journal of Advertising,* vol. 23, March 1994, 83-96.

13

Australia

A Western or Eastern Advertising Market?

Paul Gaskin

Australia in the World of Advertising

Australia conjures up various stereotypes in the minds of Europeans and Americans. Like most stereotypes, these represent part—and only part—of the truth. Whichever are held by the reader, perhaps this chapter will help to balance them.

With almost 19 million people, Australia represents a market of middle size. Using the World Bank's purchasing power parity measures, which enable us to make the most realistic economic comparisons among countries, the Australian market as a whole is of similar size to that of the Netherlands, Turkey, or Taiwan. Almost two-thirds of Australians live in the country's five

TABLE 13.1 Populations of Major Australian Cities

City	Population (in millions)
Sydney	3.9
Melbourne	3.3
Brisbane	1.5
Perth	1.3
Adelaide	1.1

major cities. In each of these, the great majority live in suburban settings of separate single-family dwellings, with only a few living in city apartments (mainly established in the past 10 years) such as exist in major European and U.S. cities. The populations of the immediate urban areas of Australia's major cities are shown in Table 13.1.

Like most developed countries, Australia has a high divorce rate and, as a result, a large proportion of single-parent families. Life expectancy is high and—although Australia's dependency ratio is not (and will never be) as high as that in Japan, Germany, or the United States—older people constitute an increasing proportion of households.

Aside from the five major cities, the remainder of the country is sparsely populated, with few other towns over 50,000 in population. The landmass of Australia is comparable to that of the continental United States, but (unlike in the United States) 90% of Australia's population lives within the coastal areas.

Gross domestic product (GDP) per capita in Australia is about two-thirds of the U.S. level (again in purchasing power parity terms), and is comparable to GDP in Britain, Sweden, Italy, and Israel. Australia's unemployment level as of late 1998 was just below 8%.

Australia's population has a very high rate of completion of secondary education—comparable with the United States—with almost 30% proceeding to university; this proportion has increased more than sixfold in 30 years.

So Australia is a highly educated market of comfortably well-paid families living around Australia's edge. With 20% of its residents being citizens of other nations (only Luxembourg has a higher proportion), it is also a multi-cultural haven. Admittedly after much soul-searching, Australia has since the 1950s welcomed waves of immigration, first of British and Western Europeans, then of Eastern Europeans, Vietnamese, and latterly of other Asians, mainly Chinese from Malaysia, regions of China, and elsewhere.

TABLE 13.2 Top 10 Australian Advertising Agencies, 1997

Agency	Income (AU$ millions)
George Patterson Bates	92.5
Clemenger Australia (BBDO)	69.5
DDB	60.1
Young & Rubicam	44.4
J. Walter Thompson	33.9
McCann-Erickson	33.5
Ammirati Puris Lintas	31.1
Leo Burnett Connaghan and May	30.0
TMP Worldwide	26.8
John Singleton	24.5

Australia's geographic position is in the Pacific Rim, yet with its European origins and culture and use of the English language, it has maintained a separate identity, albeit one that is being enriched by immigration from neighboring Pacific countries.

Advertising constitutes about 1.2% of Australia's GDP, compared with 1.7% in the United States.

Major Advertising Agency Groups

Australia's advertising agencies are both international and domestic. Among the top 20, most are members of international groups with at least some internationally aligned accounts. Yet few of them would occupy their places in the rankings if they did not also win their share of local accounts. Sydney and Melbourne remain the head offices for Australia, with most of the major accounts based in those two cities (see Table 13.2).

Most large agencies can trace their foundations to local entrepreneurs who later sold to international groups (although JWT began as a branch in the 1930s). Mojo Partners, which grew out of two highly creative local agencies, Mojo and Monahan Dayman Adams (later MDA), has changed hands twice over the past decade as international parents' strategies changed. This activity continues with the Singleton agency, in which WPP, through merging into it the local Ogilvy & Mather (O&M) offices, has recently taken a strategic holding. It is possible that a new creative force is emerging: The two creative figures who founded Mojo—Alan Morris and Allan Johnston, long separated since they sold their interests in Mojo—have now formed a new consultancy called JoMo.

Local management has been the norm. Very few international managers have been sent to manage Australian agencies; many managers from Britain, Asia, South Africa, and the United States have succeeded in agency management after being appointed to jobs in Australia. This flow has occurred in both directions; since the 1960s some Australians have been transferred to the United States, Asia, and Europe to take over senior global positions.

Some of the large agency groups have derived very significant parts of their parent companies' global profits from Australia, out of proportion to the size of the Australian market. However, this is nigh impossible to manage in the long term, given that the Australian dollar (driven by currency traders' expectations about commodity markets) has moved in value over a range from 55 to 88 U.S. cents within the past 10 years, unrelated to Australian domestic conditions.

In the mid-1990s, a substantial change in regulatory competition policy removed the privileged position of "accredited" agencies and exposed them to additional challenge from small agencies and creative specialists. Media commission, once a privilege of well-capitalized agencies, is now almost universally available, and many clients have negotiated more flexible mixes of service fees and reduced commission rates. This policy shift facilitated even more the establishment of several additional independent media-buying groups; international agency groups tended to consolidate their buying, even if planning remained in separately branded agencies.

At the same time, most major agencies, facing challenges from direct marketing, sales promotion, and sponsorships, moved to acquire at least some such skills to offer their clients. It is not yet clear whether this will prove any more successful than the attempts, 10 to 20 years ago, to cross-refer clients between public relations firms and traditional advertising agencies owned by the same group.

The account planning function, which first was established in larger agencies in Australia early in the 1980s, is now having a resurgence—after a hiatus in the early 1990s. Both Interbrand and the Added Value Group have established presences in the Australian market, and the emphasis they place on sophisticated brand positioning will further stimulate Australian managers' use of advertising and other promotional tools.

The Media Pattern in Australia

Three commercial broadcast networks dominate television advertising in Australia at present, but there are two others: a government-funded noncommercial network and a network that programs mainly community-language programs and accepts advertising between (but not within) programs. There has been a tradition of agreed-upon regulation of technical innovations—the initial TV broadcasters began transmission within a few weeks of each other, all moved from black-and-white to color on the same date, and all will begin digital broadcasting in 2001. Radio will change to digital at that time too.

Pay television has made limited progress in Australia in the past 5 years. Two competing companies—Foxtel (a joint venture of News Corporation and Telstra, the former-monopoly telephone company) and Optus (Cable and Wireless)—have wired large sections of the major cities. Penetration is currently about 12% of households where cable is available. Rationalization seems inevitable, driven also by the government's refusal to allow pay operators to convert to digital for a further 6 years after digital broadcasting begins. By the end of 1998, no ratings had been released for pay audiences, and local advertising remained scant. In the past, Australians have rapidly adopted new technologies, particularly color television, VCRs, and mobile phones; the adoption of pay TV appears to have been slow because each competitor has offered a less-than-total channel selection.

Commercial radio in Australia began in the 1920s, rose to its peak in the mid-1950s, before TV was introduced, and now is extremely strong in the major cities, each with 10 to 15 stations. There is little networking of programming because all content is focused on local city interests. Nonmetropolitan areas have 1 or 2 stations, and in the early 2000s will have still more. The pattern of programming is similar in range to that found in the United States—there are talk stations and several varieties of music stations (but no country music).

As Table 13.3 shows, newspapers are also city based. In Sydney and Melbourne, two newspapers compete. In each of the smaller cities, only one daily survives. There is only one national newspaper, the *Australian,* which was launched some 20 years ago and still has only a fraction of the readership of the major city dailies. Saturday and Sunday papers exist, and in some cases reach far more readers than do the dailies.

TABLE 13.3 Readership of Major Daily Newspapers

Geographic Area	Title (Publisher)	Readership (in thousands)
National	Australian (News Corp.)	430
Sydney	Telegraph-Mirror (News Corp.)	1,269
	Sydney Morning Herald (John Fairfax)	902
Melbourne	Herald Sun (News Corp.)	1,339
	Age (John Fairfax)	675
Brisbane	Courier-Mail (News Corp.)	594
Adelaide	Advertiser (News Corp.)	576
Perth	West Australian (Independent)	662

SOURCE: Data gathered by Roy Morgan Research Centre, April-September 1998.

Australia still has the largest per capita women's magazine readership in the world in the Australian *Women's Weekly,* with 3.1 million readers; ironically, the *Weekly* (as it is known) became a monthly during the 1980s. After a rapid expansion in the aggregate readership (and circulation) of an increasing number of magazines for women from the later 1980s to the mid-1990s, the total women's readership is now tending to decline, bringing some weaker titles under considerable pressure. Men's titles were launched in the late 1990s, but they have yet to establish a strong following. Business magazines are strong, with some titles waxing (e.g., *Business Review Weekly*) and some waning (e.g., the *Bulletin,* until its relaunch early in 1999).

Internet penetration into homes has been increasing rapidly, and Australia ranks not far behind the United States. Internet use is highest—around 40% late in 1998—among homes with children between 10 and 19 years old. As an advertising medium, the major efforts are being put in by ninemsn, a joint venture of Microsoft and the Nine Television Network; by Yahoo Australia; and by Ozemail, which is in the process of being sold to MCI.

Sources of Advertising Spending in Australia

In the grocery field, manufacturers' brands remain stronger than in many parts of Europe, with approximately 89% of aggregate sales. Among the top grocery umbrella brands listed in Table 13.4, most are internationally controlled.

TABLE 13.4 Top Umbrella Grocery Brands, 1997

Brand	Retail Sales (AU$ millions)	Category
Arnott's	548	biscuits
Kellogg	400	cereals
Cadbury	331	confectionery and ice cream
Kraft	294	various foods
Nescafé	242	coffee
Uncle Toby's	239	cereals and snacks
Kleenex	214	tissue products
Golden Circle	208	canned fruit, vegetables, juices
Heinz	201	various foods
McCain	186	frozen foods

SOURCE: Data from A. C. Nielsen.

Cigarettes, still among the largest brands in sales revenue, are not permitted to be advertised at all; promotion is restricted to small signs at the point of sale. There are no legislative threats to other categories such as alcohol. Regulatory authorities are currently giving active consideration to consumer advertising of prescription drugs.

   As Australia's economy has moved substantially into services, the list of the top 10 advertisers has come to be dominated by retailers, financial institutions, and telecommunications providers.

Australian Creativity

The Yalumba Wines advertisement displayed in Figure 13.1, from the smallish but deservedly famous agency the Campaign Palace in Melbourne, indicates some of the hallmarks of Australian creative approaches. A self-deprecating sense of irony forms a starting point. A willingness to take the customer into the brand's confidence and also to ask (politely) for the order are two of the more common approaches.

   Australians often resent people who take themselves too seriously. American creative approaches, which too-confidently enthuse about the benefits of using the brand, are believed frequently to undermine brand credibility.

Figure 13.1. Advertisement for Yalumba Wines
SOURCE: The Campaign Palace, Melbourne.

Perhaps for this reason, far fewer personalities and endorsers are used in Australian advertising. Even though Michael Jordan was the most popular advertising personality a few years ago, Nike also used Australian footballers, cricketers, and tennis players. And a rich British voice—common in Australian advertising as a mark of importance until the 1960s—is now seen as simply foreign. A series of London commercials for the Australian beer brand Castlemaine XXXX, known as Four-X, displayed the laconic Australian as envisaged by the British. But when the commercials were imported into Australia for use in the brand's home region, they were treated as amusing, but seemed to separate the brand from its core constituency. The very things that are remarkable to the British are not suitable to be stated in public in Australia, it seems.

Until the 1980s, Australian government regulations required that all TV commercials aired had to have used Australian crews. Gradually, such restrictions have eased, and international commercials are now common. Many have their voice-overs replaced with Australian accents, although a "mid-Atlantic"

accent—similar to the "educated Australian" accent dominant in the media—
is generally effective in Australia. The "broad Australian" accent—which
is the stereotype Australian accent known to British people and Americans—
occurs with equal frequency in local advertising. These two Australian accents—
"educated" and "broad"—are in fact both spread widely throughout the population, and are not related exclusively to education level; it is not unusual within
a single nuclear family for some individuals to speak broad and others to have
an educated accent.

Australia has accepted the strongly emotion-laden European style of advertising. Many young creative people in Australian agencies have spent time
in London agencies, and many London creatives have spent a few (sometimes
many) years in Australia. This has not led to some of the extremes of semiotic
referencing and the special advertising tone of voice that characterize some
British advertising. But emotion is subtly used, and is most often set in a
context of egalitarian relationships.

Two commercials for McDonald's Australia (from DDB) used James Dean
and Marilyn Monroe look-alikes (who did not speak) in richly evocative gritty
urban settings in Australia to strengthen the relationship of McDonald's with
people (mostly older, one surmises) for whom these characters are meaningful.
Later, McDonald's used a touching "first date" commercial in which a couple—both in their 70s and dressed in the formal white clothing used for the
sedate game of lawn bowling—shared 30-cent ice cream cones at McDonald's.

Compared with the United States, Australia is less frightened of references
to sexual feelings on television, in both programs and commercials. A recent
Cannes Festival Award winner was a milk commercial that featured an
extremely fit 67-year-old retired milk delivery man who maintained his
"relationships" (we see him leaving via the *front* door) with his delighted
former customers.

One television retail campaign has been uniquely successful. Target Australia's logo itself has gone through many animated tortures over more than a
decade, demonstrating brand values such as the repeated washability of
children's garments, the large sizes of women's clothing in stock, and also an-
nouncing (three or four times a year) one-day sales at only 24 hours' notice.
The branding and promotional strength of this discount department store's
campaign—without any merchandise or human presence—has built its
strong relationship with Australian shoppers across all socioeconomic groups.
The Campaign Palace in Melbourne has also been responsible for Target's
advertising.

A Source of Advertising
Research Innovations

Australia has been a theater in which the differing attitudes toward advertising and creativity of the United States (rational, learning-focused) and Europe (emotional and focused on consumer relationships) have been played out. With many Australian creative people having worked in London, and many U.S. companies controlling large Australian grocery brands, the scene has frequently been set for conflict on what advertising is intended to do and how that should be achieved, not to mention how to measure through research whether it has indeed been achieved.

It may be that this environment, plus the pressure of smaller budgets than in either the U.S. or major European countries, has provoked the development in Australia of efficient research tools. Add+Impact is an advertising pretesting system with both qualitative and quantitative elements. Developed by Michael Cramphorn and Sally Joubert of Advertising Development Solutions, it has now spread to most major markets around the world through local licensees. It uses a "spill-the-mind" question to elicit all the thoughts, ideas, and feelings provoked by an advertising execution and combines the extensively probed responses with answers to a battery of standard "agree/disagree" questions. MarketMind Technologies has developed a similarly widespread advertising tracking system. The instigators were Dr. Max Sutherland and Bruce Smith.

The Australian advertising industry is lean and competitive, and it sets high standards for itself. It has recently agonized publicly about "poor" performance at the Cannes Festival when compared with previous years. It has experienced a rapid increase over the past three decades in the proportion of staff with degree-level education—on both client and agency sides—from below 10% to a substantial majority today. It goes into the next millennium confident and well equipped: neither "Western" nor "Eastern," but Australian and unique, and likely to become more emphatically so with the passage of time.

14

The Emperor's New Clothes

A View From Australia on the Creative Process

Jill Powell

Creative minds will change the 21st century, British Prime Minister Tony Blair said recently. Creativity as the core necessity in our brave new world is the message being spread across the corporate landscape, and enthusiastic managers are answering the call. They are abandoning the romantic notion that outstanding creativity is the product of extraordinary individual acts, because now, according to the preachers, the ability is within us all.

All through history this is something we have never entertained. The Greeks believed that the gods breathed ideas into a few gifted individuals, and this wisdom was never questioned—until now. It is the nature of our democracy today to deny no one access to good things, and even though we haven't much idea what "it" is, where it is, or where it comes from, "creativity" is associated with all things good—individual fulfillment, productivity, and business enterprise. It is why the idea endures.

But creativity is like the emperor's new clothes, and organizations are investing a lot in the unseen. Creative manipulation of what little is known is seldom challenged because the question itself is mammoth, complex, and ambiguous. Nor do we care. It makes us feel good about ourselves, and, given that it can't be seen, it can't be measured or judged; it can, therefore, do us no harm.

The problem is that we have become so bedazzled by the idea that it has blocked our judgment and common sense. On the one hand, we put our faith in formulas and numbers: Coffee is bad for you; democracy is best; 51% of consumers say . . . . Yet, on the other, we willingly invest millions of dollars on training programs and the physical enhancement of workplaces despite little evidence that either of these things increases in any meaningful way the probability of high-payoff creativity. Is it not, therefore, an anomaly that we embrace something so unquantifiable, so indefinable, as the sole generator, facilitator, and savior of our new world?

Perhaps it is simply a love affair with the new. Back in 1971, 91% of U.S. managers questioned in a survey did not believe that creativity could be trained or developed at all.[1] At an Academy of Management meeting in 1994, out of the 1,000 papers presented, not one was on creativity.[2] Yet in less than a decade the notion has beaten its way to the forefront of organizational culture and is now seen as vital and fundamental to future success.

Many organizations, however, have been less interested in what creativity is and more preoccupied with finding and managing it. As a result, they have latched prematurely onto prescriptions for enhancing creativity. They have not stopped to question whether biases exist that inhibit creative contributions, what characteristics make a difference, or how the product affects the process, nor have they looked closely at why creativity flourishes in some organizations and not in others or at what kinds of organizations reliably increase the likelihood.

Creativity has allowed us to answer questions about the future that we haven't even formulated yet—answers like "Creative minds will change the 21st century." However, many managers are starting to question the rhetoric itself, because the reality on the factory floor is far from convincing. Creativity is about problems, and the fact is, few people like problems. Our natural instinct is for self-preservation rather than exploration, and problem solving involves risk. It takes a person with extraordinary amounts of courage, self-belief, tenacity, and persistence to break boundaries and confront management with new ideas, and a huge investment in time and energy is required to make it all happen. Few employees love what they do that much.

Creativity is a fairly marginal goal for most people most of the time, and they have no need or desire to push their God-given potential, whatever it may be, to the limit. And even if they do, most presume that the kind of creativity that shakes the world is off-limits to them. Companies may, in fact, be asking the majority to perform unnatural and unwelcome convolutions of the mind in the name of creativity. The subjects know the bare facts, but who will tell the emperor? Perhaps we should simply appreciate the few risk takers we have rather than scold the majority of people for their caution and common sense.

In the current climate, it would verge on blasphemy to suggest that a few great minds will move opinion and cultures in the 21st century, but it is likely to be so. All through time, in any field, there has only ever been a handful of people who have made a difference. The distribution of meaningful creative acts in any field has always been a bit like the distribution of wealth: A small percentage accounts for the largest share.

We have known for a long time that biology is, to a large degree, our destiny. People only get to be creative, athletic, musical, and/or intelligent in the first place because of certain innate characteristics—characteristics that are likely to be genetic in origin. Heredity may set the upper bounds, but whether creative capacity moves mountains depends on an entirely different set of conditions that have nothing to do with being creative.

Characteristics That Make a Difference

Ambitious, achievement-oriented, capable of self-management, flexible, enjoys learning from new challenges and approaches. Must be comfortable in ambiguous situations, socially skillful, a strategic thinker and team player able to navigate through existing power structures and committed obsessively to work.

Sounds like an ad from the corporate "most-wanted" list—not attributes usually ascribed to creatives. Yet in a recent Australian study these characteristics were found to be vital to success.[3] What was surprising was that the best did not fit the stereotype of the flaky, no-ties-to-reality creative genius we have come to believe in. And if you met one in the street you wouldn't pick him (most are men) as a shaker and mover of culture and opinion, either.

He is not intelligent in the traditional sense and his academic career is hardly worth a mention. When he left school he had had no clear goals or career direction and fell into advertising by chance. He looks and behaves like a regular Joe, which is why he goes unrecognized in the world at large. The only way you would know he is a creative hotshot is by the title on his office door.

We tend to ascribe supernatural powers to clever creative people because, unlike our ability to point to the length of a runner's legs, we are at a loss to explain how they do what they do. No one would argue that, like good athletes, they have some kind of neural or genetic advantage. But mysterious? Are they not simply people able to process and synthesize diverse information more quickly and efficiently, weed out irrelevancies, and see parallels that aren't always obvious? Biologically and neurologically speaking, they do what they are capable of doing.

What the Australian study found was that the best in advertising, like the best in any field, just play the game a lot better, faster, and harder. They organize their lives to succeed, seeking out highly visible accounts to give their work a greater chance of being seen and big budgets that allow them to hang around long enough to be remembered and applauded. They work in big agencies because big agencies have big accounts. It helps to be a writer, although there is no valid explanation for this other than the prestige afforded the written word. Age is a factor. Despite the fact that advertising is seen as a young person's industry, all outstanding contributions are credited to those between 35 and 50. This is hardly surprising when one considers that most great historical acts have come at the end of a lifetime of doing.

We run into gray areas when we move beyond the demographics and into the possible reasons. In the Australian study, the best creative people were described by their peers as having an almost osmotic membrane connecting them to people and the world around them and an intuitive ability to evoke a response. This, however, is likely to be the result of a particular interest in what they do and is possibly learned, given that many of the outcomes are past ideas repacked and re-presented in novel ways. Experience is useful—but only up to a point, because no one knows for sure whether it is biological maturity or life experience that ultimately counts. A level of education helps, but studies have found that too much education can inhibit creativity. Knowledge is useful, but what one does with what one already knows appears to matter more. "An ever open mind is no better than an ever open mouth," Oscar Wilde suggested. We do not yet know, and possibly never will, at what point it all makes a difference.

The best creative people were also described by their peers as visionary and having a greater sense of the big picture. But there may be a logical explanation for this. Their position at the front line may simply give them a great vantage point from which to see emerging market and social trends and the opportunity to visualize and mobilize a response ahead of the pack. Their acts, as a result, appear visionary. The best creatives, at the end of the day, are likely to be not only better problem finders and problem solvers, but also better capital investors. New ideas are great capital, because if you do it first you own it. David Ogilvy, however, has suggested that most creatives in advertising are not capable of recognizing great opportunities when they do come by, nor do they know how to act upon them.[4]

Biases in Agencies That Inhibit Creativity

FOR HIRE: 25-30 male—high-school diploma; no prior experience in advertising.

With so many highly qualified people in the job market, would any manager give this ad a second look? Yet the Australian study found that the best creative minds in advertising came to the job with these qualifications—or lack of them. We have always known that there is some kind of link between cleverness and creativity, but there is a lot of confusion in organizations when it comes to hiring creative people because the link is not clear—the emperor's clothes again.

We have come to equate university degrees with cleverness, despite the fact that history has revealed, time and time again, that geniuses in all fields slip through institutional cracks. In business today, it is much more acceptable to think cleverness is something that can be learned, controlled, and, as a consequence, measured. This is why we do not question the suspect outcomes of training programs and ability tests to predict future success, while, conversely, we refuse to entertain that a 30-something-year-old inexperienced and "uneducated" man could do the job better.

Organizations are fragile things, and when they are built around creative people their survival is more threatened than usual, especially in advertising, where outstanding creativity is the ultimate legitimation of what the industry does. Surprisingly, many of the same biases exist in agencies as exist in all organizations when it comes to employing creatives, because, at the end of the day, advertising is a business like any other. One could be forgiven for assuming that because creativity is their stock-in-trade, agencies are somehow better at picking potential. In some ways they are—the guy for hire is at least likely to get an interview.

Advertising is a young person's industry, true. One only has to look at the numbers of people under 30 working in agencies for proof. Young, fresh, and zesty is the image to which every advertising agency aspires. However, most of the outstanding contributions are made by agencies' older members. No surprises there. Despite the obvious dichotomy, we continue to associate youth and hip with creative. Age, it appears, has more to do with the logic of the advertising industry than aging itself. Youth, it seems, has been refashioned to fit new industry values as well as consumer ones.

Why are the most outstanding contributions acknowledged as coming from those between 30 and 50? The most obvious explanation would be that by doing something longer one is bound to get better, faster, and more able at it—but this is not necessarily true. The reality is likely driven by the same economic factors that afflict all businesses. In the 1980s, Australia fell on hard times; as a result, jobs disappeared from the bottom and middle and shrunk behind those people who were left. In the 1990s, this created a gap between those who remained and those who came after. It created an older elite whose dominance in the field has largely remained unchallenged and, according to many, has left no room for young people to come through.

Advertising is full of such contradictions. We condemn creativity as a frivolous artistic pursuit that lies beyond rational thought yet simultaneously view the commercial outcome almost reverently as the result of great mysterious insight. Despite ourselves, we feel closet admiration for anything created outside the formula. We think of great creative minds as reservoirs of great thoughts, all the while knowing that most good people in agencies have had, on average, only one or two profound ideas in a lifetime, which they have more or less embellished over an entire career. Creativity has yet to yield its secrets to the outside world, and maybe it never will. The romantic idealization of the solitary genius is so deeply lodged in our minds that we do not choose to pay close attention to the details.

In the Australian study, however, the best creative people described their abilities far more pragmatically; they did not think of themselves as creative, or as being in possession of any extraordinary capabilities. They felt that their skill was in moving elements around until they fit and making decisions about their work as it was progressing. Sometimes they got it right—sometimes they didn't. Money wasn't a prime motivator, but it was, surprisingly, a great psychological resource: "The more I earn, the more they have to listen to what I have to say," said one.

The best did not appear to work in the random, haphazard way we associate with creative action. Instead, they described their work styles as purposeful, sequential, and as goal oriented as any other. They were often thought of as egotistical by their coworkers, but they did not see egotism in themselves. Rather, they suggested that what was perceived as ego was a psychological tool they sometimes used to survive the rugged evaluation process. Criticism, they admit, hurts because they care so much about what they do. The tortured creative genius, all agreed, is a myth, but a useful one because it implies that what they do lies beyond rational thought. This gives them propriety over creative ideas in the business world and, as a consequence, affords them enormous personal leverage within the agency.

How the Product Affects the Process Itself

> If I look at something and it turns my head around, turns my heart around, turns my guts inside out and I say, "Oh my God," and you have altered me forever. That's what an outstanding idea is all about. That's the point of it all. (Scott Whybin, Whybin TBWA, Melbourne)

While many organizations explore new ways of enhancing creativity, traditional "creative" domains, such as advertising agencies, bemoan the fact that the kind of creativity that refashions a culture is a rare commodity these days. This scarcity, according to many, is responsible for creative salaries' being pushed skyward and has created an anomaly in traditional hierarchical pay structures. Nowadays, a good creative can earn more than the boss, simply because there are more good managers out there than good creatives. The notion there should be more good people out there may come, in part, from the self-serving definition of the word *creative* itself. We confuse the majority who call themselves creative with the few who are great because they all work in the place called the "creative department."

We place so much importance on creativity because, as a society, we need to know there are people around who can ensure our survival. What isn't so obvious, despite our eagerness for more, is that we, or rather our appointed judges and gatekeepers, control the numbers, because to accept too many contributions devalues our cultural capital and renders future creative investments worthless. Every now and again, when contributions are low, a newcomer is allowed to rise and shine to show that brilliance is alive and well no matter how overrated the outcome. Genius, it seems, is a title bestowed.

Creatives in a business environment don't make for harmony, and when creativity *is* the business, this effect is even greater. For a start, the very unpredictability of action that creates excitement in the creative department generates the opposite effect in the majority of more task-oriented coworkers in the agency. Creatives take up more airspace, resources, and money than anyone else. They play games, infiltrate power structures, and turn management systems upside down with all the zeal of commandos and are more concerned with glory than with personal fulfillment or reputation. In the Australian study, the best were described time and time again as having a peasant toughness, a killer instinct, and being good finishers. They make better generals than foot soldiers, which is why most are creative directors. They like to be in charge. They are not considered good on practical matters and delegate the more mundane tasks. This is not due to the lack of importance of such tasks or lack of interest, but because of shortage of time. Opportunities are limitless and time is not. They maximize their time by building and mobilizing a close network of extremely competent people to implement their visions.

Despite the fact that creations are collectively achieved, they are almost always singly rewarded. Glory is theirs alone. They are not reliant on personal approval; they question authority and are loyal only to their craft, their careers, and the task at hand. They are allowed to be like this because they are "creative," and this is tolerated in an advertising agency because what they do is vital to everyone's survival.

However, we tend to overrate creative ability and underestimate the powerful influence of circumstance. Despite the mountain of evidence, the idea endures that creativity comes from within the individual and is immune to economic ebb and flow. We understand why historic periods such as the Renaissance spawned so many great artists and thinkers, yet we choose to remain ignorant of the subtle and constant push and pull of the world around us. In our search for special "creative" qualities, we blind ourselves to the facts because they are too simple—too obvious. No matter how gifted one is, external opportunities have always determined one's creativity.

Why Creativity Flourishes in
Some Agencies and Not in Others

It's all in your network.

Great ideas don't happen in a vacuum; they require a rare confluence of person, talent, opportunity, and economic circumstance. We all like to think it will happen to us, but it rarely does because it isn't something that can be planned for. It is something that happens to a few who are lucky enough to be in the right place at the right time. Working in the right agency immersed the best creatives in the craft at its highest level, inspired them with strong company philosophies, and surrounded them with brilliant people. The best, without exception, were taken under the wings of important and influential industry figures who recognized their potential, taught them the rules, explained past achievements, introduced them to the right people, helped validate and promote their work in the field, and, on occasion, streamed them through to the top. They all said this mentorship was vital to their success and remained a forceful influence throughout their careers. As one put it:

> I was forced back by my teacher. He made me ignore all I had learned, then brought me forward slowly . . . never bending to suit me. For the first 10 years I didn't feel like I was working in advertising at all. I felt like I was just watching on. This gave me the opportunity to see how things happened and I gradually became involved in the decision making. I think having the chance to step back is what is helping me now.

Interestingly, special creative work spaces are endorsed by the industry despite little evidence that they make a difference at the level we are talking about. Most creatives in the Australian study admitted that they did their thinking outside the office, and a regular business environment, they agreed, was just as suitable for long periods of preparation and production. The idea that such things as creative work spaces increase the probability of boosting creativity is appealing and readily acceptable because it appears to offer an easy solution.

Creativity is essentially a social process, and it is the intellectual atmosphere that determines how people work. Because of our obsession with the individual, we continue to view creativity as a singular pursuit, but in reality it is probably one of the most highly interactive forms of human endeavor.

Strong social networks provide stronger ties and more credible sources of information and create greater-than-average expertise and knowledge. Challenging interdependency builds up a critical mass of believers, which in turn attracts others. The greater the density of interaction and excitement, the greater the likelihood that the environment will prompt a person already so inclined to break away.

Such an environment was described by the best as having good "human walls." Being in the right agency with the right people at the right time with the right qualifications for the job can make all the difference. According to one respondent, it can make a $33\frac{1}{3}\%$ difference and can determine whether one is considered at one time a genius or a hack.

Creativity, it seems, has a better chance of being enhanced by changing conditions than by efforts to make people think more creatively. Agencies, however, will not necessarily become more creative as a result, because at this level environment is largely a matter of choice. The best creative people actively seek out the most stimulating places to work. They gravitate toward centers of vital activity, placing their work where it has the greatest opportunity of being seen.

What Kind of Agency Reliably Increases the Likelihood?

Size matters.

The evidence is in the numbers. The top gross-billing agencies have all the best creative people. The "it" factor is overwhelmingly where one works, and it is impossible to overestimate the importance. Sure, this is a massive generalization and there are more considerations around the equation, but the facts are there.

In the 1970s and 1980s, small boutique agencies were repositories of brilliance in Australia, but the recession that followed may have been largely responsible for the move of the best people to larger agencies, because in tough economic times big agencies are better at buffering creatives from harsh economic realities. The study found that middle-sized to big agencies provided the hottest creative environments, the implication being that beyond a certain level, opportunities do not increase with size.

Why big agencies? Why now? The best in any field have always been drawn to centers of activity: Great companies and cities alike attract ambitious individuals seeking to leave their mark. Nowadays creativity is seen in the light of company sponsorship rather than individual accomplishment, and the influence of the individual is decreasing in importance as a result. Big agencies, especially those with strong global networks, are able to provide better vantage points, more credible resources and opportunities for creatives, and a greater critical mass of believers in the creative cause.

It would be easy to assume that big agencies, as a result, are full of creative clues, but at this level they are not. Only a few in any creative department ever get the chance to do great work, not because of the lack of opportunity, but because of the self-limiting prophesies of most people and the uneven distribution of available creative capital. We often do not see this link because we prefer to think that opportunity and environment are nurturing passive influences on creativity. The truth is that the relationship between a high creative and the place he works is highly interactive.

The waters are still largely uncharted. We have consensus, clues, and role models but still no answers. What is interesting is the widespread and ready acceptance of ideas that clearly have shaky foundations: Advertising is a "creative" industry; creative people have a mythical ability; youth makes one more creative; training and a delightful setting will improve the chances of creativity. These ideas appear to have more to do with convincing ourselves than anything else, and they are perpetuated by an industry that has talked to itself far too long.

The world around us is changing, and the shifts are not only in character but in pace. The fault lines are moving in advertising, too, but according to many the industry is not heeding the call. Sydney creative director Jack Vaughan questions why the industry lacks the inspiration or foresight to create a bright future for itself: "For an industry that prides itself as a 'mover and shaker,' changes are happening to us, not by us." [5] Martin Sorrell, WPP Group chief executive, threw the cat among the pigeons at the IAA Conference in 1996 by suggesting that advertising is failing to attract the best and brightest graduates who could ensure the future strength of the industry. He believes that what the industry needs is cleverer people—and he could have a point.

The future, it seems, lies not in seeing new landscapes but in having new eyes. Perhaps the industry needs to develop a more realistic model of creativity. The multimillion-dollar question is: Will the conditions favorable to the business of advertising in the future also be favorable to individual cleverness?

Notes

1. B. G. Whiting, "Managing Opinions on Creativity," *Journal of Creative Behavior,* vol. 5, 1971, 166-168.

2. Teresa M. Amabile, "Discovering the Unknowable, Managing the Unmanageable," in Cameron M. Ford and Dennis A. Gioia (eds.), *Creative Action in Organizations: Ivory Tower Visions and Real-World Voices* (Thousand Oaks, CA: Sage, 1995), 77-82.

3. Jill Powell, "The Relationship Between Environment and Outstanding Creative Performance in Advertising," unpublished master's thesis, Royal Melbourne Institute of Technology, 1997.

4. David Ogilvy, *Confessions of an Advertising Man* (New York: Atheneum, 1964).

5. Jack Vaughan, "Free Thinking," *Campaign Brief,* November 1993, 23-26.

Recommended Further Reading

Csikszentmihalyi, Mihaly, *Creativity: Flow and the Psychology of Discovery and Invention* (New York: HarperCollins, 1996).

Ford, Cameron M., and Dennis A. Gioia (eds.), *Creative Action in Organizations: Ivory Tower Visions and Real-World Voices* (Thousand Oaks, CA: Sage, 1995).

Gardner, Howard E. *Creating Minds: An Anatomy of Creativity Seen Through the Lives of Freud, Einstein, Picasso, Stravinsky, Eliot, Graham and Gandhi* (New York: HarperCollins, 1993).

15

Japan

The Advertising Agency Scene

John Philip Jones

T he most striking feature of the advertising agency business in Japan is the degree to which it is dominated by locally owned operations. In this regard, Japan is unique among the world's most important non-U.S. advertising markets.

The leading Japanese agencies are detailed in Table 15.1. Of the top 20 agencies, the only non-Japanese organizations that feature on the list are McCann-Erickson (ranked 9th), J. Walter Thompson (ranked 15th), and Leo Burnett (ranked 18th). In 12th place is Dentsu, Young & Rubicam (Y&R), an agency in which Y&R has an equity stake. The foreign agencies are therefore weaker than the Japanese agencies—in particular in their amount of media-buying "clout," which is an important aspect of agency practice in Japan. However, foreign agencies are becoming increasingly active in Japan, with WPP recently taking a stake in Asatsu (the number 3 agency) and Omnicom buying into I.& S. (ranked 8th) and Nippo (a smaller operation).[1] This trend

TABLE 15.1 Twenty Largest Advertising Agencies in Japan, 1997

Rank	Agency	Billing ($ millions)	World Ranking of Position in 50 Largest Ad Agency Organizations
1	Dentsu Inc.	11,137	4
2	Hakuhodo Inc.	5,921	10
3	Asatsu Inc.	1,671	17
4	Tokyu Advertising	1,654	18
5	Daiko Advertising	1,653	19
6	Yomiko Advertising	1,066	26
7	Dai-Ichi Kikaku	949	21
8	I.&.S. Corp.	912	27
9	McCann-Erickson, Japan	874	3
10	Asahi Advertising	622	32
11	Man Nen Sha	569	36
12	Dentsu, Young & Rubicam	542	22
13	Oricom Co.	482	41
14	Nikkeisha Inc.	444	44
15	J. Walter Thompson, Tokyo	430	2
16	Sogei	407	48
17	Nihon Keizai Advertising	334	
18	Leo Burnett-Kyodo Co.	249	
19	Dentsu Kyushu	221	
20	Meitsu	179	

SOURCE: Adapted with permission from data that appeared in *Advertising Age,* April 27, 1999, S10, S31. Copyright Crain Communications Inc., 1999.

NOTE: All of the agencies listed are headquartered in Tokyo, except for Man Nen Sha (Osaka), Dentsu, Young & Rubicam (New York), and Dentsu Kyushu (Fukuoka).

is connected with Japan's current economic problems, which I discuss later in this chapter.

Very much the largest Japanese agency is Dentsu. Randall Rothenberg, an investigative journalist who has made a special study of the advertising industry, describes Dentsu's position in the following words:

[In 1990] Dentsu placed 20% of all the newspaper advertisements in Japan and almost 17% of all the magazine ads. It produced one-quarter of the eight thousand television commercials broadcast in Japan each year. Because of its supremacy in advertising spending, Dentsu's power over media content was unparalleled; it was said the agency could persuade news organizations not to cover stories harmful to its clients. It even controlled Japan's television ratings system, and allegedly forced from the air programs of which it disapproved by claiming low ratings for them.[2]

In 1996, Dentsu still accounted for huge shares of all media advertising: 32% of television, 17% of newspapers, 16% of magazines, and 13% of radio.[3]

But although Dentsu has subsidiary companies or equity partnerships with agencies in 40 countries, 85% of its billing is in Japan. It has recently been announced that Dentsu is in negotiation with Leo Burnett to acquire a stake in that large privately owned American agency.[4] However, these moves to spread its business internationally are unlikely to change Dentsu to a significant degree. Because of its culture, not to speak of its dominance in its home market, Dentsu will continue to be a nationally focused operation—a Japanese agency first and last.

Japanese law does not make it easy for foreign-owned agencies to operate in Japan. Partly as a result, Japanese advertising has two important characteristics that differentiate it from advertising in other developed markets. First, the style of advertising is unlike what is seen in most other countries, in that the television advertising is more entertaining, emotional, and mood oriented, with less hard selling. There are very few brand comparisons. (Procter & Gamble's initial moves into Japan, using campaigns derived from American prototypes, were notably unsuccessful.) Japanese television is characterized by great profusion and density of commercials, many of very short length. Few international advertising campaigns are effective in Japan, and those that are successful (e.g., Unilever's Lux bar soap and Timotei shampoo, both created by J. Walter Thompson) use themes intrinsically similar to the general run of Japanese advertising. Another feature of Japanese advertising is the extensive use of testimonials by celebrities both Japanese and Western, all of whom command high fees.

Second, many Japanese agencies are also involved in untraditional businesses, such as book and magazine publishing and the production of communications-related computer software. They are sometimes even involved in businesses totally unrelated to media communications. The general business practice in Japan is that agencies are permitted to accept different clients that compete with one another in the same categories. As a consequence, Japanese agencies often treat their client lists as confidential.

The shape of the advertising business in Japan is governed by the features of Japanese business as a whole. These features, which are rooted in the practices of a traditionally isolated market, include a tolerance of business concentration and a lack of legal restraints on such concentration as well as a general absence of "tooth and claw" competition. (This softness toward competitors embraces "insiders" but does not extend to "outsiders" such as foreign agencies.) It is not surprising that Japanese advertising possesses characteristics that are very unusual among markets of a comparable size, and perhaps this is a minor reason for the lack of success of foreign agencies in Japan.

As already discussed, the Japanese have a unique style of advertising. Tom Sutton, who ran J. Walter Thompson Japan for most of the 1970s, often expressed the view that Japan was the only country in his direct experience in which it was virtually impossible to employ international campaigns. Successful campaigns like those for Lux and Timotei were the exceptions that proved the rule, and worked because of their similarity to locally originated advertising.

Japanese agencies, with their wide range of business activities and their ability to handle competing clients, have grown very large even by world standards. However, as a result of the special features of Japanese advertising, Japanese agency work does not travel well. Japanese agencies have gained relatively little business outside Japan—a failing that has led them to take equity positions in foreign agencies.

In spite of the size and importance of the Japanese advertising industry and the great size of many Japanese agencies, Japan is, from a world advertising perspective, less important than might appear at first glance. One result is that, as a general rule, large Japanese brands of cars and other consumer durables are in most countries supported by advertising campaigns developed by local agencies, not branches of Japanese agencies. It is a fair generalization to say that the huge size of Japanese agencies does not enable them to produce a better creative product than that of smaller agencies in other countries.

Japanese agencies offer an extensive range of communications services and collateral activities. These account for 35% of agency income in the case of Dentsu. The two oldest agencies in Japan are Hakuhodo (the second-largest agency), founded in 1895, and Dentsu, founded in 1901. The leading Japanese agencies are publicly owned. Not surprisingly, they tend to be more profitable than their American counterparts.

The recession in the Pacific Rim since 1997 has hit Japan badly. Although personal savings in the Japanese economy are very high, and unemployment and inflation are both low, the country's gross domestic product actually fell by 3% in 1998 and is not likely to show any growth in 1999.[5] As a consequence, advertising is depressed. Of the top 20 Japanese agencies, 18 posted billing declines in 1997 compared with 1996, and decline or stagnation is likely to be the outcome for 1998 billing figures and also possibly for those in 1999. The Japanese government has attempted a number of fiscal policies to jump-start the economy. Despite the originality of some of the innovations (e.g., free shopping coupons distributed by the city of Hamada), none of these policies has been effective.[6] It is unlikely in such circumstances that advertising could in any way operate to prime the economic pump.

The most likely outcome for advertising of the present economic problems is, as already suggested, a strengthening of the position of foreign agencies in Japan. Japanese agencies are finding themselves in the unaccustomed situation of facing a weak and sluggish home market. And they are also conscious of the looming presence of well-established foreign agencies that are strong in their own countries and overseas and are willing to introduce resources and expertise into the Japanese advertising market. Such agencies are likely to be given a warmer welcome than they have received in the past.

Notes

1. Roderick White, "The Sun Also Rises," *Admap,* February 1999, 20-23.
2. Randall Rothenberg, *Where the Suckers Moon: An Advertising Story* (New York: Alfred A. Knopf, 1994), 372.
3. White, "The Sun Also Rises."
4. Ibid.
5. "Economic Indicators," *Economist,* February 6, 1999, 108.
6. Jonathan Watts, "Free Money Fails to Lure Japanese," *Guardian Weekly,* February 7, 1999, 5.

16

The Asia Pacific Tigers

Michael Ewing

As we move towards 2000, Asia will become the dominant region of the world: economically, politically and culturally. Up until the 1990s the West set the rules. Now Asians are creating their own rules and will soon determine the game as well. Even Japan will be left behind as the countries of South East Asia, led by the overseas Chinese and China, increasingly hold economic sway.

John Naisbitt, Megatrends Asia, 1996

Internationally renowned art critic Robert Hughes once said that nothing dates more quickly than visions of the future. For more than two decades international investors, business commentators, and politicians alike have viewed the tiger economies of the Asia Pacific as the ultimate metaphor for success, growth, employment, and myriad other economic virtues. Today, however, adjectives such as *miracle* are being replaced with *crisis*, and *melting* is used to describe economies once considered *boiling*. The traditional Chinese character for *crisis* has two faces, symbolizing both danger and opportunity. The question is, Which face will have more influence on advertising in the region at the start of the new century?

Anyone writing about the economies of East and Southeast Asia in 1999 cannot ignore the recent financial firestorm and its sometimes devastating aftermath. At the risk of suffering the same fate as earlier soothsayers, I will offer my thoughts on the medium-term prospects for the region. But I will not focus in this chapter principally on the impact of the meltdown. My key themes are the factors that make East Asia unique from an advertiser's perspective. These include a system of networking as powerful as any in the world, an attitude toward brands that sometimes turns Western logic on its head, a younger generation that may be "X" in name but not in nature, and the existence of Asia-wide psychographic segments that transcend national boundaries.

Undoubtedly, Asia is a region in transition. My own medium- to long-term outlook is far more positive than that of the popular press, and I view the current turn of events as a serious but necessary market adjustment. Unfortunately, the situation in some countries is compounded by political instability, lack of investor confidence, and various other structural and social complications. These elements notwithstanding, one simply cannot overlook Asia's importance to multinational advertisers or overstate the region's vast potential.

Although the future may hold enormous promise, the current financial crisis is very much a reality. Before I offer a discussion of the region in any detail, it is necessary to take stock briefly of the recent economic damage and contemplate its impact on the advertising industry. Over the past 2 years, most Asian countries have experienced severe declines in their currencies and loss of confidence in their markets. The three countries most affected have been Thailand, South Korea, and Indonesia. Financial turmoil forced Hong Kong, Malaysia, Thailand, South Korea, and Indonesia into gross domestic product decline during 1998, and the Philippines and Singapore have remained economically stagnant. The International Monetary Fund estimates that Indonesia, South Korea, Malaysia, and Thailand could collectively grow by about 0.6% in 1999 and as much as 3% in 2000, whereas economists with Goldman Sachs predict positive growth in Hong Kong, Singapore, Taiwan, Malaysia, and the Philippines in 1999.[1] Needless to say, 1997 saw advertising expenditure slashed across countries, industries, and media, and the full-year projection for 1998 is equally bleak (see Figures 16.1 and 16.2).

Regional publications posted a 16% drop in revenue between mid-1997 and mid-1998. Only three publications (*Financial Times, Business Week,* and

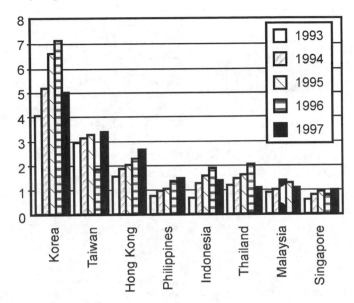

Figure 16.1. Ad Spend by Country, 1993-1997 (US$ billions)
SOURCE: Adapted from 1998 Asia Market Intelligence Ltd.; data courtesy of *Adweek Asia.*

USA Today) increased their ad revenues for the period (Figure 16.3), although this is somewhat misleading because all three derive a considerable portion of their income outside the region. In addition, media discounting has been prolific, and one can also assume that some fairly creative foreign exchange rate media deals have been struck recently.

Figure 16.2. Full-Year Ad Spend Estimate, 1998 (% change compared with 1997)
SOURCE: Zenith Media; data courtesy of *Adweek Asia.*

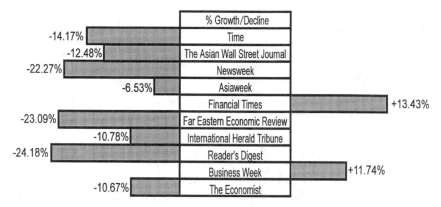

Figure 16.3. Top 10 Regional Publications, Ranked by Revenue, 1998 Versus 1997
SOURCE: CMR July 1998; data courtesy of *Adweek Asia.*

How one defines "the Asia Pacific" is open to question. The six original ASEAN trade partners of Indonesia, Malaysia, the Philippines, Singapore, and Thailand (excluding Brunei) provide a useful point of departure, to which I would add South Korea and Taiwan as well as Hong Kong, although it is now of course a Chinese special administrative region. Mainland China and Japan are excluded from this discussion, as are smaller, developing economies such as Cambodia, Myanmar, and Vietnam.

Asian Networks and the Overseas Chinese

One cannot even begin to understand the Asia Pacific region without appreciating the role of the overseas Chinese population and the enormous economic contribution of the members of that population, even in countries where they are the ethnic minority. In Malaysia, overseas Chinese account for 30% of the population but control more than half the economy. Elsewhere, the figures are even more impressive: In Thailand they are 3% of the population and control 60% of the economy; in both Indonesia and the Philippines, they are 3% of the population and control 70% of the economy. Collectively, they constitute the third-largest and arguably the most financially influential ethnic group on earth. Naisbitt calls them "the greatest entrepreneurs in the world!"[2] Ethnic Chinese residents in Asia control liquid assets of US$2 trillion, although this figure could be understated, the meltdown notwithstanding.[3] If we were to count the economic activity of all the overseas Chinese as a country in its own right, it would be outranked only by the United States and Japan. In addition, overseas Chinese account for 80% of all foreign investment in China itself.[4]

It is widely recognized that a key difference between Chinese and Western business practices lies in the relative importance Chinese businesspeople place on personal relationships, or *guanxi*.[5] *Guanxi* is a major dynamic in Chinese society and a key differentiator between Chinese companies and those of Japan and the West. *Guanxi* is literally translated as personal connections/relationships on which an individual can draw to secure resources or advantages when doing business as well as in the course of social life.[6] Arias offers a useful summary of the main characteristics of *guanxi*: (a) It includes the notion of a continuing reciprocal relationship over an indefinite time period; (b) favors are banked; (c) it extends beyond the relationship between two parties to include other parties within the social network (i.e., it can be transferred); (d) the relationship network is built among individuals, not organizations (therefore it is essentially a social network); (e) status matters—relationships with a senior will extend to his subordinates, but not vice versa; and (f) the social relationship is prior to and a prerequisite of the business relationship.[7]

Networks

The network marketing paradigm has been used by Western writers as a framework within which to examine *guanxi*.[8] A network is a metaphor for a large number of connected entities. More recently, the multicultural dimension of networks has been recognized. According to Achrol, Asian networks are held together by elaborate patterns of interdependence and reciprocity and a dense interconnection of culture and identity.[9] Networks are not exclusive to Chinese culture. The Japanese concept of *wa* and the Korean notion of *inhwa* are similar illustrations of intermarket and concentric networks.[10] Networks are equally pervasive in India, Russia, and other managed economies where intimacy with those in authority is important.[11] However, they are particularly dominant and ingrained in Chinese society. The Singapore Chinese Chamber of Commerce is reported to be launching a computer network that will link Chinese chambers of commerce worldwide and facilitate the flow of information for all Chinese entrepreneurs. Singapore's Senior Minister Lee Kuan Yew says that it would be a mistake not to use the ethnic Chinese network to increase Singapore's reach in the region.

I am not aware of any research that has examined *guanxi* from an advertising agency-client perspective, but it would be intriguing to know what influence it has on new business pitches as well as on ongoing relationships. In 1994, *Adweek Asia* (then *Asian Advertising & Marketing*) conducted a survey of 100 Asian managers on their expectations of an agency. Topping the list were "creatively very strong" (87%), "has standardized quality control procedures" (73%), "has strong media-buying skills" (78%), and "has local expertise at senior levels" (76%). An interesting finding is that 74% of the Asian managers surveyed said that they would switch to another agency if given the opportunity.[12] Whether this desire stems from the pull of *guanxi* is an open question.

Korean Chaebol

Networks are equally prevalent in South Korea. Government policy has traditionally favored local capitalists rather than transnational corporations, which has led to a concentration of private capital in the hands of a small number of conglomerates, the so-called *chaebol*.[13] With this state support, the *chaebol* have rapidly grown to dominate the local market. Before the recession, the top 10 *chaebol* (Samsung, Hyundai, Luck-Goldstar, Daewoo, Sunkyong, Saangyong, Hyosung, Hanjin, Korea Explosives, and Kia) had combined annual sales in excess of US$140 billion and accounted for almost 70% of South Korea's gross national product.[14] Not surprisingly, the concentrated economic structure dominated by the *chaebol* has had a major effect on the shape of the advertising industry, which has been typified by large in-house agencies within the *chaebol*. However, as Lesley Burt has pointed out, the economic downturn has sparked great interest by foreign agencies eagerly waiting to see whether the *chaebol* unbundle their operations and sell off their advertising arms.[15] Multinational agencies will no doubt capitalize on the favorable exchange rate and seize any opportunity to merge with or acquire Korean agencies.

Brands

As Manthorpe and Southam point out, "The great myth that Asia is a vast untapped mine of potential customers waiting for Western manufactured multinational products may turn out to be just that—a myth." [16] There is indeed vast potential, but there is no automatic guarantee of success. It depends on who you are and whom you are targeting. For certain manufacturers, Asia can be brand marketing utopia. For others, it has been an uphill struggle, with marketing strategies tried and tested in the West failing to have any impact in Asia. Perhaps the biggest mistake a multinational corporation can make is to underestimate Asian consumers. In my own experience, I have found Asian attitudes toward brands to be quite refreshing. In a marketing context, Asians are generally less inhibited than Westerners and in some respects are the ultimate conspicuous consumers. However, there is considerably more to this outward manifestation than meets the eye, and it would be a mistake to misinterpret it as a blanket adoption of "Western values." Paradoxically, Asians are highly astute shoppers and keenly price sensitive, challenging the very foundations of the value equation and keeping marketers honest.

Here are two personal observations about brands in East Asia. First, I am surprised by the scarcity of strong Asian-owned brands. There are a few notable exceptions (Acer computers, Tiger beer, Singapore Airlines, Jollibee fast foods), but generally Western and Japanese brands dominate. To some degree this may be due to much of the region's colonial roots as well as to the influence of Western media. There is also the time factor. Asia is recently developed, whereas brands like Coca-Cola, Lux, and Marlboro have been around for decades. It will be interesting to see whether more Asian brands emerge in time and, if so, how well they do both domestically and abroad. South Korea is of course an exception, and it is remarkable how quickly brands such as Samsung, Hyundai, and Daewoo have become household names throughout the world. Unfortunately, South Korea has been one of the worst hit by the recession, and it is difficult to predict what might happen in the short term in that country. In Taiwan, Stan Shih, chairman of the Own Brand

Federation, is currently working with local manufacturers to help them develop strong domestic brands. He says:

> We [Chinese] have never had our own brands. We are excellent at contract manufacturing for other brands. With the rise of Asian economies, manufacturers in Singapore, mainland China, Hong Kong and Taiwan must seriously contemplate creating world class indigenous brands. This will be the aspiration of business in the region in the next century.[17]

Second, it is both amusing and perplexing to see Asian consumers' apparent disdain of mass-market (dare I say blue-collar?) brands. The rampant brand piracy across the region provides economically disadvantaged consumers with alternatives to the "real thing." The automotive market represents an interesting case study. Ford is a dominant force in North America, the United Kingdom, and Australasia, and a major competitor in South America and most of Europe. It is undeniably a mass-market brand (Ford covers the top end of the market with Jaguar and Lincoln). Yet the company has struggled to achieve anywhere near the same penetration in Singapore, Hong Kong, and Malaysia, for example. In these countries, German and European brands dominate. In fact, BMW and Mercedes regularly posted some of their highest market shares in the world in Thailand before the recession. Similarly, consider Kmart's failed attempt to enter Singapore. Kmart is one of the most successful retailers in the United States, thanks in part to its broad mass-market appeal. However, Singaporean shoppers, who I consider to be among the most sophisticated consumers in the world, shunned the U.S. giant. By the same token, retailers who are perceived to be upmarket, such as Marks and Spencer, excel in Asia, as do the world's leading designer fashion houses, prestigious Swiss watches, and other premium brands.

Asia accounts for 34% of the world sales of the Vendome Luxury Group (Cartier, Dunhill Men's clothing, Piaget, and Baume & Mercier watches), and the group expects Asia to overtake Europe to become its largest market. Similarly, John Naisbitt observes that brand consciousness continues to rise and that those with the means will not settle for anything less than their favorite designer labels.[18] This behavior can to some degree be explained by the fact that Asian cultures revere status and power and accept the hierarchical structure of society.[19] In most Chinese societies, the upward mobility of people from the lower levels of the social hierarchy is also accepted (unlike the Indian caste system, for example). Astute marketers can capitalize on this by positioning their brands as aspirational and capable of improving some inherent quality of the user in the eyes of others.[20]

The Asian Youth Market

As a widely placed Hong Kong bank advertisement says, "There are 3 billion people in Asia. Half of them are under 25. Consider it a growing market." This is indeed, as Naisbitt suggests, a modern-day consumer miracle holding vast economic consequences. Until recently, the marketing literature dealing with 20- to 30-year-old consumers had a strong North American bias, where the cohort has been labeled "Generation X" (a name coined by post-baby boom American pop-art author Douglas Coupland). However, as Alice Pascual of Audits and Surveys Worldwide points out, "If one assumes that each generation is a product of the times, then 'the times' that brought about Generation X in America are not paralleled in Asia." [21] In fact, there have been few socioeconomic similarities between the two regions in recent years. In an analysis of 10 Asian countries, Pascual found that 20- to 30-year-old Asians share a variety of characteristics that differentiate them from their respective (national) populations at large. These differences were most pronounced in terms of media habits; hobbies and pastimes; tastes in clothing, food, and music; and travel destinations. One could argue, of course, and quite rightly, that every generation is different from the one before it. However, what makes the members of so-called Generation X particularly interesting is that in the United States they have gained a reputation as being "anti-advertising." According to the literature, American Xers appear to be completely uninterested in advertising targeted specifically at them, reject stereotypical portrayals of themselves as "young and foolish," and are generally opposed to the persuasive influence of television. Not surprisingly, they watch less TV than any other group.[22]

Given the popular sentiment regarding Generation Xers and their "attitude problem," a colleague and I decided to investigate the validity of the Generation X stereotype in Asia.[23] We set out to assess Asian Xers' overall attitudes toward advertising (i.e., advertisements) as well as their feelings regarding the *institution* and *practice* of advertising. To achieve this, we adapted Mittal's study of North American public assessment of advertising.[24] Data were collected in Singapore, Malaysia, and Hong Kong. Respondents were primarily students aged between 18 and 29. The sample was skewed toward respondents with higher levels of education, but we were not overly concerned by this as there is evidence to suggest that higher levels of education are generally associated with somewhat *less favorable* attitudes toward advertising. We found that the young people surveyed rather like advertising. Given that the sample might have been expected to show more skeptical attitudes toward advertising than the population as a whole, our sample did not overstate the general approval of advertising.[25] As Larry Light points out, "This is the age of the smarter generation, where consumers will be even more demanding, more educated, more informed and more skeptical than ever before." [26]

Contrary to "Western logic," our research confirmed an overall positive attitude toward advertising. The overwhelming majority (more than 85%) of respondents consider advertising to be at least somewhat essential, and most agreed that advertising is important to them. Furthermore, more than half of the respondents surveyed claimed actually to like advertising, which, given the plethora of literature highlighting the importance of likability in advertising, is indeed a significant and encouraging revelation for Asian advertisers. Following the broad guidelines suggested by Mittal, our research examined Asian Xers' perceptions regarding the consequences of advertising.[27] This particular focus seemed pertinent, given Xers' apparent disdain of both marketers and their advertising attempts. A total of 28 statements reflecting beliefs about advertising's desirable and undesirable consequences were explored (these statements are arranged under nine broad headings in Table 16.1).

Respondents generally considered advertising a valuable source of marketplace information, particularly in terms of keeping them up-to-date on product availability. Although respondents' confidence in advertised brands/products was not particularly high, most conceded that in the absence of advertising, decision making would in fact be more difficult. In terms of social image information, it would appear that advertising does act as a fairly good social barometer, keeping consumers in touch with the marketplace. Furthermore, most respondents acknowledged that (TV) advertising still holds entertainment value—another optimistic finding for Asian marketers.

With regard to some of the less desirable consequences of advertising, most respondents agreed that advertising is making society more materialistic. However, in terms of value congruence, a surprisingly high proportion of respondents could in fact relate to the values portrayed in advertising (possibly a slightly exaggerated finding, due to a more controlled advertising environment in many Asian countries). By contrast, most respondents held fairly strong beliefs regarding the negative effects of advertising on children. Respondents by and large echoed the fairly common economic criticisms of advertising, but as with buying confidence, they did acknowledge that advertising is at worst a necessary evil—in that consumers would not be better off in the absence of advertising.

In summary, young Asians appear to have more positive attitudes toward advertising than their American counterparts (or at least the popular stereotype of American youth). Members of the cohort are fairly eager recipients of advertising and tend to feel that if advertising were eliminated, consumers would be worse off. Advertising seems to provide them with assistance in deciding what to buy when choice is difficult and it keeps them informed and up-to-date, especially about what is in fashion and what they should buy in order to keep a good social image. The message seems to be: *We know that in some respects it isn't good for us, but isn't it great!* Advertising's ability to assist the audience in maintaining a good social image appears to be a particularly important issue in many Asian countries.

As a practitioner turned academic, I am always concerned about the external validity and managerial relevance of my research. It was therefore satisfying to learn that the Ogilvy & Mather (O&M) Genie study supports my findings. As Miles Young, Pacific president of Ogilvy & Mather Asia, said:

> Young Asian adults—tomorrow's leaders—are emerging as a very distinct phenomenon. They are more independent than their parents' generation, but they are also far more conservative and community orientated than is often recognized. It's been easy to assume that superficial adoption of Western fashions means a deeper influence of the West, and this study suggests this is not the case. Marketers and advertisers who do not recognize this are, quite simply, failing to relate to their target audience.[28]

O&M interviewed more than 7,000 individuals and conducted 66 focus groups of 20- to 30-year-olds across nine South, East, and Southeast Asian markets. In terms of their response to advertising, the agency concluded that the cohort does enjoy the entertainment aspects of advertising, but that advertising does not have the same social context it does in the West. In other words, it rarely becomes part of the vernacular in Asian communities. Con-

TABLE 16.1 Asian Xers' Perceptions of the Uses and Consequences of Advertising

Marketplace information,	
Advertising is a valuable source of information about local sales.	4.95
Advertising tells me which brands have the features I am looking for.	4.77
Advertising keeps me up-to-date about products available in the market.	5.61
Buying confidence,	
One can put more trust in products that are advertised than those that are not.	3.84
Advertising helps the consumer buy the best brand for the price.	3.48
If there were no advertising, deciding what to buy would be difficult.	4.41
Social image information,	
Advertising tells me what people like myself are buying and using.	4.13
Advertising helps me know which products will help me reflect the sort of person I am.	4.04
From advertising I learn what is in fashion and what I should buy for keeping a good social image.	4.69
Entertainment value,	
Sometimes I take pleasure in thinking about what I heard or saw in advertising.	4.83
Some advertising makes me feel good.	4.93
Sometimes TV commercials are even more enjoyable than TV programs.	4.44
Materialism,	
Advertising is making us into a materialistic society interested in buying and owning things.	5.15
Advertising makes people buy unaffordable products just to show off.	4.48
Advertising sometimes makes people live in a world of fantasy.	4.86

sumers internalize their liking and respond to the rational appeals with the "outer me" and to the more emotional appeals with the "inner me."

In summary, the O&M findings debunk three myths about young adults in Asia:

- **Myth 1:** *Young Asians are consumed by materialism; they don't care about society.* In reality, Asian values such as hard work, humility, saving, and family values are much more durable than ever previously imagined.
- **Myth 2:** *There is a "GenerAsian X," made up of young people who feel unhappy and apart from the rest of society.* In fact, Asian youth are very positive in their outlook and are grateful to society for the work and leisure opportunities afforded them.
- **Myth 3:** *There is no such thing as an "Asian" youth; there are too many cultural differences across Asian countries.* In fact, despite one or two marked differences in individual country results, there is a large degree of homogeneity across Asia in terms of the cohort's more deeply held values.

TABLE 16.1 *Continued*

Value congruence,	
In advertising I often see my own values and beliefs portrayed.	4.01
A lot of advertising is based on ideas and values which are opposite to my own.	4.20
There is too much sex in advertising.	3.17
Effects on children,	
Advertising leads children to make unreasonable purchase demands on parents.	5.58
Advertising takes advantage of children.	5.06
Advertising plays an important role in educating children about what products are good for them.	3.29
Economic effects,	
Advertising improves people's standard of living.	4.40
Advertising increases the costs of products.	5.85
It would be best for companies to save money on advertising and invest the money on improving the product.	4.67
If advertising were eliminated consumers would be better off.	3.55
Manipulation,	
Advertising makes you buy what you do not need.	4.48
Sometimes I have bought things simply because of a TV commercial.	4.17
I am never really persuaded by advertising to buy a product.	3.62

NOTE: Scores shown are averages on a 7-point scale on which 1 = low and 7 = high. Cronbach's alpha = .8167. Sample sizes: Singapore, $n = 55$; Malaysia, $n = 106$; Hong Kong, $n = 43$.

Generation "Y"

Although 19- to 30-year-olds generate considerable economic clout, one should not ignore the cohort that will shortly be replacing them. Not only are children and teenagers future consumers in their own right, but they exert a formidable influence on family consumption. Recognizing this, A. C. Nielsen and TNT/Cartoon Network recently conducted a study of Asian children ages 7 to 18.[29] A quota-controlled sample of 5,700 ensured maximum coverage across 18 major Asian cities. This study's findings confirm that "watching television" is the segment's favorite leisure activity and is something they would like to do more of. Figure 16.4 shows the percentage of respondents who watch 2 or more hours a day. Between 50% and 80% of respondents are allowed to watch television anytime they want to. Interestingly enough, most

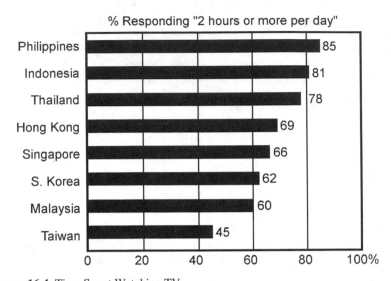

Figure 16.4. Time Spent Watching TV
SOURCE: New Generasians™; data courtesy of A. C. Nielsen, Hong Kong.
NOTE: Respondents were asked, "How much time do you spend watching TV?" Base = all respondents 7/8 to 18 years of age.

also find time to read newspapers, particularly in Malaysia, Thailand, and South Korea.

Figure 16.5 shows annual pocket money and gifts received by respondents. Although the average amounts may appear somewhat modest, particularly in Malaysia, the Philippines, and Indonesia, the total value of the "Asian kids' economy" is an impressive US$463 billion. Furthermore, as already mentioned, children wield considerable influence on family decision making. Figure 16.6 shows the top 15 product categories ranked by children's influence scores. Korean, Filipino, and Thai children exert the most influence, whereas Indonesian, Singaporean, and Malaysian children have the least "pestering power." Clearly, the message for multinational advertisers is "Don't forget the kids."

White-Collar Asia

Cross-national studies of values are potentially relevant to the explanation of differences in buying behavior. A recent study of international advertising

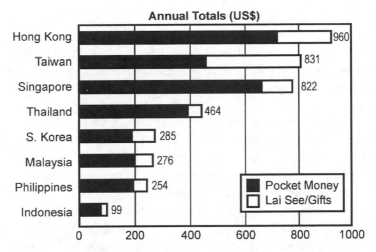

Figure 16.5. Pocket Money and Gifts
SOURCE: New Generasians™; data courtesy of A. C. Nielsen, Hong Kong.
NOTE: Respondents were asked,, "How much pocket money do you receive in a week?" and "Roughly how much money do you receive as gifts during the year?" Base = all respondents 7/8 to 18 years of age (based on US$ exchange rate at time of fieldwork).

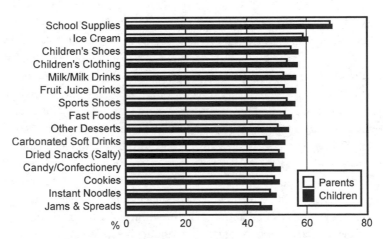

Figure 16.6. Children's Influence on Purchases (1-15 of 30 product categories ranked by children's influence scores)
SOURCE: New Generasians ™; data courtesy of A. C. Nielsen, Hong Kong.
NOTE: Base = all respondents 7/8 to 18 years of age.

decision makers found that the "Think globally, act locally" philosophy still appears to be the dominant strategy of international advertisers, but with a slight revision: "Think globally, act regionally." [30] In reality, the global/local dichotomy is actually a continuum, with many advertisers using a combination approach. For most, this entails localized execution but a degree of standardization in the message.[31] In this regard, we have progressed from product marketing to an era that Marieke de Mooij calls "value marketing": the consistent linking of brands to product-related values. Advertisers connect values with lifestyles, and every lifestyle is characterized by a number of values, which are shared to a greater or lesser extent by the members of a group. Clustering these value patterns may reveal lifestyle segments toward which advertising can be targeted. Such clustering can also be linked to media usage, which is useful in media planning.[32]

Commercial lifestyle research surveys have been conducted in Hong Kong, Malaysia, Singapore, Thailand, Taiwan, and other Asian counties. However, these studies have focused on the individual countries rather than across the region. Furthermore, they are rather out-of-date and probably of little relevance in the present economic climate.

A more recent study focused on Asian executives and businesspeople (white-collar workers). Respondents were males and females between the ages of 20 and 49. Fieldwork was conducted during May 1998 in five Asian cities: Bangkok (Thailand), Hong Kong, Kuala Lumpur/Petaling Jaya (Malaysia), Manila (Philippines), and Singapore. A total of 100 interviews were conducted in each city. In Hong Kong and Singapore, respondents were drawn from households in the top 50% in terms of gross household income; in the other three cities, they were drawn from the top 30%. Respondents were randomly selected and interviewed face-to-face, using a structured questionnaire. Only executives and businesspeople were interviewed. The client was Japanese advertising giant Hakuhodo Inc. The research supplier was Audits and Surveys Worldwide (Asia Pacific). I was involved in the data analysis.

Following is a brief summary of the study's key findings. Bear in mind that this study was exploratory in nature, and, given the modest sample sizes, generalizations should be made with extreme caution. The overriding objective of the research was to determine the feasibility of cross-national psychographic segmentation. In this context, the findings are interesting, particularly in certain product categories, under particular market conditions, and depending on the stature of the brand itself. Six psychographic segments are briefly described below. As is always the case in data reduction procedures (factor or cluster analysis), labeling of the output is a highly subjective process, and it is quite possible that there are more appropriate names for the clusters than the ones we have chosen.

Aspirationals (22%). The Aspirationals are a future-oriented segment. Even though they have attained managerial/professional status at a relatively young age, they perceive their major achievements to be still ahead of them. They are experienced in the ways of the world and admire those who have taken the opportunity to work overseas. They aspire to do the same, eventually. However, they are not yet as widely traveled as those in some other segments. They are more spiritual than those in other segments and are interested in community work and religious activities. The Aspirationals are strongly represented in KL/PJ and Manila, which explains this spirituality. Religion is a way of life in both Malaysia and the Philippines; Malaysians are brought up with strong Islamic beliefs, and Catholicism is instilled in most Filipinos from an early age. In contrast, the Chinese in Hong Kong and Singapore tend to develop their spirituality later in life. Those in this segment believe that children should be obedient and respectful to their parents. They are generally pro-Establishment. They prefer Western or pop/rock music, are keen readers and moviegoers, and favor sports such as soccer and swimming, although they are more likely to be spectators than participants.

Contented Homebodies (15%). The Contented Homebodies have already achieved many of their goals and have realized their primary ambitions. They are now content to spend more time with their families. They constitute the oldest segment and are mostly married. They are strongly represented in Singapore and Bangkok. The government policies in Singapore, in particular, provide an added feeling of security and stability for this segment. They are not as concerned about their outward appearance and are not as conspicuous a group of consumers as some of the other segments. Contented Homebodies are the most conservative segment. They adhere to the same beliefs as their parents and prefer to do things the old way. They do not believe in "rocking the boat." They are practical and cautious consumers.

Contemporary Seekers (18%). Contemporary Seekers are highly energetic. They live life to the full and are constantly looking for new things to do, places to go, people to meet. They are very socially aware. They want to be seen in the right places and to look good. They like to socialize with friends, especially at restaurants and shopping malls. Friendship is very important to the members of this gregarious segment. They are trendy, although not necessarily innovators themselves, and are highly conspicuous consumers. Contemporary Seekers have a social conscience, although they are not as spiritually inclined as the Aspirationals. They want to help people less fortunate than themselves. Contemporary Seekers are those most interested in culture and the arts. They like art, antiques, and fashion shows. Despite their energy and their interest in travel, they themselves are not yet particularly well traveled.

Cyber-Individualists (9%). Cyber-Individualists are hard workers who use the latest technology to make themselves more efficient. They still believe that success comes from hard work and ability. By making sacrifices now, they can provide better lives for themselves and their families in the future. They are globally oriented and accepting of foreign nationalities. They are well traveled, and many have studied abroad. Most Cyber-Individualists are from Hong Kong. They are independent in nature and are less conformist than the older generation. Cyber-Individualists have the latest technology at their disposal. They own their own computers, surf the Web, and are seldom without their cell phones. They also like music and own the latest audio equipment. They are time-constrained and have few hobbies outside work and home.

Network Belongers (11%). The Network Belongers are very sociable people. They have large networks of friends and acquaintances with whom they interact frequently. In fact, their personal values are strongly influenced by network/group norms. They are very conscious of their appearance and strive for peer approval and acceptance. They are outwardly happy and generally contented people. They like reading entertainment news, as this includes gossip that they can share with their friends. They like to participate in group-based activities such as sports and karaoke. Network Belongers are domestically oriented and have little interest in traveling or working abroad.

Suppressed Strivers (25%). The Suppressed Strivers are frustrated, stressed individuals and are not particularly content with life. They are motivated but have generally underachieved. This results in conflict—most likely conflict with their families and/or society as a whole. Family conflict could be caused by a need to become more independent from their parents. Societal conflict could be caused by suppression in conformity with cultural norms. Members of this segment are in a Catch-22 situation. Their beliefs are different from those of their parents, yet their ingrained respect for their elders makes it difficult for them to articulate their inner feelings.

In summary, there is evidence that the notion of a multicountry Asian typology has potential, and that there are indeed a number of characteristics that Asians share regardless of their nationalities. However, it is also equally obvious that there are differences among countries. For example, there is a higher concentration of Filipinos and Malaysians among Aspirationals, a higher representation of Singaporeans and Thais among Contented Homebodies, and considerably more Hong Kong nationals among the Cyber-Individualists. For advertisers, the challenge is to see where global advertising appeals and message strategies will be successful and where more localized approaches are called for.

Future Imperfect

As I write this chapter, most of Asia is experiencing the worst economic and/or sociopolitical turmoil in recent history. Even rock-solid Singapore, with its near-perfect infrastructure, market, and governance mechanisms, is reeling from the backlash of the regional shake-up. As a Singaporean friend once said to me, "If one of our neighbors catches a cold, we get double pneumonia!" Such is the strong level of interdependence throughout most of the region. Those in the know believe that it will take at least 3 years for the key economic indicators in Asia to start tracking northward again. Either way, it is likely that there will be at least three important issues emerging.

1. It is probable that after the dust settles, a revised Asian order will surface. If anything, the developed-developing country continuum will be more extreme. Despite the new regime in Indonesia, life there remains as volatile as ever, and marketers are being forced to devise new approaches to reach economically impoverished consumers. Unilever recently launched new soaps and detergents under the Sunlight name at discounts of up to 30%. The consumer goods giant is also selling products such as shampoo in

sample-sized containers at a fraction of the cost of full-sized ones, because consumers simply cannot afford the latter.[33]

Thailand will go to the polls soon to decide its destiny, and there are concerns that the coalition government will not retain power. In the interim, some companies are concentrating on building brand awareness in Thailand. Increased spending on hair-care advertising by both Procter & Gamble and Unilever led to a 12% increase in category advertising expenditure in the first 8 months of 1998.

Following a US$3.2 million Commonwealth Games advertising campaign and a week of being under the international spotlight, few commentators would have predicted the current Malaysian political problems, radical monetary policy, and hostile investment climate.

South Korea is another unpredictable entity. In relative terms, it has been worst hit by the economic storm, with advertising investments slashed and staff retrenchments in advertising and media organizations. However, with the IMF program in place, ever-optimistic South Korean agency heads believe their country might recover more quickly than some of its Southeast Asian neighbors.[34]

Taiwan seems to have escaped surprisingly unscathed and may well use the opportunity to catapult itself further ahead of its regional neighbors.

Singapore is a difficult case to comment on. In its own right it is practically immune to the internal problems being experienced by its neighbors. However, because Singapore is sandwiched between Malaysia and Indonesia, its future depends on the degree to which it can decrease its dependence on its neighbors and expand its relationships with China, India, and the rest of the world. Fortunately, its geographic location and world-class infrastructure will ensure that it will remain the regional hub for some time to come.

2. I firmly believe that in the long run, penny-wise and pound-foolish advertisers will pay for their shortsightedness. Serious multinational advertisers who intend to maintain a long-term presence in the region should heed David Ogilvy's advice regarding advertising expenditure during a recession. In a study of the 1974-1975 recession in the United States, it was found that companies that continued to advertise experienced higher sales and higher net income during the recession and for the 2 years following recovery.[35] I believe that this possibility is of greater-than-average importance in Asia. When the tide turns, firms that have taken a long-term view and continued

to invest in their brands will outperform those that have concentrated on survival tactics. Leo Burnett's Asia Pacific president, Steve Gatfield, agrees. His agency's consumer research shows that consumers are not ready to sacrifice health care products or nutritious food for the family, but may postpone luxuries such as an overseas holiday or a new car.[36] Hong Kong, with its currency pegged to the U.S. dollar, is a notable exception, as is Taiwan, albeit to a lesser extent.

3. My final "postdepression" prediction pertains to the new media environment and the role of technology. Cable television is expected to continue its impressive growth, paralleled by an associated boom in home shopping networks. Asian satellite television networks, such as STAR TV, offer another alternative to regional advertisers, and ad sales have been surprisingly strong for some of the regional satellite and cable networks. According to a Price Waterhouse/Multichannel Advertising Bureau report, advertisers spent an impressive US$104 million in the first 4 months of 1998.[37] STAR TV believes that there will be a major expansion in the merchandising industry as programming expands the demand for existing material.[38] *Adweek Asia* has provided a detailed summary of major satellite services in Asia, with information on footprint spans, types of programming, reach figures, and future developments.[39]

For some time now, Singapore, Taiwan, South Korea, Hong Kong, and Malaysia have all been striving to create high-tech communities. Figure 16.7 shows Internet usage across the Asia Pacific. Singapore's IT2000 plan aims to transform the community into an "Intelligent Island" by creating a computer infrastructure that covers business, education, and even family life. *Australian Personal Computing* magazine recently rated Singapore the second most IT-literate country on earth, with more than 40% of its population using computers on a daily basis. The plan to develop a broad-based integrated services digital network will see the beginning of the electronic newspaper and magazine, overlapping the activities of traditional broadcasting and print publishers.[40] Malaysia has developed its own Multimedia Super Corridor (MSC) as part of its "Vision 2020." The plan includes a paperless government, multimedia university, telemedicine hospital, international schools, and various multimedia companies. Microsoft, IBM, Sun Microsystems, Netscape, and Oracle are all involved in the project.

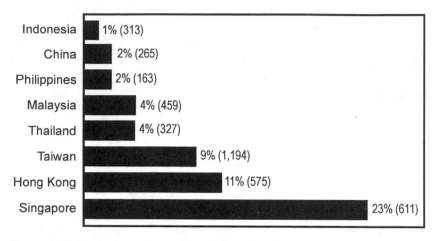

Figure 16.7. The Internet: Current User Penetration (%) and User Population (in thousands)
SOURCE: NetWatch Asia '98; data courtesy of A. C. Nielsen, Hong Kong.

Conclusion

It is now clear that some of the rhetoric about the so-called Asian miracle was overblown. We should all have known better. But as is often the case, the pendulum of opinion has swung the other way too far, too quickly. The blanket pessimism about Asia's prospects today is no more sensible than the outlandish optimism that lasted until July 1997. Asia was and is one of the most exciting economic regions of the world. It is simply too large and too dynamic to ignore. Its people are too skilled and too motivated to be held back forever.

Recovery certainly will be patchy. Some countries will fare better than others. Investors will need to pay much greater heed to the fundamentals than in the recent past. Realism and discipline, not hype, will be the order of the day. This is, of course, no bad thing.

For advertisers, the key is to understand the market. Superficial headlines should not be allowed to mislead. There are many myths about Asia, but an important truth is that the region is different from the West. Attitudes are different, the media are different, values are different. Bangkok is not Baltimore. Singapore is not Stockholm.

The best advice for marketers and advertisers is to have faith: Do your homework first, but continue to invest; the long-term rewards will be there.

Notes

I would not have been able to complete this chapter without the help of various special people. In no particular order, I would like to thank Nigel de Bussy, for his insightful comments on an earlier draft; Leslie Burt and Daniela Francisci at *Adweek Asia,* for helping me out with the facts and figures; Jansen Yeoh at Ogilvy & Mather (Malaysia), for personally taking me through the O&M Genie study; and Alice Pascual and Andrew Ammundsen at Audits and Surveys Worldwide (Philippines), for giving me the opportunity to understand the Asian marketplace better. I would also like to thank Hakuhodo Inc. (Tokyo), for allowing me to publish findings from the agency's proprietary Asian psychographics study; and Steve Garton at A. C. Nielsen (Hong Kong), for his useful comments and assistance. Even after all this help, I lay sole claim to any inaccuracies or errors.

1. Lesley Burt, "The Effects of the Economic Recession on Advertising in Asia," speech delivered to the International Advertising Association, Japan Chapter, Tokyo, October 28, 1998.

2. John Naisbitt, *Megatrends Asia* (London: Nicholas Brealey, 1996), 3.

3. Philip Kotler, Swee Hoon Ang, Siew Meng Leong, and Chin Tiong Tan, *Marketing Management: An Asian Perspective* (Singapore: Prentice Hall-Simon & Schuster, 1986), 523.

4. Howard A. Davies, Thomas K. P. Leung, Sherriff T. L. Luk, and Yiu-hing Wong, "The Benefits of 'Guanxi': The Value of Relationships in Developing the Chinese Market," *Industrial Marketing Management,* vol. 24, 1995, 207-214.

5. Kotler et al., *Marketing Management,* 523.

6. Howard A. Davies, "Interpreting 'Guanxi': The Role of Personal Connections in a High Context Transitional Economy," in Howard A. Davies (ed.), *China Business: Context and Issues* (Hong Kong: Longman Asia, 1996), 155-169.

7. Jose T. G. Arias, "A Relationship Marketing Approach to Guanxi," *European Journal of Marketing,* vol. 32, nos. 1-2, 1998, 145-156.

8. F. R. Dwyer, P. H. Schurr, and S. Oh, "Developing Buyer-Seller Relationships," *Journal of Marketing,* vol. 5, 1987, 11-27. See also Hans B. Thorelli, "Networks: The Gay Nineties in Industrial Marketing," in Hans B. Thorelli and S. T. Cavusgil (eds.), *International Marketing Strategy* (Oxford: Pergamon, 1990); J. C. Anderson and J. A. Narus, "A Model of Distributor Firm and Manufacturer Firm Working Partnerships," *Journal of Marketing,* vol. 54, 1990, 42-58.

9. R. Achrol, "The Evolution of the Marketing Organization: New Forms of Turbulent Environment," *Journal of Marketing,* vol. 55, 1997, 77-93.

10. Kotler et al., *Marketing Management,* 264.

11. U. Lehtinen, "Relationship Marketing Approaches in Changing Russian Markets," *Journal of East-West Business,* vol. 1, no. 4, 1996, 35-49.

12. Kotler et al., *Marketing Management,* 791.

13. Kwangmi Ko Kim, "Advertising in Korea: International Changes and Politics," in Katherine T. Frith (ed.), *Advertising in Asia: Communication, Culture and Consumption* (Ames: Iowa State University Press, 1996), 127.

14. Ibid.

15. Burt, "The Effects of the Economic Recession."

16. J. Manthorpe and N. Southam, "Balancing Act," *Montreal Gazette,* July 16, 1995, B5.

17. Stan Shih, translated from the Taiwan-based *Excellence* magazine and the Hong Kong-based *Yauzhou Zhoukan* magazine, as quoted in Naisbitt, *Megatrends Asia,* 19.

18. Naisbitt, *Megatrends Asia,* 41.

19. Ernest F. Martin, Jr., "Advertising in Hong Kong," in Katherine T. Frith (ed.), *Advertising in Asia: Communication, Culture and Consumption* (Ames: Iowa State University Press, 1996), 51.

20. M. L. Vittratorn Chirapravati, "The Blossoming of Advertising in Asia," in Katherine T. Frith (ed.), *Advertising in Asia: Communication, Culture and Consumption* (Ames: Iowa State University Press, 1996), 225.

21. Alice Pascual, "Decoding Generation X," paper presented at the Institute for International Research's International Conference on Generation X, Singapore, 1995.

22. S. Donaton, "The Media Wakes Up to Generation X," *Advertising Age,* January 1993, 16. See also S. Harrington, "In Between Young and Foolish & Old, Boring," *Advertising Age,* February 1996, 28; Karen Macalister, "The X Generation," *HR Magazine,* May 1994, 66-71; H. Stipp, "Xers Are Not Created Equal," *Mediaweek,* March 1994, 20.

23. Michael T. Ewing and Albert Caruana, "Communicating With the Cohort: Exploring Generation X Asia's Attitudes Towards Advertising," *Journal of International Consumer Marketing,* vol. 11, no. 1, 1999, 41-54.

24. Banwari Mittal, "Public Assessment of TV Advertising: Faint Praise and Harsh Criticism," *Journal of Advertising Research,* January/February 1994, 35-53.

25. Ibid.

26. Larry Light, "The Changing Advertising World," *Journal of Advertising Research,* February/March 1990, 34.

27. Mittal, "Public Assessment of TV Advertising."

28. Miles Young, quoted in "Enter the 'Genie!' Ogilvy & Mather Signals Arrival of a New, Distinctively Asian Generation," Ogilvy & Mather press release, Hong Kong, May 13, 1997.

29. Anthony Dobson and Duncan Morris, "The New GenerAsians," paper presented at the 2nd ESOMAR Asia Pacific Marketing Research Conference, Manila, November 17, 1998.

30. Jan Jaben, "Ad Decision-Makers Favor Regional Angle," *Advertising Age International,* May 1995, 3.

31. Ali Kanso, "International Advertising Strategies: Global Commitment to Local Vision," *Journal of Advertising Research,* January/February 1992, 10-14.

32. Marieke de Mooij, *Advertising Worldwide: Concepts, Theories and Practices of International, Multinational and Global Advertising,* 2nd ed. (Englewood Cliffs, NJ: Prentice Hall International, 1994), 160.

33. Burt, "The Effects of the Economic Recession."

34. Ibid.

35. Ibid.

36. Ibid.

37. Ibid.

38. Kotler et al., *Marketing Management,* 810.

39. "A&M Satellite Television Channels," *Adweek Asia,* February 6, 1998, 14-15.

40. Kotler et al., *Marketing Management,* 810.

17

Is India an Asian Tiger?

John Philip Jones

Marketing people in the United States, with their natural tidiness of mind and fascination with classification, tend to put the countries of Asia into three groups (countries in each group are listed here in order of population):

1. *The highly developed economies:* Japan, Hong Kong, and Singapore
2. *The rapid developers:* Thailand, South Korea, Taiwan, and Malaysia
3. *The rest:* China, India, Indonesia, Pakistan, Bangladesh, Vietnam, the Philippines, Myanmar, North Korea, Sri Lanka, and Cambodia

Measured by their per capita gross domestic product (GDP), the first group of countries generates annual wealth at a rate of US$20,000. The second group's annual GDP is in the $10,000 bracket. These are the countries often referred to as the Pacific Tigers. The countries in the third group all produce $3,000 or less—some, such as India, a good deal below this level. What worsens the disparity between the third group and the others is that the third group is by far the largest in terms of population, accounting for 2.8 billion of the 3.1 billion in the 18 countries as a whole.

Americans therefore see a picture of a relatively small collection of countries that have lifted their economies up to Western standards, another small group of countries that are moving up rapidly, and a vast and heterogeneous third group of countries that are still economically only half awake. The facts support this generalization, at least in terms of aggregates. But simple aggregates can be misleading.

For a start, it is difficult to make meaningful generalizations about the *causes* of various rates of economic development in different countries because of the many factors that influence such development and the relative importance of the factors case by case. I am thinking, inter alia, of natural resources, degree of industrial development, political and fiscal systems, education and skills, communications of all types, the entrepreneurial spirit, access to capital, and access to markets. For simplicity I shall lump all these factors together and call them the *commercial infrastructure.* If this is sound, it can have an astonishing effect over a period of a few decades—witness the relative progress since World War II of Taiwan versus China and of South Korea versus North Korea.

However, quick fixes (e.g., the injection of outside capital) are rarely effective on their own. The commercial infrastructure must be built within the country, and this is normally best done by the nation's own business and political leaders, the former generally being more effective at the job than the latter.

I believe that India represents a very special case. From some points of view India is out of place in the third group of relatively backward countries. For one thing, India represents a most significant mass. In population, it is the second-largest country on earth, and the total value of its annual GDP puts it already in the world's top 15 economies. It is among the top 10 steel producers, and it is one of the few atomic powers—itself not necessarily a desirable accomplishment but a sign of economic significance. Perhaps more important, it is one of the world's leaders in the computer industry.

The most salient economic fact about India—and something that surprises people who do not know the country—is that its commercial infrastructure is in most respects remarkably well developed. There is political freedom; India is, after all, the largest democracy in the world, although the price it pays for its vigorous system is some degree of political instability. It has a relatively well-educated population. There are many world-class Indian-born university professors, many of them working in the United States and Europe—something to be regretted, because they could be enormous contributors at home. India has a powerful entrepreneurial spirit. There is no shortage of raw materials. Investment capital is available from both internal and overseas sources, especially now that we see real advances in economic liberalization. India has reasonably effective physical communications and a good supply of news and advertising media. Knowledge of English—the international language of business—is far more common among Indian businesspeople than is the case among businesspeople in France or Germany, not to speak of Japan.

In view of all these advantages—advantages that have unquestionably protected India from the grave problems that have afflicted the Pacific Tiger economies at the end of the 1990s—what is inhibiting India's progress? And is India on the brink of something bigger? I shall argue that the latter is the case. I shall concentrate on my own specialist field—the marketing of mass-market consumer goods and services. In this, India is reasonably well advanced in all important respects except one, which I shall describe shortly.

Most top-flight international marketers sell their goods and services in India. There is no shortage of totally Indian-owned enterprises as well. The purchasing patterns of those members of the Indian population who earn enough income to buy discretionary goods and services—a group I shall call *discretionary income* or DI households—are more similar to than dissimilar from those of the better-off classes in New York, London, Paris, or Tokyo. These people have all been similarly educated; they dress in the same way; they consume food and beverages of similar quality; they use the same credit cards; their houses and apartments are similarly equipped; they watch as much television; they travel as widely, although there are, relatively speaking, fewer cars in India than in the other countries. Most important, they lead lives of similar social sophistication. It is not just a matter of having the same material possessions; they have the same educated tastes.

There are large numbers of such people in North America, Europe, and Japan. There are also large numbers of them in India. The difference is that, as a proportion of the total population, DI households represent a majority in North America, Europe, and Japan, but only a minority—albeit a substantial minority—in India.

How large a minority are the DI households in India? According to a recent estimate made by Tata Services, India has 16.2 million households classified as "high income." This is defined as an annual income of 86,000 rupees or more. At an official dollar exchange rate, this translates to a figure of less than US$3,000. Yet, as anyone who is familiar with the low cost of living in India can testify, 86,000 rupees certainly represents an income in the Indian environment large enough to be classified as a DI. With an average four-person household, we can therefore visualize a DI population in India of well over 60 million people. This is the same size as the population of Thailand. It is larger than South Korea, larger than Taiwan, and larger than Malaysia. In fact, it is almost half the size of all four of these Pacific Tigers added together.

There are two other features of this simple analysis. First, India's annual growth—6% in real terms—is comparable to that of the Pacific Tigers before the recent recession and far ahead of the fully developed economies of North America and Europe. Remember that an uninterrupted compound growth of 6% per annum—India's present level and the anticipated level for the next few years—will double a GDP in less than 14 years; it will double it again in a further 14, again 14 years later, and yet again 14 years after that. This means that such growth will bring to India, by the middle of the 21st century, a total GDP 16 times its present size. No matter how much other economies grow within their current parameters—a reasonable assumption based on general economic history—India is likely to become one of the major players on the world economic stage by the middle of the next century.

The second aspect of my analysis—something that directly stems from my growth projection—is that such an increase will inevitably mobilize the economic potential, both as producers and as consumers, of the immeasurably large Indian population whose income is at the moment below the DI threshold. This trickle down of wealth will solve India's most intractable economic problem, rural poverty. It is difficult to comprehend what such a future holds for the growth prospects of consumer goods marketers.

The important participants in such growth are already operating in the Indian market, although I doubt whether they foresee a future quite in the terms I have described. Among the internationals, Unilever has a long and distinguished history in India. Procter & Gamble, Colgate-Palmolive, Nestlé, Reckitt & Colman, Coca-Cola, Pepsi-Cola, Kellogg's, and many other world-class companies are well established. Both Ford and General Motors have begun operations. Indian enterprises, especially those well attuned to the consumption patterns and also the production capabilities of the Indian population, are often successful enough to steal major market opportunities from under the noses of the internationals. I believe instinctively that this pattern will continue.

What are the impediments to the realization of even greater growth and change in the future? I think there is only one of any importance. It is not production systems—these are already contributing to efficient large-scale manufacture, and in this, certain of the more perceptive organizations base their systems on the special characteristics of the Indian economy, in particular the large supply of semiskilled labor.

It is not marketing and advertising, which are carried out by experienced practitioners with a good understanding of local conditions—witness the relatively small package sizes, planned to accustom Indian consumers to buying prepackaged consumer goods.

Indian advertising has a special flavor. The major campaigns—almost invariably the work of the larger international agencies—are based on good research and are focused on the special characteristics of the Indian consumer. There is a highly developed Indian film industry; in terms of the output of feature films, it is the largest in the world.

There is no misunderstanding of branding. Brands are directed with considerable sensitivity at the Indian market, taking account of the differences (e.g., in food consumption patterns) between India and Western countries. Physical delivery of goods to retailers is also efficient.

The only serious difficulty impeding dynamic growth in the various consumer goods fields is the backward state of the Indian distributive trade, where the consumer confronts the brand at firsthand. I have visited a few small, well-planned self-service stores in Bombay and Madras, but there are very few such places, and nothing approaching an American supermarket, although it is premature to expect such organizations to be established in city outskirts or suburbs in India, because of the relative scarcity of personal automobiles.

There will, however, continue to be this real impediment to the efficiency of consumer goods marketing in India until the urban consumer is able to shop routinely in well-planned, clean, and, above all, air-conditioned self-service food and drug stores. Retail display is the final—and in some ways the most important—link in the marketing chain. It defeats the best-laid plans if excellent brands—products with desirable functional attributes plus the psychological added values nurtured by consumer advertising—are not available for sale in the appropriate surroundings. By *appropriate,* I mean retail environments where the shopper can take pleasure in her shopping task.

One obvious difference between India and other countries is that in Indian DI households, the family shopping is not always carried out by the lady of the house—the person who should demand and require high standards in the retail stores she uses. This is, however, a "chicken and egg" problem. If household shopping were made a more worthwhile and interesting experience, then housewives in India, like their sisters in other countries, would do such shopping themselves and accept only the highest standards. Their insisting on such standards would lend impetus to all types of marketing improvement: faster delivery, better packaging, and imaginative merchandising and sales promotions.

Preaching for advances to take place in Indian retailing from an American ivory tower is naturally a rather fruitless endeavor. I can only hope that these words will help to awaken Indian businesspeople, a group normally not lacking in either imagination or energy—the combination of qualities that is the essence of the entrepreneurial spirit. Such men and women should do some thinking about the opportunities for volume and profit that are most certainly ripe for exploitation in Indian retailing.

I noticed improvement in Indian food stores upon each of my visits in 1989, 1995, 1997, and 1998. I would be very surprised indeed if the pace of improvement has not picked up significantly before the 21st century has far advanced.

18

China

Advertising Yesterday and Today

Hong Cheng

A Brief History

Advertising in China is both old and new. It is old because it has a very long history; it is new because it did not reappear until 1979. Today, advertising is one of the fastest-growing industries in China.

Studies have found that commercial advertising in China dates back to the Western Zhou Dynasty (11th century-771 BC), when daytime trade fairs began to appear. Displays of goods and street hawking were the major forms of advertising then. By the time of the Tang Dynasty (AD 618-907), high-flying wine banners, lanterns, pictures, signboards, and decorated structures had become popular advertising media.[1] When printing was invented during the Song Dynasty (AD 960-1127), printed advertisements came into existence in

China. The Shanghai Museum displays a bronze plaque from that period that was used by a Liu family's needle shop in Jinan, Shandong Province, to print wrappers for advertising its products.

Although advertising in embryo emerged in China quite early, the traditional contempt for commerce and the long-standing self-contained and self-sufficient economic system in the country stunted its further growth for centuries. The Opium War (1840-1842), an epoch-making event in Chinese history, turned China into a society that had colonial as well as feudal characteristics. Foreigners from many countries came to China, mainly with an interest in trade. Along with foreign commodities came modern advertising media.

Although newspapers have existed in China since the 8th century,[2] those carrying advertisements first were three British-run English-language newspapers in Hong Kong: the *Friend of China and Hongkong Gazette* (1842-1859), the *Hongkong Register* (1844-1859), and the *China Mail* (1845-1911).[3] Throughout the 19th century, more than 300 foreign-owned newspapers and magazines were circulated in China.[4] Many of these publications were in Chinese, and many of them became the major modern media for advertising in the country. The first Chinese-language newspapers carrying advertisements were *Zhongwai Xinbao* (*Chinese and Foreign News Paper*), launched in Hong Kong in 1858, and *Shanghai Xinbao* (*Shanghai News Paper*), founded in Shanghai in 1861.[5]

Introduced by Westerners, modern advertising media and communications skills were soon well received by the Chinese. *Zhengzhi Guanbao* (*Political Official Gazette*), established by the government of the Qing Dynasty in 1907, became the first Chinese government newspaper to run advertisements. The competing *Shen Bao* (*Shanghai Gazette*) and *Xinwen Bao* (*News Gazette*), which eventually became Chinese owned, were the two most successful and longest-running newspapers that carried advertisements in early-20th-century China.[6]

The first Chinese magazine carrying advertisements was the British-run *Xia'er Guanzhen* (*Chinese Serial;* 1853-1856) in Hong Kong. The magazines that carried the most advertisements in the early 20th century were *Dongfang Zhazhi* (*Eastern Miscellany;* 1901-1941), *Funu Zhazhi* (*Women's Magazine;* 1915-1945), and *Kuaile Jiating* (*Happy Home;* 1935-1945), all published in Shanghai.[7]

The 1930s was a golden age for advertising in China. At that time the media available for advertising, in addition to newspapers and magazines, included billboards, posters, neon signs, streetcars (which carried advertisements on their tops as well as their sides), booklets, calendars, and (a relatively unimportant medium) radio broadcasting.[8]

The growth of advertising in early-20th-century China could also be attributed to the development of advertising agencies. Much like their Western counterparts, Chinese advertising agencies evolved from space brokers.[9] Toward the 1930s, there were around 20 agencies in Shanghai, the commercial center and the base of advertising in China.[10]

The first modern agency was the China Commercial Advertising Agency (CCAA), founded in 1926 by C. P. Ling, the U.S.-educated "father of Chinese advertising." Together with Ling's agency, Carl Crow, Inc., from the United States, Millington Ltd., from Britain, and Consolidated National Advertising Company, another Chinese-run agency, became the dominant "Big Four" in Shanghai during the 1930s. Before 1949, when the People's Republic was founded, around 100 advertising agencies were in operation in Shanghai, with a few others in Beijing, Chongqing, and Guangzhou. But the golden age was short-lived, truncated by World War II and the civil war of the 1940s.[11]

During World War II, many newspapers were moved to Chongqing, Sichuan Province, where the Nationalist government was temporarily located. The major newspapers published there included *Zhongyang Ribao* (*Central Daily News*), *Dagong Bao* (*Impartial Gazette*), *Saodang Bao* (*Collecting-Gazette*), and *Xinmin Bao* (*New People Gazette*). All these newspapers carried advertisements.[12] Meanwhile, the major newspapers run by the Communist Party of China also began to carry advertisements. These included *Xin Zhonghua Bao* (*New China Gazette*), *Jiefang Ribao* (*Liberation Daily*), *Xinhua Ribao* (*New China Daily*), and *Jin-Cha-Ji Ribao* (*Shanxi-Chaha'er-Hebei Daily*).[13]

During the first few years after 1949, the Chinese government allowed advertising to exist, although foreign participation was ended. Domestic advertising business even recovered from the war to some extent. However, the government's plans to impose strict control on production, consumption, and prices left little room for advertising. After January 1956, all the remaining advertising agencies became completely state owned. The 108 agencies in Shanghai, for example, were merged into the state-run Shanghai Advertising Corporation.[14]

In 1957, an international advertising conference attended by 13 socialist countries was held in Prague, Czech Republic. Dominated by the theme that "socialism needs advertising," this conference added some momentum to Chinese advertising.[15] Business boomed for a while, slumped during the hard times around the early 1960s, and picked up again until the Cultural Revolution (1966-1976), the final blow to the advertising industry in China.

During the period of the Cultural Revolution, advertising was labeled "bourgeois commercialism" and a "symbol of capitalism" designed to deceive the masses. Agencies that had managed to hang on during the early 1960s were reduced to producing political posters, and they finally closed.[16] Not until 1979 did the first local agency reopen for business. Nevertheless, recent studies reveal that "even the *People's Daily* (*Renmin Ribao*)—the official Communist Party newspaper—printed industrial product and raw materials advertisements, among others, every year throughout the entire period of the Cultural Revolution, albeit in very reduced numbers. In fact, advertisements never completely disappeared during the period."[17]

Chinese Advertising Since 1979

The period from 1979 to the present has been a new era for Chinese advertising, which dawned after the Third Plenary Session of the 11th Central Committee of the Chinese Communist Party held in December 1978. After this Party congress, the country's focus was shifted from the 10-year Cultural Revolution, which was dominated by class struggle, to a grand economic development program known as the "Four Modernizations," which is still going on today.

One of the most important strategies the Chinese government adopted to promote this program was the economic reform started in 1979. The essence of this reform was to legitimate the market mechanism in China, which has changed the country from an entirely planned economy into one integrated with market forces. Together with an emphasis on the role of the market mechanism in economic development, advertising—which had been treated as a capitalist symbol and had almost entirely disappeared during the Cultural Revolution—came back to life. In the past two decades, it has been officially called "an accelerator for the economic development in China." [18]

The renaissance of the advertising industry again largely began in Shanghai, the focal point of the golden age of China's advertising in the 1930s. On January 14, 1979, an editorial appeared in the Shanghai-based *Wenhui Gazette* calling for "restoring the good name of advertising." Seeing advertising as "a means of promoting trade, earning foreign exchange, and broadening the masses' horizons," the editorial writer encouraged China's mass media to carry foreign as well as domestic advertisements.[19] On the same day, the *Tianjin Daily* ran an advertisement for the Tianjin Toothpaste Factory, the first-ever advertisement in China since the Cultural Revolution.

On January 28, 1979, the *Liberation Daily*, another Shanghai-based newspaper, carried advertisements for several domestic products. On the same day, the Shanghai Television Station showed a commercial for a Chinese-made tonic wine, the first ever in China's television history. On March 5, 1979, the Shanghai Broadcasting Station transmitted a radio commercial for a photo studio. On March 15 of the same year, the *Wenhui Gazette* carried an advertisement for the Swiss-made Rado watch, the first foreign advertisement exposed in China after the Cultural Revolution.

At the same time the mass media were responding actively to advertising, advertising agencies reappeared in China. The Shanghai Advertising Corporation, the last company to cease operation when advertising was banned during the Cultural Revolution, was reactivated in late 1978. In 1979, 10 advertising agencies operated in a few major cities, such as Beijing, Guangzhou, Nanjing, Shanghai, and Tianjin. Since then, advertising agencies have spread all over the country, although the majority are concentrated in urban areas.

Since late 1979, advertising in China has experienced substantial and sustained growth. As shown in Table 18.1, which highlights advertising's growth between 1981 and 1996, 8 of the 15 years under observation had increases of 40% or more. Although the increase rate for 1990—the year after the 1989 Tiananmen incident—was 25.1%, the lowest in the 15 years, the growth rate for 1993 was 97.6%, the highest since 1981. No wonder 1993 was named "the Advertising Year of China." [20]

In U.S. dollars, China's 1996 advertising industry billings were about $4.4 billion.[21] Its 1997 billings reached an estimated $5.6 billion, more than doubling the $2.3 billion of 1993. Parsons remarked in 1993 that China's advertising industry was "witnessing its fastest growth ever." [22] His observation still rings true today. Even the recent economic crisis that some Asian countries have experienced has not affected China's advertising industry in any noticeable manner.

On the contrary, the advertising industry in China is enthusiastically embracing newcomers to the market, particularly computer technology-savvy companies, while maintaining services to their existing customers. The Beijing-based Infoshare Technology Co. Ltd. has, for example, become the exclusive

TABLE 18.1 China's Advertising Industry Growth, 1981-1996

Year	Business Volume (million yuan)[a]	Business Volume Annual Increase Rate (%)	Advertising Expenditure in the GNP (%)	Per Capita Spending on Advertising (yuan)[a]	Advertising Units[b]	Numbers of Advertising Employees	Per Capita Business Volume by Advertising Employees (yuan)[a]
1981	118.000	NA	.024	.117	1,160	16,160	7,302
1982	150.000	27.1	.028	.147	1,500	18,000	8,333
1983	234.074	56.0	.040	.227	2,340	34,853	6,916
1984	365.278	56.1	.052	.350	4,077	47,259	7,729
1985	605.225	65.7	.070	.571	6,052	63,819	9,483
1986	844.777	39.6	.087	.786	6,944	81,130	10,412
1987	1,112.003	31.6	.098	1.017	8,225	92,279	12,050
1988	1,492.939	34.3	.106	1.345	10,677	112,139	13,313
1989	1,998.998	33.9	.125	1.774	11,142	128,203	15,592
1990	2,501.726	25.1	.141	2.188	11,123	131,970	18,957
1991	3,508.926	40.3	.162	3.030	11,769	134,506	26,088
1992	6,786.754	93.4	.255	5.792	16,683	185,428	36,600
1993	13,408.736	97.6	.392	11.314	31,770	311,967	42,981
1994	20,026.230	49.4	.457	16.709	43,046	410,094	48,883
1995	27,326.900	36.5	.475	22.562	48,082	477,371	57,245
1996	36,663.710	34.2	.548	29.957	52,871	512,087	71,597

SOURCE: *Zhongguo Guanggao Nianjian* [China Advertising Yearbook] (Beijing: Xinhua, 1996), 47; *Zhongguo Guanggao Nianjian* [China Advertising Yearbook] (Beijing: Xinhua, 1998), 27.

a. In 1996, 1 *yuan* was equal to about US$0.12.

b. Advertising units include advertising agencies, advertising departments in the media, and advertising manufacturers.

advertising agency in China for Internet content provider Yahoo! According to an agreement signed between Infoshare and Yahoo! in February 1999, the former will promote Yahoo! services in China and help Chinese customers to create on-line advertisements on Yahoo!'s worldwide network. An Internet service company funded by the China International Electronic Commerce Center, Infoshare designed and built the "Made-in-China" Web market and the Web site for China's Ministry of Foreign Trade and Economic Cooperation.[23]

The growth of advertising business, however, has varied from region to region in China, with Beijing, Shanghai, and Guangdong together accounting for more than half of the total business in 1996. Table 18.2 displays a

TABLE 18.2 A Ranking of Chinese Regions in Advertising (by business volume), 1996 and 1995

1996 Business Volume Ranking	Region	1996 Business Volume (million yuan)[a]	1995 Business Volume (million yuan)[a]	1996 Increase Rate (%)	1996 Increase Rate Ranking	1995 Increase Rate Ranking
1	Beijing[b]	9,247.09	6,063.23	52.5	4	5
2	Shanghai[b]	6,420.98	4,400.04	45.9	5	7
3	Guangdong[c]	4,045.38	3,723.53	8.6	21	26
4	Zhejiang[c]	2,394.50	1,960.90	22.1	15	3
5	Jiangsu[c]	2,368.61	1,633.79	45.0	6	23
6	Shandong[c]	2,278.37	1,334.11	70.8	2	9
7	Sichuan[c]	1,314.81	1,044.95	25.8	13	10
8	Liaoning[c]	903.62	832.44	8.6	22	12
9	Fujian[c]	892.83	727.26	22.8	14	19
10	Hubei[c]	863.71	721.48	19.7	17	14
11	Tianjin[b]	724.68	548.77	32.1	9	13
12	Hunan[c]	584.36	596.42	−2.1	28	20
13	Anhui[c]	563.85	427.53	31.9	10	2
14	Hebei[c]	512.85	443.64	15.6	20	1
15	Henan[c]	507.28	422.11	20.2	16	22
16	Heilongjiang[c]	431.00	307.42	40.2	7	4
17	Jiangxi[c]	421.57	202.97	107.7	1	27
18	Shaanxi[c]	402.76	346.33	16.3	18	17
19	Guangxi Zhuangzu[d]	365.47	377.08	−3.1	29	16
20	Yunnan[c]	338.08	263.36	28.4	11	11
21	Shanxi[c]	217.17	161.73	34.3	8	30
22	Jilin[c]	200.60	187.53	7.0	24	15
23	Xinjiang Uygur[d]	161.06	161.84	−.5	27	24
24	Hainan[c]	122.46	133.50	−8.3	30	29
25	Guizhou[c]	117.81	75.23	56.6	3	28
26	Nei Mongol[d]	106.12	82.87	28.1	12	21
27	Gansu[c]	102.12	97.68	4.5	25	8
28	Ningxia Huizu[d]	29.05	26.99	7.6	23	18
29	Qinghai[c]	23.90	20.60	16.0	19	25
30	Xizang (Tibet)[d]	1.59	1.58	.6	26	6

SOURCE: Adapted from *Zhongguo Guanggao Nianjian* [China Advertising Yearbook] (Beijing: Xinhua, 1998), 28.

a. In 1996 and 1995, 1 *yuan* was equal to about US$0.12.

b. Municipality directly under the central government.

c. Province.

d. Autonomous region.

breakdown of advertising industry growth in the 30 regions of (mainland) China.

Since China reopened its doors to the West, transnational advertising agencies (TNAAs) have not lost any time in entering this new market. Dentsu was the first TNAA, opening offices in Beijing and Shanghai soon after advertising was resumed in 1979.[24] Leo Burnett has made its development in China "the highest priority of any new market in the world." [25] In 1990, there were only 17 joint-venture advertising agencies in China; by 1992, there were 98, and the number jumped to 280 in 1993.[26] Today, all major players in world advertising have set up shops in China, representing a wide array of global manufacturers and service providers.

TNAAs' significant inroads into the Chinese market are also clearly reflected in their fast-growing business over the years there. In 1986 and 1992, foreign advertising accounted for $15 million and $75 million in billings, respectively, less than 6% of China's total advertising spending in those two years. By 1997, however, the billings of the top 19 TNAAs operating in China had totaled $898.48 million (see Table 18.3), taking about 15% of the entire advertising volume in the country.

Among the top 10 advertising agencies in 1997 (ranked based on billings), 7 were entirely or partly run by the TNAAs. In that year, Saatchi & Saatchi continued to wear the crown of the number one advertising agency in the whole country which it took in 1995. However, the large chunk Saatchi & Saatchi took from the Chinese market accounted for only 2.46% of that TNAA's 1997 worldwide billings.[27]

On the other hand, only 3 domestic agencies appeared on the 1997 top 10 list: the China National United Advertising Corporation, the Guangdong Advertising Corporation, and the Shanghai Advertising Corporation.[28] Some advertising analysts in China have begun to be concerned about the "threat" of TNAAs to local advertising agencies. They have pointed out that local agencies need more agility in order to function properly in the market economy and compete successfully with their foreign counterparts.[29]

While posing challenges to the indigenous advertising agencies in China, some TNAAs provide professional help to this new market. In 1996, Dentsu signed an agreement with the State Education Commission of China and six Chinese universities to mount an advertising education program in celebration of the world's largest agency's 95th anniversary. According to the agreement, Dentsu would invest more than $6 million in the program, which would,

TABLE 18.3 Top Transnational Advertising Agencies in China, 1997

Agency	City	Equity	*1997 Gross Income ($ thousands)*	*Change from 1996 (%)*	*1997 Volume ($ thousands)*
Saatchi & Saatchi[a]	Beijing/Guangzhou/ Shanghai	MJ	21,100	35.7	175,837
McCann-Erickson Guangming	Beijing	MJ	17,436	27.7	116,301
Ogilvy & Mather	Shanghai	MJ	13,527	22.4	90,225
Leo Burnett	Guangzhou	MJ	12,221	17.0	81,475
Bridge/J. Walter Thompson Beijing	Beijing	MJ	11,588	9.5	77,251
Grey China	Beijing	MJ	9,395	26.4	62,666
DMB&B	Guangzhou	MJ	8,970	33.2	59,827
Beijing Dentsu	Beijing	MJ	7,149	13.2	44,800
Shanghai Lintas	Shanghai	MJ	5,634	28.0	37,582
Dentsu, Young & Rubicam	Shanghai	MJ	4,605	–15.3	30,715
BBDO/CNUAC	Beijing	MJ	3,530	6.4	23,703
FCB/Megacom[a]	Beijing	MJ	3,428	197.4	28,564
DDB Worldwide	Beijing	MJ	2,072	–2.2	13,823
Guangdong Guangxu Advertising (Asatsu)	Guangzhou	JV	1,652	171.9	10,950
Shanghai Asatsu	Shanghai	JV	1,503	64.4	10,950
TBWA Lee Davis	Shanghai	MJ	1,235	90.8	8,236
Bozell China	Beijing	JV	1,184	126.2	8,952
Beijing Huawen-Asatsu International	Beijing	JV	892	5.2	7,776
Shanghai Hakuhodo	Shanghai	JV	721	NA	8,876

SOURCE: Adapted with permission from data that appeared in the April 27, 1998, issue of *Advertising Age.* Copyright Crain Communications Inc., 1998.

NOTE: MJ = majority ownership; JV = 50-50 joint venture.

a. Gross income figures are *Advertising Age*'s estimates.

among other things, involve a year's residency at the agency in Japan for one or two advertising faculty members from each of the universities. As *Advertising Age* commented, "The move is in line with the agency's stated ambition to extend its influence via education."[30]

While TNAAs are trying to establish a strong foothold in China, some Chinese advertising agencies are thinking of testing the waters in overseas

markets. According to *Advertising Age,* China planned to open its first advertising agency in the United States in late 1997. Established in 1989, Hairun
International Advertising Co. Ltd., a joint venture with Hong Kong China
Advertising and Printing Co. Ltd., is intended to target Chinese Americans
and Chinese living in the United States. Hairun's first work in the new U.S.
market was for shampoo made by Chongqing Olive Cosmetics Co. Ltd., one
of the largest manufacturers of daily-use toiletries in China. This Los Ange-
les-based Chinese agency planned to promote Olive products in department
stores with specialty counters and to advertise on billboards and public
transport sites. Hairun was reported to have $48.2 million in billings in 1996
and an estimated $54.2 million in 1997. Its major clients include VV Soybean
Milk Powder, Flying Pigeon Bicycles, Master Kang Instant Noodles, Samsung, and Jinro.[31]

During the first few years after advertising came back to life in China, many
people still viewed it with suspicion, thinking that "advertised goods were
over-stocked products." [32] But soon studies found that "Chinese consumers
were very positive about advertising . . . and optimistic about advertising's
economic and social consequences." [33] Many of them were "gaining reference
from advertisements to guide their consumption." [34] However, more recent
research, although still largely agreeing with the findings of previous studies,
suggests that consumers' "support" of advertising in China should be interpreted with caution:

> The Chinese consumers may have been more sophisticated than they were given
> credit for. . . . [Although the] Chinese audience was generally supportive of the
> return of advertising, the support was less enthusiastic than previously thought.
> The general attitudes were, instead, rather reserved, conditional and somewhat
> calculated. Although Chinese consumers overwhelmingly approved the exis-
> tence of advertising, they also wanted to limit its quantity, and many did not enjoy
> the advertisements. The tendency was stronger among the more educated—they
> were more critical and distrusting of the advertisements, yet more supportive of
> the policy of permitting advertising.[35]

Advertising Industry Structure

Over the past 20 years or so, China's advertising industry has been developing
mainly along three lines: (a) through "specialized" advertising agencies, (b)
through advertising media, and (c) through advertising manufacturers (i.e.,

production houses manufacturing a variety of specialized advertising materials.[36] In 1987, for example, there were 795 advertising agencies, 5,161 advertising departments in the media, and 1,182 advertising manufacturers.[37]

Even in the early 1990s, direct expenditure in the media for advertising was the main part of the industry. In 1991, for instance, direct placement of advertisements in newspapers, television, magazines, and radio added up to 62.7% of total billings, but advertising agencies took up only 19.7%. The remaining 17.5% came mainly from advertising manufactures.[38]

The State Administration for Industry and Commerce (SAIC) initiated steps to eliminate direct advertising arrangements between clients and media and to ban the media from acting as agencies for other media. As a result, in the past few years advertising agencies have been playing an increasingly important role in China's advertising industry. Since 1995, their billings have maintained a share between 40% and 45% of the total advertising volume in the country.[39]

Advertising Agencies

The growth of Chinese advertising agencies after 1949 has gone through three phases: (a) the advertising workshops before the mid-1950s, (b) the art and design companies from the mid-1950s to mid-1960s, and (c) the professional advertising corporations since the 1980s. In the early 1980s, the business of advertising companies mainly involved the design and manufacture of product catalogs, media buying, and indoor and outdoor decoration for department stores and sales exhibitions. Since 1986, much more priority has been given to advertising creation, media planning, market research, and consulting services.[40]

Chinese advertising agencies, often identifying themselves as companies or corporations, fall into two major groups: one affiliated with the Ministry of Foreign Economic Relations and Trade (MOFERT), the other attached to various non-MOFERT departments. In addition to being bound by government regulations for advertising, all the agencies are subject to the control of the departments with which they are affiliated.[41]

Foreign Trade Advertising Agencies

Under the aegis of the MOFERT, the China International Advertising Corporation handles national foreign trade advertising and coordinates local foreign trade advertising agencies. The foreign trade advertising agencies in all provinces and major cities undertake foreign advertising as well as advertising for export products on a regional or local basis. Nowadays, some of them have even started to handle domestic advertising business.

The major local foreign trade advertising agencies include the Beijing Advertising Corporation, the Shanghai Advertising Corporation, the Guangdong Advertising Corporation, the Tianjin Advertising Corporation, and the Jiangsu International Advertising Corporation.[42] Today, most of these agencies are operating in cooperation with or as joint ventures with foreign agencies.

Domestic Advertising Agencies

In addition to the one foreign trade advertising agency in each province or major city, there are numerous other corporations mainly handling domestic advertising. In fact, many of them have also been licensed to handle foreign advertising business.

The affiliations of these agencies vary greatly. For instance, whereas the Nanjing Advertising Corporation is under the Cultural Bureau of the Nanjing Municipal Government, the Guangzhou Advertising Corporation is under the Guangzhou Municipal Administration for Industry and Commerce.[43]

Authorized by the State Administration for Industry and Commerce, the Beijing-based China National United Advertising Corporation, the largest domestic advertising company (by business volume) in 1997,[44] coordinates and oversees major local domestic advertising agencies.

Advertising Media

Conventionally, advertising media in China are divided into five categories: newspaper, magazine, radio, television, and outdoor.[45] Many media institutions have set up subsidiary companies to handle their advertising business. Typical examples are the China Global Advertising Company of the Xinhua News Agency, the China International Television Service Corporation of the China Central Television Station, and the China Broadcasting Service Corporation of the Central People's Broadcasting Station. However, most of the media institutions only have advertising departments or sections.

TABLE 18.4 Top 10 Chinese Newspapers in Advertising (by business volume), 1995

Newspaper	Business Volume (million yuan)[a]
Yangcheng Evening Paper (Guangzhou)	465.00
Guangzhou Daily	460.00
Xinmin Evening Paper (Shanghai)	324.16
Beijing Evening Paper	208.36
Shenzhen Special Zone Gazette	205.00
Liberation Daily (Shanghai)	177.70
Xinhua Daily (Nanjing)	160.00
Nanfang Daily (Guangzhou)	153.59
People's Daily (Beijing)	137.00
Chengdu Evening Paper	137.00

SOURCE: Adapted from Zhongguo Guanggao Nianjian [China Advertising Yearbook] (Beijing: Xinhua, 1997), 33.

a. In 1995, 1 *yuan* was equal to about US$0.12.

Newspapers

In 1997, there were more than 2,200 newspapers in China, compared with only 186 in 1978.[46] Most of these newspapers are open to foreign as well as domestic advertisements today, with those specializing in economic information usually carrying more advertisements than others.

Newspapers with a daily circulation of more than 1 million include *People's Daily, Reference News, Workers' Daily, Peasants' Daily, Economic Daily, Wenhui Gazette, Liberation Daily, Yangcheng Evening Paper, Xinmin Evening Paper, Chinese Youth Gazette,* and *People's Liberation Army Daily.*[47] *China Daily,* the leading English-language newspaper currently published in China and overseas, also carries advertisements.

Before 1990, the annual billings of newspaper advertising were consistently more than 30% of the total advertising business volume in China,[48] but the proportion dropped to 25.6% in 1995 and 23.1% in 1996.[49] In the first half of 1998, it continued to drop to 19.6%.[50] Table 18.4 lists China's top 10 newspapers, measured by advertising volume, and Table 18.5 shows the 1993 media rates of newspapers in some cities, municipalities, and provinces in China. Occasionally, the rates were based on the "prestige" rather than on the actual circulation of the newspapers.

TABLE 18.5 Chinese Newspaper Advertising in Selected Regions, 1993

Region and Newspaper	Rate (per column cm)	Circulation (thousands)	Remarks
Guangzhou City			
Yangcheng Evening Paper	HK$650	1,250	national, overseas
Nanfang Daily	HK$380	800	provincial
Guangzhou Daily	HK$380	500	overseas
Guangdong Television (weekly)	HK$456	2,100	provincial, neighboring areas
News Express	HK$150	180	
Guangdong-Hong Kong News	HK$150	200	
Nanjing City			
Nanjing Daily	US$22	300	
Xinhua Daily	US$25	600	
Shanghai Municipality			
Xinmin Evening Paper	US$80	1,450	
Wenhui Gazette	US$50	1,000	readership: intellectuals nationwide
Liberation Daily	US$60	650	
Radio & Television (weekly)	US$70	2,700	
Tianjin Municipality			
Tianjin Daily	US$40	450	
Beijing Municipality			
People's Daily	US$150	4,500	national, overseas
Economic Daily	US$70	1,000	readership: economic, trade organs nationwide
Beijing Daily	US$85	700	
Beijing Evening Paper	US$95	800	
Workers' Daily	US$60	1,800	national
Guangming Daily	US$60	500	readership: intellectuals nationwide
Beijing Radio & Television (weekly)	US$80	500	Tuesdays
Reference News	US$90	3,800	national, restricted
China Daily (in English, 1992)	US$26	150	national, overseas
Guangdong Province			
Shenzhen Special Zone Gazette	US$30	250	
Foshan Gazette	HK$60	100	
Shantou Special Zone Gazette	HK$100	80	
Shantou Daily	HK$150	150	
Fujian Province			
Fujian Daily	US$45	350	

TABLE 18.5 *Continued*

Region and Newspaper	Rate (per column cm)	Circulation (thousands)	Remarks
Xiamen Daily	HK$200	150	
Hainan Province			
Hainan Daily	HK$200	150	
Shandong Province			
Qingdao Daily	US$30	100	
Jinan Daily	HK$80	200	
Dazhong Daily	US$40	550	
Zhejiang Province			
Zhejiang Daily	US$30	500	
Hangzhou Daily	US$14	150	
Sichuan Province			
Sichuan Daily	US$35	700	
Chongqing Daily	US$30	300	
Hebei Province			
Hebei Daily	70 yuan	350	
Henan Province			
Henan Daily	US$30	650	
Heilongjiang Province			
Heilongjiang Daily	US$38	300	
Harbin Daily	US$35	NA	
Liaoning Province			
Liaoyang Daily	11.5 yuan	200	
Liaoning Daily	US$30	350	
Dalian Daily	US$30	250	

SOURCE: Adapted from John D. Friske (ed.), *China Facts and Figures Annual Handbook* (Gulf Breeze, FL: Academic International Press, 1994), 190.
NOTE: In 1993, HK$1 was equal to about US$0.13, and 1 *yuan* was equal to about US$0.17.

Magazines

The number of magazines in China has increased significantly in the past 20 years or so. In 1978, only 930 magazines were published in the country; this figure doubled in 2 years.[51] In 1997, more than 7,000 were in circulation,[52] about 4,000 of which carried advertisements.[53] Some magazines have circulations of more than half a million. For instance, *Culture and Life* has a circulation of around 1 million, and *Younger Generation*'s circulation is more than 5 million. *Red Flag,* official organ of the Communist Party of China, has

TABLE 18.6 Top 10 Chinese Magazines in Advertising (by business volume), 1994

Magazine	Business Volume (million yuan)[a]
Chinese Talents Pictorial	5.05
Semimonthly Talk	2.90
Shanghai Television	2.18
Observation (weekly)	2.09
China Financial Computing	1.50
Bosom Friend	1.40
Visual and Audio	1.31
World of Electricity	1.29
Beijing Review (weekly; in English)	1.17
Liaoning Pictorial	1.06

SOURCE: Adapted from Zhongguo Guanggao Nianjian [China Advertising Yearbook] (Beijing: Xinhua, 1996), 62.
a. In 1995, 1 yuan was equal to about US$0.12.

the largest circulation in the country (9.7 million).[54] Since the early 1980s, the annual billings of magazine advertising have been below 5% of the total advertising volume in China; the proportion dropped to 1.53% in 1996 and 1.34% in the first half of 1998.[55] Table 18.6 lists China's top 10 magazines by advertising volume.[56]

Radio Stations

With more than 1,000 wireless and more than 2,000 wired stations in the mid-1990s, China's radio system covers all urban and most rural areas.[57] More than 90% of the wireless and about 40% of the wired radio stations are handling advertising, which reaches nearly 80% of the population of the country.[58] Although the annual business volume of radio advertising as a proportion of total advertising billings declined from more than 7% in the early 1980s to 2.38% in 1996, its absolute volume has never gone down.[59] In fact, in early 1998, its proportion of the total advertising volume in China bounced back to 3.1%.[60]

Radio is still the third-largest advertising medium in China today, after television and newspapers. Table 18.7 lists China's top 10 broadcasting stations by advertising volume, and Table 18.8 lists the advertising media rates for a few major broadcasting stations in China. The rates vary from station to station.

TABLE 18.7 Top 10 Chinese Broadcasting Stations in Advertising (by business volume), 1995

Station	Business Volume (million yuan)[a]
Central People's Broadcasting Station	47.54
Beijing People's Broadcasting Station	45.00
Shanghai People's Broadcasting Station	45.00
Shanghai Dongfang Broadcasting Station	41.14
Guangdong People's Broadcasting Station	38.00
Guangzhou People's Broadcasting Station	32.55
Liaoning People's Broadcasting Station	20.00
Shenzhen People's Broadcasting Station	19.50
Tianjin People's Broadcasting Station	18.60
Foshan People's Broadcasting Station	15.00

SOURCE: Adapted from *Zhongguo Guanggao Nianjian* [China Advertising Yearbook] (Beijing: Xinhua, 1997), 34.

a. In 1995, 1 *yuan* was equal to about US$0.12.

TABLE 18.8 Media Rates for Selected Chinese Broadcasting Stations, 1992

Station	Broadcast Area	Rate for 30 Seconds		
		Local Enterprise	Joint Venture	Foreign Enterprise
Central People's Broadcasting Station (Channels 1 and 2)	nationwide	600 *yuan*	690 *yuan*	US$400
Beijing Radio	Beijing and vicinity	250 *yuan*	325 *yuan*	US$238
Shanghai Radio	Shanghai and vicinity	400 *yuan*	400 *yuan*	US$140
Guangzhou Radio (in Cantonese)	Guangzhou and vicinity	115 *yuan*	115 *yuan*	US$102

SOURCE: Adapted from John D. Friske (ed.), *China Facts and Figures Annual Handbook* (Gulf Breeze, FL: Academic International Press, 1993), 280.

NOTE: Local enterprises and joint ventures paid in Chinese currency, except where noted. Foreign companies were charged in U.S. dollars. In 1992, 1 *yuan* was equal to about US$0.18.

Television Stations

Growing from 52 stations in 1983 to nearly 1,000 in the late 1990s, plus more than 1,000 additional cable stations, China's television system covers more than 80% of the country's population, slightly higher than the coverage of radio broadcasting.[61] Even in the mid-1990s, nearly 90% of urban households had color television sets, and nearly 80% of rural households had either black-and-white or color televisions.[62] In 1993, more than 800 million Chinese watched television, nearly 200 million more than the figure in the late 1980s.[63]

The regeneration of China's advertising industry in 1979 also gave birth to television advertising. In that year—two decades after the launch of China's first television program in Beijing—the Shanghai Television Station broadcast the first-ever television commercial in the country. Since then, television has been the fastest-growing advertising medium in China. Its business volume in the nation's total advertising industry rose from about 5% in the early 1980s to about 25% in the late 1990s.[64] In 1991 and 1992, television surpassed newspapers in advertising volume. But in 1993 and 1994, it temporarily lost the battle to newspapers. It regained the crown as the country's largest advertising medium in 1995 and has successfully maintained its position since then.[65] In 1994, there were 1,985 television stations handling advertising business in China.[66] Table 18.9 lists the top 10 Chinese television stations in advertising terms, and Table 18.10 shows the media rates for selected television stations in China. The rate differences for stations, as presented in the table, are even sharper than those for radio advertising.

Over the years, media rates have been firming up in China simply because demand for space and time from advertisers outstrips media supply.[67] The tone of media rate increases in this seller's market is often set by the China Central Television Station (CCTV) and the *People's Daily*, the two largest and most influential electronic and print media organizations.[68] Table 18.11 presents the latest rates for several CCTV channels.

Outdoor

In addition to the four major advertising media, there are many other options for advertising in China. Major urban centers are the best places for a company to introduce its name to Chinese consumers. For example, millions of people pass through Shanghai's and Beijing's main thoroughfares on any given day. The heavy traffic and bustling crowds—also typical of other major cities—guarantee a large audience for outdoor advertising, which includes billboards, bus shelters, bus and trolley bodies, light boxes, and neon signs.

TABLE 18.9 Top 10 Chinese Television Stations in Advertising (by business volume), 1995

Station	Business Volume (million yuan)[a]
China Central Television Station	2,000.00
Beijing Television Station	358.99
Shanghai Television Station	310.00
Shanghai Dongfang Television Station	243.26
Guangdong Television Station	188.00
Shandong Television Station	150.00
Zhejiang Television Station	135.90
Guangzhou Television Station	130.00
Tianjin Television Station	115.00
Fujian Television Station	110.00

SOURCE: Adapted from *Zhongguo Guanggao Nianjian* [China Advertising Yearbook] (Beijing: Xinhua, 1997), 34.

a. In 1995, 1 *yuan* was equal to about US$0.12.

Table 18.12 displays the rates for some of the outdoor advertising media in China.

In 1994, a giant color LED audio/video screen, claimed to be the largest in the world, was put into operation in Tianjin. Costing 36 million *yuan*, this screen is 15 meters tall and 40 meters long. It offers visual displays 20 hours a day on the banks of the Haihe River.[69]

In the same year, a neon advertisement, the largest of its kind in China at that time, was set up on the Nanjing Yangtze River Bridge, the longest bridge across the longest river in the country.[70] But in size this was surpassed by another neon advertising board erected for Eastman Kodak Co. on top of the China Post Hub Building to promote Kodak film. The building is beside Chang'an Avenue, known as the First Avenue of China because the headquarters of the Chinese Central Government, Chinese Communist Party, and other government organizations are located along this street. The neon advertising board, designed by China Post Advertising Co., is more than 1,590 square meters and consists of more than 40,000 neon tubes. The board uses the advanced CPU central system—the first time in a neon advertising board in China—from Intel Corporation and Motorola.[71]

TABLE 18.10 Media Rates for Selected Chinese Television Stations, 1992

Station	Broadcast Area	Day	Local Enterprise (yuan)	Rate for 30 Seconds Joint Venture (yuan)	Foreign Enterprise
CCTV2	nationwide	Mon-Fri	4,000-10,000	6,000-13,000	US$ 4,000-8,000
		Sat-Sun	5,000-11,000	7,500-14,000	US$ 5,000-9,000
CCTV8	Beijing	Mon-Sun	4,000	5,500	US$ 3,000
BTV6	Beijing and vicinity	Mon-Fri	4,500	4,500	US$ 1,600
		Sat-Sun	5,700	5,700	US$ 2,000
BTV21	Beijing and vicinity	Mon-Sun	1,500	1,500	US$ 1,000
STV8 and STV20	Shanghai and vicinity	Mon-Fri	1,200-3,000	1,800-4,500	US$ 500-1,800
		Sat-Sun	1,400-3,500	1,800-5,250	US$ 500-2,160
GTV14 (Cantonese)	Guangdong	Mon-Fri	300-2,200	450-3,300	HK$ 1,800-12,900
		Sat-Sun	345-2,530	518-3,795	HK$ 1,800-16,770
GTV2 (Mandarin)	Guangdong	Mon-Fri	500-1,000	750-1,500	HK$ 1,800-9,100
		Sat-Sun	575-1,150	863-1,725	HK$ 1,800-11,830

SOURCE: Adapted from John D. Friske (ed.), *China Facts and Figures Annual Handbook* (Gulf Breeze, FL: Academic International Press, 1993), 280.

NOTE: CCTV2 = China Central Television Channel 2; CCTV8 = China Central Television Channel 8; BTV6 = Beijing Television Channel 6; BTV21 = Beijing Television Channel 21; STV8 = Shanghai Television Channel 8; STV20 = Shanghai Television Channel 20; GTV14 = Guangdong Television Channel 14; GTV2 = Guangdong Television Channel 2. Local enterprises and joint ventures paid in Chinese currency, except where noted. Foreign companies were charged in U.S. or Hong Kong dollars. Price ranges indicate that media rates were based on specific time spots, which had their own fixed rates. In 1992, 1 *yuan* was equal to about US$0.18 and HK$1 was equal to about US$0.13.

Advertising Manufacturers

Since the late 1980s, the increasingly diversified advertising forms in China have turned many advertising manufacturers into an independent sector in the advertising industry. Their business ranges from the designing and printing of posters and product catalogs to the manufacture of neon lights, light boxes, and electronic displays. Their business volume as a proportion of China's annual total advertising billings has varied from nearly 20% in the early 1980s to no more than 5% in the late 1990s.[72] Typical examples of advertising manufacturers are the Beijing Advertising & Art Corporation, the

TABLE 18.11 Advertising Media Rates for CCTV Channels (effective January 1, 1999)

Channel	Broadcast Time	Rates[a] (yuan)		
		5 Seconds	*15 Seconds*	*30 Seconds*
Channel 1	after 7:00 a.m.	7,000	7,000	12,000
	6:00 p.m.-10:50 p.m.	10,000-40,000	20,000-80,000	36,000-126,000
	after 11:00 p.m.	7,000	12,000	21,600
Channel 2	after 7:00 a.m.	5,000	5,000	9,000
	7:30 p.m.-11:28 p.m.	5,000-38,000	10,000-38,000	18,000-68,400
Channel 3	after 7:00 a.m.	3,500	3,500	5,000
	after 6:00 p.m.	6,000	6,000	9,000
Channel 4 (satellite)	anytime	4,500	4,500	7,000
Channel 7	6:00 p.m.-9:00 p.m.	4,500	4,500	7,000
	other time	3,500	3,500	5,000
Channel 8	after 7:00 a.m.	3,500	3,500	5,000
	after 6:00 p.m.	8,000	8,000	12,000

SOURCE: Adapted from *People's Daily,* October 15, 1998, 2.

a. Price ranges indicate that media rates are based on specific time spots, which have their own fixed rates. In 1999, 1 *yuan* was equal to US$0.12.

Shanghai Dongfang Neon Light & Advertising Corporation, the Guangdong Cultural Advertising & Decorating Corporation, and the Tianjin Art & Advertising Corporation.[73]

TABLE 18.12 Outdoor Advertising Rates in China, 1992

Type	Rate	Minimum Rental Period
Billboards	US$35-80/sq m per month	6 months
Neon signs	US$60-80/sq m per month	3 years
Bus shelter (Shanghai only)	US$7,000 per shelter	1 year
Trolleys (Shanghai only)	US$10,000 for three trolleys	6 months
Light box	negotiable	negotiable

SOURCE: Adapted from John D. Friske (ed.), *China Facts and Figures Annual Handbook* (Gulf Breeze, FL: Academic International Press, 1993), 281.

Advertising Administrations, Associations, and Regulations

Advertising Administrations

The highest administrative body in charge of advertising in China is the Advertising Office of the State Administration for Industry and Commerce (SAIC), which is under the aegis of the State Council. In turn, administrations for industry and commerce of local governments at various levels all have advertising departments or sections.

In addition to implementing the general regulations for advertising promulgated by the State Council, the Advertising Office of the SAIC drafts detailed rules governing advertising in China. Authorized by the State Council, the office inspects and registers organizations (including both enterprises and institutions) engaged in advertising business, issues advertising business licenses, examines and supervises all advertising activities, solves disputes in advertising business, encourages the disclosure of deception and other illegal behavior in advertising, and gives guidance to advertising associations.

Units that intend to be engaged in the advertising business nationally must apply to the Advertising Office of the SAIC for business licenses. Those preferring to do local advertising business must apply for licenses through local administrations for industry and commerce. Foreign advertising agencies intending to open offices in China must first apply to the Advertising Office of the SAIC for approval, and then register at all local administrations for industry and commerce in the areas where their offices are to be set up. Foreign enterprises intending to start advertising companies or joint ventures on a national scale in China must apply to the Ministry of Foreign Economic Relations and Trade for approval, and then report to the SAIC for business licenses. If the proposed companies or joint ventures are local in scope, they must send their applications for review to both local government departments of foreign economic relations and trade, and local advertising departments of the administration for industry and commerce. The applications are then forwarded to the Advertising Office of the SAIC for approval. Once an application is approved, the local advertising department concerned will issue the business license.[74]

Advertising Associations

There are two national advertising associations in China. One is the China Advertising Association (CAA), established in December 1983, which in the mid-1990s had about 10,000 corporate members from government administrative bodies, advertising agencies, the media, and advertisers. The CAA coordinates and gives guidance to local advertising associations that have so far been set up in 27 provinces or autonomous regions and 18 major cities. It has a number of affiliated committees: the advertising agency, newspaper, radio, television, railway, public transit, research, and legal consultative committees.[75]

The other association is the China National Advertising Association for Foreign Economic Relations and Trade (CFAA), set up in August 1981. Its more than 100 members include domestic advertising corporations that handle advertising for foreign trade, joint-venture advertising agencies, and publishing houses under the Ministry of Foreign Economic Relations and Trade. The CFAA participates in international activities on behalf of China's foreign economic relations and trade sector. It co-sponsored, for example, the Third World Advertising Congress (with *South* magazine of the United Kingdom) held in Beijing in June 1987. More than 2,000 representatives from 52 countries and regions attended the conference.[76] In August 1994, the CFAA and the Western Communication Group Inc. jointly held the first U.S.-Sino Advertising and Corporate Identity Strategy Symposium in New York City.[77]

The China chapter of the New York-based International Advertising Association was officially set up in Beijing in May 1987. This IAA chapter had 33 members from 13 cities when it started, each prominent in China's advertising industry.[78]

Advertising Regulations and Law

Advertising is a carefully regulated industry in China. During the years between 1949, when the People's Republic of China was founded, and 1966, when the Cultural Revolution started, there was no national advertising regulation in China. All the regulations regarding advertising were made by local governments, such as those in Shanghai, Tianjin, Chongqing, Xian, and Guangzhou. During the Cultural Revolution, all those regulations disappeared, together with virtually the entire advertising industry in China.

It was not until February 1982 that the first national regulations for advertising, the *Interim Regulations for Advertising Management,* were promulgated by the State Council. The regulations contained the following major points:

- Administrations for industry and commerce at state and local levels were authorized to control advertising.
- All enterprises and institutions engaged in advertising had to be registered and had to hold business licenses.
- The content of advertisements had to be "clear and truthful."
- The following types of advertisements were not permitted: (a) those violating state policies, laws, and decrees; (b) those jeopardizing the dignity of the various ethnic groups in China; (c) those judged to be reactionary, obscene, disgusting, or superstitious; (d) those judged to be propaganda of a slanderous nature; and (e) those violating regulations on state secrets.
- Advertising fees were to be in accord with standard rates set by local administrations of industry and commerce.

In cases of violations of the regulations, the SAIC was required to issue disciplinary warnings or impose penalties; cases of "gross violations with serious consequences" were to be handled by the People's Court according to law.

In December 1987, the new *Regulations for Advertising Management* superseded the *Interim Regulations.* Although these two sets of regulations were similar in substance, the new regulations were clearer in language and less ideological in formulation. The major changes in the new regulations included the following:

- The distinction was removed between foreign and domestic advertising enterprises.
- Monopoly and unfair competition were prohibited.
- Individuals were allowed to engage in advertising businesses so long as they held business licenses (which was absolutely not allowed in the earlier regulations).
- The list of forbidden content now included symbols of China's national flag and emblem and the tune of China's national anthem, but advertisements violating the regulations on state secrets were not mentioned.
- Clear distinction between news reporting and advertising was emphasized, and journalists were not allowed to accept payment for stories that were effectively advertisements.

- Advertisements for cigarettes were forbidden on radio and television, and also in newspapers and periodicals, though high-quality liquor could be advertised.

- Proof had to be provided for products whose advertisements featured claims regarding quality standards, awards, patents, registered trademarks, health benefits, and so on.

- Advertising rates were no longer standardized, and commission rates were decided jointly by the SAIC and the state's price control department.

- More specific punishments were listed for the violators of the new regulations, which allowed defendants to appeal to the administration at a higher level.

Empowered by the State Council, the State Administration of Industry and Commerce promulgated detailed rules in June 1982 and January 1988 to explain the above two sets of regulations for advertising. Since 1987, the SAIC has also jointly issued several dozen sets of additional rules and circulars with other government departments under the State Council, to provide guidelines for advertising business and to deal with its problems and malpractice.

As part of a continuing government effort to "standardize advertising activities across the country," [79] the *Advertising Law of the People's Republic of China,* the first of its kind in Chinese history, was passed by the National People's Congress on October 27, 1994. This new law took effect on February 1, 1995, superseding the *Regulations for Advertising Management* that were effective from December 1987 through January 1995.

When compared with the regulations of 1987, the 1994 law, which has 49 articles, has four major new features. First, it is less ideology-oriented. Although the word "socialism" is used twice (Articles 1 and 3), the more aggressive political terms, such as "the dignity of the Chinese nation" and "reactionary," used in the 1987 regulations (Article 8), do not appear.

Second, the new law is more consumer-oriented. As is stated at the outset, it is formulated to "protect consumers' legal rights." [80] The new law includes special items on advertisements for medications, medical equipment (Articles 14 and 15), pesticides (Article 17), foods, alcohol, and cosmetics (Article 19). All are products closely related to consumers' health and safety.

Third, the ban on cigarette advertising in the new law is extended from radio, television, and newspapers in the 1987 regulations to magazines, cinemas, theaters, sports venues, and waiting rooms in airports and railway stations (Article 18).

The most outstanding feature of the new advertising law is, however, its stipulation of more severe punishments for malpractice than in the 1987 regulations. In the *Detailed Rules and Regulations for Advertising Manage-*

ment promulgated by the State Administration for Industry and Commerce in 1988 to supplement the 1987 regulations, the maximum fine for malpractice in advertising was 10,000 *yuan*.[81] But this amount has become the minimum fine in the new law, and the maximum fine can be either 100,000 *yuan* or five times the advertising fee involved (Articles 37-44).[82]

It seems that the new advertising law has been enforced pretty rigidly. In a sample of 5,002 commercials broadcast by television stations in six major cities in early 1995, 32.6% were found to have violated the law to some extent. Penalties, including denying renewal requests for advertising business licenses in the middle of that year, were reportedly imposed on the parties involved. Most of the commercials in trouble included puffery and were misleading.[83]

Before the new advertising law was enforced, unregulated business covered everything from patent medicine to wrinkle-removing cream. The new law has reportedly reined in extravagant product claims because it requires that advertising claims be backed by statistics and provable facts.[84]

Following the new advertising law, more regulations on advertising for certain types of products are in the making. Since late 1996, China, both the world's largest tobacco producer and the world's largest tobacco consumer, has been planning a nationwide ban on cigarette advertising. The first step is to establish cigarette advertising-free cities while continuing to resist the attempts of the tobacco industry, domestic and foreign alike, to create an even greater demand for tobacco products in the country. In late 1996, there were already rules against public smoking in 59 Chinese cities and in the provinces of Jilin, Shandong, and Shanxi. Smoking-free schools and colleges also emerged, with 123 in Beijing alone.[85]

In 1997, a new regulation governing television commercials for liquor with high alcohol content was imposed. The new rule bans from television screens commercials for spirits containing 40% or more alcohol. Commercials for liquor containing less than 40% alcohol have to get approval from the China Distillery Association and the China Food Industry Association before they can be broadcast. But no change was made to liquor advertisements published in newspapers and magazines.

The new regulation was issued by the State Administration for Industry and Commerce, the watchdog of China's advertising industry. In recent years, an increasing number of people have criticized the growing volume of liquor commercials broadcast between television programs, especially during prime-time television programs and news reports. During the 3 years prior to the new regulation, liquor producers had been the highest bidders for commercial airtime on prime-time television. Many people have also criticized the fact that the making of liquor consumes a great deal of grain in a country where many people in remote areas still do not have enough to eat.[86]

The new advertising law, as documented in recent research, has not had much effect on the Western cultural values portrayed in Chinese advertising, particularly television commercials. Instead of diminishing Western cultural values in advertising content, the new law seems—as previous advertising regulations also intended—to control certain Western values that are regarded as either politically or culturally unacceptable in China. In fact, politically unacceptable values have never been a serious problem for advertising there. No marketers, domestic or foreign, would resort to such values as "Western democracy" and "freedom of speech" to promote their products or services in China. And culturally unacceptable values have been consistently under control in Chinese advertising. The most prominent example is sex, which has had a very low profile in Chinese television commercials both before and after passage of the new advertising law. On the contrary, some other Western cultural values, such as competition, enjoyment, and individualism, have been found to be depicted even more often in Chinese television commercials since the new law came into effect—probably because they are not its targets.[87]

The above conclusions have important implications for both international advertising professionals and researchers who are interested in China. For the former, they imply that those who want to enter and stay established in the Chinese market should select cultural values not only aggressively promoting their products, but also fitting neatly into China's sociocultural context. For researchers, these conclusions pose challenging but exciting research possibilities, calling for specially planned approaches for China in comparison with those taken in other developing countries, and even in other parts of the world influenced by Chinese cultural values.[88]

Notes

1. Linqing Liu and Jixiu Chen, *Guanggao Guanli* [Advertising Management] (Beijing: China Finance and Economics, 1989), 39. See also Youwei Sun, *Guanggao Xue* [Advertising] (Beijing: World Affairs, 1991), 37; Bai-Yi Xu, *The Role of Advertising in China,* working paper (Urbana: University of Illinois, Department of Advertising, 1989), 4.

2. Ganlin Ding et al., *Jianming Zhongguo Xinwen Shi* [A Concise History of the Chinese Press] (Fuzhou, Fujian: Fujian People's Publishing House, 1985), 2. See also Bai-Yi Xu, *Marketing to China: One Billion New Customers* (Lincolnwood, IL: NTC Business Books, 1990), xxi.

3. Frank H. H. King and Prescott Clarke, *A Research Guide to China-Coast Newspapers, 1822-1911* (Cambridge, MA: Harvard East Asian Research Center, 1965), 20-21.

4. Won Ho Chang, *Mass Media in China: The History and the Future* (Ames: Iowa State University Press, 1989), 7.

5. Xu, *Marketing to China*, xxi. See also Liu and Chen, *Guanggao Guanli*, 47.

6. Liu and Chen, *Guanggao Guanli*, 47. See also Xu, *The Role of Advertising*, 6.

7. Xu, *The Role of Advertising*, 6. See also Xu, *Marketing to China*, xxii.

8. Xu, *Marketing to China*, xxii-xxiii.

9. Ibid., xxiii.

10. Sun, *Guanggao Xue*, 47.

11. Xu, *Marketing to China*, xxiii.

12. Sun, *Guanggao Xue*, 49.

13. Liu and Chen, *Guanggao Guanli*, 55.

14. Xu, *Marketing to China*, xxv.

15. Barbara S. Baudot, *International Advertising Handbook: A User's Guide to Rules and Regulations* (Lexington, MA: Lexington, 1989), 9.

16. Xu, *Marketing to China*, xxv.

17. Lauren A. Swanson, "China Myths and Advertising Agencies," *International Journal of Advertising*, vol. 16, no. 4, 1997, 277. See also Lauren A. Swanson, "People's Advertisements in China: A Longitudinal Content Analysis of the *People's Daily* Since 1949," *International Journal of Advertising*, vol. 15, no. 3, 1996, 222-238.

18. Yinghui Wang, "Advertising: An Accelerator for Economic Development in China," *Jingji Xinxi Bao* [Economic Information Gazette] (Beijing), September 8, 1991, 2.

19. Yunpen Ding, "Restoring the Good Name of Advertising in China," *Wenhui Gazette* (Shanghai), January 14, 1979, 3.

20. Lubing Fan, "1993: The Advertising Year of China," *Baokan Guanggao Wenzhai* [Advertising Digest From the Press], no. 5, 1994, 56.

21. "China Hosts Advertising Festival," *Advertising Age*, May 29, 1997 (on-line: http://ads.adage.com /search97cgi/s97_cgi).

22. Paul Parsons, "Marketing Revolution Hits Staid Giants . . . While in China, Advertising Blooms Like a Hundred Flowers," *Advertising Age*, July 19, 1993, 18.

23. "Yahoo!'s Ad Agency," *China Daily* (Beijing), February 5, 1999, 4.

24. Mat Matsuda, "Dentsu Eases Through Open Door," *Advertising Age*, December 14, 1981, S9. See also Barbara Mueller, *International Advertising: Communication Across Cultures* (Belmont, CA: Wadsworth, 1996), 306; Swanson, "China Myths," 281.

25. Suzanne Miao, "Burnett Looks to Build in China," *Adweek*, May 3, 1993, 14.

26. *Zhongguo Guanggao Nianjian* [China Advertising Yearbook] (Beijing: Xinhua, 1995), 23.

27. "World's Top Fifty Advertising Organizations," *Advertising Age*, April 27, 1998, S10.

28. "Top Ten Advertising Companies in 1997," *Xiandai Guanggao* [Modern Advertising], no. 3, 1998, 39.

29. Tianhong Li and Feng He, "The Competition Situation of Chinese Advertising Companies Seen From Their Concentration Degree," *Xiandai Guanggao* [Modern Advertising], no. 4, 1998, 12-13.

30. "Dentsu Forges Educational Links With China," *Advertistng Age*, September 11, 1996 (on-line: http://ads.adage.com/search97cgi/s97_cgi).

31. "First Chinese Agency to Open in U.S.," *Advertising Age,* August 17, 1997 (on-line: http://ads.adage.com/search97cgi/s97_cgi).

32. Bill Britt, "State-Owned Media Offer Advertiser Benefits in China," *Advertising Age,* June 12, 1996 (on-line: http://ads.adage.com/search97cgi/s97_cgi).

33. Richard W. Pollay, David K. Tse, and Zhengyuan Wang, "Advertising, Propaganda, and Value Change in Economic Development: The New Cultural Revolution in China and Attitudes Toward Advertising," *Journal of Business Research,* vol. 20, no. 2, 1990, 83.

34. Britt, "State-Owned Media."

35. Xinshu Zhao and Fuyuan Shen, "Audience Reaction to Commercial Advertising in China in the 1980s," *International Journal of Advertising,* vol. 14, no. 4, 1995, 387-388.

36. Swanson, "China Myths," 279.

37. *Zhongguo Guanggao Nianjian* [China Advertising Yearbook] (Beijing: Xinhua, 1988), 22, 27, 31.

38. *Zhongguo Guanggao Nianjian* [China Advertising Yearbook] (Beijing: Xinhua, 1992), 24.

39. *Zhongguo Guanggao Nianjian* [China Advertising Yearbook] (Beijing: Xinhua, 1998), 27. See also Lubin Fan, "Chinese Advertising in the First Half of 1998," *Zhongguo Guanggao* [China Advertising], no. 5, 1998, 24.

40. *Zhongguo Guanggao Nianjian,* 1988, 26.

41. Lauren A. Swanson, "Advertising in China: Viability and Structure," *European Journal of Marketing,* vol. 24, no. 10, 1990, 28.

42. Ibid., 29.

43. Ibid.

44. "Top Ten Advertising Companies in 1997," 39.

45. *Zhongguo Guanggao Nianjian* [China Advertising Yearbook] (Beijing: Xinhua, 1996), 156.

46. Kenneth D. Day and Qingwen Dong, "Normative Theories of the Role of Mass Media and Mass Communication Research in China," paper presented at the annual meeting of the National Communication Association, New York, 1998, 1.

47. *Zhongguo Guanggao Nianjian,* 1988, 32.

48. Ibid., 28; *Zhongguo Guanggao Nianjian,* 1992, 30.

49. *Zhongguo Guanggao Nianjian,* 1998, 27.

50. Fan, "Chinese Advertising."

51. Xu, *Marketing to China,* 73.

52. Day and Dong, "Normative Theories," 1.

53. "China's Advertising Media, 1990-1993," *Baokan Guanggao Wenzhai* [Advertising Digest From the Press], no. 5, 1994, 57.

54. Xu, *Marketing to China,* 74. See also Mueller, *International Advertising,* 308.

55. *Zhongguo Guanggao Nianjian,* 1988, 28; *Zhongguo Guanggao Nianjian* [China Advertising Yearbook] (Beijing: Xinhua, 1997), 27. See also Fan, "Chinese Advertising."

56. *Zhongguo Guanggao Nianjian,* 1995, 18; *Zhongguo Guanggao Nianjian,* 1998, 27. See also Fan, "Chinese Advertising."

57. "Economic and Social Development in China," *Beijing Review,* October 17, 1994, 18. See also *Zhongguo Guanggao Nianjian,* 1996, 63.

58. "China's Advertising Media, 1990-1993," 57. See also *Zhongguo Guanggao Nianjian,* 1996, 45.

59. *Zhongguo Guanggao Nianjian,* 1995, 18; *Zhongguo Guanggao Nianjian,* 1997, 27.

60. Fan, "Chinese Advertising."

61. *Zhongguo Guanggao Nianjian,* 1995, 21. See also Fan, "1993."

62. *Zhongguo Guanggao Nianjian,* 1996, 63.

63. "China's TVs Tune in to Prime Time," *China Daily* (Beijing), August 30, 1993, 3.

64. *Zhongguo Guanggao Nianjian,* 1988, 29; *Zhongguo Guanggao Nianjian,* 1998, 27.

65. *Zhongguo Guanggao Nianjian,* 1995, 18; *Zhongguo Guanggao Nianjian,* 1997, 27. See also Fan, "Chinese Advertising."

66. *Zhongguo Guanggao Nianjian,* 1996, 45.

67. Suzanne Miao, "Chinese Advertisers Face Rate Hikes: Media Costs Skyrocket at TV Stations, Newspapers," *Adweek,* January 4, 1993, 32.

68. Hong Cheng, "Advertising in China: A Socialist Experiment," in Katherine T. Frith (ed.), *Advertising in Asia: Communication, Culture and Consumption* (Ames: Iowa State University Press, 1996), 88.

69. Ning Li, "World's Largest LED Screen in Operation," *Beijing Review,* November 21, 1994, 28.

70. *Zhongguo Guanggao Nianjian,* 1996, 166.

71. "Kodak Snaps Up Prime Ad Site in Beijing," *Advertising Age,* January 1, 1998 (on-line: http://ads.adage.com/search97cgi/s97_cgi).

72. *Zhongguo Guanggao Nianjian,* 1988, 31; *Zhongguo Guanggao Nianjian,* 1998, 25.

73. *Zhongguo Guanggao Nianjian,* 1998, 309, 331, 365, 445.

74. Swanson, "Advertising in China," 27-28.

75. *Zhongguo Guanggao Nianjian,* 1996, 92.

76. *Zhongguo Guanggao Nianjian,* 1995, 125.

77. *Zhongguo Guanggao Nianjian,* 1996, 86.

78. Xu, *Marketing to China,* 69.

79. *Zhongguo Guanggao Nianjian,* 1996, 68.

80. Ibid.

81. Ibid., 53.

82. Hong Cheng, "Toward an Understanding of Cultural Values Manifest in Advertising: A Content Analysis of Chinese Television Commercials in 1990 and 1995," *Journalism & Mass Communication Quarterly,* vol. 74, no. 4, 1997, 777-778.

83. "Thirty Percent of Television Commercials Have Violated the Law," *Shichang Bao* [Market Gazette] (Beijing), May 23, 1995, 1.

84. Gary Bennett (ed.), *China Facts and Figures Annual Handbook* (Gulf Breeze, FL: Academic International Press, 1996), 393.

85. "China Plans Nationwide Ban on Tobacco Advertising," *Advertising Age,* September 22, 1996 (on-line: http://ads.adage.com/search97cgi/s97_cgi).

86. "China to Ban High Proof Spirit Ads From TV," *Advertising Age,* June 11, 1997 (on-line: http://ads.adage.com/search97cgi/s97_cgi).

87. Cheng, "Toward an Understanding," 791.

88. Katherine T. Frith and James Tsao, "Advertising and Cultural China: Challenges and Opportunities in Asia," *Asian Journal of Communication,* vol. 8, no. 2, 1998, 1-17.

Part III

An International Perspective on Measurement and Evaluation

19

How Single-Source
Research First Developed

Colin McDonald

How Individuals Respond to Advertising

Here is a commonsense scenario of how we think advertising probably works.
Each of us, every day, is confronted with a lot of advertising. Much of it is for
things we don't buy and never will buy; we will ignore most of these ads, but
we may notice a few of them and even enjoy them for their own sake (without
necessarily deciding to do anything as a result). But some of the advertising
we see is for things (goods, services, and so on) that we do buy or might buy.
How do we respond to these?

Sometimes it is possible that seeing an ad may suddenly stimulate a new
idea, like when the little light bulb appears over the man's head in the cartoon.
But probably this is rather rare. Much more likely is the reiteration of what is
already familiar. Ads, assuming we notice them at all, continuously nudge us,
keeping alive the desirable images that are already in our minds, replenishing
the emotional strata laid down by all the earlier advertising we have seen
before and our experience of the products.

This process is continuous and is the source of the long-term, brand equity-building effect of advertising. But it does not make sense to think of this long-term effect as distinct (or different in nature) from the immediate response that we have to advertising each time we notice it. Much nonsense has resulted from trying to pretend that advertising somehow works only in the long term. This response may take a variety of forms: pleased recognition, an emotional lift, amusement, curiosity, possibly a negative reaction (boredom, repulsion). Occasionally (almost certainly in a minority of exposures) a person's seeing an ad may lead him or her to take some action, including buying the brand next time if it is a regularly bought category. This last evidence of response may also be affected by other factors, such as consumer offers and price promotions or the strength of competitive advertising, and it would be reasonable to expect these factors to work together in guiding the customer toward one brand rather than others the next time he or she has to think about it.

This view of advertising response is entirely common sense; that is, it is what one would construct just by looking into one's own experience before examining any evidence from outside. The important thing about it is that it does not assume anything automatic or inevitable about the response. Not only do individuals differ from each other in what they respond to, but the same individuals can vary in their responses at different times. People, one would expect, are very volatile in how they respond to the same advertising at different times; their responses depend on what happens to be uppermost in their minds (or emotions). The carrying through of mental response into buying behavior must be even more volatile still, because other factors then intervene. We might buy more of brand A this week than usual because it is on sale at the supermarket, and ads for A might well have reinforced that decision—but it probably means we will buy less of A next week (just because we have satisfied our need in advance), and our seeing more ads for A will not then make any difference. For an ad to be working, we only have to show that some people respond to it some of the time, perhaps quite rarely.

Within-Person Measurement

Unfortunately, that very randomness and unpredictability, and comparative rarity, of responses (especially if they are evaluated in terms of buying behavior) make it very difficult to be certain when one has obtained a genuine response, much less a measure of responses in quantity. Putting together the usual aggregate measures of sales, purchases, or attitudes on the one hand and advertising delivery weights on the other simply does not work. It is impossible to be sure, even when there is a correlation, that the sales movement is the result of the advertising and not of some other factor that is confounding the measurement. There is only one way in which it is possible to prove convincingly that advertising has caused behavioral or attitudinal change, and that is to take the measure down to the level of the individual and find those cases where a person's behavior is different after he or she has seen advertising than it was before; one can then add together these links, established at the disaggregated level, with confidence that we know what the resulting measure means. It is for this reason—the normal aggregate measures not working and the need for a different kind of measure at the level of the individual—that many operators have despaired of establishing short-term advertising effects, or even doubted that they exist, and concentrated so heavily on the long term.

But can short-term effects, at the individual level, be observed and measured? Yes, they can, if we have the right data.

The J. Walter Thompson Panel

Measurement of such short-term effects was first done in 1966, in an experimental project that was commissioned by J. Walter Thompson Limited (London). Housewives in the London television area kept diaries over 13 weeks at the end of the year.[1] Completed diaries were obtained from 255 housewives. On each day, the housewives recorded their purchases in 50 different product fields, the issues they had seen out of 32 newspapers and magazines, and the television segments they had seen, with each program and commercial break separately identified.

The purpose of the experiment was to seek a deeper insight into housewives' patterns of purchasing in relation to their opportunities to see (OTS) advertisements. OTS were derived through the collation of the detailed reading and viewing information in the diaries with known print insertions and transmissions of commercials for different brands.

The raw material that could be derived from each diary consisted of a day-by-day record of purchases and OTS for that person. Table 19.1 shows an

TABLE 19.1 Part of One Person's Data on Cereals

Days	Sept.	20 Tues.	21 Wed.	22 Thurs.	23 Fri.	24 Sat.	25 Sun.	26 Mon.
Purchases		J	—	Q	—	—	—	G
OTS		C		C	C	C		
		F			F			F
		J	J		J			J
		O	O	O				
			G	G			G	G
			Y					
					B	B		

example of one of these records for breakfast cereals, the code letters referring
to different brands.

The First Analysis

The question for analysis was how to find a valid relationship between these
two "time series" of ads and purchases. Simply relating the aggregate numbers
together gives a spurious matching driven by weight: the heavier buyers also
see more television and therefore more ads (for everything). As already
discussed, the relationship had to be within individuals.

An important constraint is that a causal relationship, if it exists at all, must
point forward in time. Change toward a brand must be more likely after
advertising has been seen than before if we are to say that there is a short-term
effect. The first investigation—of three product categories—therefore looked
at cases in which two successive purchases of the same brand were followed
by a change; that is, people had followed the purchasing sequence A→A→B.
If a short-term effect is operating, we would expect to find that there were
relatively more OTS for B, on average, in the second interval (when A→B)
than in the first (when A→A); conversely, there would be fewer OTS for A in
the A→B interval than in the A→A one. When we aggregate all these cases,
we in fact find the results shown in Table 19.2.

A marginal effect of the kind we have hypothesized exists. In all of the
rows except the last one, there are more B OTS, and fewer A OTS, in the

TABLE 19.2 Sequences in Which Two Purchases of the Same Brand Are Followed by a Switch (A→A→B)

	First Interval (A→A)	*Second Interval (A→B)*
Laundry detergents		
OTS B	110	128
OTS A	166	157
Cereals		
OTS B	140	150
OTS A	184	174
Tea		
OTS B	60	76
OTS A	55	64

second interval than the first. B OTS are associated with later switching to B; A OTS are associated with not switching away from A.

The Main Analysis: Change and Repeat Measures

This first-line evidence that we were seeing short-term effects led to a more general analysis using the purchase interval as the unit analyzed. One can do this, of course, only with categories that are purchased fairly frequently. A purchase interval is any two successive purchases and the space between them, which may or may not be filled with advertising OTS.

Let us consider a Brand X (which can stand for each of the individual brands in a product field in turn). The people who will give us useful information for switching analysis are those who buy Brand X and at least one other brand in the course of the panel. Let us call O all other brands bought that are not X.

In terms of Brand X, an individual can have only four kinds of purchase intervals:

- *Switching intervals:* to X (O→X)
   or away from X (X→O)
- *Loyal intervals:* X→X
- *Intervals unconnected with Brand X:* O→O

TABLE 19.3 One Respondent's Cereal Record

Purchases	J	Q	G	H	L	F	A
OTS in intervals	2J	1J	1J				
	1G	2G	1G				3G
	1F	1F	3F	4F			
	1C	3C	1C	4C	1C	1C	
		2R	4R			2R	
						1T	1T

For each brand, these intervals can be cross-tabulated against the occurrence of OTS for X, thus:

	OTS for X in Interval					
	0	1	2	3	4	etc.
O→X						
X→O						
X→X						
O→O						

Table 19.3 shows how this counting procedure works for the cereals example in Table 19.1. Counting G in Table 19.3, we find:

	OTS in Interval				
	0	1	2	3	4+
O→G			1		
G→O		1			
G→G					
O→O	2	1		1	

In this example, the housewife had two OTS for G before she changed to G and one before she changed away from G. In her other intervals, when she did not buy G at all, she had, respectively, three OTS once, one once, and none twice.

This counting is done for each brand in turn and the resulting tables are added to produce a composite Brand X. It will be noticed that each switch interval will be counted twice: an interval A→B will be taken as both O→B

TABLE 19.4 Change and Repeat Ratios

OTS in Interval	0, 1	2+
Change (% O→X out of all O→ intervals)		
Laundry detergents	20.8	29.0
Cereals	17.8	25.6
Tea	16.9	24.2
Soup	26.2	29.3
Margarine	23.3	27.9
Bread	12.7	20.0
Toothpaste	32.8	41.4
Shampoo	29.4	37.8
Milk drinks	37.1	42.2
Average	24.1	30.8
Repeat (% X→X out of all X→ intervals)		
Laundry detergents	57.9	67.5
Cereals	32.6	51.3
Tea	61.9	73.2
Soup	66.6	65.9*
Margarine	70.8	72.6
Bread	59.4	66.1
Toothpaste	50.4	60.0
Shampoo	48.1	36.4*
Milk drinks	51.6	55.9
Average	55.5	61.0

*See text for explanation.

and A→O. Double or triple purchases on the same occasion are counted separately for each brand. The analysis was done for nine separate product categories.

From these tables of purchase interval type against number of OTS, one can calculate certain ratios that reveal whether there is an effect or not:

- *Change:* the proportion of all intervals starting with a different brand that end with brand X. If this proportion increases from left to right in the table (i.e., when there are more OTS for X in the interval), we can say that this shows the attractive power of the advertising toward the brand.

- *Repeat:* the proportion of all intervals starting with X that remain loyal to X at the second purchase. If this proportion increases when there are more OTS for X, it is a measure of the power of advertising to keep existing users loyal—that is, its retentive effect.

These ratios, for the nine categories, were as shown in Table 19.4. In almost every case (except for the two marked with asterisks in the table), there was a

TABLE 19.5 Nine Product Categories (aggregated)

	OTS in Interval				
	0	1	2	3	4 or More
Number of intervals	24,897	4,809	2,039	894	966
Type of interval (%)					
O→X	12.5	13.3	16.7	14.9	18.0
X→O	12.4	15.1	14.5	13.3	17.1
X→X	14.8	21.2	24.4	27.4	24.8
O→O	60.3	50.4	44.4	44.4	40.1
Change (%)	17.2	20.9	27.3	25.1	31.0
Repeat (%)	54.4	58.4	62.7	67.3	59.2

higher likelihood both of changing to or staying with the brand when at least two OTS for that brand had occurred than when there had been only one OTS or none.

If we aggregate the nine categories together, instead of averaging them as in Table 19.4, we can enlarge the sample enough to show the OTS broken out in more detail. This can be seen in Table 19.5. From this table, it is clear how both the change and the repeat variables increase in likelihood with even one OTS and increase again with two, and how the curve tails off at three or more. The table also shows greater instability because of the decreasing sample bases. We need to remember always that it is more common for consumers not to see our advertising, even when they are heavily exposed to television.

OTS Brand Share

Another analysis, done for only one product category (laundry detergents), found that the same trends occurred if OTS are expressed in brand share terms instead of simply as numbers. This is to be expected if two or more OTS tend to "win" over one and is a useful confirmation (see Table 19.6).

Effects of OTS in a Short Period

The analyses discussed above were all based on counts of OTS in an entire purchase interval, which might have lasted from a day or two to a couple of

TABLE 19.6 Share of OTS for the Brand (in percentages)

	0-.10	*.11-.20*	*.21-.30*	*.31-.40*	*.41+*
Change	17.4	28.8	24.1	25.0	35.8
Repeat	61.6	67.3	69.5	64.2	68.4

weeks. But it seemed reasonable to expect that OTS received shortly before a purchase may have a stronger effect. Longer purchase intervals (e.g., more than a week) have more opportunity to contain large numbers of OTS (three or more), yet the effect of these larger numbers could be diluted by their being spread over a longer period; this could be the explanation of the apparent drop in effectiveness with three or four or more OTS (Table 19.5).

To check this hypothesis, a count was done in the same manner in which the OTS counted were limited to a "window" of 4 days before the second purchase in the interval. The results showed that, indeed, the effectiveness was a little stronger at the higher OTS levels, although the general shape of the response was not altered; it was still the case that the effect leveled off after two OTS.

Summary

These results from the J. Walter Thompson experimental panel of 1966 seemed to confirm a number of hypotheses about the purchasing of fast-moving consumer goods, hypotheses that were being formulated on other grounds at about the same time. They showed that it was rare for consumers to "change brands" in a drastic manner; rather, most consumers had repertoires of a few (sometimes many) brands among which they would interchange.

With at least some consumers, one could perceive directly that these switching patterns were related to opportunities to see advertising. Buying probabilities grew up to a certain level of OTS before the purchase occasion, but tended to level off after about three OTS, and the effects appeared to be stronger when the OTS occurred only a short time before the purchase. The findings were influential in the development, during the 1970s and 1980s, of the idea of "effective frequency"—the concept that one should attempt to direct advertising to target consumers in such a way that they would receive enough, but not a wasteful amount, of opportunities to see before the days when they would be doing the most purchasing.

It is important not to overstate what these findings mean. They are evidence that advertising is "working" in the sense that buying consumers are responding to it. Only some consumers, and only some of the time, respond in this visible way by actually changing their behavior immediately after seeing advertising, but that does not mean that those who do not switch in this obvious way are not also responding—we infer that, to some extent, they are. We still know very little about what is going on, and how it varies between brands, with different sorts of products and consumers, or how advertising interacts with other types of promotion. We do not have a "model" of advertising working, still less a predictive model for future sales. Much more investigation is needed before these aims can be reached.

All we do know—but it is a significant piece of knowledge—is that it is possible, by analyzing panel data longitudinally within respondents, to observe advertising as it is working. That means that we should be able to identify a brand for which the advertising is being effective and distinguish it from another brand for which the advertising is failing, even when market conditions are such that it is not possible to differentiate between the two brands in terms of short-term movements in sales. It should also be possible to relate observable short-term working with the long-term, brand equity-building effectiveness of the advertising.

Note

1. Colin McDonald, "What Is the Short-Term Effect of Advertising?" *Admap,* November 1970, 350-356, 366. This work has also been reprinted in Simon Broadbent (ed.), *Market Researchers Look at Advertising: A Collection of ESOMAR Papers 1949-1979* (London: Sigmatext, 1980); and Michael J. Naples (ed.), *Effective Frequency: The Relationship Between Frequency and Advertising Effectiveness* (New York: Association of National Advertisers, 1979), 83-103.

Editor's Note

A few comments need to be made about the preceding chapter. McDonald's contribution is important because he is a seminal figure who himself pioneered the type of research described: the ingenious method called *single-source research.*

The term *single-source research* has been used since the 1960s to describe the technique that measures consumer purchasing of a brand in the households that have received advertising for it in comparison with purchasing of that brand in the households that have not received such advertising. The phrase means that the purchasing and advertising exposure are measured at a single source: the individual household.

The concept is simple to understand. However, it is difficult and expensive to employ in the marketplace. That is why McDonald's original concept has been modified in different ways at different times, and the effectiveness of his system has to some extent been eroded. The problem has always been to establish precisely the identities of the brands whose advertisements enter the households, and when these are received. There are great practical problems in collecting this information and applying it in turn to brand purchasing. McDonald's original method, which I have subsequently called *pure single-source research,* represents the classic and best system. I use the phrase *diluted single-source research* to describe weaker methods—those in which there is no rigorous control of the relationship between advertising for the identified brand and its purchasing immediately afterward.

McDonald describes the genesis of his technique and some of the insights into advertising effects revealed and propagated during the first quarter century of irregular and rather unsatisfactory development of his system. He stops short of the most recent and broadest-scale employment of the method, which was carried out in the early 1990s by A. C. Nielsen in the United States, and which has received wide publicity.[1] This large study represented a return to McDonald's pure single-source system, and its rather dramatic results stem directly from the use of McDonald's carefully contrived technique.

Note

1. See John Philip Jones, *When Ads Work: New Proof That Advertising Triggers Sales* (New York: Simon & Schuster-Lexington, 1995).

20

Short-Term Advertising Strength

New Empirical Evidence From Norway

Thorolf Helgesen
Morten Micalsen

STAS is the well-known acronym for Short-Term Advertising Strength, a concept developed by John Philip Jones. As many people know, Jones studied the effect of advertising on sales based on a single-source panel in the United States. The panel consisted of 2,000 households with both TV meters and in-home scanners. Knowing the advertising schedule, he was able to describe the differences in purchase behavior between those exposed to TV advertising and those not exposed to TV advertising within a period of 7 days. STAS is an index describing this difference. If sales in the two groups are equal, the STAS index will be 100, meaning no difference. A STAS score of

120 indicates a sales increase of 20% generated by advertising among those exposed to it.[1]

Jones's findings and conclusions attack many established beliefs about how advertising works:

- In the past, most of us have heard the statement, "Advertising must be allowed some time to work before we can see the effects." Jones has demonstrated that the first exposure is by far the most effective—and furthermore, if advertising does not work in the short term, it will not work in the long term either. This means that a STAS score above 100 is a gatekeeper for long-term sales effects.

- Krugman's experiments in the 1960s resulted in a widely adopted belief that a frequency of three exposures was an optimum (the "effective frequency" theory). By looking at response curves, Jones found that most of the effect was in fact generated after one exposure only.

- David Ogilvy's philosophy of "concentrate and dominate" is also attacked by Jones's findings. Jones's theory supports recency planning. It stresses planning for continuous short-term reach, and it stresses reaching purchasers, not consumers.

Based on the work of John Philip Jones, we designed a Norwegian STAS project, which we describe below.

The Norwegian STAS Project

Jones used TV meters and in-home scanners in a single-source panel to study the effects of TV advertising. As this type of panel is not available in Norway, we had to use a simpler approach. We also had to cover print advertising, as print is a major advertising channel in Norway. Our study—like Jones's study—included only fast-moving consumer goods and was not intended to cover less repetitive types of purchases.

We used a diary covering 3 commercial TV channels (measuring 5-minute intervals), reading of 13 newspapers and magazines, and purchases of 126 different brands. The sample was drawn from Gallup's Consumer & Media—a study that provided us with more than 3,000 previously collected pieces of information for each respondent. Our net sample was 863 households—meaning a response rate of an impressive 75%. We also had to limit the study to 2 months' duration. Even though our study was much smaller than Jones's, we would have had to conduct about 50,000 interviews in order to collect the same information. For the samples, see Table 20.1.

TABLE 20.1 Comparison of the Jones and Norwegian Studies

	Jones Study	*Norwegian Study*
Method	scanners + TV meters	diary
Sample	2,000 households	863 households
Period	1 year	2 months
Media	TV	TV and print

Organizing the Project

In most countries, a lot of money is involved in advertising. Controversial findings such as Jones's could therefore easily lead to a lot of noise but no change in behavior. Taking this into consideration at an early stage, we tried to establish a climate for collaboration across the industry by including ad agencies, media, advertisers, and media buyers/planners in our project planning process. After nearly 2 years of planning and presentations of international research at many meetings, we were finally ready to conduct a Norwegian STAS project by the end of 1997. A total of 23 companies participated and helped finance the project by paying an entrance fee. A budget of approximately US$175,000 was collected.

The aim of the project was to get a better general understanding of how advertising works in Norway, both in general terms and more specifically for the participating companies. Would we find the same results in Norway as Jones found in the United States? What kind of short-term sales effects could be generated using different media?

The Findings

After analyzing 33 campaigns, we calculated the STAS scores (purchase of Brand X exposed to advertising indexed on purchase of Brand X not exposed to advertising, providing the baseline of 100). Given the STAS scores, we could also calculate the actual effects on sales. Because not all people exposed to the advertising will buy the brand—and not all people buying the brand have been exposed to the advertising—the actual sales increase is limited by

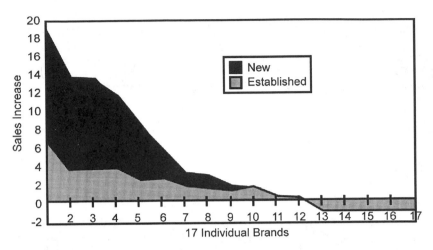

Figure 20.1 Range of Sales Increases

the number of people who are exposed to advertising for Brand X within the 7-day window.

For one-third of the established brands we found no sales increase. For the remaining two-thirds, the results range from 0.2% to about 7%. No campaign for an established brand managed to increase its sales by more than 7%. This—we know—is far less than many would have expected. We discuss the reasons in the next section.

All of the campaigns for new brands managed to increase sales. The lowest effect recorded was a 0.3% increase in sales. The highest was 21%. The range of sales increases found is shown in Figure 20.1.

Our data reveal that only a small part of an established brand's market share is driven by advertising in the short term. To some extent this also seems to be true for new brands, although advertising could play a more important role there.

In many cases, we found brands with a penetration rate in the range of 20-30% in a 2-month period. Often more than 50% of the purchases are made by less than 10% of those buying the brand. Their behavior seems quite unaffected by advertising. Occasional buyers seem to be the group in which advertising can generate some increase in sales in the short term.

This point raises the question as to whom the advertisers should try to target. In many cases, heavy users are the target—for maintenance purposes.

If so, a sales increase cannot be expected, as these people are already heavy buyers. In cases where medium or light users are defined as targets, we often find that advertisers have very little knowledge about target size and potential. Often, these groups tend to be rather small. This makes advertising goals in terms of advertising awareness a poor measure: It's not how many you reach—it's which specific people you reach.

The real problem is how to target these groups through media. They are rarely definable by demographics. This might be the reason many campaigns seem to miss target groups with potential, even though they often cover more than 50% of the population.

We have no reason to believe that TV advertising is more efficient than print advertising—or the other way around. Both TV and print campaigns have proven sales increases in our research. However, in some cases we have found evidence that print can be more cost-effective than TV, due to lower contact costs and better ability to cover specific groups.

For TV, the STAS scores varied from 55 to 329, with an arithmetic mean of 150; in five cases, the scores were negative. For print media, the scores varied from 129 to 360, with an arithmetic mean of 208; in no cases were the scores negative.

When it comes to response functions, our findings are similar to Jones's. On average, the first exposure accounts for about 60% of the effect, if any. The remaining 40% stems from the next two or three exposures, suggesting that coverage is more important than frequency. However, in real life, many media channels must generate high frequency in order to obtain high coverage. Again, it is not high coverage in general that is important, but high coverage with low frequency in, for example, groups of light users of the brand. In many cases—especially when using television—this means high frequency and high costs, making advertising an expensive tool.

A 3% increase in sales on a US$2 million campaign—a heavy campaign in Norway—is not a good investment for many advertisers, at least not in the short term. The return depends, among other things, on sales volume, profit margins, and advertising costs. In general, you need a large sales volume and high profit margin in order to make a profit on a sales increase of only 3% stemming from advertising.

But can we really expect the increase to be higher? Our research suggests that for most established brands of repeat-purchase packaged goods, a realistic expectation should not exceed 3%. The power of personal experience and habit seems to be far more important than advertising, as suggested by Andrew

Ehrenberg in the awareness-trial-reinforcement (ATR) model.[2] In our study, we found advertising for established brands to be a weak force in terms of spontaneous consumer response. For new brands, advertising can play an important role in building penetration.

STAS Scores: Some Strategic Perspectives

Measuring STAS scores is one thing; interpreting STAS scores in a strategic perspective amounts to something more. Let us take as an example a STAS score of 120. Theoretically, this score represents a 20% increase in sales of Brand X among those exposed to the advertising for Brand X at least once during the preceding 7 days. Transferred to the market at large, the size of the increase depends on how many potential buyers have actually been exposed to advertising for Brand X during the same interval. If this is 10% of the potential buyers, the sales increase in the marketplace is 2%. Even if a 2% increase in sales may be interesting in some markets, it is significantly less than 20%. The findings from the Norwegian study indicate that a much more common result is something between 0.5% and 2.0%.

The reason for these unusually low sales increases is deficiency in the advertising budgets and in the weight of the advertising media, both of which contribute to an inability to provide the reach and frequency to establish widely and then repeat positive STAS effects. These seem to be a special characteristic of Norway—perhaps because commercial television is a relatively recent innovation.

In many markets, and especially in mature markets with established brands, any increase in sales tends to be temporary. What is gained in the short term tends to be lost again soon afterward. In order to justify the advertising expenditure, the economic contribution from an increase in sales should recover the advertising costs. With a 0.5-2.0% increase in sales, this will often prove to be impossible—although, of course, it depends on the advertising expenditure, the extra income from added sales, and the net contribution stemming from those extra sales.

In Norway, we found that a number of advertising campaigns did not recover their costs by means of extra sales. Does this mean that the advertisers would be better off by canceling the advertising beforehand? Not necessarily—because our calculation rests solely on the relation between advertising costs and revenues stemming from extra sales to consumers. Indeed, advertising also has a number of secondary effects that may be equally important, or even more so. Advertising may, among other things, improve the manufacturer's relationship with dealers; in addition, it may motivate the sales force, stimulate world-of-mouth recommendations, and function as a barrier to entry into the category for other products. So, possibly, any loss on advertising could, theoretically, perform a useful function by preventing still greater losses due, for example, to new intruders in the market. Consequently, the profitability of an advertising campaign cannot be evaluated on the basis of short-term consumer impact alone. Every relevant factor must be included in the analysis if one is to reach a realistic conclusion.

Varying STAS Scores

The next issue we need to discuss concerns the meaning and importance of varying STAS numbers. At first glance, one might say that a high STAS score is preferable to a lower STAS score. But the STAS score is a function of the number of exposures. Thus any STAS score has its price. If a STAS score of, say, 150 is obtained at twice the price of a score of 140, the lower score may be more cost-effective. By definition, advertisers will always prefer a lower STAS score to a higher one—as soon as the optimum number of exposures has been passed. The problem is that advertisers seldom, if ever, know when this happens. We have seen a tendency to concentrate more on STAS scores than on their costs.

Leaving out the issue of frequency and concentrating on effects from the first exposure only, one may still ask, What are the meaning and relevance of high versus low STAS scores? As John Philip Jones has pointed out, a low STAS score indicates a weakness in advertising creativity. In many cases, this may be true. And of course, the media schedule may have its weaknesses, too. With an infinite number of alternatives, it always seems possible to increase any STAS score by changing advertising strategies. However, in practical life, the possibilities are limited for a number of reasons, especially restrictions on time and money. It cannot be stressed enough that adequate pretesting is a most valuable tool for developing cost-effective campaigns. In fact, the STAS findings from Norway would probably have been different if pretesting of ads had been carried out more frequently. This is more than a guess. At the

Norwegian School of Management, a recent study of advertising practices showed that only one-third of the largest Norwegian advertisers pretested their advertising campaigns before they were exposed. Therefore, many of the Norwegian STAS findings stem from advertising that has not been pretested. With more extensive pretesting, the average STAS scores would probably have been higher.

New Brands Versus Established Brands

In our opinion, there are factors influencing STAS scores that may be even more important than creative messages and media plans. One of these becomes evident when we compare STAS scores across different types of brands. As we have pointed out, the Norwegian STAS findings strongly indicate that high STAS scores are mainly found for advertising campaigns for new, intrinsically interesting products, whereas STAS scores for long-established brands in mature markets tend to be smaller.

Furthermore, for brands with high market shares, STAS scores tend to be lower than STAS scores for new brands with smaller market shares. And as long as brands with large market shares also tend to be long established, such brands tend to have developed a *momentum*—the ability to sustain demand for a brand without further advertising support. This tends to reduce the STAS score.

In one extreme case from the Norwegian study, 97.7% of the purchases of a brand were made in the absence of preceding advertising exposures, as contrasted to 2.3% following previous advertising exposures. The STAS score was extremely low—only 55. These findings may be more understandable if we describe this brand's history: It has been an important brand in its category for about 50 years, and during all those years, the brand had been supported by heavy advertising. Probably it has a stock of loyal users, but the brand may have less appeal to younger people today.

Against this background, one may ask to what degree advertising for long-established brands is a sensible and profitable exercise. Many long-established brands enjoying low STAS scores might just as well refrain from advertising. But advertising has a number of secondary effects, such as those discussed above, that may justify the expenditure on many occasions.

Advertising: Offensive or Defensive?

An even more important aspect of advertising effectiveness is the basic function of advertising—is it offensive or defensive? That is, does it aim at expanding sales and market share, or does it aim primarily at market share maintenance? For new products, advertising is basically attacking—it aims at increasing penetration in order to stimulate sales and increase market share. For those that succeed—possibly 1 out of 10 introductions—STAS scores tend to be high. And in some cases—as demonstrated by the Norwegian STAS study—the advertising expenditures may also be recovered in the short run.

For established brands in mature markets, the situation is different: The function of advertising is mainly to protect markets shares, not expand them. As Ehrenberg has noted, advertising is the price firms pay to stay in business.[3] The question, then, is whether this price can be justified by a longer and still profitable brand life. In the Norwegian case cited above, one might ask whether the company should continue to keep the present brand alive by means of continued advertising on a large scale or whether it should be milked or relaunched—or, possibly, be replaced by an entirely new brand—according to the Boston Consulting Group's well-known matrix. The strategic implications of the STAS findings bear on these choices.

Advertising: Strong or Weak Force?

The Norwegian STAS findings indicate that advertising may function as a strong force as far as new products are concerned. This will be the case especially in growing markets. But for long-established brands in mature markets, the situation is different. In those cases, advertising operates mainly as a weak force—one explanation being the inherent momentum for established brands, with many purchases from consumers who have not been exposed to advertising recently. It might be argued that much of this momentum stems from previous advertising. However, in our opinion, it is more likely to stem from product qualities, competitive pricing, and effective distribution.

In our view, any STAS score can be interpreted and understood only when it is related to specific brands and market situations. It goes without saying that a number of factors must also be addressed in order to reach sensible and believable conclusions—among them, advertising as a part of the company's total marketing mix, the competitors' strategies and activities, and also changing buying patterns among consumers.

STAS Scores Below 100

Before leaving the issue of STAS scores, it seems worthwhile to consider the subject of STAS scores below 100. How can they actually be interpreted?

Among the 33 measured STAS scores, varying from 55 to 360, 5 brands had scores below 100. A possible (but counterintuitive) explanation is that in these cases, advertising had a totally negative effect on sales. However, a more likely explanation is that STAS scores below 100 may be due to more effective advertising or even sales promotions for competing brands being run at the same time. In Norway, we found that out of 126 brands included in the sample, 40 were supported by advertising during the observation period. Of these, with 33 brands there was only insignificant competing advertising. Effective competing advertising seems hardly to be a factor behind the lowest Norwegian STAS scores, although we did not measure the presence of competitive promotions.

A third hypothesis is that STAS scores below 100 may be due to differences between the two groups (exposed versus nonexposed), for example, in terms of brand preferences, buying patterns, and media exposure. If so, STAS scores under 100 can be explained, but only because we are comparing two groups of consumers with different characteristics—which is rather uncomfortable from a methodological point of view.

Conclusions

Findings from the Norwegian STAS experiment are similar to those found in other countries as far as STAS scores and the corresponding response functions are concerned. A main finding is that advertising for new products seems to be more cost-effective than advertising for established brands in mature markets. This finding can be interpreted as support for the theory of advertising—as a strong force when related to new products and as a weak force when related to long-established brands in mature markets. But before conclusions are drawn, findings should be interpreted on a long-run basis, and in a wide marketing context. From the Norwegian experiment, there are also indications that print media may have a competitive edge compared with TV.

To assess the general validity of STAS scores as a measure of advertising impact and effectiveness, further research is needed. One avenue of research may be to explore in more detail the characteristics of consumers: their brand awareness, their brand preferences, the momentum of the brands they use, their brand repertoires and purchasing patterns. In Norway, we have the capability to do this because we already have so much background information about the respondents; the cost of the additional analyses is the only drawback.

Looking at the prospects for further Norwegian-based research in this area, we are optimistic. The response from the market has been very encouraging. Advertisers, advertising agencies, and media have expressed the view that this STAS study has been the most interesting and promising advertising research project they have ever experienced—not only because of the STAS findings themselves, but because the STAS exercise has stimulated a constructive discussion and an improved understanding of how advertising works, even if there is still a great need for further research.

Notes

1. For discussions of STAS, see John Philip Jones, *When Ads Work: New Proof That Advertising Triggers Sales* (New York: Simon & Schuster-Lexington, 1995); John Philip Jones, "Single-Source Research Begins to Fulfill Its Promise," *Journal of Advertising Research,* vol. 35, May/June 1995, 9-15.

2. See, for example, Andrew S. C. Ehrenberg, "Repetitive Advertising and the Consumer," *Journal of Advertising Research,* April 1974, 25-33.

3. See, for example, Andrew S. C. Ehrenberg, "Justifying Our Advertising Budgets," paper presented at a conference held by the Advertising Association, London, January 22, 1998.

21

The Effectiveness of Television Advertising in France

Laurent Battais
Laurent Spitzer

This chapter describes an area-based application of pure single-source research. This system was introduced in France under the name of TVScan (which is described in the appendix to this chapter). The research has two main purposes. The first of these is to optimize TV targeting. The idea is to integrate a brand's marketing objectives into the media strategy. We concentrate on the audience of buyers, nonbuyers, and light or heavy buyers of a whole product class or a brand, with the aim of fine-tuning the components of the media plan (channels, dayparts, weekdays) and measuring the relevance of program sponsorships.

The second but more important purpose of TVScan is the quantification of medium- and long-term advertising effects through such indicators as market share, penetration, and purchase intensity (purchase frequency)—in every case depending on media exposure. It is now possible to measure the incremental effect of a sales stimulus as precisely for advertising as for promotions.

All analyses start with the definition of the marketing target in behavioral terms—the real population for which the communication was conceived—for example, category buyers during 6 or 9 months prior to the airing and during the campaign (plus following weeks).

Each period measured usually represents 8 to 12 weeks: the postcampaign length covers the burst (4 to 6 weeks) and its carryover effects (4 to 6 weeks). Consumer panel indicators—market share, penetration, and volume per buyer— are produced for each period.

At the heart of the research is the difference between households without exposure to the advertising and households with at least one contact. Coverage figures of 90-95% are quite usual, and we often build a reference group of "very low exposure," that is, 0 contact + 1 contact (+ 2 contacts for the heaviest weights). Among households with contacts, we then build three equal-sized groups: households with low, medium, and high exposures.

The adjustment of a brand's growth or decline in the group with contact versus the nonexposed households shows the incremental medium- to long-term effect of advertising. This is the share-adjusted development index, which reflects the trend with advertising compared with the trend without it. Any in-store influence is accounted for, because both groups visit the same hypermarkets and supermarkets.

As an example, let us look at a brand with a marketing target of 1,070 households (category buyers) and pre/postcampaign periods lasting 10 weeks each. From one period to the other, among households without any contact, the brand's share goes down, to an index of 85. Meanwhile, the share develops by 30% among households with at least one contact, represented by an index of 130. The comparison of 130 with 85 yields an indexed advertising effect of 152 (45 percentaged on 85). The same calculation is made with the other main indicators (penetration, volume, or value per buyer) and comparisons are made between households with low/medium/high advertising exposures and households without contact.

Conclusions About Overall Effectiveness of Campaigns

Since 1996, 55 studies have been carried out with this methodology. All brands were well-established brands of repeat-purchase packaged goods. There was an equal split between leaders and challengers. As far as product type is concerned, the ratio of foods to drug products was approximately 3:1.

The most striking conclusion is the proportion of successful campaigns (i.e., with a share development index above 105). This success rate is approximately the same for food (68%) and beauty care (77%), as well as for leaders (71%) and challengers (69%). This 70% success rate is similar to figures found in studies in the United States, Germany, and the United Kingdom.

What were the media characteristics of these campaigns? The successful ones achieved an average of 808 gross rating points (GRPs), with a 94.6% coverage and frequency of 8.5. For the ineffective campaigns, the figures were 702 GRPs, 92.6% and 7.6, respectively. Media weight was therefore not a key factor.

Difficulties were caused by several factors. First, in half the cases, the copy was too old or was not relevant for the French market. Another important factor was the spillover effect of advertising coming on top of heavy promotions. The latter were already driving all potential purchases. This was particularly obvious for food products with very short purchase frequency and for established brands. Finally, in a few cases, competitors had advertised and/or promoted efficiently at the time of the campaign. Brands had fewer chances of success with a share of voice under 35%.

Effective Campaigns

On average, the share-adjusted development index was 148, representing an average improvement of 4.2 share points. This figure reflects the contribution of challenger brands: Starting from lower original shares, their average growth yields high indexed increases. The successful campaigns are analyzed by quartiles in Table 21.1.

Influences on Successful Advertising

Six factors that all have a potential bearing on the success or lack of success of advertising campaigns are discussed below. Five of these (extent of category growth, seasonal variability, competitive position of the brand, promo-

TABLE 21.1 Successful Campaigns Analyzed by Quartiles

	Index of Sales Growth
All successful campaigns	148
First quartile (largest brands)	107
Second quartile	118
Third quartile	157
Fourth quartile (smallest brands)	226

tional activity, and how long the copy has been used) are indeed factors of significant importance.

Extent of category growth. The average growth for drug and beauty-care products produces an index of 190; that for food products is 132. This may be a reflection of the different degrees of volatility of these two large categories. It also may be due to the fact that drug and beauty-care products can be stockpiled by the consumer more easily than food products can.

Seasonal variability. Categories with strong seasonality average an index of 133. Those with normal seasonality produce an index of 156.

Competitive position of the brand. Market leaders achieve an average index of 117; challengers average 181. But these percentage increases should be weighted according to the relative sales volumes of the two types of brands. Market leaders (which are larger) average a gain of 4.8 share points; challengers gain only 3.6 share points despite their large percentage increase.

Budget level. As we have already indicated, advertising weight is not a factor of much importance. The average index for the half of the campaigns that ran at a weight of less than 700 GRPs was 151; the figure for the other half (with a weight of more than 700 GRPs) was 145. In the first group there were more leaders than challengers; the reverse was the case in the second group. The relative size of the scores is slightly unexpected; the greater number of challengers in the second group might have been expected to generate higher scores.

Promotional activity. The advertising campaigns accompanied by increasing promotional weight from one period to another generated an average index of 157. The campaigns accompanied by decreasing or stable promotional weight produced an index of 134.

As we have explained, the two groups of households—those exposed to advertising for the brand and those not exposed—received the same promotional stimuli at the same time; that is, both received promotions for some brands, and both received no promotions for others. The higher sales performance of the more intensively promoted brands is evidence of advertising/promotional synergy. This echoes similar experience in the United States.

How long the copy has been used. Campaigns using new commercials achieved an average index of 144. With campaigns employing commercials that had been used before, the average score was 156. This higher number may be the result of greater consumer understanding of the older commercials. These data are not complete, however, because they do not cover a full enough period to evaluate the potential long-term wear-out of the campaigns.

Penetration and Purchase Frequency

The two key consumer variables driving sales are penetration (proportion of households buying the brand at least once) and purchase intensity (how much they buy it on average). The research showed that 64% of the successful campaigns boosted penetration; 46% increased purchase intensity. The increased number of users generally represents buyers from earlier periods who had been brought back rather than total newcomers to the brand. The effect of the advertising is nevertheless positive, because it brings people back earlier than they would have come back by normal rotation. On the other hand, increased purchase intensity happens only with new brands or when the campaign is reinforced by promotional stimuli.

Penetration growth is greater for drug/beauty-care brands (157) than for food brands (120), and greater for challengers (148) than for leaders (111). *Purchase intensity* is also greater for drug/beauty-care brands (129) than for food brands (109), and greater for challengers (119) than for leaders (109).

TABLE 21.2 Campaigns Analyzed by Weight of Television Exposure

	Average Sales Index
Bottom tercile (lowest TV exposure)	157
Middle tercile (medium TV exposure)	156
Top tercile (highest TV exposure)	154

The Incremental Effect of Increased Frequency

As we have discussed, taking all the households in the panel together, weight of television viewing does not seem to boost the sales effect of the campaigns (see Table 21.2). However, this flat response to additional television exposure is the result of the aggregation of two different groups of campaigns. Half the campaigns respond to increased viewing, but the other half respond in a directly opposite way, as shown in Table 21.3.

The reciprocal relationship between the two groups of brands in Table 21.3 is not determined by the competitive positions of the brand or by relative weight put behind the campaigns. The higher-viewing households of Group 2 tend to be older and of lower professional level. They show themselves less in harmony with the brand, which implies a smaller connection or reaction to it. This calls into question the correspondence between the media plan and the marketing target.

Postscript

The research described in this chapter is ongoing. By the time this volume appears, the number of campaigns evaluated will have increased from 55 to 100. Each campaign will add to the battery of valuable objective data on the sales performance of consumer advertising.

To date, this French research has provided information that broadly supports the findings of pure single-source research carried out in the recent past in the United States, Germany, the United Kingdom, and Norway. There are methodological differences among the studies from these five countries, but the harmonies in their conclusions are much greater than the differences. As

TABLE 21.3 Campaigns Analyzed by Weight of Television Exposure

	Average Sales Index	
	Group 1	Group 2
Bottom tercile (lowest TV exposure)	126	185
Middle tercile (medium TV exposure)	136	172
Top tercile (highest TV exposure)	181	132

additional empirical evidence is generated, students of advertising will come closer to an understanding of ways in which sales respond to advertising stimuli in disparate countries, and the first indications are that common patterns will become increasingly apparent.

APPENDIX
The Methodology of TVScan

TVScan is the name of the research system described in this chapter. It is operated by MarketingScan, which is a joint venture between Médiamétrie, the French leader in media research, and GfK, the leading German company associated with area test market programs.

MarketingScan has recruited a panel of 2,000 representative households in the city of Angers. Located in the western part of France, the Angers area contains more than 220,000 inhabitants and is the 20th in France in terms of size. Its demographic structures are close to national averages. Its geographic situation is without regional peculiarities, and it is far from the French borders. It offers a very suitable variety of retailers, 63% of whose business is nationally based.

The selected households are equipped with an audience metering device designed to keep track of TV viewing electronically, second by second. Household data are transmitted daily by modem to a central location.

Each family also receives one or several ID cards, with a specific number and a bar code. The card is presented at the cash desks of seven stores in Angers. Scanners read both the card and the codes of the items purchased. This enables a perfect link to be made between the panel household and its purchases. Store data are systematically collected, and incentives ensure that the ID card is presented for each purchase. Constant checks are carried out. Panel households make more than 90% of their purchases in the stores that have been signed up.

The concentration in one single area means that all households are confronted with the same marketing environment—that is, identical product ranges, pricing, and promotions. The system is an example of carefully controlled, pure single-source research.

22

Test Marketing— and Some Notes on Iceland, a Totally Isolated Marketing Environment

David Wheeler

One of the important uses of test markets is to help in the development of successful and profitable advertising campaigns. In this connection it is interesting to listen to what the CEOs of some of the biggest advertisers have to say about the role of advertising.

A survey was conducted in May 1994 by the London *Financial Times* and the Institute of Practitioners in Advertising in which interviews were conducted among the top 500 U.K. advertisers. Of those taking part, half came from the top 100 advertisers.[1] Of the CEOs interviewed, 66% saw advertising as an investment as opposed to the 30% who viewed it more as a cost. Of the total sample of 156 respondents, 59% agreed strongly that "advertising is the best marketing tool for long-term brand building," and 69% agreed that "the best use of advertising is long-term rather than short-term."

Again, among the CEOs interviewed, 79% "agreed strongly" that "strong highly creative advertising can multiply the benefits of the media spend many times over." Given the strength of these views, it is perhaps not surprising that 87% of the total sample "agreed strongly" that "it is very important to measure the effects of advertising." These were the views of Britain's largest and most successful companies that use advertising.

In a totally separate survey conducted in April 1994 among 131 member companies of the Incorporated Society of British Advertisers, 79% of respondents claimed that "advertising effectiveness was a very important issue to their Company." [2] Among the reasons given for this viewpoint were the following:

- "We need to justify budgets against our global structure, comparing commercially with other operating units."
- "All investments should be measured in terms of return/value added."
- "Given fragmented media and audiences, the accuracy of communication and targeting is questioned."

I must stress that although the findings reported above are extracted from surveys conducted in Britain, by definition many of these are multinational companies, often with U.S. parentage and operating in a global marketplace. These findings are therefore applicable throughout the marketing world.

It is for the purpose of meeting the management needs revealed by this research that resources are often devoted to test markets. This helps to explain the importance of test marketing as a management tool. It has an important part to play in the introduction of new products as well as the development of existing products. It is concerned with the whole product—physical properties, packaging, pricing, advertising—but, above all, it is concerned with consumer response.

An Example of Test Marketing

Marketing is dynamic by nature. Not only to succeed, but even to retain their present positions in the market, marketers must constantly monitor what is happening to their products and take whatever actions they judge necessary in order to at least defend their market shares.

On the basis that attack is the best form of defense, marketers are more likely trying to answer the question, How can I improve my sales? By way of illustration, an interesting case study emerged a few years ago concerning a long-established brand with a worldwide market—Lea & Perrins Worcestershire Sauce, a brand that is familiar to devotees of the Bloody Mary.[3] Although between 1984 and 1988 its U.K. brand share measured in money increased from 79.8% to 85.7%, its volume sales fell by 4% over the same period. Price increases in advance of inflation were disguising a lapse in product usage that was a threat to the brand's future. The quest then became to find out who the people were among whom this lapse was occurring, and why they were not using the product as much as before. More essentially, the question was, How could the trend be reversed?

This question highlights one of the great marketing dilemmas: Improvements in marketing inevitably involve change. But making changes in the marketplace incurs further risks to my own market position. How, therefore, can I assess the potential benefits of change at minimum risk? In other words, how do I set about assessing the marketing options open to me, in a realistic market environment, without risking my total market share? The answer is often to be found in the carefully planned, well-designed test market, and this is exactly what Lea & Perrins Worcestershire Sauce found too.

The careful planning involved a detailed analysis of market research data, first, about the product itself. This showed that on the one hand there seemed to be a hard core of "frequent" users of the brand who tended to be slightly older and more downmarket than average users and who were apparently happy splashing the sauce on their meals, particularly red meat dishes. On the other hand, however, there were "infrequent" consumers who tended to be younger and more upmarket, who used the product in cooking on an irregular basis rather than on cooked food. Again the brand was mainly associated with traditional red meat dishes.

The second type of research data concerned trends in food consumption. These showed a growing trend away from red meat dishes toward poultry and a decline in the importance of the main meal and the growth of snacks. "Overall the brand was becoming out of touch with modern eating habits. The prospects looked bleak."

On the basis of these and other research findings, a carefully thought-out marketing strategy was developed from which a statement of advertising objectives emerged:

- To increase sales by increasing the frequency of "in-cooking" usage by focusing on simple, everyday recipes
- Longer term: to position the brand as eminently suitable for white meat, fish, and vegetables as well as red meat

The creative brief identified existing infrequent "in-cooking" users as the primary market, with all other users of the brand as the secondary objective. The proposition was that Lea & Perrins Worcestershire Sauce added a touch of magic to everyday meals, and each advertisement would feature several dishes whose natural flavor had been enhanced by this touch of magic.

The campaign that emerged first found expression in the color press, but it was felt that although the relatively small size of the brand's sales had always ruled out television, that medium should be put to the test in order to gauge what level of response might be achieved. This called for the design of a test market in one TV area, and for this purpose the Central TV area in the United Kingdom was chosen.

If any findings were to be worthwhile, it was clearly going to be necessary to build into the test market design a means of comparing brand usage between the test area and a control area, in terms of both volume of product usage and type of product usage. In order to measure the latter, and based upon earlier experimental work, two panels of 300 homes were set up—one in the Central TV area, the other spread across the United Kingdom (the control).

The panels were matched in terms of their prior frequency of product use, and each home was supplied with a calibrated bottle of Lea & Perrins and a self-completion diary in which to record use of the product. In order to attempt to diffuse attention from the test product, the panel members were also given calibrated bottles and diaries for a quite different and noncompeting product. Prior experience of this type of research showed that the results of the first month's diary entries should be ignored in order to allow the novelty effect to wear off, and so placements were made a month before the start of the TV campaign.

The television campaign in the Central TV area ran from October 9 to December 3, 1989, and 682 television ratings/gross rating points (TVRs/GRPs) were obtained across all commercials. The results of this effort were quite dramatic.

TABLE 22.1 Lea & Perrins Volume Changes

	All Users	Frequent	Infrequent
Rest of United Kingdom	100	100	100
Central TV	132	139	130

Direct measurement. The most important measure was the total volume consumed, as monitored on the calibrated bottle at the start and finish of the test. This was dependent not on accurate diary keeping or on respondents' claimed usage, but on the actual measurements taken from the calibrated bottle (see Table 22.1). The order of these differences clearly indicates a statistically significant advertising effect, but were the increases due to people's (a) using the same amounts but more frequently, or (b) simply using more of the product with the same regularity? Analysis showed that the average volume used per recipe occasion was essentially *unaffected* by the advertising, which means that the *frequency* of usage had increased, as shown in Table 22.2.

Recall interviews. Prompted awareness of the television campaign reached 57% in the test area. Among the key target audience of infrequent users aged 25 to 34, this figure rose 73%. Versatility was regarded as the main message coming across from the advertising.

Retail sales data. Recorded sales showed increases in volume and rate of sale in the Central TV test area that coincided with the TV campaign, and the effects continued until early March 1990.

TABLE 22.2 Lea & Perrins Frequency of Use

	Rest of United Kingdom	Central TV
Frequents		
In cooking	100	113
On food	100	92
Infrequents		
In cooking	100	115
On food	100	119

The Lea & Perrins Worcestershire Sauce example illustrates how important careful planning and a well-thought-out design are to the successful outcome of a test market study. Success in this context is unrelated to whether or not the brand itself is a success; rather, success is achieved when the data obtained from the test market are of such a form, and sufficiently reliable, to enable marketing decisions to be made with a measurable degree of confidence.

However, examples such as the one described above are rare. That test market study had the advantage of the product's being unique, with little competition, a low purchase price, and a naturally long purchase interval. The planners of the test did not have to compete against heavy advertising budgets; they did not have to worry about media overspill influencing the test market outcome; and they did not have to fear predatory pricing from competitive brands—which would have invalidated the test market findings. So what constitutes the ideal test market?

The Ideal Test Market

The ideal test market is a microcosm of the real market. In miniature, the test market should offer the following:

- The same kinds of potential consumers as the real market, with the same spending power and the same competition, at the same prices
- The same advertising and promotion opportunities as the real market, in the same kinds of media, without the confusion of media overspill
- The same product distribution chain as the real market
- Fast and confidential information on consumer attitudes
- The ability to monitor customer purchases and product usage
- The ability to gather reliable sales data for the market rapidly

And this ideal test market would be undertaken at minimum cost:

- Of product manufacturing and packaging
- Of advertising and promotion
- Of mainstream management resources

Finally, the results of the test market research should be of such a form and degree of reliability as to make it possible to extrapolate: To take the test market data and forecast the market response, in the main market, in terms of sales benefit against cost. And all this would be achieved without the competition realizing what you have been up to.

Test Marketing: The Reality

Microcosms in the marketing context are extraordinarily difficult to find. The traditional test market towns, or regions, have usually been overworked by others, and therefore are overexposed and overresearched. They are no longer typical of anywhere in a marketing sense.

The competition, of course, knows where these test areas are likely to be. They are carefully watched for unusual marketing activity, so competitors have a good chance of finding out what is going on; they may monitor and measure the research or indulge in counteractive spoiling tactics.

These days, perhaps the biggest problem to be overcome in the selection of a test market area is the question of media overspill. With the proliferation of media choice available to the consumer in terms of numbers of broadcast television and cable and satellite television channels, of FM and AM radio stations, of magazines both general and specialist, and of newspapers, whether local, regional, or national, morning or evening, the patterns of advertising exposure have become extremely complex.

One of the key elements—and problems—in effective analysis of a test market is the need to measure the amount of advertising for the test brand and competitive brands to which individuals have been exposed and the relationship between this advertising exposure and people's subsequent market behavior. In a situation of prolific media overspill, such an analysis may prove impossible. The test market could then be invalidated.

Even supposing that the obstacles so far mentioned have been overcome, there remains the question of the costs of operating a test market. This is no small-budget item. Because much of the work involved is separate from, and additional to, the mainstream activities of the company, the set-up and operational costs of test markets are disproportionately high in several ways:

- In terms of production costs, packaging, and the like
- In cost of media and advertisement production
- In market research and analysis costs

- In demands upon management resources, because at different times the whole chain of management becomes involved

Because marketing is such a dynamic process, many factors are changing in the market all the time. These will have effects upon the test market: Plans may need to be modified, and the findings may be less clear-cut than hoped. In consequence, the test market may need to run for much longer than planned.

Even at the end of the test market, one critical risk always remains—that the results have been misread, misinterpreted, or misunderstood, in which case the marketing consequences for the position of the brand in the main market could be disastrous.

How, Then, Can Markets Be Tested?

Despite all the foregoing reservations, markets are being tested all the time, and usually with very beneficial results. How? More and more companies are recognizing that market growth comes not just from sporadic product innovations but from the development of a deep understanding of the relationship between the consumer and the market, which comes in turn from measured and continuous market assessment. This often reveals clues to possible marketing innovations that may then be tested on a small scale, even within the mainstream marketing process. It is a case of continual market testing rather than intermittent test marketing.

With the development of global brands there are increasing opportunities for marketers to adopt this approach and gain advantage from it. For example, how does the market for your brand or your market segment differ on a country-by-country basis? How do consumer habits vary in different countries? What can be learned about test markets in one country that might generate ideas that could be adopted in other markets or that might suggest new product ideas? How might the distillation of such ideas across countries help reinforce a global strategy?

Important product breakthroughs have often come from new insights that have evolved as a result of the adoption of this approach. Companies that apply this practice to their test marketing activities have better new product development records than those that do not. It is even possible to benefit from the competition on this basis by monitoring their test market activity and getting to the market before them in other geographic areas.

One of the other advantages of this approach to market testing is that it can circumnavigate some of the hazards of the single "big bang" type of test market. Less is dependent upon one throw of the dice; the risk is spread over other market areas at other times. What has been learned from market testing in other territories can help marketers develop their own plans—with all the investment involved—with more confidence. An important reason for market testing, quite apart from its econometric uses, is that it allows the consumer to be the final arbiter before a manufacturer goes to product launch. This is particularly valuable in the case of test markets for new products, where we can test whether the physical properties of the product, such as flavor, are compatible with the aesthetic characteristics of packaging and advertising image, and whether these features are consistent with the price being asked from the customer in the marketplace.

Test marketing has thus evolved into a rather more sophisticated concept of *market testing*. And this permits a wider range of geographic areas to be considered for the purpose of testing different elements of a product in realistic marketing environments. It is the international networking approach applied to market testing.

Market Testing in Practice

The international networking approach to market testing is applicable to most major brand manufacturers, particularly, but not exclusively, in the packaged goods field. A visit to a supermarket almost anywhere in the world demonstrates this very clearly: Whatever the product field, one sees the major part of shelf space taken up by the well-established, well-known international brands. It is now even becoming true of the growing number of supermarkets in Moscow—brand wars are no longer confined to a few major countries. As in the political world, there is now guerrilla warfare being fought in small markets the world over, and sometimes the results can have global impacts.

From a market testing point of view, an interesting example is provided by a small country in the mid-Atlantic, Iceland. It is a country with a population of only 260,000 and a standard of living comparable to major Western European markets. For example, Iceland has more automobiles per capita than the United Kingdom or France. It is rich in media opportunities—TV, radio, newspapers, magazines, cinemas, and outdoor advertising—and yet has virtually no media overspill problems. It has shopping malls, supermarket chains, and independent stores, all stocked with global brands. Iceland offers unique opportunities as a test market, especially for brands aimed at Europe:

1. Because of the size of Iceland's population, which is reflected in the media costs there, it is possible for the advertiser to reach the total market at a substantially lower absolute cost than in other West European markets.

2. Because of Iceland's geographic position, there is no overlap with other markets and no media overspill. This means that it is possible to collect market and media data that are not polluted by activities in neighboring market territories.

3. Iceland offers marketing conditions common to other developed European markets because Icelandic customers have the same consumer desires and seek the same services as do their counterparts elsewhere in Europe.

4. Iceland has a sophisticated distribution infrastructure and offers very talented TV and print production facilities at low cost but to a high European standard. For those who need on-the-spot advice or assistance with their advertising, there are nine member companies of the Society of Icelandic Advertising Agencies. In addition, English is a universal second language and a common business language.

5. *The Icelandic Media and Marketing Index* is a single-source database that combines audience, attitude, product-buying, and consumption measures. It aims to cover all media and all products and services on the market that are of any significance. The studies are combined together, and there are now 10 surveys with more than 10,000 respondents in the database. There are ample facilities for supplementing this marketing information with ad hoc market research.

6. Because of Iceland's isolation, it is relatively easy to maintain the confidentiality of market tests conducted there.

Earlier in this chapter, I described the properties of the mythical ideal test market. Several of the key elements in that list are met by the opportunities available in Iceland. The number available will vary from case to case, as the following examples illustrate.[4]

Brand A

For the very understandable reason of marketing confidentiality, the identity of the two protagonists in this case may not be revealed, but they are two major global brands in a fast-moving food product field. Both brands had been on the Icelandic market for many years. Brand X, the client brand, has been market leader for more than 50 years. The competition, Brand Y, has for many years been trying to take over brand leadership, and traditionally has had a higher share of voice. By 1991, the sales of Brand X had been stable for at least 10 years. Marketing activities produced no measurable sales effects, and the theory was advanced that the brand had reached a ceiling and that the advertising expenditure was going entirely toward defending and maintaining the brand's market share.

On the basis of research undertaken in 1991, it was decided that a new marketing and advertising strategy would be formulated for 1992. Brand X had been targeted primarily at children and teenagers. Market analysis showed that with consumers over the age of 25 years, consumption frequency for Brand X declined much faster than for Brand Y. Awareness levels (top of mind) were equal for both brands, as were opinions on taste. However, it was found that Brand Y was rated better on nutritional qualities and on price.

A strategy therefore emerged to identify two different target groups in the advertising plans and to divide the budget between them: children/teenagers, and adults 25+. In the first year the budget was directed at the adult sector with a "health and nutrition" campaign using TV, and by mailing an informative booklet to all women ages 30 to 60 and families with small children. In the second year, the focus was on children and teenagers and was heavily promotion oriented. In the third year, the focus was again on the health image, with new TV commercials and newspaper advertisements. The results were striking:

- *Sales volume:* Rather than remaining flat, total sales volume (in tons) increased by 30.1% between 1991 and 1994.
- *Age distribution:* Consumption frequency changed dramatically between 1991 and 1993, as shown in Table 22.3.
- *Image:* A striking improvement took place in the health and nutrition ratings for Brand X. The index of these ratings grew from 5.8 in 1991 to 6.9 in 1994, when for the first time they exceeded Brand Y.

The Samsala Bakery

The Samsala Bakery had been, for two decades, the leading producer of bread sold in supermarkets and other food stores in Iceland. In the late 1980s

TABLE 22.3 Brand X: Consumption Changes by Age Group

	Age Group				
	13-17	18-24	25-44	45-59	60+
Increase (%)	16	23	50	211	371

it started to lose market share. The competition was coming from a firm called Myllan (The Mill), which was developing strong brand images for its products. During this time the Samsala Bakery was ignoring brand image development and instead had become dependent upon promotion-oriented activities. In 1992 it was obvious that something had to be done.

Market research conducted in 1992 revealed a disturbing situation:

- The Samsala Bakery had an inferior image compared to its competition.
- The consumer had minimum knowledge of Samsala Bakery's product lines.
- The Samsala company itself had a negative image, and the main competitor was perceived as a much more modern bread producer.

From the same research, important information about the bread market emerged:

- The consumption of bread was on the increase, and bread was seen as a healthy, nutritious, and essential part of a modern diet.
- When the consumer evaluated brands, the most important perceived quality concerned health, followed by taste and freshness. Price was of only secondary importance.

It was decided that Samsala's slipping market share would be tackled by a shift in marketing emphasis from promotion back to building the brand image, and at the same time improving the corporate image of the Samsala Bakery.

The company's two bread lines, which had not been distinguished in any meaningful way, were repositioned. One, called Big Sandwich Bread, was aimed at satisfying the appetite of the younger, male-dominated market. This target group was seen as eating bread on the basis of quantity to satisfy hunger. These people judged the bread on the basis of its volume and filling properties. The other line, called Bakery Bread, was aimed at an older, female-dominated market. This target group was seen as choosing bread on the basis of health and nutrition.

Television commercials and print advertisements were produced for the two bread lines, each directed at its own target group. At the same time, television and print campaigns were produced that stressed the general quality of Samsala bread. The overall marketing budget was not much changed, but now most of it went toward advertising instead of promotion.

The results were very positive. After the first full year (May 1993 to June 1994), sales and brand image had both improved markedly:

- *Sales:* Samsala Bakery products increased in sales volume by 38% over this period.
- *Top of mind:* The top-of-mind rating for the corporate Samsala Bakery increased from 22% to 35%, and it was closing in on its main competitor.
- *Brand awareness:* Recall of the Samsala Bakery bread lines increased from 42% to 62%.
- *Brand image/quality:* Between 1992 and 1993 the health and nutrition images of the Samsala Bakery brand name improved substantially to reach parity with the competition. The "softness" and "freshness" associations improved even more drastically and surpassed the other brand.
- *Purchasing habits:* The proportion of consumers who claimed that they "usually buy" Samsala Bakery breads increased from 33% to 44%.

In summary, the repositioning of the brand had reversed its decline and opened new opportunities for continuing market growth. For an international brand these findings would have offered valuable pointers for many other market territories.

Much can be learned from market testing about how to market a brand more successfully. Within established marketing companies, there are normally good facilities for undertaking market tests of different types: large and small, complex and simple, prolonged and brief. On occasion, fully structured test markets may be necessary, but it is often more cost-effective first to review the alternative ways of market testing to find simple methods. These are often less costly, less risky, and more immediate indicators than textbook methods of high sophistication and scientific purity.

Notes

1. Financial Times and Institute of Practitioners in Advertising, *Financial Times/IPA Marketing and Advertising Survey* (London: Institute of Practitioners in Advertising, 1994).

2. Institute of Practitioners in Advertising, *IPA Survey of Incorporated Society of British Advertisers (ISBA) Members on Advertising Effectiveness* (London: Institute of Practitioners in Advertising, 1994).

3. Michael Llewellyn-Williams, "Adding a Little Magic to Lea & Perrins' Worcestershire Sauce," in Paul Feldwick (ed.), *Advertising Works 6* (London: IPA/NTC Publications, 1990).

4. The examples that follow come from the Icelandic Market Testing Studies conducted by YDDA Advertising (Grjotagata 7, Reykjavik, Iceland, 1994).

23

Modeling the Marketing Process

Innovation From Japan

Roger M. Brookin

Editor's Introduction

This chapter describes an intuitively persuasive and sophisticated model of the marketing process as it operates in the field of repeat-purchase packaged goods. The model is a proprietary device developed by a marketing consultancy named Petal, the founder of which is the author of this chapter, a practitioner with significant international experience. Although the model was developed by the Petal organization for the Japanese market, much of the empirical and conceptual work on which it is based was generated in Europe—in France and the United Kingdom in particular.

The Petal model is not static. It moves forward in response to successful use in the marketplace and has even evolved since this chapter was written. Because of its international viewpoint, the Petal model confronts marketing practitioners in the United States with unorthodox concepts that I believe they will find valuable in the American environment.

Golf is a game I never took to, but because I have lived and worked in Japan for more than 20 years, it has been thrust into my consciousness. I have noticed that golfers, wherever they hail from, have varying degrees of (a) natural golfing talent, (b) coaching by qualified instructors who understand the game, and (c) top-quality equipment. I have also note that naturally talented golfers are few, but that, given the right coaching and equipment, almost anyone can play a creditable game.

Marketing is my sport, and the parallel with golf is striking. Talented amateurs invented marketing, but now it is an activity in which tens of thousands seek to earn their living and need to play at least a creditable game. Marketing modeling can be likened to coaching in golf: Flair can provide excellent results, but focused flair delivers best.

My purpose in this chapter is to provide some simple coaching to marketers: upgrade the bases from which they work and offer guidance as to how to make the best use of the myriad excellent tools available today, without blinding them with science.

The golfing analogy bears one more extension: A golfer is not independent of his or her environment. On any day, a golfer's expected, normal (or par) performance is dependent on the course he or she is playing and the weather. Whether the golfer achieves—or beats—par will depend upon flair, honed skills, equipment, and training. Whether the golfer wins a hole depends upon his or her opponents.

So it is in marketing. Brand performance has a "par for the course" that is dependent on the "course" of market structure and the "weather" of the market environment. And market share depends not on absolutes, but on performance relative to competitors. We all live by our revenue and profit: Those are absolutes. But their components are driven by our relative performance as we mold brand equities within and across the changing environment of the world's markets.

The Petal Model

Petal is the name of the marketing agency that I have founded in Tokyo. As well as extended sporting analogies, the agency has developed a simply expressed model to guide management of brand equity, both within and across markets. The model attempts to provide guidance on how to implement better marketing through a total understanding of why people buy one brand rather than another.

The Petal model is not meant to be definitive, nor is it necessarily right in all aspects. It has, however, shown itself to be robust and practical in helping marketers learn how to focus and guide their efforts to understand and manage brand properties efficiently. The model suggests the following:

- Marketing management involves manipulating stimuli (elements of the brand mix, such as advertising, price, and promotion) that are intended to influence the sales of a brand.
- The stimuli work in a complex manner, affecting different consumers differently depending on the "filters" through which they are perceived and become triggers of consumers' desire to purchase the brand (or drivers of their preference).
- Preference in turn is modified by price, promotions, and advertising (or drivers of behavior).
- The effect of stimuli and drivers is conditioned by the structure of the market, which determines the most likely performance of an average in any market (the par).
- Par will be exceeded—or not achieved—according to the robustness of the mix itself: the degree to which it coherently manipulates the stimuli and drivers relative to competitive brands.

This is a holistic model. It looks at a brand as a totality and attempts to measure the effect on sales of manipulating any one of the available triggers. The most important triggers—in terms of both effect and resources consumed—are price and advertising. Both are too often managed in isolation, with scant respect for their effects on the marketing mix as a whole. The Petal model enables a marketer to put them in context, providing tools for their description and understanding both in isolation and as components of the total brand performance. They can then take their place as contributors to the development and maintenance of great brands.

Great Brands

Mass marketing is variously defined, but probably as good an economist's description as any is *managing the flow of goods and services from producers to users*. And I like this practical working description: *making or maintaining a coherent, impactful character for my brand that is different from, and better value than, my competitor's*. Each word is pregnant with implications:

- *Making or maintaining:* This highlights the difference between "attack" and "defend" modes of marketing. The former is higher-profile new brand work, thrusting new products into markets. This is an appropriate attitude for new entrants into a category or country. Defense, on the other hand, implies maintaining existing equity—an activity that is often underestimated but vitally important. A subsidiary posture between the two—brand extension—requires a delicate balance; such a position is fraught with peril but offers tremendous opportunities if handled sympathetically.

- *Coherent:* All aspects of the brand mix need to work together and contribute synergistically to the whole. Much of the brand engineering work done on major brand equities identifies dissonance in the mix that, if rectified, can result in powerful increases in brand equity.

- *Impactful:* One of the most common weaknesses of brands is that they do not stand out from the crowd. The fault for this lies squarely with advertising. An awful lot of time is spent in many companies on crafting the right message and not enough on making sure it is communicated powerfully and memorably. Advertising has two principal functions: that of communicating a message (of which impact is a necessary component) and that of generating salience (or raw impact). Given the amount of resources that advertising consumes—and the multiplier that effectiveness has on each dollar of advertising expenditure—it is unforgivable for marketers to forgo the opportunity to maximize the effect. The Petal model helps to identify an appropriate balance between the components of advertising.

- *Character:* It is commonplace to talk about brand characters. But a character implies that there be no abrupt and unexpected changes in the brand "personality" that can confuse people, that all aspects of the character work together to create a whole and single impression—and that different members of the family share similar traits.

- *Different:* Me-too brands abound. A great brand must be seen by the consumer as offering different satisfactions from those offered by competitors. Rarely will a completely new need be satisfied—more often, a new way of satisfying an old need will be found. This is another hallmark of a great marketer—not copying competitors' claims, but outflanking or leapfrogging them.

- *Better value:* Value is a key concept; it is a combination of what consumers see the brand as offering and the price they think they have to pay for it. The offering is not only whether the brand objectively and physically performs a task better than another, but that the potential purchaser finds that the total bundle of satisfactions offered by the brand is more desirable than the bundle offered by the competition. The nature of these satisfactions can be broadly defined as physical, sensory, or emotional. This more desirable product must then be offered at the right price—not too expensive, and not too cheap.

- *The competitor:* Relative measures are important—absolute measures less so. What matters is that the brand on offer is seen by the consumer to be the best available. It is a wise manufacturer who holds back product improvements if they are not necessary to create or maintain a leading position.

The DUM Process

I suspect that it was Albert Einstein who said that imagination is more important than knowledge. Certainly, organizations spend a great deal of time and money collecting Information, much less turning the information into knowledge, and hardly any time at all applying imagination to it. So it is with marketing.

Petal models are gleaned from the world's leading marketing practitioners to help turn data into catalysts for the imaginative application of knowledge. As an aid to getting the best out of these models, I have found it useful to divide our involvement with information into three stages: *describing* what is going on, *understanding* why those things are going on (identifying drivers), and *manipulating* the drivers of those events to achieve our ends. Giving names to these three stages helps me both to clarify the process and to ensure that I do get around to manipulation and don't lose myself in the addictive area of data description. The naming process also helps me to communicate these concepts to others.

Description is not difficult to understand, and has been the target of most of the intellectual and financial investments in marketing over the years. Describing market shares, loyalty analyses, penetration, habits, and the results of product tests is vitally important to our ability to manage a brand, and it is on this that the marketing research industry has been founded. But description alone is not sufficient "better to manage better brands."

Understanding entails recognizing why things happen as they do—understanding the real "drivers" of activities. It is here that models come into their own: They provide frameworks that can help us to understand, communicate, and implement agreed-upon actions. The actual model used is of less importance than that a model is used—any modeling discipline confers significant rewards.

Manipulating the stimuli to generate the desired outcome is the objective of the exercise. The reason for developing a detailed understanding of what is going on in the market and why (i.e., an understanding of the drivers) is to be able to focus and maximize the impact of talent and intuition on the process of creating or maintaining a better brand.

Although these three stages may appear intuitive and self-evident, confusion among them leads to a lack of control in expenditure on data collection and diffusion of scarce talent. There is a company that spends more than $3 million a year on marketing research, yet its managers cannot express the consumers' views of its brands' strengths and have no clear idea of where the brand portfolio is heading. The company buys plenty of descriptive data, yet has practically no understanding, and so is hampered in its attempts to manipulate its brands.

The implications of DUM thinking for the marketing process can be quite profound. Such thinking can be used to impose a tight intellectual discipline on the description and understanding elements of the marketing task while leaving free those areas of creativity and invention that demand imagination for brand manipulation.

When used properly, marketing research can be a great boon to a company. But incorrectly managed, it can be a drag on innovation, constraining where it should encourage freedom. Research must not be a dusty data collector or simply a crutch for justifying decisions made on other grounds. The researcher must earn the respect of the marketing team, see its function as a continuous accretion of understanding of his or her brands, their stimuli, drivers, and results. DUM thinking can lead to a revision of the types of data collected and of the balance between data collection and analysis. And it can help describe a process to investigate those phenomena in any specific situation.

An important concept in this regard is that of *zoom*—the ability to use a level of data aggregation appropriate to the decision to be made. This may be compared to the scale of a map—a globe helps you to choose a Great Circle route, an atlas to determine which cities to visit, and a street map to decide when to turn left. Simple abstractions, where appropriate, of complex phenomena can be as important to strategic direction as details to the perfection of implementation.

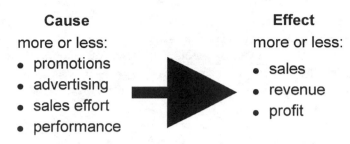

Figure 23.1. The Intuitive Model

When applied to understanding drivers of behavior, I refer to this as the "I love you" effect. Why one person loves another is exceedingly difficult to model. That one person believes that he loves another, and acts under those constraints, is, however, simple to demonstrate, subject only to trivial measuring procedures. So it is in marketing—complex phenomena will have a matrix of complexity of expression: The description of an effect may often benefit from being simple (as long as it is not simplistic), even though the process of understanding may be ever so convoluted.

Cause and Effect

The implicit model under which most people operate (Figure 23.1) is not complex. It assumes, not unreasonably, that a cause produces an effect. This model is intuitive, and can be seen operating in most companies on most days—and is evident in many learned papers and company transactions. Indeed, it is the intellectual rationale behind advertising pressure tests, the call for a "sales component" of advertising pretesting, and much amateur marketing theory.

What is unreasonable about it, of course, is that it assumes that the cause-effect relationship is direct and one-to-one. Unfortunately, real life is not as simple as that. The model represents a very wide zoom: Although causes do clearly stimulate effects, they tend to do so in what appears at first sight to be a convoluted and mysterious way—there are all sorts of intermediate stages in between. Understanding those stages in as much detail as necessary to do them justice, but as simply and elegantly as to make them readily comprehensible and actionable, is the task that Petal modelers have been addressing.

Causes are in reality those elements of the marketing mix that managers manipulate as they manage the brand—a set of stimuli, designed to affect consumers in specific ways. Presenting and adding value to these stimuli is effected largely through advertising and packaging—thus any work undertaken to understand brand equity must have its impact largely on the advertising process.

Consumer psychology tells us two things about these stimuli as they operate in repeat-purchase packaged goods:

- Consumers rarely carry more than a couple of impressions about a brand in their minds.
- Different consumers see and react to different stimuli in different ways, according to their environments.

Therefore, the stimuli that we attempt to link to our brand had better be good—and *good* in this context means simple, different, meaningful, and coherent.

Management of great brands requires that we find stimuli (advertising and promotions, sales efforts, and product performance) that, while being striking and appealing to an individual consumer, have the breadth of appeal to work across a broad group of people—unique enough to differentiate the brand from its competitors and important enough to appeal to a sufficiently large group of potential buyers.

The Petal model (see Figure 23.2) helps to do this by postulating a process of marketing that is complex enough to permit worthwhile modeling but simple enough to be grasped easily. It says that the stimuli generated and manipulated by the marketer are screened by the consumer through sociopsychological filters. Each group of consumers understands something a little differently from another group—even if the stimuli are identical—because of their upbringing, experience, and situation. This unique understanding of what has been communicated becomes the consumer's own understanding of what the brand is and does: each individual's bundle of triggers or "real causes" as seen by the customer.

The bundle of triggers has a simple mechanism that enables the consumer to recognize and summarize it—usually the brand name, but sometimes the logo or the package. This is analogous to a person's name and is a key element in the mix. The role of advertising is twofold: to keep the brand salient, at the top of consumers' minds, and to endow that name with the desired benefits.

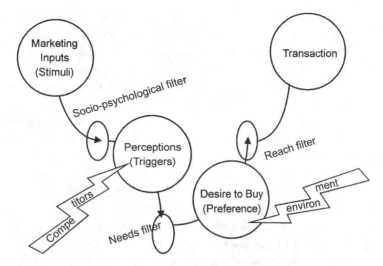

Figure 23.2. The Petal Model

The user matches this bundle of triggers against what she wants from the category and forms a judgment about the suitability of the brand to her needs. This results in a change in preference for the brand. Rarely is this done logically, explicitly, or even consciously, which is why unsophisticated motivational research can be misleading. But good research tools can be used with confidence as long as we stick to two principles: that the place of the stimulus-preference model in the whole marketing model is respected (beware cause-effect) and that triggers are not confused with stimuli.

The tools that the Petal model employs liken this process to a series of response functions. (A change in one of the triggers will lead, through a nonlinear response function, to a change in preference based on that stimulus. Simply add up the effect of all the stimuli, adjust for synergy, and the preference can be assessed.)

"Adolf Hitler" is a powerful brand name—just hearing or seeing it produces a significant reaction in most people. It also, incidentally, demonstrates the Petal model well: The stimulus is the same for everybody, but different people bring different filters to interpreting that stimulus into rational and emotional triggers, which—having been processed through the drivers of preference— lead to a wide range of individual reactions on exposure to the name.

As a result of these first three stages, the consumer has a preference for the brand that can be measured using relatively simple tools. She may be indifferent (an effect that is quite common and not often recognized, but must be built into any model; the only people to perceive some brand engineering subtleties are its advertisers) or may be more or less likely to want to buy the brand—consciously or subconsciously.

This desire to buy the brand (preference) is then subjected to a further set of drivers, those that determine whether the desire to purchase is exercised or not. Examples of these drivers are the quality of distribution of the brand through its sales outlets (ease of access), the effect of special promotion offers or coupon deals, and short-term price deals, all of which affect purchasing transactions without affecting preference at that time.

I will not discuss these drivers of behavior further in this chapter. Much has been written about them, and in the Petal model these phenomena are also treated as response functions of behavior to the various stimuli.

Figure 23.2 also demonstrates that the process is affected by the environment—the norms of behavior at each stage. Note that the par for a market is determined neither by country nor by product category, but by the market's competitiveness and brand structure. Second, note that brand performance within the model is not an absolute; it is relative to other brands' performance, which indeed in turn modifies the norm for the marketplace.

As a result of all this, we should have been able to model a transaction—a person buying or not buying the brand in question.

Stimulus to Trigger: Sociopsychological Filters

The area of the model between stimulus and trigger can cause a great deal of confusion. It is the heartland of the advertising process, yet one that has received less than its share of attention. It includes processes that seek to complement behavioral understanding with emotional insights, but is mainly an examination of a translation process—the translation from the world of the marketer (who is crafting the stimuli) to the world of the consumer (who is reacting to the triggers). These worlds have many manifestations: perceptual, social, economic, and demographic.

Although it is of course an artifice to consider the stimulus and the trigger as different phenomena, this approach is justified by the clarity it brings to a complex process. Sociopsychologists bring a whole discipline to understanding the filters consumers use as they translate our stimuli into their triggers. Petal tries to tame some of these devices.

Stimuli can be viewed in three broad ways:

- *Physical:* the product itself, the chemicals and physical properties that give it function—adhesives in a glue, cleansers in a detergent, absorbents in a diaper
- *Sensory:* those elements of the product or its mix that are included primarily not for their direct physical effects but for their indirect effects—perfumes connoting efficiency, tastes connoting refreshment, colors connoting softness
- *Emotional:* the elements that develop the character or ambience of the brand and the tone and symbolic environment of the advertising

Advertising is viscerally involved in all three—creating, molding, or presenting them. But what goes in does not necessarily come out: Twice as much bleach does not necessarily mean whiter shirts; 30% more citric acid does not necessarily result in a tarter taste; music in a minor key does not necessarily induce a mournful mood. This may be because the consumer sees triggers in different terms—they are placed in her world, seen in her context. This involves the translation process, which can be understood as passing the stimuli through a series of filters that are unique to each set of consumers.

The filters that operate on people's motives and needs, as well on brands' perceived images, which are driven by the stimuli, are broadly of four types:

- *Rational:* These are those areas that the consumer believes to be "concrete," "hard facts." They result in triggers that are justifications, such as efficiency or physical performance, price, and value for money.
- *Emotional:* These are self-directed needs that result in triggers concerned with how the individual feels inside—sensations such as indulgence and self-confidence.
- *Social:* These are other-directed motivations, resulting in triggers concerned with how the individual looks to others and relates with society—individuality, conformity, and youth are examples, as indeed are body odor and style.
- *Cultural:* These result in role and value fulfillment and the enactment of the person's role in society—cohesion to moral values, acceptable expressions of glamour, and puritanical drives are examples.

To perceive the world from another's point of view is notoriously difficult, but the Petal model helps us to do so through the use of a number of devices, among them representing different groups of people in two-dimensional abstractions from reality that we can hope to grasp. The objective of all this is to understand the needs and wants of consumers relating to the task that the brand is designed to tackle and how consumers' perceptions of those needs and wants are changing. This will help us as marketers to understand how consumers are able to differentiate between brands and products, how they place them in relation to each other and to their perception of the environment. At the end of the day, what words and concepts can be used to trigger the desired associations for the brands?

It is an interesting observation that the global/local debate can be viewed as a result of misapprehension of the stimulus-trigger phenomenon. The marketer looks for "glocal" brands: those that use a profound understanding of filters at work in different markets to generate global triggers from local stimuli.

Triggers to Preference:
Drivers of Preference and of Behavior

Drivers of preference are sometimes called *pull factors* (that is, when consumers pull the brand through the retailer pipeline because they want so much to buy it), and drivers of behavior are often called *push factors* (when the marketer pushes the product through the pipeline by offering nonbranding incentives to consumers). Figure 23.3 shows this by transforming the Petal model from a circular flow model into a branching tree format—which is easier to draw and can show more clearly the relationships and pathways between the elements.

The figure demonstrates yet again that things are not as simple as they first appear. Sales of a brand are affected by two very different sorts of drivers. There is rarely a unidimensional answer to the question, Why did this brand do well?—whatever the level of zoom. Performance in the market is always a combination of push and pull—so some brands that are crafted in a merely average way sell phenomenally well, whereas excellent brands can be disappointing in sales. There is, however, some justice in the world: Push tends to be a modifier of pull, with the implication that sheer logistical strength cannot

Figure 23.3. Pull and Push

make a great, sustainable brand. Weak logistics can, however, kill a potentially great brand.

Not only are the effects of marketing stimuli complex and indirect (Figure 23.2), they are also multitudinous. Using the tree diagram approach, we can pursue the idea of push and pull in more detail and attempt to quantify the contribution of each, as well as each of their constituent parts, on sales of the brand. It will help to understand the effect of each of these parts, and how to deploy them, and is complementary to the sociopsychological analysis, which aims more to understand their makeup and hence how to fashion them more effectively.

The model differs depending on whether we are reviewing existing brands (where the emphasis is on reviewing the repeat-purchase process and defending against encroachments) or new brands (where the emphasis is on reviewing the diffusion of the new brand into the target population).

Existing Brands

Figure 23.4 displays the outline of the model at low-resolution zoom for existing brands. Push is divided into two components in this example—the effect of price and the effect of distribution. In a real working model, we would see the subcomponents of these elements, including the different types of

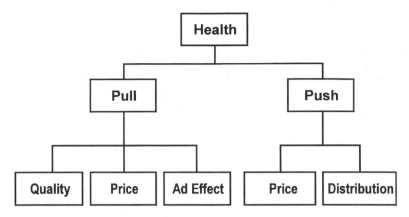

Figure 23.4. A Working Tree for Existing Brands

promotions, couponing, quality as well as depth of distribution, and a range of other drivers of behavior. This level of abstraction is justified here, as the details of any model are specific to the time, the place, and the category.

Components of pull (when consumers want to buy the brand so much that it is metaphorically pulled through the pipeline) are here abstracted to the quality, the price, and the advertising effect. Each of these has a special definition in the Petal model. *Quality* is what would more normally be called brand image. It is that component of preference that is derived from the effect of the consumer's perception of the brand (the triggers) on the needs and wants of the consumer. In order to measure quality, it is necessary to measure the importance of each of the components of brand preference and how the brand performs relative to all the other brands the consumer would consider to satisfy the task. There is a massive and deliberate overlap here with the sociopsychological model, as this model attempts to quantify the way in which each driver affects pull (or preference); the other attempts to understand more intuitively the ways in which these drivers work. Quality combined with price gives the value of the brand.

Price is what consumers think they have to pay for the brand (perceived price). It differs from price in the push side of the equation, which is the short-term offer price. A Rolls-Royce is an expensive car (in pull terms), but its short-term appeal may be enhanced by a short-term offer of "several thousand dollars off—for this week only." Only in the short term can these two prices be seen as independent of each other. They do, of course, interact

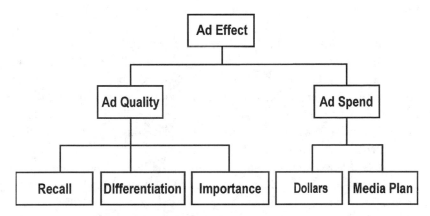

Figure 23.5. A Working Tree for Advertising

over time—too much short-term price promotion will weaken the prestige image even of a Rolls-Royce (e.g., recall the recent fortunes of some prestige brands such as haute couture names used for inexpensive luggage).

Advertising effect also works in complex ways. Advertising is one of the principal sufferers of the inability to zoom. The gross effects of advertising are relatively easy to measure—Petal models have found that a remarkably powerful way to describe the effects of advertising is to ask consumers simple questions such as "Is what this ad is saying important to you?" Indeed, the submodel for advertising within the Petal model appears to be disarmingly simple (see Figure 23.5). This is not, of course, to deny the incredibly complex way in which advertising works: Simplicity of description does not imply naïveté of understanding or ease of manipulation.

It should come as no surprise that the two principal drivers are the quality of the advertising and the ad spend (the level of advertising exposure). What often does come as a shock to some marketers (but less so to advertisers) is the relative importance of the advertising quality—it has been shown that the effectiveness of each dollar spent on advertising can be multiplied by up to five times depending on the quality of the advertising.

And quality of the advertising can be measured using only three simple dimensions: recall (that the advertising links whatever effect it has with the bundle of triggers—usually the brand name—that the consumer uses to identify the brand), differentiation (that people find the advertising to be clearly identified with the brand and different from the advertising of other brands), and importance (that what is being said and how it is being said are meaningful to the consumer).

Quality of the advertising, however, is much more complex to understand. There are many examples in which the problem is easy to identify, but fiendishly difficult to solve. In these circumstances, access to a single model offering both the diagnosis and the explanation can be very important. This figure does not address the very important question, What is the ad affecting? That is partly because the diagrams that explain this are very difficult to express in two dimensions without color. Advertising has two major tasks—the first is to communicate something about the brand. This would put an arrow in Figure 23.5 from the ad effect box to the ad quality box (or rather to its constituent parts). The second task is a separate line right up to somewhere between push and pull—the salience of the advertising. This is often not recognized for the important driver that it is. This I refer to as the "sandwich board man effect," and is the element of advertising that operates by forcing the brand into the consciousness of consumers, reminding them that the brand, or the category, is available, and a candidate for their disposable cash. It has been shown that the biggest influence on brand choice is whether the brand's advertising has been seen in the past week. This is salience in operation.

The model illustrated in Figure 23.6—or a simplified version of it—can be used as an indicator of the health of a brand. If each box of the tree diagram is coded (a simple code is a tick for "okay," an X for danger), this can be used as a simple but effective method of signaling the relative strength or weakness of each component of an ongoing brand's performance. If the contribution of a mix element represented by the box is positive to the brand's sales (above par for that market), it gets a tick; if negative, an X. This concept is of particular benefit for disentangling push and pull factors—as in Figure 23.6, where a strong brand is overpriced—and can be used routinely and company-wide as a tool for reporting on the health of the various brands in the company's portfolio, as well as how they compare to the competition.

New Brands

For new brands, the structure of the model will be somewhat different—although the principles behind it are identical—to describe, understand, and manipulate the complexities at just the right level to permit understanding without oversimplification. The Petal model (Stimulus–Trigger–Preference–

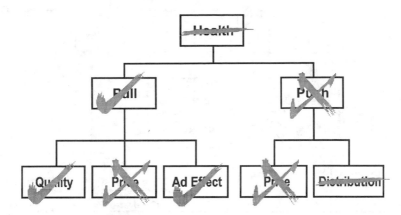

Figure 23.6. Simple Brand Health

Transaction) applies, and indeed, the drivers may be the same. But instead of looking to describe and eventually sustain an established presence in the marketplace, the objective is to introduce a new brand into the market. To do this, the drivers will initially be those affecting adoption and trial, secondarily those of repeat purchase, and finally of ongoing repeat.

Although push and pull are important in the case of new brands, the crucial factor is whether a new brand can insinuate itself into the market. The main determinant of whether a new brand is capable of achieving its potential is its robustness—that is, whether the new brand has the four crucial characteristics of IDQV:

- *Impact:* Is the brand identified by its name, package, and advertising?
- *Differentiation:* Does it have a unique, dominating mix?
- *Quality:* Does it live up to an appealing promise?
- *Value:* Does it do all this at the right price?

Figure 23.7 shows the components of each of I, D, Q, and V and the relationships among them. The relationships among these elements and those operating in existing brands are clear, as is the reorganization of the hierarchy to reflect the importance of trial and repeat phases of the diffusion process. Again, some of these measures (such as uniqueness) are relatively simple, and some (such as the image) are very complex. This diagram ignores completely

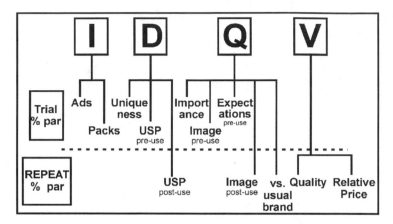

Figure 23.7. New Brand Robustness

the push side of the equation—the focus of management during the development phase is on getting pull right, and push elements can be assumed at this stage to be constant, to be dealt with later in the mix development.

An examination of a very large number of cases has shown that new brands that score high on IDQV will do well in the marketplace, but those with any weakness will not succeed. Table 23.1 shows an abstract from the experience database. The cases in the database were divided into three groups according to whether they were in the top-scoring 33% (high), the middle third, or the lower third (low) for each of I, D, Q, and V. The percentages of the high and low groups to achieve targets are displayed in Table 23.1. Thus 99% of products that scored well on value hit their targets, but none of those with poor value hit their targets.

As a predictor of marketplace performance, this is a very striking correlation, and it leads to a clear action guideline: Any new product mix that underperforms on any one of the IDQV boxes needs to be reengineered until it has been rid of these flaws. This is a robust measure of whether the brand has the capacity to live up to its potential in the vicissitudes of the real marketplace.

The components of the IDQV chart can be measured and coded in much the same way as the brand health check, to give an instant and powerful measure of the potential of a new brand. Full diagnostics are essential to understand why the new brand is performing as it is on these measures, and, in conjunction with the sociopsychological models, to help to put them right.

TABLE 23.1   The Marketplace Effect of IDQV-Proportion of Brands That Reached Target

	% Low Scoring on Each Measure	% High Scoring on Each Measure
Impact	27	73
Differentiation	31	71
Quality	0	87
Value	0	99

Pars

The Petal model is based on the sequence Stimulus–Trigger–Preference–Transaction. Robustness, or IDQV, is a measure of how likely the preference is to turn into the optimum transaction. Par measures what is the optimum transaction level for a particular preference mix in different markets.

In its simplest conception—in the golfing analogy—par describes how the average brand would fare if launched into a particular market environment. Par derives from an examination of the performance of newly launched brands in a host of markets and an attempt to find out why they did well or badly. This examination looks at all the expected drivers—country, product category, advertising spend, pretest scores, and so on. But they are not the things that worked: The things that drove performance were all linked to the competitive structure of the market.

Indeed, so strong is the influence of market structure on share of a new entrant that if you knew only the market structure, you could forecast the share of market obtained by a new entry to within 30% (e.g., 10% plus or minus 3%). Add in measures of the robustness of the brand mix, and the accuracy of the prediction is narrowed significantly to within about 10%. These findings gave rise to the tool that is widely used in evaluating the strategic potential of markets and the actual performance of brands—the market par.

Pars vary more than may be expected. Par shares for one type of food product in one country range from 1.6% to 18.6%—based only on the market's competitive structure. The par discriminates, has variance, and is of value.

There are many ways to use a par in practice: It can be used to calibrate the performance of a new brand—is the 5% share achieved by a new brand good or bad? Pars can be compared across countries, or across new categories within a country, and used to judge whether "most likely" sales of a brand would justify the start-up investment needed. Add in a simple profit calculation and margins, and the par profitability for a market can be measured. This provides a strategic view of the relative opportunities in different categories.

Conclusions

Marketing models are useful tools for the operating manager. They provide frameworks within which to classify the various phenomena that are encountered in marketing operations, checklists within which to channel the creative energy generated in marketing, and structure and vocabulary that permit excellent dissemination of ideas and plans, both laterally to advertising and marketing agencies and vertically within the management structure.

Marketing is a complex and dynamic process, and not merely an exercise in applied statistics or marketing science. The Petal model aims to maintain the organic flair of the practitioner in harmony with insights from a disciplined approach. The Petal model suggests that both existing and new brands can be thought of as going through a process whereby

the marketer applies a stimulus to the marketplace,
which is perceived by consumers through filters and acts as a trigger,
to change (or not) relative preference for competing brands,
which will be modified by in-market activities before affecting transactions.

The process is controlled by the environment, which determines par response functions to stimuli and triggers.

To return to the golfing analogy, consumer marketing is indeed a bit like golf—the environment defines the par, using the right driver improves your score, and so on. But whatever your level, do take lessons from a pro!

Glossary

DUM: Acronym for the process of conducting an activity: The stages are describe, understand, and manipulate. This mnemonic has become shorthand for building on information properly to guide action.

Experience database: A collection of market situations, fully analyzed, held in a form that permits lessons to be drawn.

IDQV: Acronym for the four components of robustness of a brand: impact, differentiation, quality, and value.

Norm: See par.

Par: The most likely performance of an average brand, all other things being equal, derived from reference to an experience database (by analogy to the game of golf, in which par is the number of strokes a scratch player should require for a hole).

Petal: The author's marketing agency, based in Tokyo, Japan.

Petal model: A hypothesis that marketing activity can be characterized as a flow in which stimuli (sociopsychological filters) trigger perceptions (drivers of preference) and preferences (drivers of behavior) that lead to transactions. The whole model applies in any environment having an equilibrium (par) state determined by the environment. A brand's performance against par is determined by its robustness.

Robustness: The likelihood that a new brand will achieve its potential (in terms of trial and repeat), or that an existing brand will maintain its position (in terms of sales); composed of IDQV.

Zoom: The ability to use a simple level of abstraction, where appropriate, to communicate a complex process.

Note

The ideas in this chapter, although my responsibility, have been inspired and hugely influenced by Jacques Blanchard, president of Novaction and head of a talented team of brand engineers. Peter Cooper of CRAM has been seminal in stimulating the concepts addressed in the sociopsychological sections. I do not intend to imply here that Novaction and CRAM methods are the only way to use the concepts outlined, but they do work in practice—and they did inspire them.

24

Media Synergy

Evidence From Germany

Rolf Speetzen

$\mathbf{I}$n Germany, as in many Western economies, household products that are routinely purchased and of a low level of housewife interest are advertised mainly on television. To assess how far the effectiveness of advertising expenditure could be improved by the additional use of magazines, the Axel Springer Publishing Company employed (a) a research facility linking household panels with point-of-sale collection of purchasing data at specific stores and (b) a facility for test/control exposure to advertising in *Hörzu,* the leading television/radio program journal.

This chapter reports on an experiment on Procter & Gamble brands in three product fields. The three brands had formerly been advertised exclusively through the electronic media, but 10 advertisements in *Hörzu* for each, over a test period of 22 weeks, resulted in increases in brand shares of from 15% to 23%, from 30% to 37%, and from 50% to 64%. Subsequent analysis of media schedules suggested that a major reason for these changes was the substantial increase in coverage that the addition of print provides, whereas an increase in television expenditure does not extend the coverage but merely increases the dosage given to those who are already heavily exposed.

The Research Program

The research project "Plus *Hörzu*" had three characteristics:

- It was research confined to a single media vehicle, in which the additional use of print was confined exclusively to *Hörzu*.
- It was an intermedia inquiry to research the effect of adding print to promote brands that had formerly used the electronic media exclusively for their advertising.
- It was a study into *advertising effectiveness,* as we wanted to determine the results of a mixed media schedule on a brand in the market.

A considerable body of knowledge has been built up over the past few years on *Hörzu* as a medium: knowledge on the quality of exposures to *Hörzu* and the effectiveness of communicating through *Hörzu*. The most important new objective of this study was to reveal the advertising effectiveness of *Hörzu*. An indicator, perhaps the cause, of a journal's advertising effectiveness is the quality of the reading situation and how it is read.

We examined the influence of reading situations and reading times in an earlier piece of research titled "Lesequalität" ("Reader Quality"). It was established that magazines read at home, such as *Hörzu,* are studied more extensively than are those read outside the home environment. We also found that there was effective communication with the reader when a magazine was seen at home, whereas there was virtually no bond set up between magazine and reader when it was read away from home.

The emotional components that could influence the effectiveness of communication were examined for the first time in our survey "Leseklima" ("Matching Mind With Matter"). It was demonstrated that magazines that offer a broad range of material touching on the emotional experiences of their readers' lives have high reading scores and above-average bonds between the magazines and their readers.

However, all this earlier evidence provided only indirect indicators for advertising effectiveness, measured indirectly through reading time, reading situation, or reader loyalty. It was highly desirable for research to provide proof of advertising effectiveness, but concrete proof was available only in regard to one market segment: advertisements of department stores for merchandise usually carefully selected by the consumers. Department stores direct their efforts at increasing turnover by selecting periodicals that produce the best coupon or other direct responses. Here *Hörzu,* with its 44% of department store budgets, has a strong lead over its competitors.

But direct evidence relating to everyday products has been missing in the past, such as evidence for products like detergents. It is less easy to monitor sales performance of such products following campaigns than it is to record coupon response. In addition, everyday products are often advertised exclusively or almost exclusively through electronic media and are therefore not available for research into print media.

Survey Method

We can test actual advertising effectiveness only by coming as close as possible to the real-life situation of advertising in action. The panel for our research included four test stores in Hanover, Cologne, Darmstadt, and Nuremberg. These stores are major supermarkets of different trading groups. All the stores are in relatively isolated locations and have no strong competition in their areas. This gives them a high proportion of regular customers who use these stores for their normal purchases. The four stores are fitted with special cash registers so that all merchandise purchased can be clearly identified and the data stored. We can also track movements in sales of identified brands.

The test was carried out by the prominent German market research organization GfK, and personnel from this company were present in all the test stores to supervise the data collection.

Test Purchasers

For the test panel, GfK selected 600 households from the regular customers of each of the four test stores. These households buy regularly in these stores, on average twice or three times a week. Their sociodemographic characteristics conform broadly to those of the average population in western Germany. The particular panel is a combination of a retail trade panel with a recording of purchasing at point of sale and a consumer household panel. In total, the survey comprised 2,400 test households using the four test stores.

Each household in the sample was given an identity card with an ID number to make it possible to track buying habits. On production of this card at the checkout, the ID number was printed on the receipt and stored. The duplicate went to GfK for processing. The data collected included information on all purchases of the brands concerned in the survey, quantities purchased, and prices.

As an inducement to sample members to produce their identity cards with each purchase, a lottery was staged every month; as further encouragement, each household received a free copy of *Hörzu* every week.

This method is not particularly new. For some years, *Hörzu* has been distributed to this household panel, so that the offer of a free copy was neither unusual nor particularly influential in their participation—it was already part of their normal lives. Thus we were able to achieve our goal of normality and participation in an everyday part of people's activities.

The sample copies offered to the test households as a sort of thank-you for participating in the panel had an important test function that the panelists could not detect. In these copies, an additional four-page advertising spread was included, just like a conventional campaign for a normal brand. Because this was a constituent part from the start of the test program, the test advertisements did not seem out of place, but gave every impression of being an integral part of a familiar medium.

Other households whose purchasing was also monitored did not receive *Hörzu* and acted as the control.

Procedure

As before, the test households got their free copies of *Hörzu* on production of their identity cards every week. In one particular copy of *Hörzu,* three brands were advertised regularly on the four-page product advertising spread. Purchasing habits and possible changes in purchasing behavior could be determined from analysis of the purchase receipts.

According to the survey design, monthly figures were available for the following:

- Number and characteristics of first-time buyers
- Number and characteristics of repeat buyers
- Increase in sales of the test brands, with a comparison of the performance of competitive brands

In order to determine the effect of advertising on the test brands in *Hörzu,* we compared the sales to the test households with the purchases of those same brands by customers from other households using the test shops, but not included in the test group. The stimulus of additional advertisements in *Hörzu* was the only difference between the test households and the households not included in the test panel. All other influences exerted on behalf of the test brands, whether through advertising or some other promotional activity, impinged equally on test and nontest households. The research system closely resembles the pure single-source research technique.

Survey Timing

What we wanted to determine was the advertising effect—that is, the influence exerted by the additional advertisements carried in *Hörzu*—through a comparison of the progress of sales among the test households and the nontest households. A preliminary phase was essential. This allowed a starting baseline to be established for both groups. In this way there could be confidence that no structural differences between the two groups would distort the measurement of the advertising effect.

During the 16-week preliminary phase, we observed the purchasing habits of the test households, particularly in regard to the three test products, in order to analyze the progress of the test brands and the competitive brands without the influence of the advertising in *Hörzu.* During this preliminary phase, the advertising of the test brands followed the normal schedule—almost exclusively through radio and television commercials.

Within the actual 22-week test phase, a total of 10 advertisements for the test brands were specially printed in the copies of *Hörzu* passed to the test households. To show positive results, the effect of the advertising in *Hörzu* had to result in overall sales increases for the test brands in the 2,400 test households.

Test Brands

Our major concern for this experiment was to acquire a suitable partner, with suitable test brands. We would like to express our appreciation to Procter & Gamble and its advertising agency for their support and cooperation.

The actual brand names of the test products cannot be revealed; we can say, however, that they were a fabric softener, a washing powder/detergent, and a household cleanser. They are all well-known and well-established brands, with large advertising budgets behind them. All three brands were advertised mostly through the electronic media.

The three test brands had different shares of market (SOM). Brand A held a market share of 15%; Brand B, 30%; and Brand C, 50%. All three brands were priced at above-average levels, and all were supported with individual advertising budgets of DM20 million to DM25 million per year. The print share before the experiment was generally insignificant.

Brand A accounted for 25% of share of voice (SOV). For Brands B and C there was parity between SOM and SOV, with Brand B's SOV at 30% and Brand C's at 50%.

Results

The results were surprising in their magnitude. Brand A increased its market share from 15% to 23%. Brand B reached 37% from 30%. And even Brand C, with a major share of 50% at the start of the test phase, scored an increase of 14 percentage points, to a 64% market share. This was all achieved within 22 weeks.

Figure 24.1 shows the development of the brands over time. At the start, from the 45th week of one year to the 8th week of the following year, was the 16-week preliminary phase. Then followed the 22-week test phase with the 10 insertions per test brand in *Hörzu*. It can be clearly seen how the sales to the test households climbed sharply above the levels of the nontest households.

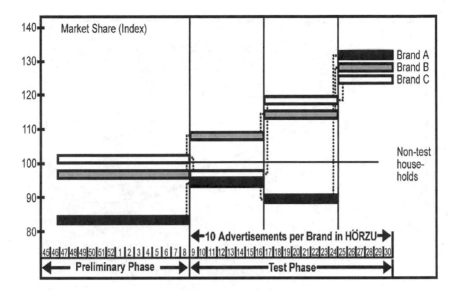

Figure 24.1. Sales Over Time: Three Test Brands

The steps in the figure represent the intervals at which the data were analyzed. The shares for the two biggest brands were about the same during the preliminary phase for both the test households and the nontest households. Brand A showed a different pattern and needed to catch up within the preliminary phase. There was a major change, however, for all three brands, with massive sales increases after the "Plus *Hörzu*" activity started to bite.

The magnitude of the results shows the surprising effectiveness of "Plus *Hörzu*." This naturally prompted us to try to explain why this should have happened. The obvious question is whether this result could be applied generally. A small handicap is that the ideal test situation, with regular readers only—who were exposed to virtually all the 10 advertisements of each of the brands—can hardly be projected into the total population. But television/radio program journals have a large aggregate penetration, and it became possible to estimate the effect of adding all six TV/radio program magazines in Germany, each carrying 10 insertions, in addition to an existing television-based advertising schedule.

The most important point is that "plus *Hörzu*" or "plus TV/radio program magazines" brings increased reach, and this increased reach is qualitatively

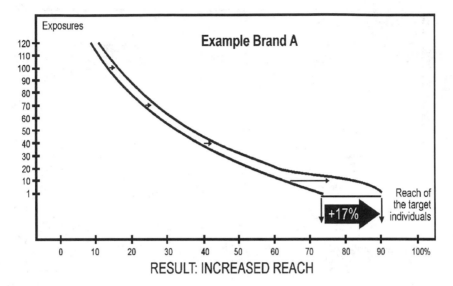

Figure 24.2. Net Reach Estimates: Electronic Media Plus TV/Radio Program
Magazines

very interesting. We took the normal media plan for Brand A and analyzed it
in terms of net reach. In this actual plan (an exclusively electronic media plan),
we established that 73% of all target individuals were subject to at least one
exposure per year. To put it another way, 27% of all target individuals were
not reached at all, but nearly 30% were dosed with 50 exposures or more via
television.

In a second statistical computation, we inserted 10 advertisements into the
six TV/radio program magazines in addition to the all-television plan for
Brand A. The result, shown in Figure 24.2, is clear: All the target individuals
are given additional exposure to the advertising, and, more important, the
number of target individuals reached by this combination climbs from 73%
to 90%. This means an increase of 17 percentage points.

A third statistical analysis shows that the absolute amount spent is not the
key determinant. Instead of adding the cost of print advertisements to the
expenditure for print media, we applied it as an addition to the existing
expenditure for the electronic media. Figure 24.3 shows that the target
individuals who receive a high rate of exposure are merely given an increased
dosage, whereas virtually none of those who do not see the advertising would

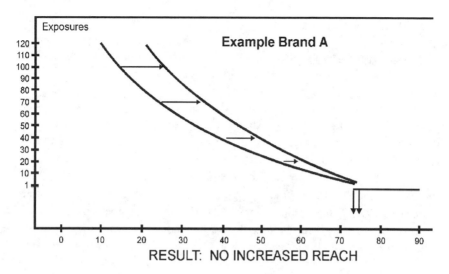

Figure 24.3. Net Reach Estimates: Electronic Media Plus More Electronic Media

be brought into the net. Despite an increased expenditure of around DM3 million, 26% of the target market is still untapped.

Share of Mind

A media strategy different from that of competitive brands (e.g., by the inclusion of print media in addition to the normal use of television) can make a difference to a brand's *share of mind*—that is, the degree to which the brand dominates the consumer's thoughts about the product field.

Share of mind can be calculated, and it can be reasonably assumed that share of mind is related to share of market. An increase in Brand X's share of mind is likely to boost its share of market, and an increase in the share of mind for a competitive brand will have a negative effect on Brand X's market share.

How to react in a marketing-oriented and sensible fashion, and how to improve the chances of advertising communication for a brand, may be demonstrated through the results of share-of-mind evaluations for Brand C. For this brand, we calculated the consumer's share of mind resulting from three alternative media schedules:

1. The normal television schedule
2. The normal television schedule plus an additional electronic budget
3. The actual media schedule plus an addition of 10 insertions in each of the six German TV/radio program magazines

The share-of-mind value for Brand C without increasing the budget (media schedule 1 in this list) is 64.4%. All the competitors can claim a score against this of 29.5%. If this budget is boosted by DM3 million and applied to the electronic media (media schedule 2), the share-of-mind estimate increases to 68.6% for Brand C and 25.4% for the competitors. However, if this budget increase is placed in the TV/radio program magazines, then the share of mind increases to 72.1% for Brand C, against 24.9% for the competitors.

In summary, therefore, the mixed media schedules we examined had the following results when compared with the former television-only schedules:

1. Increased share of market in all cases
2. Increased net reach of the target audience
3. Increased share of the consumer's mind

These favorable outcomes were the result of the changed media mix and not of the increased net advertising investment.

We believe that the findings of the study reported above have a universal relevance. They echo and reinforce the findings of similar studies in other countries as well as in Germany.

25

What Do We Know of Mixed Media Effects?

More Evidence From Germany

Adrian Weser

The Growth in Classical Media Advertising

With market maturity in most product categories, competition replaces aggregate growth as the main dynamic. According to Nielsen S+P Advertising Research, there was advertising for 57,000 products and services in Germany in 1997. Ten years before, the figure was about 41,000.

Classical mass-media advertising is almost certainly the most effective instrument to build the consumer's goodwill. With this background, it is no longer surprising that German advertising expenditures doubled within one decade. In 1996, Nielsen S+P registered gross advertising expenditures in

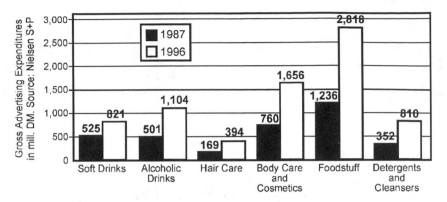

Figure 25.1. Development of Advertising Expenditures on Fast-Moving Consumer Goods

Germany of DM25.2 billion, compared with DM11.9 billion in 1987—an increase of 229%.

The percentage increase of advertising expenditures in the sector of repeat-purchase packaged goods (fast-moving consumer goods, or fmcg) corresponds to the market trend. In 1996, the six fmcg categories spent DM7.6 billion on advertising in classical media. This was 30.2% of the advertising total from all the 26 categories measured by Nielsen S+P Advertising Research. Food alone accounted for DM2.8 billion. The growth in all categories can be seen in Figure 25.1.

Analysis of Effects

Anyone wanting to analyze the economic effects of advertising will be confronted with an extremely complex communication reality. The number of possible influences and their combination during consecutive periods cause big problems for every manager searching for reliable and valid answers covering time and cost aspects. But a formula of high empirical and theoretical quality can compress the reality to a few known and measurable numbers and can express a mathematical correlation between these numbers. Within limits, models of this type can explain advertising effects.

The model discussed in this chapter was initiated and published by Verband Deutscher Zeitschriftenverleger (VDZ). It is called WerbeWert 97, and it concentrates on the following variables: market share, changes in distribution, share of advertising, and media mix. The model is based on a study of 147 brands of repeat-purchase packaged goods, employing data from (a) the A. C. Nielsen trade panel, giving information about market shares and changes in distribution; and (b) A. C. Nielsen S+P Advertising Research, giving information about the advertising expenditures and the media mix of the individual brands.

The classical media types—print media, TV, radio, and poster advertising—were measured for the period between 1991 and 1996. The model assumes that a brand's market share in the current period is determined by (a) the market share of the period before, (b) changes in distribution, (c) the share of advertising, and (d) advertising media mix. And the market share of the period before is also influenced by (e) changes in distribution and (f) advertising expenditures. A multiple, nonlinear regression is used to measure the correlations between the input variables.

The general conclusions from the experiences of these 147 brands are as follows:

1. Advertising works. All the four media types have similar effect curves. Brands with high market shares have to advertise disproportionately as much in order to avoid losses of share.
2. All the four media types have a heavy starting effectiveness. A share of 15-19% of advertising leads to an increase of market share.
3. In the case of an increase in share of advertising, decreasing returns become evident for each medium separately. Therefore, mixed media advertising offers advantages.
4. Print media work very effectively relative to other media.

These points are illustrated in Figure 25.2.

The quality of a regression can be assessed using the explainable variance. The WerbeWert 97 model explains 98.6% of the variance of market shares between two periods; 93.3% of the variance is derived from the market share of the period before; and 5.3 percentage points of the remaining 6.7% variance are caused by the advertising expenditures within the two following months. Only the 1.4% that remains cannot be explained. A comparison of measured and calculated changes of market shares has a correlation of +0.99.

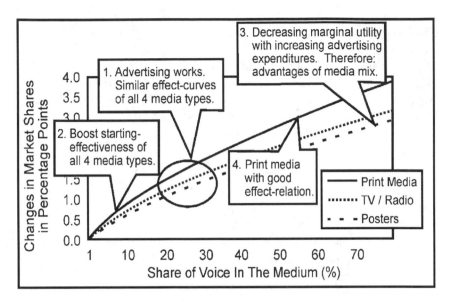

Figure 25.2. Main Results From 147 Brands

The model can be used to provide empirical support for six groups of hypotheses regarding the sales effect of advertising. The examples that follow all relate to specific individual but typical brands.

Hypotheses About Advertising Weight and Market Share

Advertising can boost market share through a continuous presence. The brand in Figure 25.3 spent 55% of its budget in television, 35% in print media, and 10% on radio. The brand's share of voice was 9% and its initial market share was 10%. Distribution level was constant. Sales progress is shown in Figure 25.3: a gain of 3 percentage points over 6 months.

With the brand in Figure 25.4, a cessation of advertising caused a gradual erosion of market share. This brand also started with a market share of 10%. Distribution level was constant. (To emphasize the extent of the erosion, the figure makes a comparison with the rising bars, which show the performance of the continuously advertised brand that we saw in Figure 25.3.)

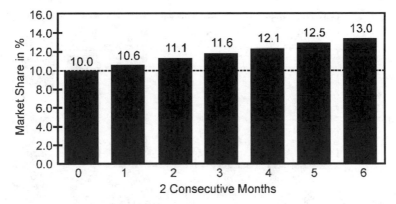

Figure 25.3. Effect of Continuous Advertising

Hypotheses About Use of Mixed Campaigns

The brand illustrated in Figure 25.5 started with a 20% share of market and a 15% share of voice. Distribution did not change over the advertised period. With a preponderance of the budget in television (80%) and a minority in print (20%), the brand made only slow progress over the 12-month period monitored.

The brand in Figure 25.6 also started with a 20% market share and 15% share of voice. Again distribution did not change. However, the media budget was balanced among four media: television (45%), print (40%), radio (10%), and outdoor (5%). The sales performance was significantly better than for the brand in Figure 25.5 (represented by the lower bars in Figure 25.6).

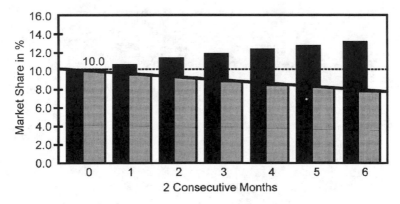

Figure 25.4. Effect of Stopping an Advertising Campaign

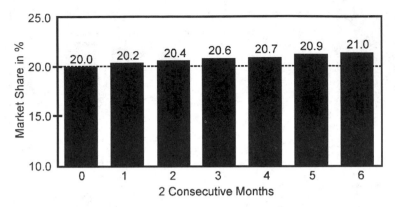

Figure 25.5. Effect of Two Media

Hypotheses About Share of Voice

Figure 25.7 shows a brand that was undersupported by advertising (2% share of voice for an initial market share of 14%). Media were distributed 55% television, 35% print, and 10% radio. Distribution was unchanged.

In Figure 25.8, we also see a 14% brand, with a distribution of the advertising budget in the same proportions as the brand in Figure 25.7, and similarly no change in distribution. But in Figure 25.8, the brand had a 5% share of voice—an underinvestment, but a sufficient support level to maintain

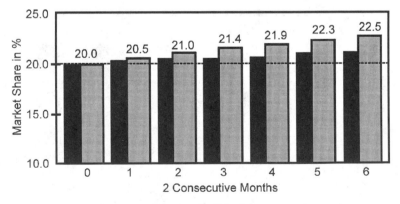

Figure 25.6. Effect of Balanced Multimedia Schedule

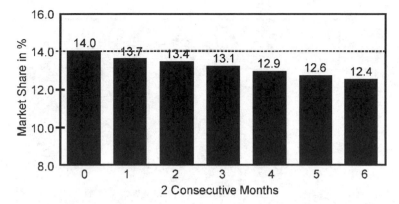

Figure 25.7. Advertising Expenditure Too Low to Support Sales

sales. (The lower bars are a repeat of the data in Figure 25.7, showing the poor performance of the underadvertised brand.)

Hypotheses About the Advertising for Large Brands

With a schedule concentrated in one medium, share of voice must exceed share of market in order to maintain a large brand's market share. In Figure 25.9,

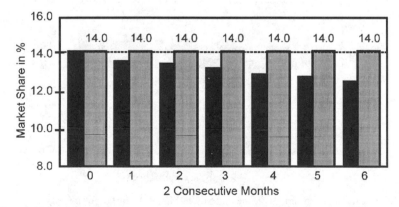

Figure 25.8. Advertising Underinvestment at Sufficient Level to Maintain Sales

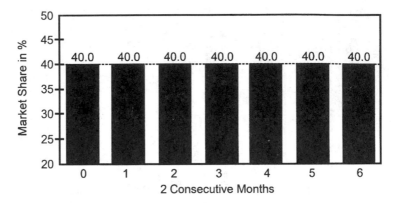

Figure 25.9. High Share of Voice and Stable Share of Market for a Large Brand With Polarized Media Schedule

the brand's schedule was 90% in television. The initial market share was 40% and share of voice 43%. Distribution did not change during the year described.

With a mixed media schedule (45% print, 40% television, 10% radio, and 5% posters), market share can be stabilized for a 40% brand with a share of voice as low as 27%, with distribution unchanged. The flat series of bars in Figure 25.10 describe this brand (compared with the rising bars, which refer to the brand in Figure 25.11).

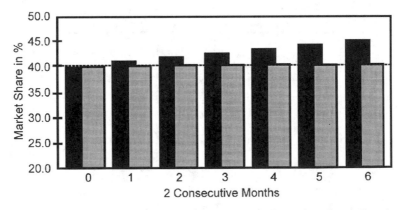

Figure 25.10. Low Share of Voice and Stable Share of Market for a Large Brand With Mixed Media Schedule

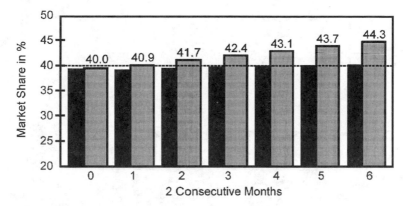

Figure 25.11. High Share of Voice and Increasing Share of Market for a Large Brand With Mixed Media Schedule

With a mixed media schedule (45% print, 40% television, 10% radio, and 5% posters), market share can be increased for a 40% brand with a share of voice (43%) above share of market, with distribution unchanged. See the rising bars in Figure 25.11, which should be compared with the flat series of bars that are a repeat of Figure 25.10.

Hypotheses About the Distribution of New Brands

Figure 25.12 shows a modest increase in the market share of an unadvertised new brand, but with a 5% boost in retail distribution.

The addition of advertising (Figure 25.13) gives a sharp boost to the sales effect of 5% increase in distribution. In this case the advertising schedule was mixed (45% print, 40% television, 10% radio, and 5% posters). The rising bars in Figure 25.13 should be compared with the relatively flat series of bars that refer back to the brand described in Figure 25.12.

Hypotheses About Advertising Continuity

In the three examples presented in this section, the advertising schedule was mixed in the same proportions (45% print, 40% television, 10% radio, and 5% posters). In all cases, distribution remained unchanged.

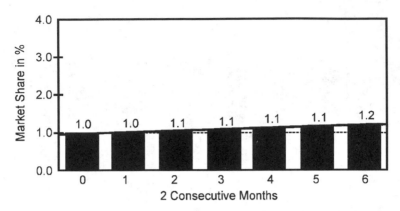

Figure 25.12. Market Share Responds to Increased Distribution for Unadvertised New Brand

In Figure 25.14, a brand with a 16% market share and an initial 12% share of voice lost share when the advertising was stopped after the first two bimonthly periods.

Figure 25.15 shows that a *substantial* increase in share of voice (to 22%) can restore market share to 16% for a brand that had sunk to below 15%. In Figure 25.16, the brand (unlike those in Figures 25.14 and 25.15) maintained a constant 12% share of voice for an initial market share of 16% and succeeded in increasing it significantly.

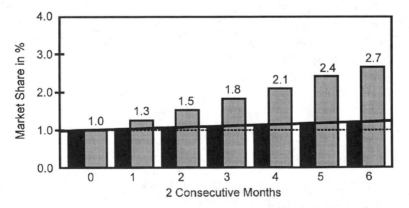

Figure 25.13. Market Share Responds Sharply to Increased Distribution Supported by Advertising for New Brand

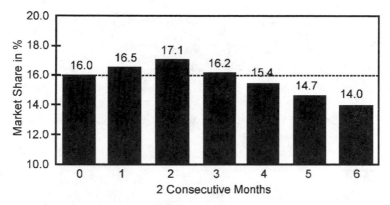

Figure 25.14. Effect of Cessation of Advertising

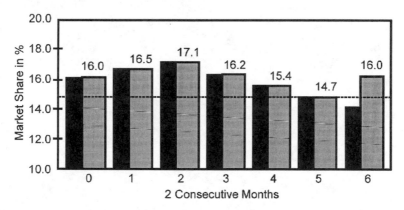

Figure 25.15. Effect of Substantial Boost in Share of Voice

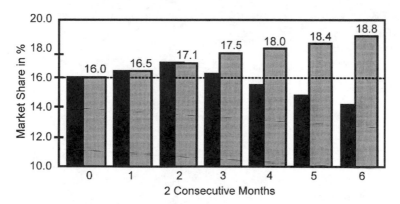

Figure 25.16. Effect of Continuous Advertising

In summary, the findings of this research point to strong endorsement of the following:

- The general relationship between advertising and sales.
- The value of continuous advertising in preference to intermittent exposure. (The value of continuity is reinforced by the use of mixed media schedules.)
- The ability of large brands to be undersupported in terms of share of voice—*if they employ mixed media schedules.*
- The ability of advertising (particularly mixed media advertising) to boost sharply the sales effects of increasing distribution for new brands.

26

Advertising Likability

A View From South Africa

Erik Du Plessis

One reason advertisers still debate whether it is important to make advertising that consumers like is that they do not understand what advertising likability is or how it works. In this chapter, I bring all the dimensions of advertising likability into perspective. I examine modern views about the physiology of the brain, scientists' views of the role of emotions in attention, and the empirical evidence for ad liking. I also try to define ad liking and comment on the implications of research in this area.

NOTE: This chapter was originally published as an article in ADMAP (April 1998), and is reproduced by permission.

How Advertising Likability Works

Let us start with how the brain interprets advertising—or any other stimulus. Each neuron in the brain is connected to up to 5,000 others. A neuron's function is to conduct an electronic impulse (40MHz) along its dendrites to the neurons it is in touch with. The point of contact between neurons is called the synapse. Depending on the sensitivity of the synapse, the receiving neuron will "fire"— transmit an impulse to the neurons it is in touch with—when it is stimulated.

The sensitivity of a synapse is determined by the number of times the two neurons for which it is the connection have fired in the past. The more they have done so, the more sensitive the synapse becomes, and the higher the likelihood that the receiving neuron will fire when stimulated by the sending neuron.

If you read the words *Margaret Thatcher,* the neurons in your eyes are stimulated by the black and white areas of this page, which stimulate certain neurons in the occipital region at the back of your brain. These in turn stimulate other neurons—neurons that are sensitized to certain patterns (letters)—which stimulate others that have "learned" from repeated stimulation of certain combinations of letters to recognize words, and these again stimulate other memories you have about the concepts the words represent. If you have never heard of Margaret Thatcher, the memory will probably only go as far as silently enunciating the words phonetically. If you are illiterate, you will simply see black lines on white. If you are a staunch Tory, a very developed memory will come to the fore.

The direction of propagation (recruitment of other neurons) is from the back of the brain toward the front, because the occipital areas are at the back. The frontal lobes are where logic, reason, and consciousness are seated. As the signal propagates to the frontal lobes, it is increasingly "interpreted," based on the neuronal "cloud" that develops. This process of interpretation is also the process of recall of memories and, at the same time, of reaffirming memory. All these processes are the same thing, and are the result of stimulation of one set of neurons leading to the recruitment of still more neurons. I can illustrate this by asking the reader "not to think of an elephant." It is quite impossible, reading this, not to think of an elephant, and the more you try, the more complete the picture you get.

Interpretation is involuntary. Attention is largely involuntary. The laying down of memories is mostly involuntary, except where someone decides to learn something by concentrating on it and repeating it until the memory is laid down.

This outline of how advertisements become interpreted and become consciousness has one shortcoming: It assumes that all stimuli will become consciousness, yet we know that the brain receives millions of stimuli at any moment, and only one or two become consciousness.

The Importance of Emotion

Emotion is the key to understanding how stimuli reach consciousness. In the brain, the amygdala controls bodily reactions to emotion. It is the center of flight-or-fight reactions and controls the readiness of muscles, adrenaline production, heart rate, and so on. The functions under its control ready the body for action.

Neurologists, led by Professor LeDoux, now see the amygdala as performing a vital part in interpretation: It stands between the frontal lobes (where "thinking" occurs) and the occipital region (where the stimuli start). This is both its physical location and its role in interpretation, consciousness, and other functions.

What you see is transmitted directly to the occipital region via the optic nerve, which has no real contact with other parts of the brain. Then the signal is transmitted toward the frontal lobes. On the way, the route is defined by synaptic sensitivities—memories are recruited and interpretation takes place. En route, the signal passes through the amygdala, which makes a cursory examination of the developing memory/interpretation. If necessary, the amygdala will prepare the body for an emotional response, and so adds an "emotional component" to the memory/interpretation.

LeDoux explains that when you walk through trees and see a twig shaped like a snake, you freeze for a moment, then realize it is only a twig and continue walking.[1] Neurologically, the amygdala does a cursory examination of the visual perception and adds a fear/flight/freeze emotion to the forming perception. Only when the frontal lobes provide a more developed interpretation do you move on.

It is more important for the organism's survival to mistake a twig for a snake than to mistake a snake for a twig. It is more important for us to react and then interpret in detail than it is for us to interpret in detail and then react.

We have all experienced how we "get a jolt" when we think we see a loved one and then realize we have made a mistake. We all stop talking when we are driving and a tricky situation arises. We know how we stop talking when a certain ad appears on television. The amygdala has added an emotional value to the forming memory and thus determined its potential for being the forming neuronal cloud that dominates—the one we give attention to. This means that LeDoux proposes that *the emotional element of a memory recall, and therefore its interpretation, is formed before its "rational" or detailed interpretation.*

Damasio has shown that when people lose the ability of emotional evaluation, they also lose that of rational interpretation.[2] Unless you can attach an emotional reaction (or memory) to a new experience, you fail to exhibit a rational reaction to it. Emotional reactions are necessary to drive our attention to new stimuli, but are also necessary for us to exhibit rational reactions to them—to interpret them sensibly. This is because we evaluate everything in terms of the emotional reward of past similar experiences.

Emotional and Rational Reactions

Based on left-brain/right-brain theories, Krugman has proposed that some types of advertising are left-brain oriented, and therefore susceptible to certain types of research approaches.[3] Zielske published an experiment that seems to confirm this,[4] but Thorson has shown that Zielske misinterpreted his results, and the opposite was true.[5]

Many still argue that there is a division between emotional and rational reactions, and copy-test methodologies show this division, with some claiming a "persuasion" or "conversion" measure that relies on rational reactions only. However, the model that neurologists and cognitive scientists are working under is one in which every perception has both an emotional valuation and a rational content, and in which the emotional reaction is formed first, and then rational reaction. This should change a lot of our thinking about the way advertising works and the way it should be researched.

Empirical Evidence Favoring Ad Likability

Before considering empirical evidence about ad liking, think about what happens in group discussions. When respondents are asked what they think of a brand or an ad, they will say, "I [don't] like it, because . . . ." To most evaluative questions, our first response is an emotional (like/dislike) response, followed by rationalization.

Electroencephalograms show that when a person is exposed to a visual stimulus, there is activity in the occipital region, followed by a decrease in activity, followed by more activity, 0.03 seconds later—sufficient time for the original stimulus to travel to the amygdala and for a message to come back to direct further attention to the stimulus. Franzen states that it takes an individual 0.03 seconds to decide whether or not to read a print ad.[6]

The strongest empirical support for the effect of ad liking comes from the Advertising Research Foundation's Copy Research Validation Project. The researchers set up an experiment to find out which copy-testing questions best predicted in-market results. Although all the popular measures showed some predictive ability, the mere fact that people liked the ad was the most predictive. This prompted Alexander Biel's *Admap* paper "Love the Ad. Buy the Product?"[7]

From our South African database of more than 17,000 ads, in which in-market awareness was measured for all ads in the country over 10 years— the measurement taking place in the second week after the ad's first appearance—we found that ad liking predicts an ad's ability to lay down a memory trace better than its length or even the media weight behind the ad. The same was found in an experiment with 180 U.K. ads.

Thorson has listed a number of academic papers that have predicted the importance of ad liking, and John Philip Jones (a proponent of persuasion measures) has reanalyzed his Nielsen database and concluded:

> The advertising campaigns shown by my pure single-source research to have the greatest effect in the marketplace were certainly not hard-selling in the conventional sense. . . .
>
> The successful campaigns have three general characteristics: 1) they are likable and offer a reward for watching because they are entertaining and amusing; 2) they are visual rather than verbal; 3) they say something important and meaningful about the brand being advertised.[8]

The evidence in favor of ad liking is overwhelming.

What Is Ad Likability?

Most practitioners mistakenly believe that ad likability equates with entertaining advertising, but it is a more complex phenomenon than that. Like Millward Brown, we concluded that clutter reels, and any form of research for which respondents are specially recruited, preclude the measurement of an ad's ability to attract attention—which is a major part of the function of ad likability. To determine ad likability, we need questions that the respondent can answer introspectively.

We developed in South Africa a predictive model and applied it to 26,000 respondents in copy tests, and then used it at the respondent level to evaluate its ability to predict ad liking: We got an R^2 of 0.86! This model says the following:

- People like advertising that entertains them. Entertainment is the opposite of being familiar with the ad or the style of advertising—the ad must not be "the same old thing." (There are exceptions—well-loved campaigns that run forever and are regularly refreshed can work, but most ads cannot aspire to this.)
- People like ads they can empathize with, that show them how they would like to be. This is the opposite of ads that alienate them, talk down to them, or mock them or their values.
- People like ads that give news about products, how these can be useful to them, and what they can do with the products. This is the opposite of advertisements that confuse them, require an effort to understand, and are not credible. (In many ways, this is the "persuasion" measure used by many companies—persuasion is part of liking, not a separate dimension.)

Looking at this complex and multidimensional definition of ad likability, we can understand why some authors who simply equate ad liking with entertainment are negative about the empirical evidence on ad liking.

"Love the Ad. Buy the Product?" and Ehrenberg

Every student of advertising theories is aware of Ehrenberg's work, which says that users remember better the advertising for the brands they use, which leads to a virtuous spiral: Ad awareness leads to bigger brands, and bigger brands lead to higher ad awareness (mostly the latter).

This work by Ehrenberg seems to stand outside arguments about advertising memories, and especially those about ad liking. But neurological understanding of the brain brings Ehrenberg into the mainstream: People will have more positive feelings toward brands that they use, so that mention of the brand will evoke more positive emotional evaluation of the forming message. This ensures it a better chance of getting attention, causing a better memory lay-down.

Interestingly, the opposite also has to hold true. When people have a positive feeling about an ad, then, when memories are stimulated by mentions of the brand—or seeing it at point of sale—the first emotional response will be positive.

Researching Ad Likability

Because of the apparent simplicity of ad likability, it is very tricky to create likable ads and to research ad likability. (In South Africa, only about 4% of ads receive a consumer liking score of more than 8 out of 10. Such scores are lower in the United States and the United Kingdom.)

- We have to understand that because all answers by respondents are based on both emotional and rational reactions, and rational reactions are determined by initial emotional reactions, any pretesting research we do should lead to a better ad in terms of emotional reactions. It should lead to more liked ads—as long as we understand the multidimensional nature of liking.
- It is a mistake to think that the use of focus groups will necessarily lead to greater "depth," in the sense of uncovering subsconscious reasons for all types of projects. In the case of trying to find out why people like an ad or a brand, focus groups will usually simply lead to greater postrationalization.
- Focus groups are, therefore, best employed in the development of campaigns, to find out what might create ad liking, what the potential areas are for empathy or relevant news that could be the basis of the campaign.
- Posttesting (and pretesting of concepts) is best done through quantitative research to determine ad liking and to develop introspective questions to identify why an ad has received low likability scores.
- It is essential to recognize that interpretation is a personal process. How the advertiser and the creative director interpret the ad, and the emotional values they give their experiences, may be very different from the values viewers will give. That is why it is important to gain insight into the viewers' experiences that lead to ad likability, and then to test whether the ad succeeds in provoking the right interpretations and emotions.

- Because most people react to ads in a personal environment—people discuss few ads with their friends or family members—reactions to ads are always personal. It is misleading to try to evaluate ads through group discussions.

- We use models to explain an ad's likability that are based not only on quantitative research but on normative databases.

Conclusions

Emotional responses are the "gatekeeper" to advertising effectiveness, because the way our brains work dictates that emotional responses precede rational analysis. This means that the likability of an ad—a complex phenomenon that goes beyond mere entertainment—is key to its success. Therefore, copy testing should focus on liking, and almost any testing we do should help to illuminate the way in which real people respond to ads. Decent copy testing is even better.

Notes

1. Joseph LeDoux, *The Emotional Brain: The Mysterious Underpinnings of Emotional Life* (New York: Simon & Schuster, 1996).

2. Antonio R. Damasio, *Descartes' Error: Emotion, Reason, and the Human Brain* (New York: Putnam, 1994).

3. Herbert E. Krugman, "How Potent Is TV Advertising?" presentation made at the Association of National Advertisers Workshop, October 1972.

4. H. A. Zielske, "Does Day-After Recall Penalize 'Feeling' Ads?" *Journal of Advertising Research,* vol. 22, no. 1, 1982, 19-23.

5. Esther Thorson, "Likability: 10 Years of Academic Research," presentation made at the Advertising Research Foundation Copy Workshop, September 1991.

6. Giep Franzen, *Advertising Effectiveness* (Henley-on-Thames, UK: NTC, 1994).

7. Alexander L. Biel, "Love the Ad. Buy the Product?" *Admap,* September 1990.

8. John Philip Jones, "Is Advertising Still Salesmanship?" *Journal of Advertising Research,* vol. 37, no. 3, 1997.

27

Pioneer Work on Advertising Evaluation

The Institute of Practitioners in Advertising's Advertising Effectiveness Awards

Chris Baker

The Awards Scheme and Its Context

The Institute of Practitioners in Advertising's Advertising Effectiveness Awards are presented biennially based on a competition run under the auspices of the Institute of Practitioners in Advertising (IPA), the U.K. advertising agency trade association. The aims of the IPA in presenting these awards remain the same as when they were set up in 1980:

1. To generate a collection of case histories that demonstrate that, properly used, advertising can make a measurable contribution to business success

2. To encourage advertising agencies (and their clients) to develop ever-improving standards of advertising evaluation (and, in the process, a better understanding of the ways in which advertising works)

The evaluation of advertising effects will never be easy. Advertising works generally via indirect means, performing different roles in different ways over differing timescales, usually in concert with other elements of the marketing mix. Nevertheless, the future health of the advertising industry rests on the provision of convincing proof of the commercial value of its product, as well as the creative skills that create this value.

Prior to 1980 there was virtually no case history material demonstrating advertising effectiveness, anywhere in the world, that was both published and sufficiently rigorous in its analysis and presentation of data to be convincing. This was a major barrier both to justifying the industry's services to its customers and to promoting best practice and an increasingly accountable culture within advertising.

The IPA Advertising Effectiveness Awards were designed to help fill this vacuum and have done so very successfully since 1980, producing a fresh batch of effectiveness cases every two years. The demands for proof are considerably more rigorous than those made by organizations presenting effectiveness awards in the United States and in continental Europe. Elsewhere, the Advertising Federation of Australia (from 1990) and the Canadian Congress of Advertising (from 1992) have based their awards on the U.K. IPA format.

Entries for the IPA awards are required to be in the form of written papers, up to 4,000 words in length, not counting appendices and charts. Entry forms must be countersigned by the authors' agencies' chief executives and by competent representatives of the clients, by which act copyright is passed to the IPA.

Each paper provides the full background of the business context and strategic thinking behind the advertising concerned, a description of the advertising itself, and a detailed analysis isolating the specific contribution made by the advertising to overall business success. (This necessarily means that the author must take into account the impact of other variables potentially affecting sales and other business success factors.)

The 20 best case histories from each competition are published in full in a volume of the *Advertising Works* book series (10 of which have been published to date). However, many other valuable case histories are entered, and the IPA

Data Bank now makes available more than 650 cases, representing the finest collection of advertising case histories in the world.[1]

Judging Criteria

It is not enough for advertising to be coincidental with overall marketing success. To win an IPA Advertising Effectiveness Award, a paper must isolate the particular contribution made by the advertising and make a convincing case for its value as an investment.

Ultimately, success is judged in terms of commercial criteria. Image, awareness, and behavioral data may play an important part in building the link between advertising and business performance—and indeed be indicative of the future value of the activity concerned—but the case must ultimately be related to sales and profit.

Judges are asked to play the role of skeptical observer. The dictum is "ineffective until proven effective," and the fundamental question the judges pose is, "How convincing is the case put for the specific contribution of advertising to business success?" So the onus is on the author, not only to produce strong evidence of a link between the advertising and business results, but also to anticipate and address the questions and counterinterpretations of a skeptical reader. Papers fail if they present only selective facts, either to make the case seem better than it is or from a lack of thought about the possible counterarguments.

Allowance is made for the intrinsic difficulty of the task, and in particular how difficult it is in each case to isolate advertising effect. In some cases, such as car campaigns, it is fiendishly difficult. Allowance is also made for small brands, and for other cases in which data may be limited by few resources or the nature of the market concerned. "Bonus points" are awarded to papers that add something new to our understanding or make an original point.

These criteria clearly establish the difference between the IPA awards and other advertising industry awards (which generally focus on the recognition of original thinking and craft skills)—that is, a single-minded focus on the rigorous proof of effectiveness. This difference is reinforced by the fact that the majority of the judging panel is drawn from outside the advertising industry.

The Evolution of the Awards

The world has changed a lot since the IPA Advertising Effectiveness Awards were initiated in 1980—and with it we have seen considerable changes in the nature of business, marketing communications, and the roles for advertising. Although the core purpose of the awards has remained the same over the past two decades, the IPA has aimed to reflect these changes in the context within which advertising operates through the types of cases called for and awarded most highly.

The cornerstone on which cases must be built has remained advertising's effect on consumer demand across three broad contexts for advertising:

- *Launch:* new products or services, or those with no significant history of advertising
- *Change:* new campaigns for previously advertised brands, resulting in short-term impact on sales or behavior
- *Build and sustain:* advertising that has benefited a business by maintaining or strengthening a brand over a long period

Over time, the IPA has encouraged specific types of cases demonstrating advertising's contribution to business success: the integration of advertising with other marketing tools, direct-response advertising, multicountry campaigns, ingenious responses to limited advertising or research funds, innovations in media planning, innovative strategic thinking, new learning on how to isolate advertising effects.

The 1998 awards saw a more specific focus on cases that looked not only at advertising's effects on consumer demand but also at advertising's ability to add value to a brand's other key stakeholders. Several of the 1998 cases highlighted advertising's unique ability to talk to multiple communities of interest for a brand simultaneously and thereby align and influence those groups in a common understanding of the brand's purpose: a common pursuit. Examples include the impact of a company's (primarily consumer-directed) advertising on shareholders and the financial community, which directly affected the company's value and share price. Several cases included the impact of advertising on a company's employees in terms of job satisfaction, recruitment, motivation, and productivity.

Another major theme emerging in the 1998 awards was advertising's contribution to overall competitive efficiency—advertising that was not just highly cost-effective in its own right, but also more efficient than that of its competitors.

Overall, the IPA is committed to ensuring that the Advertising Effectiveness Awards represent not just best practice in advertising and its evaluation, but the evolution of best practice.

Note

1. The *Advertising Works* books and details on the IPA Data Bank are available from the Institute of Practitioners in Advertising, 44 Belgrave Square, London SW1X 8QS, England (telephone 0171 235 7020; fax 0171 245 9904); or on-line at http://www.ipa.co.uk (e-mail: lesley@ipa.co.uk).

Index

About the Contributors

Chris Baker is a well-known British advertising analyst. Following extensive experience at the British Market Research Bureau and Saatchi & Saatchi, he became a founding member and Planning Director of the agency Bainsfair Sharkey Trott (BST) in 1990. He is now director of Strategic Consultancy at the Omnicom-owned, top-five London agency TBWA GGT Simons Palmer, which was formed from a series of mergers (including BST) in 1998. He is also a past winner of the Institute of Practitioners in Advertising (IPA) Advertising Effectiveness Award. He served as a judge for the IPA Advertising Effectiveness Awards in 1990 and as a convenor of judges in 1992 and 1994, and he is the editor of two volumes of the IPA Advertising Effectiveness Awards papers, *Advertising Works 7* and *Advertising Works 8*.

Ashish Banerjee has worked on an extensive range of major multinational brands across diverse product categories, in central, panregional, and local capacities, in three countries on three continents. Since February 1998, he has been with McCann-Erickson Romania as Vice President-Client Services Director. He joined McCann-Erickson Worldwide in New York in 1990, after completing his master's degree in advertising at Syracuse University, where he wrote his thesis on multinational advertising under John Philip Jones's supervision. He started his advertising career with J. Walter Thompson Worldwide in Bombay, India, in 1986. Prior to joining JWT he earned an M.S. in economics and an M.B.A. in marketing from the MIT-affiliated Birla Institute of Technology & Science in India.

Rena Bartos wrote the groundbreaking book *The Moving Target* in 1982, which introduced a fresh perspective for tracking (and reaching) a rapidly changing women's market in the United States. In *Marketing to Women Around the World,* she extended her unique approach across borders to help marketers target female consumers in North America, Latin America, Europe, and the Far East. She has held the positions of Senior Vice President and Director of Communications Development at J. Walter Thompson. In addition to her books, she has written many articles, including three for the *Harvard Business Review.* She is Past Chairwoman of the Advertising Research Foundation and former President of Advertising Women of New York, the New York Chapter of the American Marketing Association, and the Market Research Council. She was named Advertising Woman of the Year in 1980 and was elected to the Market Research Council Hall of Fame in 1989. In June 1998 the American Marketing Association named her as one of 10 pioneers who "made the marketing research industry in this century."

Laurent Battais is a French market research executive. He took a master's degree in marketing and began his professional career in 1987 working for Intercor Etudes (a prominent retail panel, a subsidiary of Secodip). He became Account Director on consumer and retail panels and joined Information Resources Inc. in 1993 as Account Director, where he played a leading role in the development of scanner-based trade panels in France. In 1996 he was appointed a member of the General Direction of MarketingScan, a branch of Médiamétrie and GfK AG. (MarketingScan has introduced the BehaviorScan experimental micro test market in France, in parallel with the United States and Germany. It also created the TVScan single-source database.) He is a member of the French Marketing Association and the European Society for Marketing and Opinion Research.

Jonathan Brand, the son of two authors, graduated from Middlebury College in 1955. He spent a Fulbright year in Norway, got drafted into the U.S. Army, and eventually came back to New York City with his Swedish wife. He started at J. Walter Thompson in 1960, left for *Time* magazine in 1962, and then returned to JWT in 1964. From 1968 to 1977 he was JWT's Creative Director in Scandinavia and "unofficial troubleshooter" to the continent. Back in the

United States, he worked in agencies in Boston, Philadelphia, and San Francisco, then taught copywriting at the University of Oregon, advertising creativity at the University of Texas, and marketing in Poland. He was an obsessive photographer in the 1960s and 1970s and studied with Bruce Davidson, David Vestal, Garry Winogrand, and Richard Avedon. He writes and develops in Portland, Oregon, and Rockport, Maine.

Roger M. Brookin was with Unilever for almost 30 years in Europe, South America, and Asia. Resident in Japan since 1978, he was Director of Marketing Services for Asia and a member of the board of management of Unilever in Japan. As a result of his considerable experience in the field of marketing during those years, he established Petal KK in Tokyo in 1994, which specializes in brand equity management. He cofounded TheMarketingPartnership, a Singapore-based consultancy specializing in Southeast Asian business. He has helped develop the Achievement Model in the Asia Pacific and its marketing applications. He is British; his wife is Japanese. His interests center on brands, the family, languages, and music, and he has lectured widely on both cultural and marketing topics.

Jeremy Bullmore was born in 1929. He was educated at Harrow School and afterward served in the British army before going to Oxford University, where he spent 2 years not reading English. His first job, in 1954, was as a trainee copywriter with J. Walter Thompson in London, and he stayed with that agency until his retirement in 1987. He became, successively, Copywriter, Writer/Producer, Creative Group Head, and Head of Television; then, from 1964 to 1975, he was Head of the Creative Department, and from 1976 to 1987, Chairman of the London agency. He was a member of the J. Walter Thompson worldwide board, and, from 1981 to 1987, Chairman of the (British) Advertising Association. In 1985 he received a decoration from the British government for his services to the advertising profession. Throughout his time in advertising he wrote and spoke frequently on the subject. Since 1988, he has remained active in the business as a nonexecutive director of the British newspaper organization the Guardian Media Group plc. and WPP Group plc. (the parent company of J. Walter Thompson and Ogilvy & Mather).

Hong Cheng is Assistant Professor of Communication at the Slane College of Communications and Fine Arts, Bradley University, Peoria, Illinois. He received his Ph.D. in mass communications from the Pennsylvania State University. His research interests include cross-social and cross-cultural studies of advertising, mass-mediated intercultural communication, and new news media. His works involving advertising in China have appeared in the *International Journal of Advertising, Journal of Advertising Research, Journalism & Mass Communication Quarterly,* and *Media Asia.* He has also written a book chapter on advertising in China for *Advertising in Asia: Communication, Culture and Consumption* (edited by Katherine T. Frith). He is a member of the American Academy of Advertising, the Association for Education in Journalism and Mass Communication, the International Communication Association, and the Society of Professional Journalists.

Harold F. Clark, Jr., is President of Smith Clark Associates, a communications and marketing consulting firm in Amenia, New York. Among his clients are Johnson & Johnson, the Bechtel Corporation, the American Association of Advertising Agencies, J. Walter Thompson, and the American Soybean Association. He spent 28 years at J. Walter Thompson, from which he retired in 1988 as Executive Vice President and member of the Board of Directors, responsible for advertising standards and training and development worldwide. He is a graduate of Amherst College (B.A.), Stanford University (M.A.), and Columbia University (Ph.D.).

Marieke de Mooij was born in the Netherlands and draws from 25 years experience in both advertising practice and education: at an international textile company, in an advertising agency, and as a Director of the Dutch Foundation for Education in Advertising and Marketing. She has been involved in international advertising education since 1980, as Director of Education, International Advertising Association, and as Managing Director of BBDO College. She is President of Cross Cultural Communications Company, her own consultancy based in the Netherlands, which focuses on international advertising and cross-cultural communications. She is also an Associate Professor at the University of Navarra, Spain. She lectured in international advertising and culture for professionals and at universities in various parts of the world. She is the author of *Advertising Worldwide: Concepts, Theories and Practices of International, Multinational and Global Advertising* (second edition, 1994) and *Global Marketing and Advertising: Understanding Cultural Paradoxes* (1998).

Erik Du Plessis is a well-known market researcher based in South Africa. He was formerly Media and Marketing Director at BBDO in that country. In 1984 he founded Impact International, which has become the leading South African advertising research company, based in Johannesburg, and which has amassed a large database of research results from tested advertisements. His work is widely known within and outside South Africa. He has published in the *Journal of Advertising Research* (New York) and *Admap* (London). He won the award for the best research paper at the South African Marketing Research Association Conferences of 1991, 1993, and 1995, and in 1998 he received the prestigious Telmar Award in New York for his contributions to media research.

Michael Ewing received his doctorate in marketing from the University of Pretoria, South Africa, and spent 4 years as marketing research manager with Ford Motor Company's South African subsidiary, SAMCOR. In 1996 he moved to Western Australia to join the marketing faculty at Curtin University of Technology, where he leads the advertising group. He frequently visits the Pacific Rim, either teaching in Hong Kong, Malaysia, and Singapore, or consulting in the Philippines. He has published in various international journals, including *Asian Journal of Marketing, Journal of Advertising Research, Journal of Business Research,* and *Journal of Global Marketing,* as well as in the proceedings of the Academy of Marketing Science, American Marketing Association, and International Advertising Association. He has more than 70 peer-reviewed articles and conference papers to his credit.

Rosemary Ford is a Senior Associate Director at the British Market Research Bureau (BMRB) International, which she joined in 1979 after graduating from Southampton University. She worked at BMRB for 10 years, including 1 year seconded to the Indian Market Research Bureau in Bombay and Calcutta. Her experience covered social, financial, and media research during this period. She became a Senior Associate Director in 1988, and her paper presented at the (British) Market Research Society Conference in that year received the award for all-around "best paper." In 1989 she left BMRB to work with Booz, Allen and Hamilton management consultants in Philadelphia, Pennsylvania, and to start a family. She rejoined BMRB in 1993, and is now part of BMRB's media unit, MEDIA@BMRB.

Paul Gaskin is a Senior Lecturer in the Department of Marketing at Monash University in Melbourne, Australia. He has been Planning or Research Director at three major Australian advertising agencies—J. Walter Thompson (Sydney), McCann-Erickson, and Young & Rubicam—and held senior positions in market research with Roy Morgan Research Centre and Reark Research. He also taught advertising at Queensland Institute of Technology (now a university). He has a Bachelor of Commerce degree in economics from the University of New South Wales, and an M.B.A. from Cranfield University in the United Kingdom.

Thorolf Helgesen is Professor of Marketing Communications at the Centre of Media Economics, the Norwegian School of Management. He is a previous Research Director at Lilleborg (Unilever). Later, he held the position of Managing Director at the Norwegian Association of Advertising Agencies until he joined the Norwegian School of Management in 1987. He is also a past Chairman of the Norwegian Market Research Society. He received his Ph.D. from the University of Lund, Sweden.

John Philip Jones is a British-born American academic and a graduate of Cambridge University (B.A. with honors and M.A. in economics). He spent 27 years in the advertising agency business, including 25 years with J. Walter Thompson in Britain, Holland, and Scandinavia, managing the advertising for a wide range of major brands of repeat-purchase packaged goods. In 1981, he joined the faculty of the Newhouse School of Public Communications, Syracuse University, where he is now a tenured full Professor and former Chairman of the Advertising Department. He is also Adjunct Professor at the Royal Melbourne Institute of Technology, Australia. His published works include seven books and more than 70 journal articles. He specializes in the measurement of advertising effects, and is an active consultant to many advertisers and advertising agencies in the United States and overseas. He travels extensively in connection with his work. He has been the recipient of a number of professional awards.

Colin McDonald is a British research pioneer. A graduate of Oxford University, he worked for Reckitt & Sons and for the British Market Research Bureau and was Chairman of Communication Research Ltd. He now runs his own consultancy. In 1966 he carried out the first classic experiment of pure single-source research. During more than 30 years' experience of a broad range of research, he has published extensively. His book *How Advertising Works* appeared in 1992, and *Advertising Reach and Frequency* was published in 1995. His other publications include *Sampling the Universe* (with Stephen King; 1996) and *A History of Market Research in Britain,* published by the (British) Market Research Society for its 50th anniversary. He is also coeditor (with Phyllis Vangelder) of ESOMAR's *Handbook of Opinion and Market Research* (fourth edition, 1998). He is a Fellow and Gold Medalist of the (British) Market Research Society.

Morten Micalsen was born in Oslo, Norway, in 1966. He has a B.A. in marketing and a master's degree from the Norwegian School of Management in the fields of strategic management, marketing management, and marketing communication. He is currently Account Director at Bold Advertising in Norway. Prior to taking his current position, he worked at Gallup Norway for 8 years as Manager for the Consumer Department and Manager for the Advertising and Communication Department. He is also a Lecturer at the Norwegian School of Management in market research, consumer behavior, and marketing communication. At the time he wrote the chapter that appears in this volume, he worked for Gallup Norway and was responsible for a strategic alliance between Gallup Norway and the Norwegian School of Management, an alliance that culminated in one of the largest cross-industry research projects ever conducted in Norway.

Adam Phillips is Managing Director of Euroquest and an Executive Director of British Market Research Bureau (BMRB) International. He has more than 25 years' experience in marketing and social research. In addition to his experience at BMRB, he has worked on the client side of research and also at research agencies in the Netherlands and the United States. He has been Chairman of the (British) Market Research Society and an AMSO Council Member, and he was recently elected to the ESOMAR Council. He was the recipient of prizes at the ESOMAR Congress in 1990 and 1991. He has a degree in electronic engineering from Cambridge University. In his spare time he is a sailor and beekeeper.

Jill Powell completed a Master of Arts degree in advertising at the Royal Melbourne Institute of Technology (RMIT), Australia, in 1997. Her research paper addressed the phenomenon of outstanding creativity in advertising. As an independent creative recruitment specialist from 1980 to 1990, she developed close associations with many creatives and their agencies and had a unique opportunity to witness their progress through their careers. Further interest in this subject was generated by her teaching in the undergraduate creative advertising program at RMIT and, as a committee member of the Melbourne Art Directors Club, taking charge of the Mentor Scheme for 2 years. In 1989, she presented a paper on the changing face of employment in advertising at the Asia/Pacific Design Conference. She has lived and worked in the communication industry in the United Kingdom, Australia, New Zealand, and Taiwan and is now living in Detroit, Michigan, with her husband, Ted, who is International Creative Director on the Ford business at J. Walter Thompson. She also freelances as a travel writer and has written more than 50 stories in 20 countries.

Rolf Speetzen was born in 1940 in Kiel, Germany, and was educated in Germany and England, obtaining a degree in sociology at Hamburg University. He started his career in media research at Informarkt, at that time the German Politz research agency. Between 1970 and 1973 he was head of media research at Wolfgang Schaefer Markforschung, the Politz follow-up organization in Hamburg. He joined Axel Springer Publishing Company in 1973 as Head of the Magazine Division of the Market Research and Planning Department and was appointed Senior Research Executive in 1982, responsible for all of Axel Springer's activities: newspapers, magazines, and electronic media. In this role he also headed the research of SAT-1, at present one of the largest private TV channels in Germany, from the launch in 1985 to 1990. He is part-time Lecturer in Social Sciences at Hamburg University and has been on the program committees of and spoken at many international events, including Worldwide Readership Research Symposia, ESOMAR seminars and congresses, and ARF and CARF conferences. His articles on media research appear frequently in many European trade magazines. He is the author of an English/German-German/English dictionary of media and marketing terms.

Laurent Spitzer is a French market research executive. He took a master's degree in marketing and began his career at Médiamétrie, the leading firm in the French media research industry. He was much involved in developing international business, conducting a number of standard surveys in Eastern and Central Europe and also coordinating and harmonizing the firm's European television ratings. He joined MarketingScan on its foundation in 1994 and became Client Service Director in 1996. He is a member of the French Marketing Association and the European Society for Marketing and Opinion Research.

Ludmilla Gricenko Wells has 20 years of professional administrative and teaching experience in advertising copywriting and design, corporate marketing communications management, and advertising agency account super-vision. Her area of expertise is the advertising industry in the former Soviet Union. She is a consultant to Avrora Advertising Agency, Tovarich Advertising Agency, and professional advertising associations in Moscow. She is also Assistant Professor of Marketing in the College of Business, Florida Gulf Coast University. She earned a B.A. in commercial art and a B.B.A. in marketing from Eastern New Mexico University, an M.B.A. in marketing from Fairleigh Dickinson University, and a Ph.D. in communications from the University of Tennessee. Her research interests focus on the development of the advertising industry and advertising as an institution in Russia and the Commonwealth of Independent States. She has published in the *Journal of Advertising, International Journal of Advertising,* and *World Communication* as well as in the proceedings of leading academic advertising and historical conferences.

Adrian Weser was born in Hamburg, Germany, in 1948. He studied business administration and psychology at Hamburg University, focusing on market research and the buying behavior of consumers. In 1977 he worked for Lintas Werbeagentur in the Market Research Department, and from 1980 to 1993 he was with Grüner & Jahr, first in media research, and then as Advertising Manager. Since 1994 he has been at Bauer Verlag, and in 1996 he became Head of Research and Media Marketing. He is also spokesperson for the VDZ Media Research Team.

David Wheeler is a graduate of London University. He is former Director of J. Walter Thompson, London, and Vice Chairman of the British Market Research Bureau. He ended his professional career as Director General of the Institute of Practitioners in Advertising, where he originated the IPA Advertising Effectiveness Awards. Allegedly retired, he is active in applying his 40 years of marketing experience to the assistance of a number of U.K. charities and to the Icelandic marketing community.

Roderick White, a graduate of Oxford University, is editor of *Admap* and Research Director of London Conquest, a subsidiary of WPP Group plc. He has spent more than 30 years in advertising and marketing consultancy, mostly with J. Walter Thompson, London. In this time he has been involved in planning advertising internationally for a variety of major advertisers, includ-ing Alfa Romeo, Bordeaux Wines, De Beers, Ferrero, Ford, Gillette, Kellogg's, Kodak, Marks & Spencer, Parker Pen, and Unilever. His consultancy work for the United Nations has included the development of multinational marketing campaigns for the producers of a variety of primary commodities. He is author of *Advertising: What It Is and How to Do It* (fourth edition, 1994) and has written extensively in the U.K. advertising and marketing press.